THE CHRISTIAN RELIGION

The Other Voice in Early Modern Europe:
The Toronto Series, 24

The Other Voice in Early Modern Europe: The Toronto Series

SERIES EDITORS Margaret L. King *and* Albert Rabil, Jr.
SERIES EDITOR, ENGLISH TEXTS Elizabeth H. Hageman

Previous Publications in the Series

MADRE MARÍA ROSA
Journey of Five Capuchin Nuns
Edited and translated by Sarah E.
Owens
2009

GIOVAN BATTISTA ANDREINI
Love in the Mirror: A Bilingual Edition
Edited and translated by Jon R. Snyder
2009

RAYMOND DE SABANAC AND SIMONE
ZANACCHI
Two Women of the Great Schism: The
Revelations *of Constance de Rabastens
by Raymond de Sabanac and* Life of
the Blessed Ursulina of Parma *by
Simone Zanacchi*
Edited and translated by Renate
Blumenfeld-Kosinski and Bruce L.
Venarde
2010

OLIVA SABUCO DE NANTES BARRERA
The True Medicine
Edited and translated by Gianna
Pomata
2010

LOUISE-GENEVIÈVE GILLOT DE
SAINCTONGE
Dramatizing Dido, Circe, and Griselda
Edited and translated by Janet Levarie
Smarr
2010

PERNETTE DU GUILLET
Complete Poems: A Bilingual Edition
Edited by Karen Simroth James
Translated by Marta Rijn Finch
2010

ANTONIA PULCI
*Saints' Lives and Bible Stories for the
Stage: A Bilingual Edition*
Edited by Elissa B. Weaver
Translated by James Wyatt Cook
2010

VALERIA MIANI
*Celinda, A Tragedy: A Bilingual
Edition*
Edited by Valeria Finucci
Translated by Julia Kisacky
Annotated by Valeria Finucci and
Julia Kisacky
2010

The Other Voice in Early Modern Europe: The Toronto Series

SERIES EDITORS Margaret L. King *and* Albert Rabil, Jr.
SERIES EDITOR, ENGLISH TEXTS Elizabeth H. Hageman

Previous Publications in the Series

Enchanted Eloquence: Fairy Tales by Seventeenth-Century French Women Writers
Edited and translated by Lewis C. Seifert and Domna C. Stanton
2010

Leibniz and the Two Sophies: The Philosophical Correspondence
Edited and translated by Lloyd Strickland
2011

In Dialogue with the Other Voice in Sixteenth-Century Italy: Literary and Social Contexts for Women's Writing
Edited by Julie D. Campbell and Maria Galli Stampino
2011

SISTER GIUSTINA NICCOLINI
The Chronicle of Le Murate
Edited and translated by Saundra Weddle
2011

LIUBOV KRICHEVSKAYA
No Good without Reward: Selected Writings: A Bilingual Edition
Edited and translated by Brian James Baer
2011

ELIZABETH COOKE HOBY RUSSELL
The Writings of an English Sappho
Edited by Patricia Phillippy
With translations by Jaime Goodrich
2011

LUCREZIA MARINELLA
Exhortations to Women and to Others if They Please
Edited and translated by Laura Benedetti
2012

MARGHERITA DATINI
Letters to Francesco Datini
Translated by Carolyn James and Antonio Pagliaro
2012

The Other Voice in
Early Modern Europe:
The Toronto Series

SERIES EDITORS Margaret L. King *and* Albert Rabil, Jr.
SERIES EDITOR, ENGLISH TEXTS Elizabeth H. Hageman

Previous Publications in the Series

DELARIVIER MANLEY & MARY PIX
English Women Staging Islam,
1696–1707
Edited and translated by Bernadette
Andrea
2012

CECILIA DEL NACIMIENTO
Journeys of a Mystic Soul in Poetry and
Prose
Introduction and prose translations by
Kevin Donnelly
Poetry translations by Sandra Sider
2012

LADY MARGARET DOUGLAS AND
OTHERS
The Devonshire Manuscript: A
Women's Book of Courtly Poetry
Edited and introduced by Elizabeth
Heale
2012

ARCANGELA TARABOTTI
Letters Familiar and Formal
Edited and translated by Meredith K.
Ray and Lynn Lara Westwater
2012

PERE TORRELLAS AND JUAN DE
FLORES
Three Spanish Querelle *Texts:* Grisel
and Mirabella, The Slander against
Women, *and* The Defense of Ladies
against Slanderers: A Bilingual Edition
and Study
Edited by Emily C. Francomano
2013

BARBARA TORELLI BENEDETTI
Partenia, a Pastoral Play: A Bilingual
Edition
Edited and translated by Lisa Sampson
and Barbara Burgess-Van Aken
2013

FRANÇOIS ROUSSET, JEAN
LIEBAULT, JACQUES GUILLEMEAU,
JACQUES DUVAL AND LOUIS DE
SERRES
Pregnancy and Birth in Early Modern
France: Treatises by Caring Physicians
and Surgeons (1581–1625)
Edited and translated by Valerie
Worth-Stylianou
2013

The Christian Religion,
as Professed by a Daughter of the
Church of England

MARY ASTELL

Edited by

JACQUELINE BROAD

ITER

Iter Inc.
Centre for Reformation and Renaissance Studies
Toronto
2013

Iter: Gateway to the Middle Ages and Renaissance
Tel: 416/978–7074   Email: iter@utoronto.ca
Fax: 416/978–1668   Web: www.itergateway.org

Centre for Reformation and Renaissance Studies
Victoria University in the University of Toronto
Tel: 416/585–4465   Email: crrs.publications@utoronto.ca
Fax: 416/585–4430   Web: www.crrs.ca

Iter and the Centre for Reformation and Renaissance Studies gratefully acknowledge the generous support of James E. Rabil, in memory of Scottie W. Rabil, toward the publication of this book.

Library and Archives Canada Cataloguing in Publication

Astell, Mary, 1668–1731, author
The Christian religion, as professed by a daughter of the Church of England / Mary Astell ; edited by Jacqueline Broad.

(Other voice in early modern Europe. The Toronto series ; 24)
This volume offers the first complete modern version of the 1717 second edition.
Includes bibliographical references and index.
Issued in print and electronic formats.
Co-published by: Iter.

ISBN 978-0-7727-2142-6 (pbk.).
ISBN 978-0-7727-2143-3 (pdf)

1. Feminism—Early works to 1800. 2. Christian women—Conduct of life—Early works to 1800. I. Broad, Jacqueline, editor II. Victoria University (Toronto, Ont.). Centre for Reformation and Renaissance Studies III. Iter Inc IV. Title. V. Series: Other voice in early modern Europe. Toronto series ; 24

HQ1201.A87 2013   305.42   C2013-903808-6
C2013-903809-4

Cover illustration:
Portrait of Lady Frances and Lady Catherine Jones (oil on canvas), Wissing or Wissmig, William (1656–87) / Private Collection / Photo © Philip Mould Ltd, London / The Bridgeman Art Library MOU 162570.

Cover design:
Maureen Morin, Information Technology Services, University of Toronto Libraries.

Typesetting and production:
Iter Inc.

Contents

Acknowledgments

I am extremely grateful for the generous financial assistance of the Australian Research Council, who awarded me a Future Fellowship in 2010 in order to carry out research on Mary Astell, and for the tremendous support of my department, the School of Philosophical, Historical, and International Studies at Monash University, Melbourne. Without their help, this volume would not have been possible. I would also like to thank the Centre for Reformation and Renaissance Studies at the University of Toronto for providing me with a Visiting Fellowship in September 2012; this fellowship enabled me to complete the research for the introduction to this work. In addition, I wish to extend my gratitude to librarians at the Watkinson Library, Trinity College, Hartford; the British Library, London; the University of Cambridge Library, Cambridge; the Yale Divinity School Library, New Haven; the Jessie Ball duPont Library, University of the South, Sewanee; the William Andrews Clark Memorial Library at the University of California, Los Angeles; the University of Pennsylvania Rare Books and Manuscripts Library, Philadelphia; the Thomas Fisher Rare Books Library at the University of Toronto; and the Lambeth Palace Library, London. For her invaluable assistance in preparing the original typescript of Astell's *Christian Religion*, I am extremely grateful to Michelle de Stefani. For answering all my bibliographical queries with patience and understanding, I am deeply indebted to Patrick Spedding. For a number of good and sensible suggestions for improvement, I am grateful to both Elizabeth H. Hageman and the anonymous referee for the press. Finally, for their terrific advice and support, I would like to thank Jeremy Aarons, Peter Anstey, Dirk Baltzly, Sandra Broad, Sally Dickinson, Margaret English-Haskin, Amyrose McCue Gill, Graham Oppy, Al Rabil, and Paul Salzman.

Cover Illustration

The cover to this volume features an oil painting, "Portrait of Lady Frances and Lady Catherine Jones" (1687), attributed to the Dutch artist Willem Wissing (1656–87). This image is provided courtesy of the Bridgeman Art Library (MOU162570). The two women in the painting are Frances and Catherine Jones, the daughters of Richard Jones, the first earl of Ranelagh, and his wife Elizabeth. Catherine Jones was one of Astell's closest friends and the most likely addressee of her *Christian Religion*, which is written in the style of a letter to a lady with the initials "C. I." The portrait title would appear to suggest that Catherine is the figure standing to the right of the seated woman. In a 1691 mezzotint image of the same painting, however, the title remains the same while the sitters are reversed—the standing figure is to the left of the seated woman (see National Portrait Gallery, D31354). The child in the foreground is unidentified.

Introduction

The Other Voice

At first glance, the title of Mary Astell's longest treatise, *The Christian Religion, as Professed by a Daughter of the Church of England* (first published in 1705), gives the impression of a deeply religious work. This impression is not misleading. True to its title, *The Christian Religion* is a devout, almost evangelical, piece of writing: an impassioned justification for belonging to the Anglican church (and no other) in early eighteenth-century England. The title, however, belies the rich philosophical nature of the text and its deeper feminist message. In one key passage, Astell (1666–1731) announces:

> Perhaps I may be thought singular in what I am about to say, but I think I have reason to warrant me, and till I am convinced of the contrary, since it is a truth of great importance, I shall not scruple to declare it, without regarding the singularity. I therefore beg leave to say, that most of, if not all, the follies and vices that women are subject to (for I meddle not with the men) are owing to our paying too great a deference to other people's judgments, and too little to our own, in suffering others to judge for us, when God has not only allowed, but required us to judge for ourselves.[1]

In Astell's view, women should not be treated like either children or fools—they ought to be permitted to form their own judgments about right and wrong. To support these claims, she appeals to her own immediate experience of an internal power of reason, "that light which God Himself has set up in my mind to lead me to Him" (§6), and the belief that her fellow women have the same capacity for rational

---

1. See below, §45. Following Astell's lead, I use section symbols—§ in single form and §§ in plural—to refer to subsections (numbered paragraphs) in her work. All my subsequent in-text references to Astell's *Christian Religion* are to subsections in the present volume, which is based on the 1717 second edition of the text.

thought. Undoubtedly, she says, some women are naturally clever and accomplished, while others are inherently slow and dull-witted. Both types of women, however, can benefit from further moral and intellectual improvement: the first because they are most capable of such improvement, the second because they *need* it most (§259). *The Christian Religion* aims to provide all women with the tools they require to judge for themselves and avoid being led astray by others. To achieve these ends, Astell draws upon the entire edifice of early modern philosophy, including not only epistemology, theology, and metaphysics, but also ethics and politics. In this text, she puts forward Cartesian-Platonist theories about the true source of knowledge, ontological and cosmological arguments for the existence of God, a rationalist argument for the real distinction between mind and body, and a counterargument to the Lockean view that God might endow matter with the power of thought. While many of Astell's contemporaries employ similar philosophical theories and arguments, few of them do so in order to raise the consciousness in women that they should exercise their rationality toward noble ends, for "it can never be supposed that God created us, that is our minds, after His own image, for no better purpose than to wait on the body, while it eats, drinks, and sleeps, and saunters away a *useless life*" (§107). *The Christian Religion* thus represents a uniquely female-centered counterpart—an "other voice"—to the works of great male philosophers of the period.

The Christian Religion is also the crowning achievement of Astell's career. Today Astell is best known as the author of three popular feminist works, *A Serious Proposal to the Ladies, Parts I and II* (1694 and 1697) and *Some Reflections upon Marriage* (1700). The first *Proposal* details her plans for an all-female academy or a "religious retirement" for women,[2] the second offers her "method of improvement" for women to practice at home, and the *Reflections* provides her thoughts concerning the common causes of unhappy marriages in early modern society. In all three works, her emphasis is upon the

2. Mary Astell, *A Serious Proposal to the Ladies, Parts I and II*, ed. Patricia Springborg (Peterborough, ON: Broadview Press, 2002), 1:73. Hereafter I refer to the first and second parts of this work as *Proposal I* and *Proposal II* respectively. A new modern edition of Astell's first *Proposal* (1694) and her *Some Reflections upon Marriage* (1700), edited by Sharon L. Jansen, is forthcoming in the Other Voice in Early Modern Europe: Toronto series.

importance of women's cultivating a certain strength of mind and a disposition toward happiness, regardless of their material circumstances. *The Christian Religion* provides a further elaboration of the same themes. More than this, the treatise provides the reader with a sophisticated philosophical context in which to place the feminist arguments of the earlier works. We might think of this volume as a rather long "third part" to her famous *Proposal*. The first part of the *Proposal* outlines her view that in order for women to attain purity of mind and acquire truth and virtue, they must (temporarily, at least) withdraw themselves from the business of the wider world and devote their attention to the study of religion and philosophy. The second part gives women a provisional method of thinking to attain this purity, based upon the rules of René Descartes (1596–1650) and his followers Antoine Arnauld (1612–94) and Pierre Nicole (1625–95)—a method whereby women might withdraw their minds from sensory prejudices and regulate their passions in accordance with reason. This final "third part" shows her readers how that method might be applied to the study of God, the self, and other people and material beings. Building on the principles of thinkers such as the French Cartesian Nicolas Malebranche (1638–1714) and his English follower John Norris (1657–1711), Astell offers both theoretical and practical guidelines about how women can attain a Christian tranquility of mind in the midst of outward troubles and disturbances. She proposes to show that living in conformity with the will of God can bring happiness in both this life and the next. She provides moral arguments in favor of treating other people from motives of disinterested benevolence rather than petty self-interest, and she recommends psychotherapeutic techniques for the governance of the passions, those disturbing perceptions that occur in the soul as a result of its close intermingling with the body. Above all, Astell offers advice on how a woman can cultivate a virtuous disposition of character and live up to the dignity and perfection of her nature as a rational, thinking being. *The Christian Religion* thus spells out what Astell's female students would have come to understand, had they been given the opportunity to attend her academy. It represents the culmination of Astell's feminist project to teach her fellow women how to lead the good life and attain happiness.

Astell's Life and Works

When *The Christian Religion* first appeared in print in February 1705,[3] Astell was at the height of her literary fame in London. She had already published seven works, including both her *Proposals* and the *Reflections*, to general public acclaim.[4] Although these works were all published anonymously, her authorship seems to have been an open secret.[5] Among her contemporaries, she enjoyed a reputation as a woman of great piety and wisdom. She was admired by leading literary figures such as John Evelyn, Daniel Defoe, and John Dunton, as

3. [Mary Astell], *The Christian Religion, As Professed by a Daughter Of The Church of England* (London: S.H. for R. Wilkin, 1705). The *Term Catalogues* record that Astell's *Christian Religion* was first published in octavo in Hilary term (February), 1705. See Edward Arber, *The Term Catalogues, 1668–1709 A.D.; with a Number for Easter Term, 1711 A.D.*, 3 vols. (London: Professor Edward Arber, 1903–6), 3:434. "Octavo" refers to the size of the pages of the book, brought about by folding a standard printing sheet three times in order to produce eight leaves.

4. In order of publication, these works are: (1) [Mary Astell], *A Serious Proposal to the Ladies, For the Advancement of their True and Greatest Interest. By a Lover of her Sex* (London: R. Wilkin, 1694); (2) [Mary Astell] and John Norris, *Letters Concerning the Love of God, Between the Author of the Proposal to the Ladies and Mr. John Norris* (London: J. Norris for Samuel Manship and Richard Wilkin, 1695); (3) [Mary Astell], *A Serious Proposal to the Ladies, Part II: Wherein a Method is Offered for the Improvement of their Minds* (London: Richard Wilkin, 1697); (4) [Mary Astell], *Some Reflections Upon Marriage, Occasioned by the Duke and Duchess of Mazarine's Case; which is also considered* (London: John Nutt, 1700); (5) [Mary Astell], *Moderation truly Stated: Or, A Review of a Late Pamphlet, Entitled, Moderation a Vertue* (London: R. Wilkin, 1704); (6) [Mary Astell], *An Impartial Enquiry Into The Causes Of Rebellion and Civil War In This Kingdom* (London: E. P. for Richard Wilkin, 1704); and (7) [Mary Astell], *A Fair Way with the Dissenters and their Patrons* (London: E. P. for Richard Wilkin, 1704). The following Astell works are available in modern editions: Astell, *Proposals I and II*; Mary Astell and John Norris, *Letters Concerning the Love of God*, ed. E. Derek Taylor and Melvyn New (Aldershot, UK: Ashgate, 2005); Mary Astell, *Reflections upon Marriage, Impartial Enquiry*, and *Fair Way with the Dissenters*, in *Astell: Political Writings*, ed. Patricia Springborg (Cambridge: Cambridge University Press, 1996). Unless otherwise stated, my references are to these modern editions.

5. Only one year following the publication of *The Christian Religion*, a book catalogue advertised her work as "Mrs. Astyl's Religion of a Church of England Woman, new 1705." See *Bibliotheca Selectissima; or, A Catalogue of Curious Books Contained in the Libraries of the Reverend Dr. Thomas Bayley late President of St. Mary Magdalen Coll. and the Reverend Dr. Henry Parkhurst, late Fellow of Corpus Christi Coll. in Oxford* (London: n.p., 1706), 39.

well as the prominent religious writers John Norris, Francis Atterbury, and George Hickes. Her works were also known to the great philosophers, Gottfried Wilhelm von Leibniz and John Locke. And she was an inspiration to other defenders of women in her day, including Mary Chudleigh, Elizabeth Thomas, and the anonymous author known as "Eugenia." In her private life at this time, Astell was also extremely fortunate: she had a close circle of friends and patrons—a small group of wealthy gentlewomen who provided her with much-needed emotional support and financial assistance.[6]

Only a few decades earlier, Astell had faced a rather lonely and dismal future. Born in Newcastle-upon-Tyne on November 12, 1666, she was the eldest child of Mary (née Errington) and Peter Astell, both of whom hailed from respectable Northumberland families. Her father was a member of the Company of Hostmen, an elite coal merchants' guild that held a powerful sway over the flourishing Newcastle coal trade. In her childhood, Mary had enjoyed the privileged lifestyle of a respected gentleman's daughter. Alongside her younger brother Peter, she was educated by a clergyman uncle, Ralph Astell, the curate of St. Nicholas Church in Newcastle. She was apparently taught "all the accomplishments which are usually learned by young gentlewomen of her station,"[7] and she may also have had some tuition in religion and philosophy. In 1678, however, Mary Astell's father died and her life prospects were dealt a significant blow. Peter Astell's untimely death left the family in serious financial trouble, and in the ensuing years her mother was forced to rely on charity and loans to supplement her pension. By 1684, both Astell's mother and her uncle were dead. In a short period, then, Mary Astell went from being the daughter of a prosperous gentleman to an impoverished orphan with little chance of finding a suitable husband. By her own estimate, she was a rather poor

---

6. For these biographical details (and those below), I am indebted to Florence M. Smith, *Mary Astell* (New York: Columbia University Press, 1916); Ruth Perry, *The Celebrated Mary Astell: An Early English Feminist* (Chicago, IL: University of Chicago Press, 1986); and Jacqueline Broad, "Mary Astell (1666–1731)," *British Philosophers, 1500–1799*, ed. Philip B. Dematteis and Peter S. Fosl, *Dictionary of Literary Biography* 252 (Detroit, MI: Gale, 2002), 3–10.

7. George Ballard, *Memoirs of Several Ladies of Great Britain (Who have been Celebrated for their Writings or Skill in the Learned Languages, Arts, and Sciences)*, ed. Ruth Perry (Detroit, MI: Wayne State University Press, 1985), 382.

candidate for marriage anyway: not only was she penniless, she was apparently bereft of both beauty and charm.[8] Instead she developed "a certain ambition to be an author,"[9] and shortly after her mother's death, she moved from Newcastle to London, most likely with the aim of pursuing this ambition. Once there, she received some assistance from the nonjuror William Sancroft (1617–93), the archbishop of Canterbury, who was kind enough "to receive a poor unknown, who hath no place to fly unto and none that careth for her soul."[10] One of her earliest written pieces, a manuscript of religious poetry titled "A Collection of Poems" (1689), is dedicated to Sancroft out of esteem and gratitude.

In the 1690s, Astell turned her hand from poetry to philosophy. Her childhood tutor, her uncle Ralph, had been educated at the University of Cambridge at the time of the religio-philosophical movement known as Cambridge Platonism.[11] In her published works, Astell evinces a sympathy for the moral and religious doctrines of the Cambridge thinkers—especially those of Henry More (1614–87), who

8. In an early poem, "In emulation of Mr. Cowley's Poem called the Motto page I" (1688), Astell's speaker laments: "What shall I do? not to be Rich or Great, / Not to be courted and admired, / With Beauty blest, or Wit inspired." This poem is in "A Collection of Poems humbly presented and Dedicated To the most Reverend Father in God William By Divine Providence Lord Archbishop of Canterbury & c" (1689), Rawlinson MSS Poet. 154:50–97, Bodleian Library, Oxford. For a transcription, see Perry, *Celebrated Mary Astell*, 400–454 (402).

9. [Mary Astell], *Bart'lemy Fair; or, An Enquiry after Wit; In which due Respect is had to a Letter Concerning Enthusiasm, To my LORD **** (London: Richard Wilkin, 1709): "It will *plainly appear* to the reader, without an advertisement, that I had a certain ambition to be an author: whether for my own *private* glory, or for public good, or both together, if he be an artist he will discern" (17). There is no modern edition of *Bart'lemy Fair.*

10. Astell, "A Collection of Poems," in Perry, *Celebrated Mary Astell*, 401. In this context, "nonjurors" refers to those members of the clergy who refused to swear allegiance to William III and Mary II in 1689.

11. Astell later inherited her uncle's library, a collection of books that includes a number of religio-historical texts now housed at the Northampton Records Office in the United Kingdom. Among the surviving works bearing her inscriptions are William Cave's *Antiquitates Christianae* (1675) and his *Apostolici* (1677). See E. Derek Taylor, "Mary Astell's Work Towards a New Edition of *A Serious Proposal to the Ladies, Part II*," *Studies in Bibliography* 57 (2005–6): 197–232 (200n6); and Taylor and New, introduction to Astell and Norris, *Letters*, 8n18.

was well-known for his reasoned defenses of the immaterial soul and the existence of God. In 1693, Astell initiated a correspondence with a man sometimes now known as "the last of the Cambridge Platonists," the Oxford theologian-philosopher John Norris. Inspired by Norris's reputation as a man who was "not so narrow-souled as to confine learning to his own sex," she wrote to him with a puzzle concerning the love of God.[12] Their ensuing correspondence was a long and lively discussion on Norris's distinction between the love of desire (a love that we owe exclusively to God) and the love of benevolence (the love that we owe to other people), and the Malebranchean metaphysics underlying these views.[13] During this exchange, from 1693 to 1694, Astell published her *Serious Proposal to the Ladies*, an instant success that ran to four editions in her lifetime. When the correspondence with Norris was eventually published in 1695, the title page announced that the *Letters Concerning the Love of God* were "Between the Author of the *Proposal to the Ladies* and Mr. John Norris."

Over the next decade, Astell proceeded to establish herself as a writer. She took lodgings in Chelsea, a respectable suburb of London, where it seems that her clever wit and cheerful disposition won her several friends. Her most intimate and long-lasting relationship was with Lady Catherine Jones (d. 1740), the well-to-do daughter of the first earl of Ranelagh. Astell permitted Norris to publish their letters only on the proviso that he dedicated them to "the truly honorable lady, the Lady Catherine Jones, in due acknowledgement of her merits." Astell describes her friend as someone who, from an early age, shunned the temptations of birth and beauty and chose instead to remain a virgin and pursue God's work. She adds that she loves Jones "with the greatest tenderness, for all must love her who have any esteem for

12. Astell and Norris, *Letters*, 69. In the late seventeenth century, Norris was tremendously popular with female readers. His name is connected, by either personal acquaintance or correspondence, with a number of English women—including Damaris Masham, Mary Chudleigh, Elizabeth Thomas, Catharine Trotter Cockburn, and Sarah Fyge Egerton—many of whom read and commented on his writings. On Norris, see Flora Isabel MacKinnon, *The Philosophy of John Norris*, Philosophical Monographs 1 (Baltimore, MD: Psychological Review Publications, 1910); Richard Acworth, *The Philosophy of John Norris of Bemerton (1657–1712)* (New York: Georg Olms Verlag, 1979); and W. J. Mander, *The Philosophy of John Norris* (Oxford: Oxford University Press, 2008).

13. For details, see Taylor and New, introduction to Astell and Norris, *Letters*.

unfeigned goodness, who value an early piety and eminent virtue."[14] Jones is the most likely addressee of Astell's *Christian Religion*, which is written in the style of a letter to "the Right Honorable, T. L. C. I."[15] In the final years of her life, Astell lived with Jones in her home in Jew's Row, Chelsea.

When Astell's female academy failed to win support, she followed up her *Proposal to the Ladies* with a second part, "Wherein a Method is Offered for the Improvement of their Minds," in 1697. According to Astell's friend Elizabeth Elstob (1683–1756), a "good lady" had expressed interest in providing financial backing for the academy but was dissuaded by Gilbert Burnet (1643–1715), the bishop of Salisbury.[16] Astell's second part is dedicated to Princess Anne of Denmark (later Queen Anne of England), in the hope that she will not "deny encouragement to that which has no other design than the bettering of the world, especially the most neglected part of it."[17] In her later works, Astell's royalist sympathies come to the fore, not only in her *Reflections upon Marriage* (reprinted with a long preface in 1706), but also in three Tory political pamphlets of 1704: *Moderation truly Stated, An Impartial Enquiry Into The Causes Of Rebellion and Civil War,* and *A Fair Way with the Dissenters and their Patrons.*[18] Astell's final work, *Bart'lemy Fair: Or, An Enquiry after Wit* (1709), is a critique of *A Letter concerning Enthusiasm* (1708) by the Whig thinker Anthony Ashley Cooper, third earl of Shaftesbury.

14. Astell and Norris, *Letters,* 66.

15. In this period, the letter *i* was still interchangeable with the letter *j*. It is therefore likely that "T. L. C. I." stands for T[he] L[ady] C[atherine] J[ones]. The cover of this present volume features a late seventeenth-century portrait of Jones with her sister Frances (later Lady Coningsby), attributed to the Dutch artist Willem Wissing.

16. In a letter to George Ballard, dated July 16, 1738, Elstob reports: "I don't remember that I ever heard Mrs. Astell mention the good lady's name, you desire to know, but I very well remember, she told me, it was Bishop Burnet that prevented that good design by dissuading that lady from encouraging it" (Ballard MS 43:53, Bodleian Library, Oxford).

17. Astell, *Proposal II,* 117.

18. For a detailed account of Astell's political views, see Patricia Springborg, *Mary Astell: Theorist of Freedom from Domination* (Cambridge: Cambridge University Press, 2005). For a brief overview, see Jacqueline Broad and Karen Green, *A History of Women's Political Thought in Europe, 1400–1700* (Cambridge: Cambridge University Press, 2009), 265–87.

Shortly after publishing *Bart'lemy Fair*, Astell partly retired from her writing career in order to devote herself to the organization of a girls' charity school in Chelsea. In her later years, she developed breast cancer and underwent a crude mastectomy. Astell died soon after this operation, on May 9, 1731. One month later, a notice appeared in the *London Evening Post* advertising the 1730 reissue of *The Christian Religion*, this time openly attributed to "the Ingenious Mrs. Astell."[19]

Historical-Intellectual Context

The Christian Religion was written in the early years of the reign of Queen Anne (1665–1714), the Stuart monarch who acceded to the throne of England upon the death of William III in 1702. This was an era of fierce political antagonisms between Whigs and Tories, two political parties distinguished at the time by their attitudes toward Protestant dissenters (Quakers, Independents, Baptists, and so on). The majority of Tories stood for the doctrine of passive obedience, the view that subjects ought to submit quietly to any penalties for disobedience to unjust authority. They were also supporters of High Church Anglicanism, or the strict adherence to those doctrines and rituals distinctive of the Church of England (and not the dissenting churches). Above all, the Tories sought to defend the spiritual monopoly of the Anglican church in the lives of English subjects. By contrast, the majority of Whigs placed a high value on "English liberties," including liberty of conscience or freedom of religious worship for dissenters, and they supported the subject's right to resist unjust or tyrannical political authority. In 1704, hostilities between Whigs and Tories came to a head over an issue known as "occasional conformity." This was the practice of some Protestant dissenters who would occasionally take communion in Anglican churches solely in order to qualify for government posts, such as mayor and justice of the peace. In 1704, the Tories put forward a second Occasional Conformity Bill in Commons (the first bill of 1702 was defeated), seeking to punish occasional conformists for what they saw as an affront to the Anglican church. In her short pamphlets of 1704, Astell aligns herself with the Tory side of

19. *London Evening Post*, no. 553, June 12–15, 1731.

this debate. In *The Christian Religion*, she expresses the same religious and political sympathies—she defends a High Church Anglican, anti-toleration, and antidissenter point of view—but with some important qualifications.

In this treatise, Astell provides a sustained critique of three religio-political works: the anonymous *A Lady's Religion* (1697), another anonymous pamphlet titled *The Principle of the Protestant Reformation Explained* (1704), and John Locke's *Reasonableness of Christianity* (1695).[20] There has been some speculation about the authorship of the first two works. *A Lady's Religion*—the text that inspired Astell to write her *Christian Religion* in the first place (see §1 below)—was supposedly written by "a Divine of the Church of England." But despite this ascription, Astell seems to have suspected Locke's involvement.[21] In one part of the text, she drily observes that "the *Lady's Religion* seems to be little else but an abstract of the *Reasonableness of Christianity*, with all those disadvantages that usually attend abridgments" (§368). Years later, upon reading *The Christian Religion*, the antiquarian William Parry (1687–1756) praises Astell for stripping Locke of his disguise "in [im]personating a clergyman, and yet writing like a Socinian."[22] His attribution of *A Lady's Religion* to Locke is not unreasonable given that a French translation of the work, *La religion des dames*, appeared in the same volume as the French translation of Locke's *Reasonableness of Christianity* in 1715, 1731, and 1740. The translator of both texts was a young Frenchman named Pierre Coste (1668–1747), French tutor

---

20. Astell addresses these specific editions: *A Lady's Religion: In a Letter to the Honorable My Lady Howard. The Second Edition. To which is added, a Second Letter to the same Lady, concerning the Import of Fear in Religion. By a Divine of the Church of England*, 2nd ed. (London: A. and J. Churchill, 1704); *The Principle of the Protestant Reformation Explained In A Letter of Resolution Concerning Church-Communion* (London: n.p., 1704); and [John Locke], *The Reasonableness of Christianity, As delivered in the Scriptures*, 2nd ed. (London: Awnsham and John Churchill, 1696).

21. See Perry, *Celebrated Mary Astell*, 90–91.

22. William Parry to George Ballard, February 12, 1743, Ballard MS 40:158, Bodleian Library, Oxford.

to the son of Sir Frances and Lady Damaris Masham, at whose manor house of Oates in the Essex countryside Locke also resided.[23]

Locke, however, was not the author of *A Lady's Religion*. In his prefatory "Discours sur la Religion des Dames," Coste directly attributes the work to a "Mr. Stephens."[24] This Stephens is most likely the Whig clergyman William Stephens (1647–1718), also the reputed author of a defense of Locke's *Reasonableness of Christianity*, titled *An Account of the Growth of Deism in England* (1696). It seems that Stephens's colleague, the Irish philosopher John Toland (1670–1722), might have also had a hand in the work. The first edition of *A Lady's Religion* includes a "Prefatory Epistle to the same Lady, By a Lay-Gentleman," signed "Adeisidaemon" (meaning "the unsuperstitious man"). Toland uses this same pseudonym in another piece, *Clito: A Poem on the Force of Eloquence* (1700). The prefatory epistle to *A Lady's Religion* also contains a number of positive reflections on the intellectual capacities of women and their natural ability to overcome the errors and prejudices of a poor education. Similar sentiments are expressed, in strikingly similar terms, in Toland's *Letters to Serena* (1704).

There is no evidence that Astell had read Toland's "Prefatory Epistle" of the first edition (she refers only to the second edition of *A Lady's Religion*). Recently, however, Sarah Apetrei has argued that Toland ought to be numbered among Astell's interlocutors in *The Christian Religion*.[25] Apetrei bases her case on the grounds that the anonymous *Principle of the Protestant Reformation* has also been attributed to Toland. "It is in the light of this radical foe [i.e., Toland and the deist movement]," she says, "that Astell's revilement of biblical

23. On Coste, see John Milton, "Pierre Coste, John Locke, and the Third Earl of Shaftesbury," in *Studies on Locke: Sources, Contemporaries, and Legacy*, ed. Sarah Hutton and Paul Schuurman, International Archives of the History of Ideas/Archives internationals d'histoire des idées 197 (Dordrecht: Springer, 2008), 195–223.

24. See Jean Yolton, "Authorship of *A Lady's Religion* (1697)," *Notes and Queries* 38, no. 2 (June 1991): 177. The paragraph in which Coste identifies Stephens as the author is omitted in the English preface to the 1704 second edition (the edition to which Astell responds).

25. See Sarah Apetrei, *Women, Feminism, and Religion in Early Enlightenment England* (Cambridge: Cambridge University Press, 2010), 123.

criticism in *The Christian Religion* should be interpreted."[26] Though Astell never explicitly names Toland in this work, Apetrei is right to suggest that Astell addresses the popular debate about "Christian mysteries" arising from Toland's deist ideas (see below, §§58–66). But it must be noted that some of the reasons for attributing *The Principle of the Protestant Reformation* to Toland are questionable. Michael Brown, for example, merely observes that *The Principle of the Protestant Reformation* "can be attributed to Toland on the grounds that, as was common practice for him, it puffed another of his works [i.e., it referred with approval to *Christianity not Mysterious*]."[27] To be more circumspect, it might be proposed that the author is "one of Mr Toland's club," if not Toland himself, as one of Astell's contemporaries suggested.[28]

On the whole, however, Astell was right to treat all three works—*A Lady's Religion*, *The Principle of the Protestant Reformation*, and *The Reasonableness of Christianity*—as thematically on a par. In these tracts, each author represents a certain Whig, pro-toleration, and pro-dissenter point of view, and they each aim to reduce the Christian religion to plain and simple articles of faith, in accordance with so-called Socinian or deist principles. In his *Reasonableness of Christianity*, Locke proposes to demonstrate that, according to the scriptures, the primary article of faith required to make anyone a Christian is the belief that Jesus Christ is the Messiah. For Locke, the Christian religion is designed by God to be accessible to the "lowest capacities of reasonable creatures," including those of the uneducated and laboring classes:[29]

26. Apetrei, *Women, Feminism, and Religion*, 124.

27. Michael Brown, *A Political Biography of John Toland* (London: Pickering and Chatto, 2012), 83.

28. [Edward Stephens], *Necessary Correction for an Insolent Deist: In Answer to an Impious Pamphlet, the Principle of the Protestant Reformation Explained in a Letter of Resolution concerning Church Communion* (London?: n.p., 1705?), 2.

29. Locke, *Reasonableness*, 284. For a modern edition, see John Locke, *The Reasonableness of Christianity as Delivered in the Scriptures*, ed. John C. Higgins-Biddle (Oxford: Clarendon Press, 1999), 159. Henceforth, I provide page references to this modern edition in square brackets following references to the 1696 second edition of *Reasonableness*.

> The bulk of mankind have not leisure for learning and logic, and superfine distinctions of the schools. Where the hand is used to the plough, and the spade, the head is seldom elevated to sublime notions, or exercised in mysterious reasonings. It is well if men of that rank (to say nothing of the other sex) can comprehend plain propositions, and a short reasoning about things familiar to their minds, and nearly allied to their daily experience. Go beyond this, and you amaze the greatest part of mankind.[30]

The fundamental articles of saving faith must therefore be few and simple, plain and intelligible—or, in short, they must be reasonable. This argument for the "way of fundamentals" in the Christian faith is consistent with Locke's now well-known Whig stance on the toleration of nonconformists in England. In his *Letter concerning Toleration* (first published in Latin as *Epistola de Tolerantia* in 1689), he points out that God has placed each man's salvation in his own hands, and that attaining this salvation requires individuals to come to the true religion through their own efforts, and not through the compulsion of others. On this view, the attainment of eternal happiness depends not on the outward observance of ceremonials but upon an inward persuasion of mind—the individual's assent, that is, to certain fundamental religious propositions. In keeping with his irenicism, in *The Reasonableness of Christianity* Locke highlights the fact that many points of difference between Protestant sects are simply not fundamental enough to justify separate communion.[31]

In response, one of Locke's earliest and harshest critics, the Cambridge preacher John Edwards (1637–1716), accused *The Reasonableness of Christianity* of being "all over Socinianized."[32] Though the term has variable usage in England during this period,

---

30. Locke, *Reasonableness*, 305 [169–70].

31. Locke, *Reasonableness*, 306 [170].

32. John Edwards, *Some Thoughts Concerning the Several Causes and Occasions of Atheism, Especially in the Present Age. With some Brief Reflections on Socinianism: And on a Late Book, Entitled The Reasonableness of Christianity as delivered in the Scriptures* (1695), facs. ed. (New York: Garland, 1984), 113.

there are certain heterodox ideas that Astell's contemporaries associated with "Socinianism."[33] To begin with, Socinianism is typically characterized by the denial of religious beliefs that are inconsistent with reason—a Socinian refuses to accept any proposition that fails to withstand the test of reason. In this respect, Socinians were seen as natural allies to deists, those theists who reject revelation (revealed religion) altogether in favor of religious rationalism (natural religion). Socinians also support the reduction of the Christian religion to a few fundamental articles of faith: they hold that there are a minimal number of religious beliefs required to make someone a Christian, many of which have nothing to do with traditional church doctrines and practices. In keeping with their extreme reverence for reason, Socinians also deny the mystery of the trinity, the doctrine that three divine persons, the father, son, and holy ghost, are one. They do not explicitly own that the death of Christ is an atonement or satisfaction for the sins of humanity, they do not openly acknowledge the divinity of Christ (his incarnation as God), and they tend to reject the view that God inflicts eternal punishment on sinners. In Astell's day, next to the term "atheist," "Socinian" was one of the most damaging and derogatory labels that could be applied to an author's work.

Like Locke's *Reasonableness of Christianity*, *A Lady's Religion* was also labeled Socinian.[34] This short tract was addressed to Lady Howard, a woman who had apparently requested the author's opinions about how to live in accordance with the Christian religion. Despite being an Anglican clergyman, the author elects to promote the "common cause" of Christian piety rather than defend the Church of England against dissenters. He advocates a highly moralistic approach to religion, one that places an emphasis upon practical duties rather than the observation of outward formalities. To lead a virtuous life, he says, we do not need to study obscure and unintelligible doctrines of divinity, but only to understand those moral laws that are intelligible to all reasonable persons. When in doubt, Lady Howard might consult

33. See Higgins-Biddle, introduction to Locke, *Reasonableness of Christianity*, lx–lxi. The following account of Socinianism is indebted to Higgins-Biddle's analysis in this introduction.

34. See John Gailhard, *The Epistle and Preface to the Book against the Blasphemous Socinian Heresie Vindicated; And the Charge therein against Socinianism, made Good* (London: J. Hartley, 1698), 82–83.

her own reason to inform herself "wherein you are justly dealt with, and wherein you receive wrong." Likewise, when dealing with other people, she might consult the same principle to "know when you deal justly or wrongfully, and when you do kind or ill offices to another."[35] It is fitting that the moral law is so easily intelligible, he says, echoing Locke, because "the greatest part of mankind being necessarily employed in making daily provisions for themselves and families, and discharging the common offices of life, cannot attend to any religious institution which is either difficult or tedious."[36]

Like the author of *A Lady's Religion*, the author of *The Principle of the Protestant Reformation* also endorses Locke's position on the way of fundamentals. In this work, the author advises an unknown lady that it is not necessary to take public communion in any particular church in order to be a good Christian. In his opinion, all the good lady need do is receive the doctrine of Christ into her heart. To illustrate his point, the author puts forward a rhetorical supposition. Let us suppose, he says, that a "Mahometan" (a Muslim) from Morocco were converted to Christianity in England, and then returned home to the African continent, where no Christian communion could be found. Wouldn't we all agree that it is unnecessary for this African to attend church in order to be considered a good Christian? The outward form of his worship would be irrelevant: the African could save his soul regardless of where he resided, whether that be Morocco, Holland, Geneva, or England. This work was later reissued with the provocative title *Liberty of Conscience, or Religion a la Mode. Fitted for the Use of the Occasional Conformist* (1704). As this new title suggests, the pamphlet had obvious implications for the occasional conformity debate in England: in essence, it explained why occasional conformists should not be persecuted for unorthodox communion practices.

All of the principal targets of *The Christian Religion* were the subject of heated controversy in Astell's lifetime. *The Principle of the Protestant Reformation* was despised among Tories. In *The Necessity of Church-Communion Vindicated* (1705), the nonjuror Robert Nelson (1656–1715) denounced the pamphlet as "one of the vilest this age has

---

35. *Lady's Religion*, 16.

36. *Lady's Religion*, 19.

seen."[37] In 1697, in a presentment to the grand jury of Middlesex, both *The Reasonableness of Christianity* and *A Lady's Religion* were charged alongside Toland's *Christianity not Mysterious* (1696) with being works of "Socinianism, Atheism, and Deism."[38] The same document calls for these authors to be punished "according to the utmost severity of the laws," the death penalty. In his *Christianity not Mysterious*, Toland claims that "no Christian doctrine can be properly called a mystery," in the sense of being above or contrary to reason.[39] Using Lockean terms, he defines reason as the clear perception of the agreement or disagreement of ideas, and then points out that we cannot reason about mysteries of faith because we have no clear ideas of them. If the Christian religion allows such mysteries that are above or contrary to reason, then this opens the floodgates to any number of absurd religious doctrines. Almost immediately upon publishing these ideas, Toland earned for himself an unparalleled infamy: his name became a byword for freethinking atheism in the period, his book was burned by the common hangman in Ireland, and for at least a decade following its publication, *Christianity not Mysterious* was the subject of numerous refutations in print. One of Toland's first and most influential critics was Edward Stillingfleet (1635–99), the bishop of Worcester. In the tenth chapter of his *Discourse in Vindication of the Doctrine of the Trinity* (1696), Stillingfleet interprets Toland's rejection of Christian mysteries as a necessary consequence of Lockean empiricism. Stillingfleet accuses Locke's *Essay concerning Human Understanding* (1689) of providing the philosophical groundwork for heretical ideas, including not only denial of the trinity but denial of the soul's immateriality and immortality, and even of the very existence of God. In particular, he highlights the negative implications of Locke's

---

37. [Robert Nelson], *The Necessity of Church-Communion Vindicated, From the Scandalous Aspersions of a late Pamphlet, Entitled, the Principle of the Protestant Reformation explained* (London: A. and J. Churchil, 1705), 27.

38. See Gailhard, *Epistle and Preface*, 82–83.

39. [John Toland], *Christianity not Mysterious: Or, A Treatise Showing, That there is nothing in the Gospel Contrary to Reason, Nor Above it: And that no Christian Doctrine can be properly called a Mystery* (London: n.p., 1696), 6. For a modern edition, see John Toland, *John Toland's Christianity not Mysterious: Text, Associated Works, and Critical Essays*, ed. Philip McGuinness, Alan Harrison, and Richard Kearney (Dublin: Lilliput Press, 1997), 17.

view that neither sensation nor reflection can provide us with a clear idea of substance (the substratum underlying perceived qualities). This attack on the *Essay* drew Locke into what is now regarded as "one of the most memorable controversies in the history of philosophy," the Locke-Stillingfleet debate.[40] In response to Stillingfleet, Locke pointed out that he had never in fact denied the existence of substance, but only affirmed that we have an imperfect and inadequate idea of it. For Stillingfleet, this disclaimer was beside the point. In his subsequent replies, he reiterated his initial charge: in his mind, Locke's epistemology could have nothing but dangerous consequences for the articles of the Christian faith.

Astell can be counted as one of many writers who came out in support of Edwards's and Stillingfleet's cries of heresy against Locke. In *The Christian Religion*, her discussion of Locke addresses the relevant passages in both the *Essay* and *The Reasonableness of Christianity*, as well as Locke's subsequent response to Edwards, the first *Vindication of the Reasonableness* (1695), and Locke's *Reply to the Bishop of Worcester* (1699).[41] She also touches upon topics in his now well-known political work, *Two Treatises of Government* (1689). Much of *The Christian Religion* is an attack on supposedly Socinian doctrines in the works of Locke and his fellow Whig authors.

But Astell also focuses on something other critics of her time overlook or downplay: she charges both Locke and his followers (namely, Coste) with harboring unfairly prejudicial attitudes toward women's intellectual abilities. This charge is justified. In his *Reasonableness of Christianity*, Locke says that the majority of men, "to say nothing of the other sex," have neither the time nor the capacity for demonstration and that they cannot "carry on a train of proofs."[42]

---

40. H. O. Christopherson, *A Bibliographical Introduction to the Study of John Locke* (New York: Burt Franklin, 1968), 35.

41. See [John Locke], *A Vindication of the Reasonableness of Christianity, & c. From Mr Edwards's Reflections* (London: Awnsham and John Churchil, 1695); and John Locke, *Mr. Locke's Reply to the Right Reverend the Lord Bishop of Worcester's Answer to his Second Letter* (London: H.C. for A. and J. Churchill, and E. Castle, 1699). In subsequent notes, I use a short title for Astell's idiosyncratic title for Locke's reply to Stillingfleet, *Third Letter to the Bishop of Worcester* (i.e., *Third Letter*).

42. Locke, *Reasonableness*, 282, 305 [157, 169–70].

He once again includes women among "the bulk of mankind" when he observes, "you may as soon hope to have all the day-laborers and tradesmen, the spinsters and dairy maids perfect mathematicians, as to have them perfect in ethics this way."[43] The only sure way to bring women to obedience and practice, he suggests, is for them to hear plain commands. Because they are incapable of understanding difficult concepts, they must be presented with fundamentals: "The greatest part cannot know, and therefore must believe."[44] Echoing Locke, in his preface to the French translation of *A Lady's Religion*, Coste observes that the Christian religion has obviously been accommodated to the meanest capacities. It is "easy to be explained, and every way adapted to the capacity of the illiterate, *of women*, and of the meanest sort of people, that is to say, of the greatest part of mankind."[45] Like Locke, Coste implies that the female sex are among those who are "incapable of a long application of mind, and who have neither penetration nor leisure enough to give up themselves to the study of curious and subtle inquiries, not easy to be resolved."[46]

Such negative attitudes toward women's mental abilities are not unusual for the times. At the start of *The Christian Religion*, Astell expresses her admiration for an anonymous work titled *The Ladies Calling* (1673). This advice manual for women was written by the Anglican clergyman Richard Allestree (1621/22–81), now thought to be the author of the tremendously popular *Whole Duty of Man*

---

43. Locke, *Reasonableness*, 282 [157].

44. Locke, *Reasonableness*, 282 [158]. In a posthumously published work, *A Paraphrase and Notes on the First Epistle of St Paul to the Corinthians* (1706), Locke's sexism becomes even more apparent. When it comes to public religious worship, he suggests, women must submit to the spiritual authority of men and never presume to act according to their own knowledge or abilities. This is because the Christian religion does not permit women to break free from their natural subjection to men. See John Locke, *A Paraphrase and Notes on the Epistles of St Paul to the Galatians, 1 and 2 Corinthians, Romans, Ephesians* (1706), ed. Arthur W. Wainwright, 2 vols. (Oxford: Clarendon Press, 1987). In the preface to her 1706 third edition of *Reflections upon Marriage*, Astell takes Locke to task for assuming that women are naturally subordinate to men. For details, see Mark Goldie, "Mary Astell and John Locke," in *Mary Astell: Reason, Gender, Faith*, ed. William Kolbrener and Michal Michelson (Aldershot, UK: Ashgate, 2007), 65–85.

45. *Lady's Religion*, A4v; my italics.

46. *Lady's Religion*, A5v.

(1657). In his *Ladies Calling*, Allestree argues that, in terms of their souls, women are equal to men and just as capable of attaining eternal happiness. Toward this end, he recommends that women be properly educated so that they may cultivate the feminine virtues of modesty, meekness, compassion, affability, and piety. His work thus forms part of the Anglican reformation of manners movement in this period, a movement committed to educating both men and women in the Christian religion.[47] In the course of expounding his educational program, however, Allestree frequently highlights the "natural imbecility" and "native feebleness" of women.[48] At the start of the work, for the sake of argument, he concedes that in respect of their intellects, women are inferior to men. Later, he refers to women's natural talkativeness ("a kind of incontinence of the mind, that can retain nothing committed to it"), their changeability, and their easy credulity (an "impotency" and "defect" in their nature).[49] On the whole, it must be said, if his work is directed toward women's learning to form rational judgments, it is not for themselves, not for the sake of their own moral and intellectual enlightenment, but rather so that they will adopt Anglican liturgical and devotional practices. Despite holding progressive views about women's education, Allestree does not challenge the prevailing sexism of the times. By contrast, Astell does.

To appreciate why, we must look to Astell's deeply held philosophical beliefs, and to the influence of Cartesianism on her opinions about the female intellect. Descartes's philosophy had a profound impact on English thought from the 1640s through the end of the seventeenth century. Every aspect of the Cartesian program—from Descartes's rationalist theory of knowledge, his dualism (his theory of the mind-body distinction), his concept of matter, his mechanical science, his cosmology, and his ethical thought—was picked up, analyzed, and dissected in print by prominent English intellectuals of this

---

47. On Astell's part in the Anglican moral reform movement, see Hannah Smith, "Mary Astell, *A Serious Proposal to the Ladies* (1694), and the Anglican Reformation of Manners in Late-Seventeenth-Century England," in Kolbrener and Michelson, *Mary Astell: Reason, Gender, Faith*, 31–47.

48. See [Richard Allestree], *The Ladies Calling In Two Parts. By the Author of the Whole Duty of Man, &c. The Seventh Impression* (Oxford: at the Theater, 1700), 36, 48.

49. Allestree, *Ladies Calling*, 12, 80, 88.

period.[50] In her *Proposal*, Astell implicitly follows the method of thinking promoted by Descartes in his *Discourse on the Method* (1637), and she explicitly draws on later versions of that method in the works of Norris, Arnauld, and Nicole.[51] Underlying the Cartesian methodology is the assumption that every human being naturally has freedom of the will and a capacity to discern the truth. Descartes's key insight was that by using these natural faculties to the best of their abilities, all human beings could attain clear and certain knowledge. According to his way of thinking, the attainment of knowledge does not require an intensive education in Latin, Greek, or logic; and it does not require rigorous book learning or a strong familiarity with ancient sources. In her writings, Astell follows up the egalitarian implications of this new philosophy. If women can reason about a romantic intrigue or the settlement of an estate, she points out, then they can also reason about religion and morality—despite their lack of higher education. In terms of their capacity for judgment, she suggests, women are on a par with men; both sexes are at liberty to accept or reject, affirm or deny, the ideas of the intellect in accordance with their reason. While there are no named references to Descartes in *The Christian Religion*, this Cartesian background is essential to understanding Astell's positive attitude toward women's reasoning abilities in the text.[52]

The Text

The Christian Religion is Astell's most profound and significant scholarly achievement.[53] In its original form, the text amounts to more than

50. The classic study on this subject is Sterling P. Lamprecht, "The Role of Descartes in Seventeenth-Century England," *Studies in the History of Ideas* 3 (1935): 181–240.

51. See Astell, *Proposal I*, 77–78; *Proposal II*, 166, 184, 189.

52. For recent studies on Astell and Cartesianism, see Deborah Boyle, "Mary Astell and Cartesian 'Scientia,'" in *The New Science and Women's Literary Discourse: Prefiguring Frankenstein*, ed. Judy Hayden (New York: Palgrave Macmillan, 2011), 99–112; and Alice Sowaal, "Mary Astell's *Serious Proposal*: Mind, Method, and Custom," *Philosophy Compass* 2 (2007): 227–43.

53. More than one scholar has referred to *The Christian Religion* as Astell's "magnum opus." See Perry, *Celebrated Mary Astell*, 215; Springborg, *Mary Astell*, 32; and Christine Mason Sutherland, *The Eloquence of Mary Astell* (Calgary, AB: University of Calgary Press, 2005), 93.

four hundred pages and includes a lengthy table of contents, numbered paragraphs, extensive marginal notes, and an index. The work ostensibly takes the form of a long letter addressed to a female friend (most likely, Catherine Jones). In this choice of genre, Astell follows the lead of her main targets, *A Lady's Religion* and *The Principle of the Protestant Reformation*, both of which were addressed to single female audiences.[54] In the 1717 second edition, however, Astell addresses a number of remarks to the "ladies" in general rather than "her ladyship" alone. These changes bring Astell's work closer to the *Proposal* in overall tone. In that earlier work, Astell highlights the dangers of encouraging the female sex to have implicit faith. Women are taught to repeat their catechism by rote, "to read a chapter and say their prayers," she says, "though perhaps with as little understanding as a parrot."[55] This is a precarious road to salvation, because without a true understanding of the basis of their beliefs, it is only by chance that women are led to the good life: "We are their property into whose hands we fall, and are led by those who with greatest confidence impose their opinions on us."[56] Instead, Astell argues in that work, a woman must be permitted the free exercise of her reason, and to inquire deeply into the foundations of her religion, to become "a Christian out of choice, not in conformity to those about her."[57]

The Christian Religion has the same instructive purpose as the *Proposal*. In the opening advertisement to the second edition, Astell declares that her chief design is "to put women upon thinking, upon an examination of their principles, the motives and grounds of their belief and practice, and the frame and temper of their minds."[58] She proposes to defend their "just and natural rights" of judging for themselves in matters concerning their ultimate happiness (§3). Toward this end, it is important that women recognize that they are free and reasonable agents, with the capacity for understanding and choice. If God had not intended for women to use their reason, she says, then he would not have bestowed it upon them, for an infinitely wise being

54. On Astell's choice of genre more generally, see Sutherland, *Eloquence of Mary Astell*, 94.
55. Astell, *Proposal II*, 124.
56. Astell, *Proposal II*, 200.
57. Astell, *Proposal I*, 70.
58. See below, p. 45.

does nothing without end or purpose (§5). Women are obliged to use their faculty of rational judgment in order to determine their duties toward God, other people, and themselves.

One difficulty for Astell, however, is that she does not want her fellow women to make erroneous judgments or endorse unorthodox religious ideas. She is no friend to Quakerism, for example, a religious philosophy that also urges women to turn to the "candle of the Lord," or the "light within," to attain salvation. Astell rejects all forms of enthusiasm, or any extravagant claims to religious inspiration that cannot be defended by the light of reason. For her, then, it is important that women have a properly trained judgment. They must be educated to use their reason to discern where the "true" and the "good" really lie. This is why, in the second part of her *Proposal*, Astell urges women to familiarize themselves with the methodological principles of Cartesian philosophy. According to the Cartesian method of judgment, women must reason only according to their pure nonsensory perceptions, or those "clear and distinct" ideas of the intellect, if they wish to attain knowledge. They must reason in a logical, orderly manner from simple to complex ideas; they must avoid being drawn into irrelevant considerations; and they must never judge anything to be true that is not clearly known to be so.[59] In *The Christian Religion*, Astell reiterates these points. "If we would judge to purpose," she says, then "we must free ourselves from prejudice and passion, must examine and prove all things, and not give our assent till forced to do so by the evidence of truth" (§4). But while Astell maintains that the principles of religion are accessible to reason, she does not claim that we should accept *only* those principles of religion that will withstand the test of reason. Her book demonstrates how women can use their reason to take a middle path between enthusiasm and Socinianism and come to endorse the moral theology of the Anglican religion.

The natural structure of the work falls into two parts. The first (section I) deals with the theoretical underpinnings of religious belief, or Astell's *theoretical theism*: it explains what "a woman ought to believe" by the light of her reason (§2). The second part (sections II–IV) deals with issues of *practical theism*, or what a woman ought to practice in light of her religious beliefs. In the first, theoretical part,

---

59. See Astell, *Proposal II*, 176–78.

Astell considers the subject of what a woman can judge for herself, relying on her natural reason alone, and she inquires how far reason can carry her in her religious beliefs and practices. Astell quickly comes to the conclusion that reason can assure her of the existence of an infinitely perfect being. Though her subheading refers to a single "proof for the existence of God" (§8), she provides at least two arguments in the relevant paragraphs (§§7–10). The first is an ontological argument, or an argument based on premises that can be known a priori or without sensory experience; the second is a cosmological proof, an argument based upon observations about the world or "cosmos." Following the pattern of Descartes's ontological proofs in his *Discourse on the Method, Meditations on First Philosophy* (1641), and *Principles of Philosophy* (1644), Astell's first argument begins with her idea of God as "a being infinite in all perfections" (§7). She then proceeds to identify necessary existence or "self-existence" as a perfection, before concluding that an infinitely perfect being must have the perfection of existence: God must exist. Her second argument relies on a brief hypothetical supposition. Let's suppose, she says, that I was "shut up in a den from my infancy" and then, once my reason had matured, I asked myself: "from whence had I my being?" (§10). If I ever came into contact with my fellow creatures, my reason would assure me that they could not be the cause of my existence, because their existence is as contingent as my own. Instead, I would be compelled to trace my origins—and the origins of the entire human race—back to "a last resort," a necessary or self-existent being. "That there is a self-existing being," she says, "is evident to the meanest understanding, for without it there could have been no men, no world, no being at all; since that which once *was not*, could never make itself; nor can any being communicate that to another which it has not itself" (§8).

Reason leads us not only to the belief that God exists, but also to belief in divine revelation—the Bible. To support this claim, Astell argues that no sober person could reasonably doubt that the Old and New Testaments are the word of God. Our natural intuition tells us, she says, that it is reasonable to accept the testimony of others with respect to matters of fact that we cannot witness in person. We believe that there were once men called Julius Caesar and Marcus Aurelius, and we accept that they were the authors of the works known as the

Commentaries and *Meditations*, even though we have never met them and never saw them write those works. When it comes to the Bible, we must be consistent in our application of reason. We must acknowledge, she says, that "no objection can be made against the holy scriptures but what are stronger against all other writings and facts" (§22). If we were to reject the scriptures as the word of God, then, to be consistent, we would also have to disbelieve everything that we did not see or hear. But this is a most untenable and unreasonable position.

In addition to this argument, Astell presents a Pascal's Wager-style argument for the rationality of believing that revelation is the word of God. In one "thought" of his *Pensées* (first published posthumously in 1670), Blaise Pascal (1623–62) argues that it is in the interests of all individuals to believe in God. To demonstrate this point, Pascal invites his readers to a game of chance. Granted that either God does or does not exist, he asks, what will you wager? "Let us weigh the gain and the loss in wagering that God is," he says. "If you gain, you gain all; if you lose, you lose nothing."[60] In his view, the most reasonable course of action is to believe that God exists. Along similar lines, Astell calculates the risks associated with believing or not believing that the Bible is the word of God. For the sake of argument, she grants her atheistic opponents their "most unreasonable demands" (§41). Let us suppose that reason *cannot* assure us beyond reasonable doubt that the Bible is the word of God. She then weighs up the "hazard of receiving" and the risks or "dangers of rejecting" the scriptures as divine revelation. According to Astell, even the infidel must agree that the most reasonable course of action is to receive the Bible as the word of God. This course of action would be most desirable *even if* the Bible turned out to be a forgery, "since nothing could be more for my present interest, safety, and pleasure" (§41). If I believe in the Bible, and it is a fake, then I am imposed upon, that is true; but this is a small price to pay. By contrast, if I were to take the alternative course of action and reject the authenticity of the Bible, this risks bringing upon me the worst possible state of affairs: eternal opposition to God. To be prudent, I should not take that risk.

60. Blaise Pascal, *Pensées* (1670), trans. W. F. Trotter, online edition (Adelaide: University of Adelaide Library, 2012), http://ebooks.adelaide.edu.au/p/pascal/blaise/p27pe/index.html (accessed October 31, 2012), §233.

Having established the foundations for belief in both natural and revealed religion, Astell then considers our practical duties to God (section II), to our fellow human beings (section III), and to ourselves (section IV), before providing further detailed refutations of Locke, the author of *A Lady's Religion*, and two further authors, Damaris Masham and John Tillotson (section V, her appendix). Of our duties to God, Astell observes that we are clearly obliged to live in conformity with the will of an infinitely perfect being, or, in other words, in accordance with the divine law as revealed through reason and revelation. Conforming ourselves to God's will requires not only a "sincere and constant endeavor after our own perfection" (§94) but also a due regard for God's other creatures: our neighbors. In keeping with the scriptures, Astell advises that women ought to regard all their fellow human beings as members of one body, the Christian community in general, and to recognize that the good of their neighbor is not separate from their own but rather an integral part of it. Above all, she recommends acting in accordance with a principle of benevolence in our interactions with others, or from motivations of disinterested love and good will toward all. In this respect, *The Christian Religion* provides a further explication of the moral-theological themes of *Letters Concerning the Love of God*.

Though Astell employs the language of deontology (the language of duties and obligations), she also articulates an ethics of virtue in so far as she recommends the cultivation of certain excellent character traits (or virtues) in her readers. In her interactions with others, according to Astell, a wise and virtuous woman always endeavors to keep the true good and eternal interest of all human beings in mind. In her personal interactions with men, she resists adopting the character of a "coquette" (in modern terminology, a flirt), not only because she risks scandal and the ruin of her reputation, but because she tempts a fellow human being to vice and sin (§§196–98). In her close friendships with others, a wise and virtuous woman endeavors to perfect the moral well-being of her friend. Toward this end, she does not turn a blind eye to the other person's faults or encourage the friend's pride through flattery; rather she engages in friendly admonition and offers gentle moral guidance. In turn, the wise and virtuous woman is willing to accept such admonition herself, for the sake of her own moral advancement (§§203–6).[61] In her wider social interactions, this woman strives to live peaceably with her fellow human beings and is forgiving rather than resentful of other people's shortcomings and faults.

In these passages and in her later appendix, Astell provides a defense of the love of benevolence against the criticisms of a fellow woman writer, Damaris Masham (née Cudworth, 1659–1708), the author of the anonymous *Discourse concerning the Love of God* (1696).[62] Masham was the daughter of the Cambridge Platonist Ralph Cudworth (1617–1688) and one of Locke's closest friends in the last years of his life. Locke (1632–1704) lived with Masham and her husband from 1691 till his death. In her *Discourse*, Masham dismisses Norris's theory that we are obliged to love other people with only a disinterested kind of love, and that we ought to reserve our love of desire (a self-interested love) for God alone. Her main point is that Norris's theory of love renders the duties of a moral life impractical. Human beings simply do not have the capacity to withdraw their desires from material things and other people. Her concern is that a religious theory that requires impossible performances, such as complete emotional disengagement from the world, might lead some people to abandon religion altogether. The same religious theory might also drive others to live in "monasteries, and hermitages; with all those sottish and wicked superstitions which have accompanied them wherever they have been in use."[63]

In her *Discourse*, Masham refers in passing to Astell as "a young person ... biased by the affectation of novelty," but most of her sharpest comments are reserved for Norris and Malebranche.[64] In *The Christian Religion*, however, Astell interprets a number of Masham's remarks as

---

61. For a study of Astell's concept of friendship in this work, see Jacqueline Broad, "Mary Astell on Virtuous Friendship," *Parergon: Journal of the Australian and New Zealand Association for Medieval and Early Modern Studies* 26, no. 2 (2009): 65–86.

62. [Damaris Masham], *Discourse concerning the Love of God* (London: Awnsham and John Churchil, 1696). For a facsimile reprint, see Damaris Masham, *The Philosophical Works of Damaris, Lady Masham*, intro. James G. Buickerood (Bristol, UK: Thoemmes Continuum, 2004).

63. Masham, *Discourse*, 120.

64. Masham, *Discourse*, 78.

criticisms of her own opinions.[65] This is not surprising given that, like Norris, Astell also extols the benefits of a contemplative life, a life of disengagement from the desire of material things and other people. The main gist of Astell's response to Masham is that it is absurd for anyone to think that such a contemplative life is "destructive of all religion, and even of morality" (§378). Norris's theory of love does not necessarily lead to either atheism or enthusiasm. Rather, the contemplative life enables one to avoid a vacuous materialistic lifestyle, in favor of spiritual goods and long-lasting benefits. In Astell's view, this is also one of the chief benefits of a female monastery, or "a reasonable provision for the education of one half of mankind" (§379). An academy for women could be a "generous design for the glory of God and the good of mankind" (§379)—a way of advancing human nature in general. In this work, then, Astell once again revives her plans for a female academy. In one key part of the text, she calls on Queen Anne in the hope that "she will not do less for her own sex than she has already done for the other" and offer her bounty to "the most helpless and neglected part of her subjects," the women (§380).

In the final part of her main text, Astell considers the nature of our duties to our "selves" or our souls. For the moral benefit of her readers, she proposes to show that the soul is naturally immortal

65. There are a number of articles on Astell's response to Masham. See Patricia Springborg, "Astell, Masham, and Locke: Religion and Politics," in *Women Writers and the Early Modern British Political Tradition*, ed. Hilda L. Smith (Cambridge: Cambridge University Press, 1998), 105–25; Springborg, *Mary Astell*, 67–80; E. Derek Taylor, "Mary Astell's Ironic Assault on John Locke's Theory of Matter," *Journal of the History of Ideas* 62, no. 3 (2001): 505–22; Jacqueline Broad, *Women Philosophers of the Seventeenth Century* (Cambridge: Cambridge University Press, 2002), 114–40; Jacqueline Broad, "Adversaries or Allies? Occasional Thoughts on the Masham-Astell Exchange," *Eighteenth-Century Thought* 1 (2003): 123–49; Catherine Wilson, "Love of God and Love of Creatures: The Masham-Astell Debate," *History of Philosophy Quarterly* 21, no. 3 (2004): 281–98; James G. Buickerood, "What Is It with Damaris, Lady Masham? The Historiography of One Early Modern Woman Philosopher," *Locke Studies* 5 (2005): 179–214; Eileen O'Neill, "Mary Astell on the Causation of Sensation," in Kolbrener and Michelson, *Mary Astell: Reason, Gender, Faith*, 145–63; and Joanne E. Myers, "Enthusiastic Improvement: Mary Astell and Damaris Masham on Sociability," *Hypatia: A Journal of Feminist Philosophy* 28 (forthcoming). For details on Astell's response to Malebranchean philosophy more generally, see Sarah Ellenzweig, "The Love of God and the Radical Enlightenment: Mary Astell's Brush with Spinoza," *Journal of the History of Ideas* 64, no. 3 (2003): 379–97.

by virtue of its nonmaterial and indivisible nature. Toward this end, she provides an argument for the view that the soul and the body are two distinct substances, an argument that closely resembles that of Norris in the second part of his *Theory of the Ideal or Intelligible World* (1704).[66] At the conclusion to this argument, Astell dismisses Locke's controversial claim that we cannot know by the mere contemplation of our ideas of *matter* and of *thinking* that an omnipotent being "has not given to some systems of matter fitly disposed, a power to perceive and think."[67] In her view, the idea that matter can think is as repugnant as the idea that a triangle can be equal to a square. In his *Essay*, Locke himself maintains that we can be certain of the repugnancy or incompatibility of certain ideas. To be consistent, Astell says, he ought to maintain that we can be certain that matter cannot think.

Having established that the human subject is a vital union of two distinct substances—an immortal, immaterial soul and a corruptible, material body—Astell proceeds to develop a theory of the passions. The passions are those emotions, such as love, hatred, desire, and so on, that arise involuntarily in the soul as a result of its intimate connection with the human body. The passions are a problem for the attainment of virtue and wisdom because they cloud and obscure our rational judgments. In a lengthy passage (§254), Astell offers recommendations about the best way to remedy the disordering effect of the passions on the soul. Her advice closely resembles that of the final chapter in her *Proposal II*, where Astell explicitly refers her reader to Descartes's *Passions of the Soul* (1649) and Henry More's *Account of Virtue* (1690).[68] In *The Christian Religion*, her position is further ar-

66. See below, §§226–32.

67. John Locke, *An Essay Concerning Human Understanding*, ed. Peter H. Nidditch (Oxford: Clarendon Press, 1975), IV.iii.6. My references to Locke's *Essay* are to book, chapter, and section numbers in this edition. For details on the controversy surrounding Locke's claim about "thinking matter," see John Yolton, *Thinking Matter: Materialism in Eighteenth-Century Britain* (Minneapolis: University of Minnesota Press, 1983). On Astell's critique of Locke's views, see Kathleen M. Squadrito, "Mary Astell's Critique of Locke's View of Thinking Matter," *Journal of the History of Philosophy* 25 (1987): 433–39; Kathleen M. Squadrito, "Mary Astell," in *A History of Women Philosophers*, ed. Mary Ellen Waithe (Dordrecht: Kluwer, 1991), 3:87–99; and Taylor, "Mary Astell's Ironic Assault."

68. Astell, *Proposal II*, 218, 219–20. For details, see Jacqueline Broad, "Astell, Cartesian Ethics, and the Critique of Custom," in Kolbrener and Michelson, *Mary Astell: Reason,*

ticulated in response to the religious writings of an Irish clergyman named Charles Hickman (1648–1713). Though Astell never explicitly names Hickman, her quotations (§§327, 334–44) are taken verbatim from the ninth sermon in his 1700 work, *Fourteen Sermons*. Against Hickman's view, she states that human beings are obliged to eradicate their most excessive and destructive passions—pride, anger, hatred, and overwhelming sorrow.

The upshot of Astell's philosophical examination of theoretical and practical theism is, ultimately, the affirmation of complete conformity to the Anglican religion. Against the author of *The Principle of the Protestant Reformation*, she declares that reason evidently requires one to live in Christian communion, or to be a participating member of a local Christian church. She defends the reasonableness of distinctive articles and creeds of the Church of England, including the doctrine of the trinity, belief in Christ's divinity, in Christ's satisfaction for our sins, and in the other articles of the Athanasian and Apostles' Creeds. In her view, reason itself recommends all those beliefs and practices that her target authors—Locke and the authors of *A Lady's Religion* and *The Principle of the Protestant Reformation*—had rejected as nonfundamental to the Christian faith. At the very end of the work, Astell briefly addresses a sermon on the divinity of Christ by John Tillotson (1630–94), archbishop of Canterbury, where she reiterates many of these same points.

Nevertheless, Astell's deference to the Anglican church is qualified. As an Anglican and a Tory royalist, she is strongly committed to the doctrine of passive obedience, the idea that subjects are obliged "to render active obedience to just authority, in all instances that are not contrary to God's commands, and to submit quietly to the penalty where they cannot actually obey" (§149). Importantly, however, this is a position that *allows disobedience* when one's superiors sin against right reason or require something that is "contrary to God's commands" (§§149, 174). In Astell's view, subjects are not required passively to accept any dictates or commands from clerical authorities that might jeopardize their salvation. In *The Christian Religion*, she applies these ideas about the permissible bounds of resistance to the situation of women in subordination to men. Somewhat radically

---

Gender, Faith, 165–80.

(for the time), she calls on her female readers not to obey those male authorities who would enslave their capacity for rational judgment about moral and religious matters. She emphasizes that a man is not wiser than a woman merely because he is a man (§141), and that no woman is obliged to submit to a man's opinion "on his bare word, nor to swallow his arguments without examining them" (§404). She pointedly asks:

> How comes it that we are chained down to the slavery of all the silly customs of the age, to the waste of our time, the expense of our fortunes, nay even to the depraving of our very reason, but because we must do as others do, and are afraid of the singularity of being wiser and better than our neighbors? So that we force ourselves to practice those follies, which while we practice we condemn! What is it that engages women in crimes contrary to their reason, and their very natural temper, but being over-persuaded and over-ruled by the men to whose conduct they commit themselves? (§47)

Keeping within the permissible bounds of Anglican political theology, Astell invokes the moral law—the law of God and reason—against those designing men who would endeavor to make women their "dupes" or their "properties" (§266).[69] In her view, a man's dictates or commands must conform to this moral law before a woman can accept them as principles for her own actions. Strictly speaking, Astell says, a woman must "call no man master on earth" (Matthew 23:9–10), but rather submit only to that "great master" in heaven, God himself (§3). "The more entirely we depend on God," she warns, "we are so

---

69. We might think that Astell's book is an expression of the political theology of the Anglican revolution, c. 1685–88, in so far as she offers the same ideological bulwarks against *men* that Anglican writers offered against the *crown* in the reign of James II. Mark Goldie observes that the Anglican reformists invoked not their political or legal rights but rather the moral law. This law gave them a "considered case for resistance," based on the "presumption that there are discernible principles of right which, with the guidance of a sound conscience, may be invoked to overcome a wrongful sovereign." See Mark Goldie, "The Political Thought of the Anglican Revolution," in *The Revolutions of 1688: The Andrew Browning Lectures 1988*, ed. Robert Beddard (Oxford: Clarendon Press, 1991), 102–36 (esp. 107, 112–13).

much the wiser and happier, but the less we depend on men so much the better" (§267).

Afterlife of the Text

In a 1705 correspondence with the nonjuring bishop George Hickes (1642–1715), Astell repeats a number of these same points.[70] Her comments appear in a letter to an unknown woman who had appealed to Hickes for help in a matter of religious concern. This "devout lady" wanted to know if she could, in good conscience, attend services at her local parish church despite the fact that it was "schismatic" (or complying) and she herself was a Jacobite (or noncomplying). The lady, "having read some of Mrs. Astell's books, and having a great opinion of her," asked Hickes to request Astell's advice about the matter.[71] In response, in a letter dated September 21, 1705, Astell counsels the woman to rely principally on her own capacity for reflection and judgment about religious matters. Echoing her advice in *The Christian Religion*, she says:

> I pretend not to convince your Ladyship, or to bring
> you over to my opinion, nor do I desire you should take
> my word for anything. You know it is my principle, and
> ought to be everyone's for it is our Lord's command,
> to call no man 'master upon earth,' to be concluded by
> no authority but that of our master who is in heaven. I
> would have women as well as men to see with their own
> eyes as far as they will reach, and to judge according to
> the best of their own understandings.[72]

70. "The Controversy betwixt Dr. Hickes & Mrs. Mary Astell," in "The Genuine Remains of the late Pious and Learned George Hickes D. D. and Suffragen Bishop of Thetford," ed. Thomas Bedford, Papers of George Hickes, MS 3171, Lambeth Palace Library, London. These letters were recently discovered by Sarah Apetrei. For an in-depth analysis of the correspondence, see Apetrei, "'Call No Man Master Upon Earth': Mary Astell's Tory Feminism and an Unknown Correspondence," *Eighteenth-Century Studies* 41, no. 4 (2008): 507–23; and Apetrei, *Women, Feminism, and Religion*, 135–52.

71. Astell and Hickes, "Controversy," 171. I have expanded the seventeenth-century abbreviations and modernized the spelling in these letters.

72. Astell and Hickes, "Controversy," 197.

Upon reading this letter, Hickes was outraged. He accused Astell of espousing "suspicious" and "skeptical" principles concerning clerical authority, and he bluntly informed her that she wrote more like a heretic or a Protestant dissenter than an Anglican.[73] He challenged Astell to spell out the difference between her views and those expressed in the scurrilous *Principle of the Protestant Reformation.*[74] Presumably Hickes was unaware that Astell had written a critique of the work. At the time, her authorship of *The Christian Religion* seems to have been in doubt. In the same year, George Stanhope (1660–1728), the dean of Canterbury, presumed that *The Christian Religion* was the work of Astell's neighbor, Francis Atterbury (1662–1732), the dean of Carlisle. On December 17, 1705, he writes to Atterbury that "I am informed this day, that you have put out in print a mighty ingenious pamphlet, but that you have been pleased to father it upon one Mrs. Astell, a female friend and witty companion of your wife."[75]

On the whole, however, *The Christian Religion* enjoyed a good reception—it was not reviled as skeptical or subversive of all orthodox religion. While Hickes might have disapproved of Astell's apparent anticlericalism, a few years later he openly admired her treatise. In the postscript to his translation of François Fénelon's *Instructions for the Education of a Daughter* (1707), Hickes advises a young lady to read both the *Proposals* and *The Christian Religion*, observing that "these being written by one of her own sex, may probably serve to make a deeper impression upon her."[76] In his *Orthodoxy in Faith* (1713), the

---

73. Hickes says: "Madam, say you to the Lady, 'I pretend not to convince your Ladyship, or to bring you over to my opinion, nor do I desire you should take my word for anything. You know it is my principle and ought to be everyone's for it is our Lord's command, to call no man master upon earth, and to be concluded by no authority but that of our master who is in heaven.' This, Madam, is the very language of the Quakers who are heretics, and had I known it had been your principle as it is theirs, I would have had no dispute with you." Astell and Hickes, "Controversy," 204.

74. Hickes tells Astell to "read the *Letter to a Lady concerning Church Communion* … and then tell me the difference between your principles and theirs" ("Controversy," 204).

75. Francis Atterbury, *The Miscellaneous Works of Bishop Atterbury*, ed. J. Nichols, 5 vols. (London: J. Nichols, 1799) 1:391.

76. George Hickes, "The Postscript by the Translator. To Antiope," in François Fénelon, *Instructions for the Education of a Daughter, By the Author of Telemachus. To which is added A Small Tract of Instructions for the Conduct of Young Ladies of the Highest Rank. With*

religious writer John Howard observes that Astell's book provides an admirable answer to *A Lady's Religion.*[77]

Notwithstanding such commendations, Astell made certain changes to the second edition. In his critical letter of 1705, Hickes writes to Astell:

> Madam, comparing of women with men in your emulous manner, is an affectation which your best friends observe runs through most of your excellent writings. The great Hypatia, who I admire as well as you, I am confident was a greater genius of a woman than to reflect and couch such childish reflections in her lectures and writings on the other sex.[78]

While the thematic focus of the second edition of *The Christian Religion* is substantially the same as that of the first, Astell did tone down the harshness of her words. In §88, "block-heads" becomes "impolite persons," and in §266, "their dupes" becomes "their properties." In this same edition, Astell also qualifies some of her invectives against men. When lamenting that men deprive women of all useful learning, she concedes that some men have permitted women to study history. In the first edition, she sharply observes that history can serve only as a trifling amusement for women:

> For though it may be of use to the men who govern affairs, to know how their forefathers acted, yet what is this to us, who have nothing to do with such business? Some good examples indeed are to be found in history, though generally the bad are ten for one; but how will this help our conduct, or excite in us a generous emulation? Since the men being the historians, they seldom condescend to record the great and good actions of

Suitable Devotions Annexed. Done into English, and Revised by Dr. George Hickes (London: Jonah Bowyer, 1707), 292.

77. John Howard, *Orthodoxy in Faith, and Uprightness in Life and Conversation* (London: Jonah Bowyer, 1713), xvii.

78. Astell and Hickes, "Controversy," 204.

women; and when they take notice of them, it is with
this wise remark, that such women 'acted above their
sex.' By which one must suppose they would have their
readers understand, that they were not women who
did those great actions, but that they were men in petticoats! (§260)

In the second edition, Astell adds that history can be useful to women
if "we take a greater compass than they [i.e., the men] allow us language and leisure to reach, that we may trace divine providence, and
admire it in the government of the world, and conduct of the church"
(§260). Nevertheless, Astell was not completely cowed by Hickes's
criticisms. There are some alterations that emphasize the gender-crit-
ical nature of her work. In §46, her reflections on "those who have
made themselves our governors" is altered to "*men* who have *made
themselves* our governors" (my added italics), and in §47 she writes,
"What is it that engages women in crimes contrary to their reason ...
but being over-persuaded and over-ruled by the *men* to whose conduct they commit themselves?" instead of simply "by *those* to whose
conduct they commit themselves" (my italics).

Surprisingly, the only later records of good opinion about *The
Christian Religion* come from the men themselves. In his *Miscellany
of Ingenious Thoughts and Reflections* (1721), Tamworth Reresby observes that "no person has distinguished herself in a finer and more
commendable manner, than she who writ a book some years since,
called, *The Principles of a Daughter of the Church of England*, as well as
several other ingenious tracts, which show her equally devout, ingenious, and learned."[79] In a letter to George Ballard, dated February 12,
1743, William Parry expressed these glowing sentiments about "Mrs.
Astell's performance" in her *Christian Religion*:

I cannot but esteem Mrs. Astell's account of her religion
as an excellent treatise; it is written with that strength,
perspicuity, and smoothness, with such elegance of dic-
tion, such refined judgment, such an uncommon spirit

79. Tamworth Reresby, *A Miscellany of Ingenious Thoughts and Reflections* (London: H.
Meere, 1721), 415.

of true Christianity and orthodoxy, and supported with such clear, solid, full, and convincing arguments, that I have scarcely ever read a book with greater delight and satisfaction. In my opinion, the learned authoress has with great dexterity and success retorted Mr. Locke's metaphysical artillery against himself, confuted his whimsical idea of 'thinking' matter, and given him a genteel foil. She has stripped him of his disguise in personating a clergyman, and yet writing like a Socinian; and has fairly shown the imperfections and erroneous tenets contained in those two tracts of his, *The Reasonableness of Christianity* and the *Ladies' Religion*: and has convinced me, that he had no honest design in writing either of them, since notwithstanding those specious titles he has given them, instead of promoting Christianity, they tend rather to undermine and subvert the true faith, and are derogatory to the honor of the savior. But in my judgment she has justly and handsomely disclosed and defeated his false and fallacious reasonings, and defended the cause of the primitive faith with a zeal becoming a true professor of it.[80]

Though Astell's critique of Tillotson appears only as an afterthought in *The Christian Religion*, in later years she was also remembered for her comments on his sermons. In his *Advice to a Young Student* (1730), Daniel Waterland recommends Tillotson's writings but refers his reader to Astell's *Christian Religion*, noting that the archbishop's views concerning Christ's satisfaction are "modestly and judiciously examined by an ingenious lady, in a very good book entitled, *The Religion of a Church of England-Woman*."[81] In 1753, Thomas Birch also reports that

Mrs. Astell in one of her works, which do honor to her understanding as well as piety, and give her an eminent

---

80. William Parry to George Ballard, February 12, 1743, Ballard MS 40:158, Bodleian Library, Oxford. Parry's letter is reproduced in Ballard, *Memoirs of Several Ladies*, 389.

81. Daniel Waterland, *Advice to a Young Student. With a Method of Study for the Four First Years* (London: John Crownfield, 1730), 24.

rank among the writers of her sex, has made some remarks upon the archbishop's doctrine of the satisfaction
in his *Sermons concerning the Divinity and Incarnation
of our Blessed Savior*; though she treats him with the
highest respect, styling him a 'great author, so deservedly celebrated for his good sense and just expression, the
strength and clearness of his reasoning, and his natural
and unaffected eloquence.'[82]

A number of the copies of *The Christian Religion* in rare book librar-
ies were once owned by men, including the Anglican clergymen John
Conybeare and (possibly) Laurence Fogg,[83] the historian George
Tracy Buckingham,[84] the conservative politician Leonard Brassey,[85]
the surgeon and bibliophile Geoffrey Keynes,[86] and Charles Quintard
Wiggins III.[87]

On the whole, there is little surviving evidence that Astell's
work achieved its stated aim "to put women upon thinking, upon
an examination of their principles." But while no woman openly acknowledges *The Christian Religion*, some early modern women do
echo Astell's themes in their writings. There are remarkably similar
topics, for example, in the works of Astell's friends Ann Coventry
(1673–1763) and Mary Chudleigh (1656–1710). In her *Meditations,
and Reflections Moral and Divine* (1707), Coventry discusses how
short life is, how present things cannot satisfy us, how riches and titles
do not bestow happiness, and how true and lasting felicity lies with

82. Thomas Birch, ed., *Additions in the Second Edition of the Life of Archbishop Tillotson* (London: n.p., 1653?), 13.

83. Call no. BV4500.A8 1717 and BV4500.A8, Watkinson Library, Trinity College, Hartford. The copy of the first edition in the Watkinson Library bears the inscription "the gift of D. Fogg to his friend, C. Hutchinson, 1782." On one flyleaf, the words "C. Hutchinson 1770" have been written over the top of a rubbed-out inscription, faintly suggestive of the name "Fogg."

84. Call no. BV4500.A8, University of Pennsylvania Rare Books and Manuscripts Library, Philadelphia.

85. Call no. B-11 07050, Thomas Fisher Rare Books Library, University of Toronto.

86. Call no. Keynes c.8.20, Cambridge University Library.

87. Call no. 248.483 A853c, 1717, Jessie Ball duPont Library, University of the South, Sewanee.

God alone.[88] In her *Essays upon Several Subjects* (1710), Chudleigh argues that women ought to be recommended the study of virtue and persuaded "to improve their understandings, to prefer wisdom before beauty, good sense before wealth, and the sovereignty of their passions before the empire of the world."[89] There is no conclusive evidence that Chudleigh was indebted to *The Christian Religion*, but her essays do cover the subjects of knowledge, pride, humility, life, death, fear, grief, riches, self-love, anger, calumny, friendship, love, avarice, and solitude—topics that are discussed at length in Astell's work. Some surviving copies of *The Christian Religion* in rare book libraries also bear the marks of female ownership. The copy of the second edition at the Watkinson Library was once owned by Jemima Conybeare, wife of the Anglican writer John Conybeare, who then passed it down to her nephew's wife, Mary Conybeare.[90] The 1730 reissue at the Yale Divinity School Library was owned by Elizabeth H. Nichols.[91] A copy held at the Cambridge University Library was once owned by Ann Burrill (1740) and Elizabeth Anne Herbert (1805).[92] Markings in some of these books (such as crosses and underlining) indicate an attentive reading of the text.

Note on the Text

There has never been a modern edition of Astell's *Christian Religion*.[93] This present edition contains a complete text of the 1717 second edi-

88. Ann Coventry, *The Right Honourable Ann Countess of Coventry's Meditations and Reflections, Moral and Divine* (London: B. Aylmer and W. Rogers, 1707).

89. Mary Chudleigh, *Essays upon Several Subjects in Prose and Verse*, in *The Poems and Prose of Mary, Lady Chudleigh*, ed. Margaret J. M. Ezell (New York: Oxford University Press, 1993), 247–48.

90. Call no. BV4500.A8 1717, Watkinson Library, Trinity College, Hartford.

91. Call no. LS60 As82 Kc46, Yale Divinity School Library, New Haven.

92. Call no. Keynes c.8.20, Cambridge University Library.

93. There are, however, excerpts in the following works: Mary Astell, *The First English Feminist: "Reflections Upon Marriage" and Other Writings by Mary Astell*, ed. Bridget Hill (New York: St. Martin's Press, 1986), 197–202; Lynn MacDonald, ed., *Women Theorists on Society and Politics* (Waterloo, ON: Wilfrid Laurier University Press, 1998), 19–22; Hilda L. Smith, Mihoko Suzuki, and Susan Wiseman, eds., *Women's Political Writings, 1610–1725*, 4 vols. (London: Pickering and Chatto, 2007), 4:36–48, 340–41; and Taylor and New, appendix

tion, including the author's index.[94] *The Christian Religion* was re-published three times in Astell's lifetime: the first edition appeared in 1705, the second in 1717, and the so-called third in 1730. All the available bibliographical evidence suggests that the 1730 work is simply a reissue of the second edition with a cancel title leaf (a new leaf in place of the old one)[95] and a sixteen-page bookseller's advertisement at the end. There are no variations between the 1717 and 1730 texts: the errata, the main text, the watermarks in the paper, the setting of type in each gathering, and the press figures are all identical. Accordingly, it is highly improbable that there was ever a third edition of the text, and so I regard the second edition as Astell's final and considered opinion on the topics under discussion—this is why I have used it as the basis for my edition.

In my footnotes, I provide definitions of obscure or archaic terms, as well as bibliographical information about Astell's sources, references to similar topics in her other works, and further historical-intellectual details that might assist the reader. I also highlight variations between the first and second editions. I do not note minor variations in spelling and grammar, but I do indicate any alterations that

---

to Astell and Norris, *Letters*, 221–58. Copies of the original first and second editions of *The Christian Religion* can also be found in the online database, *Eighteenth-Century Collections Online*.

94. [Mary Astell], *The Christian Religion, As Professed by a Daughter of the Church of England* (London: W.B. for R. Wilkin, at the King's-Head in St. Paul's-Church-Yard, 1717). This edition was printed by the well-known Bowyer printing house of London. The work appears in the Bowyer Ledger A7 for February 11, 1717: "Mrs Astells Religion of a Daughter of a Church of England ~~Woman~~." For details, see Keith Maslen and John Lancaster, eds., *The Bowyer Ledgers: The Printing Accounts of William Bowyer Father and Son. Reproduced on Microfiche. With a Checklist of Bowyer Printing 1699–1777, a Commentary, Indexes, and Appendices* (London: Bibliographical Society; New York: Bibliographical Society of America, 1991), entry no. 373.

95. The title page of the 1730 reissue reads: *The Christian Religion, as Professed by a Daughter of the Church of England. Containing Proper Directions for the due Behavior of Women in every Station of Life. With a few cursory Remarks on Archbishop Tillotson's Doctrine of the Satisfaction of Christ, &c. and on Mr. Locke's Reasonableness of Christianity. By the Author of the Proposal to the Ladies; and Reflections on Marriage, &c. The Third Edition* (London: W. Parker, at the King's-Head in St. Paul's Church-Yard, 1730). This reissue was produced by William Parker, the bookseller who took over Richard Wilkin's old stock. For details on Parker, see Perry, *Celebrated Mary Astell*, 68, 70, 481, and 532.

might have come from Astell's hand and that might have bearing on her meaning, such as significant changes in wording and the rewriting or addition of whole sentences. Some of the variations have bearing on the structure or ordering of the work as a whole. In the second edition, Astell's extended critiques of her contemporaries, Locke, Masham, the author of *A Lady's Religion*, and Tillotson (§§75–88, 137–52, 262–69, and 393–407 in the first edition), are gathered together in a new appendix at the end, and the subsections are renumbered accordingly. In her advertisement to the second edition, she explains that she placed these paragraphs in the appendix to separate "what was matter of controversy" from "the practical part" of her treatise. As a result, the main narrative of the second edition proceeds in a much more natural and easy manner than that of the first. Another noteworthy revision in the second edition is the inclusion of marginal glosses (brief descriptive statements in the form of shoulder notes) at the start of each numbered subsection. In the first edition, these glosses make up a lengthy table of contents at the start of the work. In this present volume, I have included the glosses in italics at the start of each individual subsection in the text. I have not turned them into footnotes, as I have for other types of marginalia, because I think that Astell intended these glosses to be headings.

I have modernized the spelling, punctuation, and typography of the text. In doing so, my guiding principle was to provide a text that was accessible to the modern reader but at the same time faithful to the author's original meaning. To preserve the idiosyncrasies of Astell's writing style, and to avoid inadvertently changing her meaning, I have made minimal alterations to punctuation. By comparison with modern works, however, eighteenth-century texts are rife with commas, colons, and semicolons. Accordingly, I have made some small amendments: occasionally, for the sake of clarity, I have changed some commas, colons, or semicolons to hyphens or parentheses, and I have deleted some punctuation that may have confused the modern reader. I have used inverted commas instead of italics to indicate quotations, though I have retained Astell's use of italics for emphasis. I have expanded contracted words (I use "would" instead of "wou'd," for example) and spelled out some archaic abbreviations (I use "and so on" instead of "&c."). I have silently incorporated the original *errata*.

I have placed Astell's original marginal comments and citations in the footnotes and preceded them with the phrase "Astell's marginal note" to distinguish them from my own editorial comments. I have modernized Astell's citations following the principles used in the rest of this volume. In accordance with the *Chicago Manual of Style*, I insert the name of an author or a short title in those places where they are omitted. I have retained Astell's references to the King James version of the Bible, but I use Arabic rather than Roman numerals in the citations, such that "Acts xvii.27, 28" is now "Acts 17:27–28," and so on. Where possible, I provide page references to modern editions of cited works in square brackets following Astell's original marginal note. I have retained Astell's use of the section symbol (§) when cross-referencing individual subsections in her work.

My dictionary definitions and synonyms are taken from the *Oxford English Dictionary Online* (Oxford: Oxford University Press, 2012), http://www.oed.com, hereafter referred to as *OED*. I use biographical information from the *Oxford Dictionary of National Biography*, online edition (Oxford: Oxford University Press, 2008), http://www.oxforddnb.com, hereafter cited as *ODNB*.

THE

Chriſtian Religion,

As Profeſs'd by a

DAUGHTER

OF THE

Church of ENGLAND.

by Mrs Aſtell.

Thus ſaith the Lord, Stand ye in the ways and ſee, and ask for the Old Paths, where is the good Way, and walk therein, and ye ſhall find Reſt for your Souls. Jer. 6. 16. *Whoſoever ſhall be aſham'd of me, and of my Words, in this adulterous and ſinful Generation, of him alſo ſhall the Son of man be aſhamed, when he cometh in the Glory of his Father, with the holy Angels.* Mark 8. 38.

LONDON:

Printed by *W. B.* for R. Wilkin, at the *King's-Head* in St. *Paul's-Church-Yard.* 1717.

Title page. [Mary Astell,] *The Christian Religion*, second edition (1717). Original size 7.6 x 4.7 inches. Courtesy of the Watkinson Library, Trinity College, Hartford, Connecticut.

THE
CHRISTIAN RELIGION,
AS PROFESSED BY A
DAUGHTER
OF THE
CHURCH OF ENGLAND

"Thus saith the Lord, stand ye in the ways and see, and ask for the old paths, where is the good way, and walk therein, and ye shall find rest for your souls." Jeremiah 6:16.

"Whosoever shall be ashamed of me, and of my words, in this adulterous and sinful generation, of him also shall the son of man be ashamed, when He cometh in the glory of His father, with the holy angels." Mark 8:38.[1]

---

1. The second quotation does not appear on the title page to the first edition, and neither quotation appears on the title page to the 1730 reissue.

ADVERTISEMENT[2]

The Christian religion being designed for practice not dispute—though disputes are sometimes necessary to obviate those errors which by corrupting our faith and principles deprave our manners, and while they leave us the name of Christian, render our Christianity quite different from what is delivered in the gospel of Christ—it seemed proper, not wholly to suppress what was said against some prevailing errors, but to disengage it from the practical part in the ensuing treatise, and to put what was matter of controversy in an appendix, little being added but for connection.[3]

There are without doubt, many better systems of religion, composed by the learned divines of our church, and others. The main design of this is to put women upon thinking, upon an examination of their principles, the motives and grounds of their belief and practice, and the frame and temper of their minds. To the end their religion may be their *own*; their faith divine, and not merely human; their hearts and disposition of spirit truly Christian, wherein consists "the power of godliness," and without which all outward performances are no better than "form."[4] And if they can be prevailed upon to do this, it matters not what regard they pay to the following discourse, the writer will have gained her end.

---

2. This advertisement, which is on pages A[2]r–v of the second edition, replaces the 26-page table of contents in the first edition.

3. For the appendix, see below, §§356–408.

4. 2 Tm 3:5: "Having a form of godliness, but denying the power thereof: from such turn away."

THE CHRISTIAN RELIGION, AS PROFESSED BY A DAUGHTER OF THE CHURCH OF ENGLAND.

IN A LETTER TO A LADY.[1]

Section I

Madam,

1. *Introduction: the occasion of this letter.*[2] When I borrowed *The Lady's Religion*,[3] your Ladyship I believe had no suspicion of being troubled with such a long address, nor had I any design to give you this trouble. Though if there be anything peculiar in "a lady's religion," to distinguish it from that of other Christians, a woman I should think is as like to be acquainted with that peculiarity as a man. But I suppose, Madam, that the religion which everyone but yourself concludes you practice with a primitive piety, is neither more nor less than what was formerly taught and practiced by St. Peter and St. Paul, and so on, and is still by all orthodox guides and truly Christian people. For though the press has helped us to the religion of a "physician," a "layman," a "gentleman," and a "lady," yet in my poor opinion, they have all of them but one religion if they are Christians.[4] There are some peculiar duties indeed, suited to their several conditions of life, which so far as

1. The heading of the first edition reads "In a Letter to the Right Honorable, T. L. C. I." The addressee of the letter (referred to as "Madam" or "your Ladyship" throughout the work) is most likely the Lady Catherine Jones, one of Astell's closest friends. For details on Jones, see the "Astell's Life and Works" section of the introduction to the present volume.

2. As indicated in the "Note on the Text," these italicized subsection headings appear as shoulder notes or glosses in the margins of the second edition.

3. Astell's references are to the 1704 second edition of the anonymous *A Lady's Religion*, attributed to a clergyman named "Mr. Stephens," most likely William Stephens. For details, see the "Historical-Intellectual Context" section of the introduction to this present volume. For details on Stephens, see Stuart Handley's biography in *ODNB*, s.v. "Stephens, William," http://www.oxforddnb.com/view/article/26395 (accessed March 4, 2011).

4. It is not possible to pinpoint the specific publications Astell has in mind. She may be referring to Thomas Browne's *Religio Medici* [The Religion of a Physician] (1642), John Dryden's

47

they relate to a gentleman and to a lady, are very piously and ingeniously described by an excellent author in the *Gentleman's* and *Ladies' Calling*,[5] without supposing that they are to have different religions; for their creed must be the same and their practice in the main, if they hope for the same end, even the salvation of their souls.

2. *The design.* But if the *letter* does not suppose that a lady's religion is different from that of other people, then it is to be supposed the *writer* means, that what is contained in his letter is religion enough for a lady, and according to the "French Prefacer," for everybody; for he calls it "an excellent portraiture of the Christian religion."[6] It is said to be writ "by a divine of the Church of England," and my catechism has taught me "to submit myself to my teachers and spiritual pastors."[7] But since they don't require a blind obedience, since the Bereans are commended for refusing to take the doctrine even of an apostle upon trust,[8] and because St. Peter would have us "ready to give a reason of

---

"Religio Laici" [The Religion of a Layman] (1682), and Edward Synge's *A Gentleman's Religion* (1693), as well as the aforementioned *Lady's Religion*.

5. *The Gentleman's Calling* (1660) and *The Ladies' Calling* (1673) were published anonymously. Scholars now concur that Richard Allestree is the likely author of both works. Allestree was an Anglican clergyman and a writer of moral and devotional works in the seventeenth century, including the tremendously popular *Whole Duty of Man* (1657). For details, see John Spurr's biography in *ODNB*, s.v. "Allestree, Richard," http://www.oxforddnb.com/view/article/395 (accessed February 28, 2011). In her *Proposal II*, Astell also praises the writer of the *Ladies' Calling* as "an excellent author" who offers "ingenuous and kind advice" to women (*Proposal II*, 222).

6. *Lady's Religion*, "The Preface to the French Translation," A11v. The author of this preface is the French translator himself, Pierre Coste.

7. See Church of England, *The Book of Common Prayer, and Administrations of the Sacraments and other Rites and Ceremonies of the Church according to the Use of the Church of England* (Oxford: Oxford University Press, [1952–70]), "A Catechism": "My duty towards my neighbor, is to love him as myself, and to do to all men, as I would they should do unto me: To love, honor, and succor my father and mother. To honor and obey the queen, and all that are put in authority under her. To submit myself to all my governors, teachers, spiritual pastors and masters" (298).

8. According to Acts 17:11, the inhabitants of Berea received the word of St. Paul "with all readiness of mind, and searched the scriptures daily, whether those things were so." In his *Ladies' Calling*, Allestree also urges women "to apply their understandings" to religion: "for we find the Bereans commended, not only as more diligent, but as 'more noble' too, Acts

the hope that is in us,"[9] the making a confession of my faith, and such a modest examination of that letter as this will lead me to, while I compare it with the word of God, the only infallible guide, can't justly be reckoned a going beyond my sphere. I shall therefore presume so far on your Ladyship's patience, as to tell you what I think a woman *ought* to believe and practice, and consequently what she *may*. That she may have it in theory, is evident from a woman's writing this, and whoever would be convinced that the practice may be equal to the theory, need only turn their eyes to a lady that I could name, would your Ladyship give me leave.

3. *Everyone must judge for themselves.* I pretend not to dictate to any, leaving this to spirits more magisterial than mine, because it is like they think themselves more illuminated, and therefore cannot bear a dissent from their opinions. My design is only to tell your Ladyship my thoughts; they are at the service of such as like them, and those who dislike are as welcome to reject them. For as I know of none but my lawful governors in church and state who have a right to judge for me in any case, and therefore they only shall do it; so on the other hand, I should be very unjust if I denied to others a liberty I think fit to take. For to pretend to dictate to our fellow rational creatures (whether directly, or which is worse, because it makes them the greater *dupes*, by all the artifice of a feigned modesty and seeming humility) unless where God has given a special commission and authority to command, is an assuming of His prerogative, and an usurpation upon their just and natural rights,[10] who have as much right to abound in their own sense as we have to abound in ours. And to submit to such dictates is an affront to God, by despising or at the best neglecting the talents He has given us, and a direct disobedience to that command

---

17:11, because they attentively 'considered,' and strictly examined the 'doctrine preached to them'" (262).

9. 1 Pt 3:15.

10. Here Astell appears to subvert Locke's remarks about "just and natural rights" in the preface to his *Two Treatises of Government* (1689). In §372 and §383, Astell repeats the phrase among other direct quotations from the *Treatises*. See John Locke, *Two Treatises of Government*, ed. Peter Laslett, Cambridge Texts in the History of Political Thought (Cambridge: Cambridge University Press, 1988), 137.

of Christ's, "call no man master upon earth";[11] that is, follow no man's judgment or authority any further than as he brings his credentials from the great master who is in heaven. Were other people to answer for us in the next world, they might reasonably expect to judge for us in this. But since "we must all stand before the judgment seat of Christ";[12] "and every one of us shall give an account of himself to God,"[13] and must "stand or fall to his own master,"[14] it is as unreasonable to take upon us to *judge for*, as it is to *judge* another's servant. God never requires us to submit our judgments to our fellow creatures, except in cases wherein He makes them, and not us, answerable for the error and all its evil consequences. And we may observe, if we please, that a man never sets up himself to be anyone's oracle or director, but out of some selfish and base design.

4. *And how.* But then if we would judge to purpose, we must free ourselves from prejudice and passion, must examine and prove all things, and not give our assent till forced to do so by the evidence of truth.[15] And when we are sure we have found the truth, we ought to stick to it with a heroic constancy and immovable resolution; which is a valor that does not misbecome a woman, let it be nicknamed pride or obstinacy, or what folks please. For without it we can never be good Christians, we are hardly rational creatures, but shall be "blown about with every wind of doctrine, by the cunning craftiness of those who lie in wait to deceive."[16]

5. *Women as well as men.* If God had not intended that women should use their reason, He would not have given them any, for He does nothing in vain. If they are to use their reason, certainly it ought to be employed about the noblest objects, and in business of the greatest consequence, therefore in religion. That our godfathers

11. Mt 23:9–10.

12. 2 Cor 5:10.

13. Rom 14:12.

14. Rom 14:4.

15. Astell echoes her rules for thinking in *Proposal II* (176–78), a set of rules founded upon the method of judgment advanced by René Descartes and his followers, Antoine Arnauld and Pierre Nicole. For details about this method, see "The Text" section of the introduction to the present volume.

16. Eph 4:14.

and godmothers answered for us at the font,[17] was an act of charity in *them*, and will be a great benefit to us if we make a right use of it, but it will be *our* condemnation if we are Christians merely upon this account, for that only can be imputed to a free agent which is done with understanding and choice. A Christian woman therefore must not be a "child in understanding,"[18] she must serve God with "understanding" as well as with "affection," must "love Him with all her mind and soul," as well as "with all her heart and strength";[19] in a word, must perform "a reasonable service" if she means to be acceptable to her maker.[20]

6. *Why the writer of this letter is a Christian.* I am a Christian then, and a member of the Church of England, not because I was born in England, and educated by conforming parents, but because I have, according to the best of my understanding, and with some application and industry, examined the doctrine and precepts of Christianity, the reasons and authority on which it is built. I say authority, because, though reason will never permit me to submit to any mere human authority, yet there is not anything more reasonable than to submit entirely to that authority, which I find upon a strict enquiry, has all the evidences that reason can ask, to prove that it is divine. Reason is that light which God Himself has set up in my mind to lead me to Him, I will therefore follow it so far as it can conduct me. And as for further illumination, as it would be the height of folly and a great injury to myself to reject it, so it would be the utmost ingratitude to almighty God not to be thankful for it. Let me see then how far reason can carry me, and next what further light God has been pleased to afford.

17. the font] the baptismal font, a receptacle for holy water.

18. 1 Cor 14:20.

19. Mt 22:37.

20. Rom 12:1.

Of natural religion[21]

7. *Our natural notion of God.*[22] I can as soon question my own being, as the being of a God, for I am only because He is. And when I think of God, I can't possibly think Him to be any other than the most perfect being; a being infinite in all perfections.[23] We need not be told wherein perfection consists, for let us be ever so skeptical, we must needs acknowledge, that wisdom and goodness, justice and holiness, are perfections, and indeed the greatest perfections: therefore an intelligent nature defective in these can't be perfect, but destitute of them must needs be miserable. Knowledge and power without them would not be beauties but blemishes; nor can a being be *infinitely* wise and good, just and holy, unless he be also omnipresent and omnipotent. So that when I examine my idea, or rather according to the apostle's expression, my perception of God, who is "not far from every one of us, for in Him we live, move, and have our being,"[24] as the very heathens owned, I find that the notion I have of God contains these and all other perfections. Among which self-existence[25] is most remarkable, as being the original and basis of all the rest.

21. This heading appears in the margins of the second edition. By "natural religion," Astell means religion based purely on reason or observation, and not divine revelation. Later, in §115, she claims that Christianity is an improvement on natural religion because it also harkens to the declared will of God, as expressed in the New Testament (that is to say, Christianity takes account of both natural and "revealed" religion).

22. In this paragraph and in the first few sentences of §8, Astell gives an ontological argument for the existence of God, an argument based upon premises that can be known a priori. She offers a similar proof in *Proposal II* (180). The ontological argument enjoyed a brief revival in popularity following Descartes's reformulation of the traditional argument in his *Discourse on the Method*, the *Meditations*, and the *Principles*.

23. Astell's marginal note (second edition only): "A fitting apprehension and faith of God, is the basis and foundation of all virtues." So Origen as cited in King on the Creed, 53, third edition. [Astell refers to Peter King's citation from Origen's *Dialogue with Heraclides*, in King, *The History of the Apostles Creed: With Critical Observations on its Several Articles*, 3rd ed. (London: W. B. for Jonathan Robinson and John Wyat, 1711), 53.]

24. Astell's marginal note: Acts 17:27–28.

25. In this context, "self-existence" means ontologically independent existence rather than self-caused existence. God has self-existence in the sense that He is uncreated and does not depend on any other being for His existence.

8. *Proof of the existence of God.*[26] For if God derived His being from any but Himself, there must be something greater and more perfect than God, which is absurd, since God is by the supposition the most perfect being, and consequently self-existing, because there can be no absolute and infinite perfection but where there is self-existence; for from whence shall it be derived? And self-existence is such a perfection as necessarily includes all other perfections. That there is a self-existing being is evident to the meanest understanding, for without it there could have been no men, no world, no being at all; since that which once *was not*, could never make itself; nor can any being communicate that to another which it has not itself. Therefore the self-existing being must contain all other perfections, therefore it must be an intelligent being, and therefore it must be God. Hence I conclude, "that God only is," and that all beings beside His, are only the mere creatures of His will.

9. *From the consideration of the universe.* Thus far, and even further I might have gone, though I had never been instructed, never heard a word of divinity, provided I had made a right use of my reason, had withdrawn from the noise and hurry of the world, to apply myself to serious reflections. For it must be a strange sort of rational creature that can live in such a beautiful fabric as we inhabit, without thinking how it came here, and who was the maker of the universe.

10. *And of our own, and fellow creatures' being.* Nay, had I been shut up in a den from my infancy, if reason had ever budded, I must have thought "what am I? And from whence had I my being?" If I had been admitted to converse among my fellow creatures, the next thought must have been, certainly I do not owe my being to those who are as weak, as precarious as I am; mankind must have had a beginning, and there must be a last resort to a self-existing being: and this being which is so liberal in its communications, must needs possess in the utmost perfection all that good which it bestows.

---

26. In the following paragraphs (§§8–10), from "That there is a self-existing being" onward, Astell gives a cosmological argument for the existence of God, a proof for the existence of God based upon observations about the world or "cosmos" (in this case, the fact that "I exist" and that there is a world and other people). She provides similar arguments in her *Proposal II* (181) and *Bart'lemy Fair* (117).

11. *Our desire of happiness prompts us to inquire after God's will.* The next natural thought would be, what obligations am I under? What acknowledgments am I to make to that being from whom I hold my all; and who can certainly resume His gift, whenever my ingratitude makes it requisite? But since He gave me being without my knowledge, much less desert, and upon no other motive but His own goodness, consequently this goodness intended I should be happy, for I find He has planted in my nature an incessant desire after happiness. But what is happiness? And how shall I attain it? I cannot but passionately desire that this wise, this good, this communicative being, would be pleased to discover His pleasure to me, for surely the only way to be happy is by conforming myself to His will.

12. *Both that and reason excite us to worship and serve Him.* I find indeed a light in my mind, directing me to the author of my being, making it necessary to adore, to love, to devote myself to Him, if I would avoid the reproaches of my own mind. How happy am I when thus employed! How uneasy, how wretched when it is neglected! But who is the gainer by this service? Not this all-perfect being, for there can be no addition to infinite perfection. It is I only who get by it, I do what is fit, I answer the end of my being, and oh that I might ever do so!

13. *Immortality proved by our desire of endless happiness.* Ever! What is that? Can I who had a beginning, who am but of yesterday, presume that I shall have no end? Why may not I suppose it? Since I find that I desire not only *happiness*, but *endless happiness*, and that without any reproach from my reason, which never fails to reproach me grievously for every improper and irregular desire. And since my maker is goodness itself, far be it from me to think He would have given me this desire, if He had intended to disappoint it. I may have some appetites which it may not be fit to gratify, because the pursuit of them may be beneath the dignity of my nature; they may interfere with the common good; it may not be for my true good to satisfy them, but much to my advantage to deny them, since it manifests the freedom and empire of my mind, it gives me a sacrifice to offer up to my maker, by bowing my will to His, and resigning my inclinations to my reason. But the desire of endless happiness has no defect, it is

conformable to reason. Surely then my maker's goodness designed me an endless felicity; but what shall I do to attain it?

14. *And the corruption of human nature, from the degeneracy of mankind.* Reason that has led me thus far also tells me, that mankind who are creatures of the same nature with myself, ought to be treated as myself, I should be as solicitous for their happiness as for my own; for this is certainly the will of our maker, and it is thus that I would have them deal with me. But is this sufficient to lead me to happiness? Alas they will neither do, nor receive the good I wish them! Jarring designs, and angry passions, whence come ye? You can't proceed from the God of order and love. There is a charming harmony among inanimate creatures, whence is it that man is the only dissonant string?

15. *Which natural reason shows us, but neither the cause nor cure.* Oh that I had a more perfect and explicit knowledge of Thy ways and of Thy will, Thou great and good author of my being! Shall I presume too much by imploring it humbly and earnestly? Not but that I am infinitely obliged to Thee for reason, which distinguishes me so much from the rest of Thy creatures. But neither my body nor my mind will endure to be always upon the stretch. I cannot always act up to that, which if neglected, my reason always bitterly reproaches me for the neglect. Oh that Thou would therefore take compassion on Thy creature, and impart to me more light and more strength, that I may fully know and always do Thy will, oh God!

16. *This prompts us to desire divine revelations.* I believe your Ladyship will agree with me, that though we had never heard of religion, yet if we use our reason at all, we must needs have such thoughts as these. Nor is it hard to give instances of heathens, who if they have not thought in this very manner, have at least come pretty near it. But yet how far so ever my own reason may lead me, I will not refuse any assistance that is offered. Nay I will most gladly and thankfully receive every divine revelation. For certainly the sun of knowledge, the light that enlightens every man, the supreme and universal reason, must make greater discoveries than my feeble taper[27] can pretend to.

17. *How far reason is to judge of revelation.* All I have to do is to enquire whether that which is called divine revelation is so in reality, for thus far my own reason is a proper judge. But when she is

27. taper] a wax candle, generally used for religious purposes.

once satisfied that God has declared His will, she has no more to do but humbly and readily to acquiesce in what He has been pleased to reveal. For she who can't give me a full and satisfactory account of my own nature, who can't inform me what are the ties that hold body and mind together, nor answer a hundred questions about matters of fact and things that are demonstrably true, shall she pretend to sit as sovereign judge of the reasonableness and possibility of what God has revealed? Would she not be extravagantly impertinent and silly beyond measure, should she pretend to comprehend the divine nature, and account for that abyss of perfection, whose greatness confounds and whose light blinds her?

18. *Reason can judge only of its own ideas.* Reason can judge of things which she can comprehend, she can determine where she has a complete, or at least a clear and distinct idea,[28] and can judge of "a contradiction in terms," for this is within her compass. But she must not affirm in opposition to revelation that there is any "contradiction in the nature of things that are infinitely above her," nor deny a truth because it is out of her reach. An Indian[29] or a plowman may as peremptorily[30] as he pleases deny all the propositions in Euclid,[31] but they don't cease to be true because the poor ignorant does not understand them.

19. *How a reasonable person will act with respect to the Bible.* I am therefore to examine the proofs that are brought for the Bible's being the word of God. And if I can but find as good evidence that this is what it pretends to be, as I can have of any other ancient book or fact, that holy men of old spoke and writ as they were inspired, and

---

28. According to Descartes and his followers, clarity and distinctness are the distinguishing marks of what is certain and indubitable. In his *Principles of Philosophy*, Descartes says that "I call a perception 'clear' when it is present and accessible to the attentive mind—just as we say that we see something clearly when it is present to the eye's gaze and stimulates it with a sufficient degree of strength and accessibility. I call a perception 'distinct' if, as well as being clear, it is so sharply separated from all other perceptions that it contains within itself only what is clear" (part I, §45). See René Descartes, *Principles of Philosophy*, in *The Philosophical Writings of Descartes*, trans. John Cottingham, Robert Stoothoff, and Dugald Murdoch, 3 vols. (Cambridge: Cambridge University Press, 1985), 1:207–8.

29. Indian] a native American.

30. peremptorily] emphatically.

31. Euclid (c. 300 BCE) was a mathematician of Alexandria and author of the *Elements*, one of the most influential works in the history of mathematics (especially geometry).

that God has owned and set His seal to their testimony, I have no more to do but firmly to believe and carefully to practice all that it enjoins. But if there be fuller and clearer evidence that the Bible contains a religion revealed and attested by divine authority than there is of any other fact whatsoever, if then I disbelieve it, or if professing to believe it, I neglect to conform myself to it in all things, I don't deserve to be disputed with, I ought first to be put into Bedlam[32] and brought to my sober senses, ever I can be thought capable of a rational conviction.

20. *The two testaments mutually prove each other.* If I can prove the Old Testament to be the word of God, this proof, together with the facts that are mentioned in history concerning Jesus of Nazareth and his disciples, and which no sober person can reasonably doubt of, sufficiently prove the New. So again reciprocally, the proof of the New Testament proves the Old, *that* referring so often to *this*, as to a book writ by divine authority. And therefore, not to say all that this subject is capable of, I shall only tell your Ladyship what it is that satisfies me, that the New Testament is the word of God. Or which is the same thing, a divine law promulged[33] to mankind, to which God requires their obedience under the highest penalties.

Of revealed religion[34]

21. *Revelation possible.* It is not to be doubted but that God can, if He pleases, reveal His will by a supernatural influence, either upon the mind of every particular person, or else upon the minds of certain men by whom He thinks fit to convey it to others. I shall not enlarge so much as to show why God has not taken the first way. If it can be proved that God has indeed done the other, His making choice of this way sufficiently proves it to be the best and most becoming the divine majesty. For though it will not follow that God has done so or so, because we presume that this is best, yet when we have clear evidence as to matter of fact that God has acted thus and thus, we may then safely and justly conclude that this is best, because God always does what

32. Bedlam] Bethlem Royal Hospital, an asylum for the mentally ill in London, England.

33. promulged] proclaimed.

34. This heading appears in the margins of the second edition.

most becomes Him, and it is the perfection of His nature to do always
and freely that which is absolutely and entirely the best.

22. *Wherein the difference between reason and revelation consists.* By what was said above we may discern, how very desirable it is
that God should reveal His will more particularly than natural reason
can attain unto it. Not but that reason is one sort and degree of divine
revelation, for it is from the father of lights that we derive our illumination of any kind. So that reason may not improperly be called
a natural and universal revelation, and those further manifestations
of God's will which we usually term revelation, may justly enough be
said to be a supernatural and improved reason. There being a difference between reason and revelation such as is between the less and
the more, but no sort of opposition in any respect. Reason being the
candle of the Lord set up in everyone's heart, revelation that broad
daylight which appeared in due time and season.[35]

23. *Reasonable creatures are obliged to obey God's revealed will.*
Nobody will be so absurd as to deny that it is the indispensable duty
of all reasonable persons to conform themselves entirely to God's will,
so soon as they can be informed of it. Not one of us poor worms,
who agree with our fellow worm for his service in consideration of
the food and money we give him for a season, would endure to have
our commands disputed; we can't then be so audacious as to dispute
our maker's. So that for the better color to our disobedience, we pretend that God has not given us those commands which we do not care
to obey. Why we do not care to obey them is a question indeed that
reason can never answer, any further than thus: that there are many
sorts of madmen, abundantly more than Bedlam can hold, everyone
of which has his particular *resvery*.[36] And though reason is the same in
everyone, and so far as we follow it, we all act alike, yet taste and fancy
are not to be accounted for or disputed, they are as various as our
faces, and when they are pursued will lead us into all extravagancies.

24. *And therefore must be able to distinguish it from imposture.*
But since it is our duty to obey divine revelation, we are sure that God

35. "Candle of the lord" (originally from Prv 20:27) was a common expression in the
literature of this period, sometimes used to denote the natural law of reason, and sometimes
a supernatural principle. Astell regards it as the former.

36. *resvery*] French for reverie, "fanciful or impractical idea" (*OED*).

does not oblige us to anything either impossible or unreasonable, consequently there must be some determinate characters whereby we may distinguish divine revelation from all pretenses to it. Evidences which though they are not irresistible, because God having made us free agents, can't be supposed to destroy His own work, yet are sufficient to convince all reasonable persons who examine them as the weight of the matter, and their own personal interest in it, requires. If then the Christian religion as delivered in the New Testament has all those characters and evidences, it must needs be received as divine; since it can never consist with the justice and goodness, the wisdom and holiness of God, to give His testimony to an imposture, or which is the same thing, to leave us without sufficient light to distinguish it from the truth.

25. *This evidence not irresistible, but sufficient for conviction.* Yet be this light ever so bright in itself and sufficient for conviction, it is not to be supposed that it will have any effect on those who advise only with their libertine inclinations or their wild fancies and extravagant humors, for these are unaccountable and are to be laughed at and not argued with. But if any sober man or woman seriously consult their reason, laying aside prejudice (as they must not only in this, but in every other case if they would come at truth) and especially those indispositions they have contracted by their vices, there is no question to be made but they will find it highly reasonable to believe that the holy scriptures are the word of God.

26. *The Christian religion has this evidence, as appears from the subject matter of it.* Thus then I proceed. Having implored the divine assistance, I read my Bible with attention and reverence, and consider it carefully, and I find nothing there that offends reason. It is true there are some things in the gospel very sublime, such as natural reason could never have discovered, but now that they are revealed, it finds no impossibility, no incongruity in them. For who can know the divine purpose, but they to whom God is pleased to declare it? Who can pry into the divine essence or understand any more of it than God condescends to impart? Whatever He has revealed concerning Himself is true; if it be too high for us, it calls for our admiration, not our frivolous and presumptuous disputes. In a word, the Christian institution has so little of worldly wisdom, human passions, and contrivance in

it, is in itself so majestic, so divine, so worthy of God, so admirably well fitted to lead us on to perfection, by teaching and enabling us to despise and triumph over this world, and by preparing us for the glories of the next, which is the great end of a rational nature, that everyone who has either good sense, or even a good taste and relish of genuine pleasure, must needs to be charmed with its beauty, and be fully convinced that if God did at all design to give mankind a perfect institute suitable to His own glory and His creatures' good, it must needs be such a religion as this.

27. *Which is a good, but not the chief proof.* But though this is a very natural and easy proof of the divine authority of the holy scriptures, and such as everyone to whom the gospel is preached may come at, yet it is far from being the only proof, much less that in which all other proofs determine. Were everyone to believe not "only our English translation" but even "the original copy" of holy scripture, no "otherwise" than as they think "they see cause so to do," being at liberty to reject as spurious all that which does not sort with their "conceits," we should have wise work![37] And most people would have a wise religion!

28. *Some errors corrected.* It is, according to some, "unworthy of God" to lay restraints upon the creatures He has created and not to allow them the full swing of all their appetites.[38] Others, how much so ever they talk against popery,[39] have taken a fancy that St. Peter and St. Paul were very Jesuitical when they commanded "every soul to be subject to the higher powers, not only to the good and gentle,"

---

37. Astell's marginal note (first edition only): *Letter concerning Church Communion*, 26. A pamphlet which does not *deserve*, but which may *need*, one's notice. [Astell disparagingly refers to the anonymous work *The Principle of the Protestant Reformation Explained In A Letter of Resolution Concerning Church-Communion* (1704), sometimes attributed to John Toland. Here she challenges the author's contention that "you are not bound to believe our English translation, any otherwise than as you shall see cause so to do; for if you shall read anything in our translation which tends to support any conceit unworthy of God, or any immoral practice between man and man, you will have sufficient reason to believe the translation to be false" (26). In all subsequent references to this work, I use Astell's short title, *Letter concerning Church Communion*.]

38. *Letter concerning Church Communion*, 26.

39. popery] in the period, a common derogatory term for Roman Catholicism.

but even "to the froward,"[40] to a persecuting Nero, who at that time reigned.[41] For according to those men's "conceits," the apostles meant no more than that Christians should not attempt to throw off the yoke, but when they had power to do it effectually. Some "deliberate so maturely," and are so well instructed in "immoral practices," that they call even "nonresistance, a traitorous doctrine," though it may be presumed that governors would be very glad to find all traitors governed by this principle.[42] There are twenty more "conceits" as extraordinary as these, and perhaps there's scarce a text in scripture which somebody or other will not find occasion to object against. Must we therefore suppose it is a corruption in the original or a mistake in the translation? God forbid! For at this rate we should have no scripture at all, nor anything to trust to but our own wild fancies.

29. *How to judge of the subject matter of a revelation.* Indeed should ever so many people tell me that the Alcoran[43] is a divine revelation, and bring what they call evidence, the very reading of it would convince me that they are mistaken, its doctrines not being suitable to our natural notions of the divine purity and perfections.[44] Yet it is no wonder that a religion accommodated even to the lees and dregs of sense obtains among sensual men. The prejudices of sense and irregular appetites being the main hindrance of obedience to the gospel in countries where it is professed. And perhaps one of the best rules whereby to judge of the truth of a revelation from the subject matter of it may be this: whatever doctrine or precept tends to the humbling of our proud understandings, the subduing of our stubborn wills, and the restraining of our exorbitant affections (though we may call these

40. froward] perverse or refractory.

41. 1 Pt 2:18; Rom 13:1. Astell refers to the Roman emperor Nero (37–68), a notorious persecutor of Christians.

42. Astell's marginal note (first edition only): *Letter concerning Church Communion*, 16. [Astell refers to that part of the *Letter* in which the author challenges the Anglican royalist doctrine of passive obedience, the view that subjects are obliged to submit patiently to the penalty for disobedience to unjust authority. "As to the particular point of non-resistance," the author says, "I take it to be a traitorous doctrine here in England, where we have rights and liberties of our own, which are not at the king's disposal" (16).]

43. Alcoran] the Qur'an, the sacred book of Islam.

44. The words "its doctrines not being suitable to our natural notions of the divine purity and perfections" are not in the first edition.

"reason," "liberty," and the "rights of human nature") does indeed proceed from God. Who as He *may* do this in His own right and by that authority He has over us, so He kindly vouchsafes[45] to do it for our advantage.

30. *The sublimity of holy scripture.* I find then that the holy scriptures have in themselves a divine character, both in respect of the sublimity of the matter and the majesty of the style, even without those allowances which certainly ought to be made for the antiquity of the books, the obsolete customs and manners of the times in which they were composed, the difference of idioms, and the infirmities of the translators. For I question not but that if I could read them in their original, they would appear even yet more beautiful and divine. Let me enquire then whether God has attested these writings which are highly valuable in themselves, whoever was their author, and which I can't but wish may be found to come from Him.

31. *This a reasonable presumption in its favor.* If it be said that I am already prepossessed in their favor, be it so; mine is a prepossession that no reasonable person needs be ashamed of, for reason led me into it. But it must also be granted that if upon examination it does not appear that they have the authority they claim, this prepossession will turn more to their disadvantage than it does now to their service. For though all imposture is provoking, yet none is so odious as that which would pass upon us under the appearance of the greatest piety and simplicity.

32. *What sort of proof ought not to be expected, and what may.* What evidence therefore ought in reason to satisfy me? Should I have stood by the holy pen-men when they wrote? I ought to consider that the gospel was not published only for me, but for all Christians in all succeeding ages of the church, and it is impossible that they should all have this proof. Do I desire to have a miracle wrought in my presence for its confirmation? So may every other person. And if miracles were so frequent, we should take no more notice of them than of the ordinary course of nature, which is indeed stupendous to all who consider it, only our being used to it takes off our wonder. Would I have an inward and irresistible impulse compelling me to believe? Where then were the reward and excellency of my faith? This would be for God

---

45. vouchsafes] condescends.

to destroy His own work, to make me a necessary instead of having made me a free agent. Besides, it is not decent, it does not become the great God, nor can I in modesty expect that He should do a particular act for me; I am not worth it. That I partake in His common mercies is more than He owes me, but all the service I can ever pay is due to Him for this, and were too little to be paid, were it possible to render more. I ought therefore to be abundantly satisfied with such proof and evidence as may extend to all mankind. I would not cavil or chicane[46] with my prince concerning the bounties and favors shown me, much less will I have the greater insolence to do it with my God.

33. *No objections can be made against the holy scriptures, but what are stronger against all other writings and facts.* How do I know that the emperor Marcus Aurelius wrote those meditations that bear his name, for such great princes do not use to spend their time in contemplation, nor do they commonly think so justly of the world and its apparent grandeurs?[47] How can I be sure that Plato and Hierocles, Plutarch and Epictetus, Tully and Seneca, were the real authors of those books that are ascribed to them, in which are many things that seem to be above a heathen's reach?[48] What ground have I to believe that Cæsar wrote his commentaries and gives a true account of himself and his affairs?[49] Or that other histories are authentic? But should I set up to discredit and ridicule those heathen writers, does your Ladyship think that it would pass with the world as an argument of my wit and reach, and that I was less credulous and more reasonable

46. chicane] quibble.

47. Marcus Antoninus Aurelius (121–80) was a Roman emperor and author of *The Meditations* (c. 170–80), a work that espouses the Stoic philosophy of detachment from worldly concerns.

48. Astell names philosophers in the Platonic and Stoic traditions: Plato (429–347 BCE), Hierocles (fl. second century), Plutarch (45–120), Epictetus (c. 50–135), Marcus Tullius Cicero (106–43 BCE), and Seneca (c. 1 BCE–65 CE).

49. Gaius Julius Caesar (100–40 BCE) was a Roman statesman and author of the *Commentaries on the Gallic and Civil Wars*. Here Astell uses a common argumentative strategy of the time. For a similar line of reasoning, see Locke, *Essay*: "when there can be no supposition ... that there is as fair testimony against, as for the matter of fact attested; which by inquiry, is to be learned, e.g., whether there was 1700 years ago such a man at Rome as Julius Caesar: in all such cases, I say, I think it is not in any rational man's power to refuse his assent" (IV.xx.15).

than my neighbors? Should I not rather be laughed at for my folly and self-conceit, and would not the humor be despised as the whimsy of a "very woman,"[50] according to the civil phrase of some "very men," equally just and mannerly?

34. But I doubt I should not come off so well as the being only laughed at, should I aver[51] that those noble peers who glory in the antiquity of their titles have no sufficient proof whereby to make good their claim. Or that my rich neighbor's deeds and evidences are insufficient to convey his estate to him and his heirs, since nobody knows but they may be forgeries? But woe be to me, should I dare to affirm that *Magna Charta*[52] is a forgery, though there is a learned person who tells us "that we have not one true copy of it."[53] And yet, setting these hazards aside, if the humor of disbelieving takes me, what should hinder but that I may doubt, or even positively deny, that there was ever such a man as William the Conqueror,[54] or those successors of his who granted the people their rights and privileges?

35. *The holy scripture better attested than any other facts, and so on.* None of those facts, records, evidences, or books are so well attested as the things that were done by Jesus Christ and his disciples. They have not the concurrent testimony of so many persons of all nations, ages, ranks, interests, tempers, enemies as well as friends. Men of good understandings, sobriety, and learning as well as multitudes of all sorts and conditions have not quitted all their expectations in this

50. very woman] a common derogatory phrase of the period, usually describing a knowing or crafty woman. See, for example, Richard Steele, *The Lying Lover; or, The Ladies Friendship* (London: Bernard Lintott, 1704): "Thou art no goddess, thou'rt a very woman, with all the guile" (21).

51. aver] assert the truth.

52. *Magna Charta*] a charter spelling out the liberty and political rights of freemen in England, first issued in 1215.

53. I am unable to locate the source. For a similar point, see Richard Allestree, *The Causes of the Decay of Christian Piety*, in *The Works of the Learned and Pious Author of the Whole Duty of Man* (London: Roger Norton, 1704): "how easy were it to suggest that in so long a succession of its [i.e., the *Magna Carta*'s] keepers, some may have been prevailed on by the influence of princes to abridge and curtail its concessions; others by a prevailing faction of the people to amplify and extend it? Nay, if men were as great skeptics in the law, as they are in divinity, they might exact demonstrations that the whole thing were not a forgery" (259).

54. William I, king of England and duke of Normandy (1028–87).

world, even life itself, to bear witness to the truth of those facts, and so on, as they have to confirm their testimony of the holy scripture.

36. *The manner and simplicity of holy scripture, a further proof of its divinity.* Nor could it be a vainglorious[55] desire of leaving a name behind them that made Christ and his apostles attest their doctrine with their blood. For there runs a native simplicity through their writings which proves them to be above such a design. They are as free in publishing the poverty of their master, and that shame and contempt He underwent, and even their own faults and infirmities, as they are in declaring what may recommend them, and yet there is nothing labored and artificial in what they say. The *manner* of these holy books is such as no human art can counterfeit: whoever has a taste must needs distinguish them from all other writings and give them the preference.

37. *The holy scriptures can't be rejected on any principle, but what will lead us to disbelieve everything we did not hear or see.* It follows then, that if we mean to act like reasonable creatures, since the principles of reason are general, we ought to be guided by them, not only in some particular cases, but in all. For if we will govern ourselves by a certain principle upon one occasion, and take no notice of it, nay, even act contrary to it in parallel cases, it is plain that we follow our humors, or passions, or follies, but by no means our reason. If therefore I discard the holy scriptures for want of proof, I must upon the same principle, and for much stronger reasons, disbelieve and reject everything that has passed in the world before my time, or of which I have not been an eye or ear witness. How the wise men may make a shift to govern themselves by such measures I know not; sure I am, that it is above the understanding and skill of any woman to live in the world and conduct herself by such rules.

38. *Love to vice, and not want of evidence, the true cause of unbelief.* But what evidence can one have that those books were writ by the men whose names they bear, and that these men were really commissioned by God to deliver them as His word and will? I must either have been an eye and ear-witness of what they said and did, or else I must receive it upon sufficient testimony. The first it's like might have pleased one better; but besides, that it is not possible that every

55. vainglorious] boastful or extremely vain.

Christian should have that proof, as was already said, the latter is full as well and throughout as rational. And it is not to be doubted but that they who will not be convinced by the one would never have been persuaded by the other. For the Pharisees confessed that Christ did "many miracles," against the truth of which they could not object, at the same time that they agreed to "put Him to death."[56] They did not at all question that Jesus had raised Lazarus from the grave, but this was so far from converting them to the faith of Christ that it only enraged their malice, so that "they consulted to put Lazarus to death also," the better to stifle their own and the people's convictions.[57] For it is plain that their pride, and vainglory, their covetousness, malice, envy, and the like vices were the true causes of their unbelief, as they are still of modern infidelity, whatever pretenses may be made for it.

39. *The holy scripture as well asserted as any matter of fact can be.* A matter of fact is so much the more confirmed by how many more competent witnesses are brought to attest it. Hence it follows that they who shall live in the last ages of the world will not have less but more reason to believe the gospel than they who lived earlier. Nor were those things done in a corner; Christ came into the world in a learned and inquisitive age; there was a whole nation, and their rulers more especially, concerned in point of interest and honor, to detect the apostles if they were impostors. And we find that they omitted nothing that either bribery or malice, cunning or power could do to hinder the preaching of the gospel. So that we cannot with any tolerable pretense deny that there were such men as the apostles and evangelists, who wrote such books, and attested them by the miracles which are there recorded. For Jews and gentiles, the polite as well as the barbarous, the learned and the ignorant, the great and the little, multitudes of all ranks have acknowledged it for above this 1600 years.

40. *The sum of the evidence.* And therefore since the matter of fact, that is, that there were such men, and that they wrote such books, and did the miracles therein recorded, for the confirmation of the doctrine they taught, is better attested than any other fact whatsoever; since the holy scriptures are in possession of the title of the word of God, have been received as such by different nations, during

---

56. Astell's marginal note: Jn 11:47. [Astell also refers to Jn 11:53.]

57. Astell's marginal note: Jn 12:10–11, 18–19.

a succession of many ages, and in spite of all opposition; since there is nothing in them but what is highly agreeable to the natural notions we have of God and of religion, nothing contradictory to reason, but such discoveries of truth as much improve it; since God Himself has confirmed this revelation, both by the prophecies that went before, by the miracles that attended, and by the agreement there is between the doctrine it teaches, and a reasonable and uncorrupted mind; since God cannot deceive us, nor give His testimony to an imposture, and yet upon the best use we can make of our understandings, we have no way to discover any imposture in this revelation, but must confess that it comes attended with all the marks and evidences of truth; what can I plead for myself if I presume to reject or despise the holy scriptures?

41. *Were it less full, the hazard weighs down the balance.*[58] But let it be supposed that the proof is not so clear and full as I have represented it, for we may allow our adversaries their most unreasonable demands, without any injury to our cause, whose triumph will only be so much the more glorious; yet I ought to be very clear and full in my proof, before I presume to charge the holy scriptures with forgery: because there is no manner of proportion between the hazard of receiving, and the danger of rejecting them. For upon supposition, that they have no just pretense to divine authority, and I receive them as the oracles of God, what do I lose by it? I am imposed upon it is true (and so we are all of us in twenty matters) but not to my hurt. For though the gospel were only a mere human invention, to live according to its rules would be the wisest course I could take, since nothing could be more for my present interest, safety, and pleasure: if there be a future state, I am prepared for it; if there be none, I shall not be sensible of any loss. On the other side, if the scripture is indeed the word of God, and I disbelieve it, can I offer a greater affront to the divine majesty than by rejecting those commands which He graciously affords[59] me for my good? And since God is essentially holy and just, how can I appear in His presence having abused His goodness? How can I endure His

---

58. In this subsection, Astell offers a prudential argument for belief in revelation, based on a calculation of the risks associated with either believing or not believing that the Bible is the word of God. In doing so, she follows the logic of "Pascal's Wager," in Pascal, *Pensées*, §233. For details, see "The Text" section of the introduction to the present volume.

59. "allows" in first edition.

displeasure! Or to be in eternal opposition and enmity towards Him? Shall I run this risk because, forsooth,[60] I would not be thought credulous, I would not be imposed upon, I would distinguish myself though it were by my folly! I would have my own will, however unreasonable, and follow my own devices, however ridiculous! Notwithstanding all disappointments I would run giddily after pleasure in those ways in which nobody ever found it certainly and without regret; and would not follow the divine directions, which are as full of goodness as they are of wisdom and equity!

42. *The common objections and the persons who make them not worth a serious answer.* Supposing then that I could not answer all that pert and pretending men may object; will it follow that I must lessen my reverence for the holy scriptures? Not at all; any more than that I ought to forbear eating when I am hungry, because some learned and witty man might harangue with much art and flourish that the meat was poisoned, or fantastical, or that it was not agreeable to my present constitution but would certainly breed diseases and death; for much more I am sure might be urged on this topic, than can be offered against the holy scriptures. But I shall not enter into a particular consideration of those objections, which would carry me further than I design, and besides it is already done to very good purpose by better pens. Indeed the common discourses are too trifling to deserve a serious answer, and one may in general observe, that they proceed either from men's vanity or their vices; some take upon them to talk irreligiously because they have the folly to think that it shows their wit; others to countenance[61] their immoralities. And one may lay it down as a rule, that no man attempts to speak disrespectfully of God, or of the holy scriptures, but he is at the bottom a vain and wicked man; and whenever we find a man endeavoring to corrupt a woman's faith, we may without breach of charity conclude, he has a design to ruin her in this world as well as in the next.[62] If she has too much virtue to be as-

60. forsooth] in truth.

61. countenance] support.

62. In the first edition, this sentence reads "and whoever he be who endeavors to corrupt a woman's faith, he has a design to ruin her in this world as well as in the next" instead of "whenever we find a man endeavoring to corrupt a woman's faith, we may without breach of charity conclude, he has a design to ruin her in this world as well as in the next."

saulted directly, the way is to undermine her religious principles, these being the only firm foundation of real honor and moral honesty, nor can any virtue stand firm against all attacks, but that which is founded upon a Christian principle.

43. *The holy scriptures our only rule of faith and manners.* It appears then that the holy scriptures are our rule of faith and manners, and for our better direction in both, we have no more to do but to study them. Whatever therefore I have to add must be drawn from this fountain, for neither I, nor any person whosoever, ought to be credited any further in religious matters, than as what we say is agreeable to the word of God.

44. *Blind submission to human guides not necessary.* I know it is very frequently, but very sillily said, who shall be judge of this agreement? One great man says *this*, another *that*, and a third differs from them both, and a great many more from all these, and everyone of the number has his followers. What then can a poor woman do but follow that opinion which is most in vogue? As if one was to tell noses[63] to find out truth! Or else depend upon some one or more wise men, whom chance, or her kind neighbor, or her circumstances of life have recommended to her? For sure she is to make as little use of her own judgment in choosing her guide, as in following him! But as the diversity of opinions in matters of religion is so far from being an argument against religion, that it strongly proves the great importance of that which all the world so warmly contends about, so whatever helps error may stand in need of, the truth laid down in holy scripture shines by its own light, and may be attained by all reasonable, honest, and unprejudiced enquirers, whose vices and worldly interests have not darkened their minds, nor warped their understandings, and who humbly implore and depend upon the divine assistance in their diligent enquiries.[64]

45. *Authority and example the cause of most of our mistakes.* Perhaps I may be thought singular in what I am about to say, but I think I have reason to warrant me, and till I am convinced of the

63. to tell noses] to count heads in order to reckon the number of people.

64. In the first edition, this sentence appeals to a single masculine enquirer: "every reasonable, honest, and unprejudiced enquirer, whose vices and worldly interests have not darkened his mind, and warped his understanding."

contrary, since it is a truth of great importance, I shall not scruple to declare it, without regarding the singularity. I therefore beg leave to say, that most of, if not all, the follies and vices that women are subject to (for I meddle not with the men) are owing to our paying too great a deference to other people's judgments, and too little to our own, in suffering others to judge for us, when God has not only allowed, but required us to judge for ourselves.

46. *Judging for ourselves no prejudice to lawful authority.* How men[65] who have *made themselves* our governors may like our withdrawing from their yoke I know not; but I am certain that this principle of judging for ourselves in all cases wherein God has left us this liberty, will introduce no disorder into the world, or disobedience to our *lawful* governors. Rather, it will teach us to be as tractable and submissive to just authority, as we are careful to judge rightly for ourselves, in matters wherein God has not appointed any to judge for us. The insinuations of those who have no right to be our directors, but who have only usurped an empire over our understandings, being one of the principal causes of our disobedience to lawful authority. Both by their rendering us disaffected to our proper governors, as is their usual practice, that so they themselves may entirely command us. And also because sooner or later, we shall be convinced of the dishonor and damage of being anyone's property, and thence grow suspicious of, and uneasy at the just commands of those who have a right to prescribe in some cases.

47. *The mischief of being led by others.* How comes it that we are chained down[66] to the slavery of all the silly customs of the age, to the waste of our time, the expense[67] of our fortunes, nay even to the depraving of our very reason, but because we must do as others do, and are afraid of the singularity of being wiser and better than our neighbors? So that we force ourselves to practice those follies, which while we practice we condemn! What is it that engages women in crimes contrary to their reason, and their very natural temper, but

---

65. "those" in first edition.

66. In the first edition, this question begins "What is it that chains us down" instead of "How comes it that we are chained down."

67. expense] spending.

being overpersuaded and overruled by the men[68] to whose conduct they commit themselves? And how do they excuse these crimes, but by alleging the examples and opinions of other people?

48. *Singularity how far commendable.* I do not deny that singularity in trifles and indifferent things is a folly and a vice; but to be singularly wise and good in the midst of a crooked and perverse generation, and in spite of all the persecutions we suffer for being so, is the most exalted pitch of heroic virtue. And is very well consistent both with the care that Christians are obliged to take, that they "do nothing but what is of good report," that they "avoid the very appearance of evil," and give no just "offence" either to the strong, or to the weak, to the charitable or to the censorious: and also with that obedience and submission that is due to lawful authority.[69]

49. *Of the authority of the church.* But how much so ever I am (and I am as much as anyone can be) against private doctors and directors, who are often but corrupt and muddy streams which withdraw us from that "well of life"[70] that is freely offered to all who will apply themselves to it; false lights who lead us into bypaths, and turn our eyes from that "sun of righteousness," who "enlightens everyone" who humbly and reverently looks up to Him,[71] and am of opinion that guides, though when prudently chosen they may be of excellent use to men, can never unless upon an extraordinary occasion, and under great caution, be proper for women because of scandal, yet none can pay a greater deference to the church universal, or to that particular national church, by whose charity through the blessing of God, I am a member of the catholic or universal church,[72] the body of Christ. Who

68. The first edition reads "by those" instead of "by the men."

69. Astell paraphrases Phil 4:8, 1 Thes 5:22, and 1 Cor 10:32. She makes similar remarks in her *Proposal II* (225) and *Reflections upon Marriage* (73).

70. Jn 4:14: "But whosoever drinketh of the water that I shall give him shall never thirst; but the water that I shall give him shall be in him a well of water springing up into everlasting life."

71. Astell paraphrases Mal 4:2 ("But unto you that fear my name shall the sun of righteousness arise with healing in his wings") and Jn 1:9 ("the true light, which lighteth every man that cometh into the world").

72. catholic ... church] in this context, "the whole body of Christians" (*OED*), not the Roman Catholic Church.

has been pleased to constitute a church, and has ordained an order of men to admit into this society and to shut out of it, to direct and persuade, and to minister to all its wants, as it is a spiritual community; as the scripture teaches us, and as is also evident from the reason of things. For there must of necessity be an established government, where there is a formed society; nor can it be imagined that the God of order, the wisdom of the father, by whose commission temporal governments are settled for the good of mankind, should leave His church, whom He so dearly loves, in anarchy and confusion, and not constitute diverse "orders in it, for the work of the ministry, for the edifying of the body in love."[73] And therefore let the men that execute this office be what they may, the order and the authority is God's, and as such I reverence it, considering Him who "sent them."

50. *In what case to be sought and submitted to.* So that if through the sublimity of the subject, my ignorance of the sacred languages, of ecclesiastical history, and the ancient usage of the church, any point in controversy be too difficult for me, and that after all my diligence I can't clear up the matter with evidence and certainty, but that all I can attain to is probabilities on both sides: if it is a matter in which a final decision is not necessary, I will suspend my judgment in hopes of further information; but if there is a necessity to determine, I will with all humility submit to God's authority in His church. Not to the man whom I may fancy or choose, for this were to follow my own way, and not God's; but to him or them who shall have lawful authority over me. For though they should happen to lead me into error, yet in this case they, and not I, must answer for it; as for me, I am safer in my obedience, than I could have been even with truth in a disorderly way. I will consult the bishop of the diocese in which I live, if it be a matter of great concern, but upon less occasions, the parish priest, to whom he has committed the cure of souls. For it is not because a man talks finely in a pulpit, or has an agreeable way in private conversation that I depend on him; or because I think he is a man of learning; or which is better, of good sense; or which is best of all, of great integrity of mind, and of a holy and unblemished conversation, as well as of a sound judgment;[74] but in pure obedience to God, who has commanded me

73. Eph 4:12.

74. The words "as well as of a sound judgment" are not in the first edition.

to "obey them who have the rule over me," and who "watch," or at least ought to watch, "for my soul."[75] And in this way because it is His own, I may humbly yet confidently expect His blessing.

51. *Church communion how far necessary.* As for church communion, I can't say it is impossible for a "man" or woman to be good Christians, though they "do not join themselves in public communion with any church," because it is possible that this may not be in their power. But if we receive the scripture, "it is" certainly "necessary" for me, and for every Christian man and woman, who live in Christendom, to "join" ourselves "publicly to some one or other church communion of Christians."[76] And if the established national church where we reside, enjoins no terms of communion evidently sinful, it is our duty to join ourselves to her. She may require it, for she has an authority over us, Christ having delegated His own power to the governors of His church. So that he who refuses to hear the church, does hereby renounce Christianity, and becomes a heathen man and a publican,[77] as our Lord tells us, Matthew 18:17. To talk of being members of the universal church, and yet not live in communion with some particular church when this is in our power, is much the same as to value ourselves on being freemen at large, free of some place or other, but we know not where, for no corporation will own us, or allow us its privileges.

52. *Why it is necessary.* And therefore, though "no man or number of men," have a right "to impose" on my "belief," yet the church has a right to my obedience in everything that is not sinful, and that for this plain reason, because the holy scripture commands me to live in union and communion with her.[78] What else can be the meaning

---

75. Heb 13:17: "Obey them that have the rule over you, and submit yourselves: for they watch for your souls."

76. Astell answers to her own satisfaction the two opening queries of the *Letter concerning Church Communion*: "Is it necessary for a Christian man to join himself publicly to some one (or other) church communion of Christians? Or, whether a man might not be a good Christian, though he did not join himself in public communion with any church?" (3).

77. publican] heretic.

78. Astell refers to the *Letter concerning Church Communion*: "Nor can any man, or number of men, claim authority to *impose* his or their *interpretations* of the holy scripture upon his [i.e., a lone African convert's] belief" (4).

of those many texts which enjoin us, "not to forsake the assembling of ourselves together, as the manner of some is," but to "glorify God with one mind and with one mouth"?[79] Why are we so pathetically exhorted to "be of one accord," "of one mind," "to keep the unity of the spirit in the bond of peace," to "mark those who cause divisions, and to avoid them"?[80] Why does our Lord pray that "we may all be one," and that "we may be made perfect in one, that the world may know that God has sent Him"?[81] Which design of our Lord is pursued by His apostles, when they enjoin us to "walk by the same rule, to mind the same things," "in the unity of faith," and that because we are but "one body in Christ, and everyone members one of another."[82] Division, therefore, and separating ourselves from the Christian community upon any account but absolute necessity, is destructive to the body; as on the contrary, order, decency, unity, and church communion, tend to the "perfecting of the saints," to the edifying of the "body of Christ."[83] Christians being under solemn obligations, as they are Christians, and as they hope for any benefit by this profession and divine institution, to be *one* in their inward affections and outward worship, so far as it is naturally and morally possible, that is, so far as lawfully and innocently they can.

53. *Wherein it consists.* Now I think myself in catholic communion with the church of God, if I live in *constant communion* with the bishop in whose diocese I reside. The scripture having told us, that the holy ghost has made the bishops "overseers of the flock," "to feed the church of God,"[84] and it being their business to maintain communion with all their fellow governors, that so the universal church may be united under Christ the head. And as it would not avail me to be called by the name of Christ, or even to have been one of His immediate followers, and to have done miracles by His power, if I did not obey His commands: so this of church communion being one of

79. Astell's marginal note: Heb 10:25; Rom 15:6.

80. Astell's marginal note: 2 Cor 13:11; Phil 2:2; Eph 5; 1 Cor 1:10; Rom 16:17. [The reference to Ephesians should be Eph 4:3.]

81. Astell's marginal note: Jn 17:21, 23.

82. Astell's marginal note: Phil 3:16; Eph 4:13; Rom 12:5.

83. Astell's marginal note: 1 Cor 12; 1 Cor 14:26, 40; Eph 4:12.

84. Astell's marginal note: Acts 20:28.

them, and very pressingly enjoined, I can by no means pretend obedience to Christ, if I despise or neglect it.

54. *Desired by all sincere Christians.* Supposing then that I had been an African, and converted by the Christian slaves who were lately in captivity "upon the coasts of Barbary."[85] It is confessed that upon the redemption of these captives, I could not have had communion with Christians in religious offices, and yet I might have enjoyed spiritual communion with Christ the head of the church, and so with the whole body. The mercies of God not permitting Him to punish any of His creatures, for the breach of any law which it is not in their power to keep. But if I had preferred heaven to earth, I must have been desirous to quit all my temporal advantages in my native country upon the first opportunity, rather than not place myself where I might receive the advantages of Christian society. For if I had only consulted my New Testament, left with me by some good captive for my instruction and comfort, and had been unacquainted with any "commentator thereon,"[86] and ignorant of the lives of modern Christians, I must needs have concluded, that to quit all for Christ's sake, for the "one thing necessary," and to think myself a very great gainer if "by losing the world" I could procure any advantage to "my soul," is a fundamental Christian doctrine.[87]

55. *The church of Rome corrupt, and that of Geneva imperfect.* What's to be done then? I transport myself into Spain or Italy, there I meet with numbers of Christians, and as they tell me the Catholic Church under the government of Christ's vicar.[88] An office that I do not find in any part of my New Testament, nor do many of the doctrines they would oblige me to receive, appear in the sacred pages, but quite the contrary. Surely then, say I, if these are Christians, they are mightily degenerated from their first institution. I'll enquire further,

---

85. Astell refers to a passage in the *Letter concerning Church Communion* about an agent who comes to negotiate with William III for the ransom of English captives "on the coast of Barbary" (4). In subsequent paragraphs, Astell adopts the author's same strategy of supposing that an African is converted to Christianity, but takes the unusual step of supposing that she is that African.

86. *Letter concerning Church Communion*, 5.

87. Astell alludes to Lk 10:42 and Mt 16:26.

88. Christ's vicar] the pope.

and so I take a journey to Geneva and Amsterdam, where I do not find such a superstructure of hay and stubble,[89] as I was scandalized at in the other churches.[90] But endeavoring to inform myself more perfectly in the Christian religion, and examining further into the reasons why we receive the holy scriptures[91] as the word of God, which is the very foundation of my faith, as faith is of my Christianity; I find upon strict enquiry, that the same catholic tradition whereby the holy scriptures are conveyed to us, and proved to be what they pretend, does likewise deliver to us another form of government than that which is established in the churches among whom I am.[92]

56. *A lawful priesthood necessary*. And further, consulting my New Testament, I find that "no man can lawfully preach unless he be sent," sent, according to divine institution and designation as "Aaron was," and that God has instituted diverse orders in His church, giving to them different offices and powers.[93] Thus Philip, one of the seven ordained by the apostles to a particular ministration, Acts 6, and who is called an evangelist, preached the gospel to the Samaritans, but his authority did not extend to the "laying on of hands"[94] (whether this signifies what we now call confirmation, or the ordaining of ministers for that church, or both, as is most likely) and therefore St. Peter and St. John were sent to perfect what Philip had so well begun. In like manner, St. Paul in his epistles to Timothy and Titus, having asserted his own commission and authority, directs them how to behave themselves in the government of the church of God, how to use that power they had received from the apostle, and how to convey it to others.[95]

---

89. Astell alludes to 1 Corinthians 3:12, a passage exhorting believers to build their foundation on Jesus Christ and not substances that can be consumed by fire ("stubble" is the straw left by grain stalks after the harvest).

90. Again, Astell responds to the author of the *Letter concerning Church Communion*, who notes that "a good Christian may save his soul in Holland or Geneva, although their forms of worship and discipline be different from ours" (7).

91. In the first edition, this sentence reads "the reasons of our receiving the holy scriptures" instead of "the reasons why we receive the holy scriptures."

92. "inhabit" in first edition.

93. Rom 10:15; Heb 5:4.

94. Acts 6:6.

95. Astell's marginal note: 2 Tm 1:6; 2 Tm 2:2; Ti 1.

So that though I will not blame any church for the want of this apostolic government, not knowing what difficulties they labor under; yet if there be a Christian church, at once free from the corruptions of Rome, and the imperfections of Geneva, I shall most gladly join myself to her communion.

57. *Church of England most agreeable to God's word and the primitive church.* Now I am told of a renowned church, to which all the reformed churches give the right hand of fellowship, thither then, I direct my course. And when I come to England, what find I there? Different ways of worship, which I was not so much scandalized at while I remained at Amsterdam, because of the different nations that inhabit there. But different ways of worship and separate congregations among natives, because of some external modes not held unlawful, and though all profess the same doctrine, must needs be matter of offence to an honest African. The doctrine of the established national church I find to be exactly agreeable to my testament; and her government and public worship most conformable thereto, and to what I have learned of antiquity; and the whole is more orderly and edifying, than any I have hitherto met with; here then I fix, and I think it worth my while, whatever the journey or examination may have cost me. I lament indeed to see the lives of too many of her members, so little conformable to the doctrine she teaches them. But our savior has prevented my being scandalized at this, by comparing the kingdom of heaven, that is the church of God, to a field in which are tares[96] as well as good corn, and to a net, wherein are bad as well as good fishes.[97] Thus might I have become a member of a particular national church, and of the episcopal church[98] in this kingdom, even without the good fortune of being born in England; and thus I should have done if affected with a due concern for my salvation.

58. *Of the mysteries of the Christian religion.* As for "controversies in divinity,"[99] though I will not "condemn" a man as a "her-

96. tares] injurious corn weeds.

97. See Mt 13:24–30, 36–43, 47–50.

98. episcopal church] church constituted on the principle of episcopal government, or government by bishops.

99. Astell alludes to the "Preface to the French Translation" of *A Lady's Religion*, where the prefacer urges readers to shun "controversies in divinity" (A4v), but acknowledges it would

etic" without examining his opinions, yet I hope I may establish my *own* faith, without taking the trouble to read or hear all that talkative men may have said about the matter. And as to the mysteries of the Christian religion, if I did not find them in my Bible, I should never seek them elsewhere. Nor do I wonder that there are mysteries in it; I should wonder greatly if there were none.[100]

59. *What is a scripture mystery.* For what is a scripture mystery? What but a sublime truth concerning the nature of God, or His manner of acting, which we could never have discovered by mere human reason; and which, though it should happen to be above our weak understandings, so that we can't fully comprehend and account for it, is not therefore the less true, or less intelligible in itself, or less distinct and manifest to a higher understanding and superior reason. For as *my* reason is not the standard of truth and knowledge, and I should be very ridiculous and presuming did I pretend that a proposition was false and absurd, for no better reason than because I did not comprehend it; so neither is the most exalted human understanding, no nor the highest order of created intelligences, the standard of truth and reason. For it is the prerogative of infinite wisdom, the supreme and divine reason, and of this only, to be the measure of truth.

60. *Christianity mysterious only as it is sublime.* But the Christian religion is very far from being "dark" and "affectedly mysterious";[101] its revelations are as clear and as plain as the sublimity of the matter will admit. Nobody will call the mathematics an obscure and mysterious science, and yet it proposes theorems which will appear as abstruse and mysterious as any doctrine in the gospel, to those who know

---

be "an act of great temerity to condemn those whom the chiefs of any party are pleased to style *heretics* without reading them" (A6r).

100. Astell obliquely refers to the controversy surrounding John Toland's *Christianity not Mysterious* (1696), a work briefly discussed in the *Letter concerning Church Communion* (19–20). In his book, Toland argues that there are no mysteries, or any propositions "above reason," in the gospel. Some modern scholars have attributed the *Letter concerning Church Communion* to Toland himself. For details, see the "Historical-Intellectual Context" section of the introduction to the present volume.

101. Astell invokes the language of *A Lady's Religion*: "And it has been the observation of wise men, that when anyone affects to be dark and mysterious in his conversation, either he has some indirect design in so doing, or else whilst he makes an ostentation of wisdom, he does in reality but discover his folly" (10).

nothing of that science, nay even to such as have some smattering in it. Theorems that will pass for direct nonsense and impossibilities to an unskillful person, who yet it's like may have confidence enough in his good understanding to pass his verdict on them; and which even a modest and ingenious person may look upon as strange and incomprehensible. For would not your Ladyship think I bantered[102] you, should I affirm, that there are certain lines which though they infinitely approach, yet will never meet?[103] And that there are finite and determinate spaces equal to infinite?[104] And yet that there are such lines and such spaces, may be demonstrated.

61. *A mediator necessary, and not to be found but by revelation.* I should have felt the weakness of human nature, and its inability to live according to right reason, and to arrive at that perfection it incessantly desires, though I had never seen the scriptures. But I should not have known that Adam's sin was the cause of this, and that since I spring from him, he could derive no other than his own depraved and degenerate nature to me. My deviations from right reason, or the sins that I am conscious of, and that regret, fear, and disorder of mind which naturally and necessarily attends them, would have raised in me passionate desires of pardon and reconciliation with my maker.[105]

102. bantered] teased.

103. Astell refers to the geometrical idea of an asymptote, defined for example by Nehemiah Grew as lines that "though they may approach still nearer together, till they are nearer than the least assignable distance: yet being still produced infinitely, will never meet." See Nehemiah Grew, *Cosmologia Sacra; or, A Discourse of the Universe As it is the Creature and Kingdom of God* (London: W. Rogers, S. Smith, and B. Walford, 1701), 55.

104. A similar mathematical example appears in Antoine Arnauld and Pierre Nicole, *Logic or the Art of Thinking* (1662), trans. and ed. Jill Vance Buroker (Cambridge: Cambridge University Press, 1996), a work that Astell cites approvingly in her *Proposal II*, 166, 184, 189. The authors of the *Logic* observe that the idea of "an infinite space equal to a finite space" seems impossible, but can be demonstrated thus: "If we take half of a square, and half of this half, and so on to infinity, and then we join all these halves along their longest sides, we will form a space of an irregular shape that will continually decrease to infinity along one end, but that will be equal to the entire square. For a half and half of the half, plus half of this second half, and so on to infinity, make the whole" (Arnauld and Nicole, *Logic*, 232).

105. Astell's marginal note (second edition only): See King's *History of the Apostle's Creed*, 363. Third edition. [In the passage in question, King observes that, in the time before the gospel, "the very heathens themselves" were capable of recognizing their sinfulness and desiring God's mercy and forgiveness.]

But I could not have told on what terms He would vouchsafe to be reconciled, if He had not been pleased to declare them. For that God would send His son, at what time, and in what manner, to reconcile the world unto Himself, was what no created understanding could ever have attained the knowledge of, unless God had thought fit to reveal it. We have a natural and general perception of God, but our particular notions and fuller knowledge of the divine nature, is wholly owing to revelation. And therefore I dare not be so audacious as to question the truth of anything revealed by Him, or to object against any sort of worship or obedience which He requires, or to receive so much and no more of it, than suits with my fancy, or what I call my reason. On the contrary, having once sufficient proof of the truth of the revelation, I have no more to do but to receive the divine pleasure, and to submit to the "whole will of God," with the utmost humility and prostration of soul.[106]

62. *The mysteries of Christianity plainly affirmed in holy scripture.*[107] Again, though I do not understand the philosophy of the union between the divine and human nature (neither do I comprehend the vital union between my soul and body, nor how and in what manner they are joined, though I am sure that so it is); yet since the scripture very frequently calls Jesus of Nazareth the son of God, and also the son of man, I must believe that these two distinct natures do in Him make one person; and that that holy child who was born of the Virgin Mary, is "God with us."[108] That the father is God, the son is God, and the holy ghost is God, is plain from scripture, the name of God being ascribed to each of these divine three, in such a manner as it is never imparted to any creature. Now we know that there can be no inequality in the divine nature; as the scripture says nothing of a "made God," so right reason explodes it; and to pay divine worship to any but God

106. Acts 20:27.

107. In this subsection, Astell follows in the footsteps of Edward Stillingfleet, the bishop of Worcester, by defending the doctrine of the trinity against Socinian arguments. See Edward Stillingfleet, *A Discourse in Vindication of the Doctrine of the Trinity* (London: J. H. for Henry Mortlock, 1697), the work that initiated the famous Locke-Stillingfleet debate. For details, see the "Historical-Intellectual Context" section of the introduction to the present volume.

108. Mt 1:23: "Behold, a virgin shall be with child, and shall bring forth a son, and they shall call his name Emmanuel, which being interpreted is, God with us."

is gross idolatry. And therefore since we are taught in scripture that God is one, and are also taught to worship father, son, and holy ghost, and since we are even baptized in their name; the divine three are but one God, whose nature we must adore, but can never fully comprehend. Nor can any similitudes drawn from natural things, of which there are several, help us to a proper and worthy idea of the divine nature, though they may give us a faint resemblance of it. "God is great, and we know Him not, we cannot find Him out, with Him is terrible majesty, we should therefore fear Him, He respecteth not any that are wise of heart."[109]

63. *The divine nature is incomprehensible.* Who among us will pretend to a complete and perfect knowledge of the mystery of God's love to mankind? Is there not a length and breadth, a height and depth in it, which we can't fathom? As indeed there must be in everything that God does, much more in what He is, for "who can search out the almighty to perfection"?[110] But I hope no man will say that God's love to us is less true, or less evident, because it is so mysterious? Were it not a wise inference should I conclude that there is no God, or that it is not necessary for me to *concern* myself about Him, because I can never hope to comprehend Him? Is it not much more reasonable to affirm, that that being which I can fully understand is not God, because the very nature of God speaks Him incomprehensible? I wonder therefore why wise men give themselves so much trouble in solving difficulties, and explaining articles and the like; for in my mind such sublime truths cannot be more intelligibly, more rationally, more consistently, and clearly expressed to an honest, unprejudiced, and attentive mind, than the catholic doctrines are delivered in holy scripture, and as the church has summed them up in her creeds.

64. *The mysteries of Christianity tend to the improvement of our morals.* As for those "nice speculations or profound mysteries which have no direct tendency to improve our morals,"[111] they may very well be passed by. But all mysteries are not nice and needless speculations, for the scripture teaches us a "mystery of faith"; "a mystery

109. Astell's marginal note: Jb 36:26 and 37:22, [24], and so on.
110. Jb 11:7.
111. Astell's marginal note (first edition only): *Lady's Religion*, 9.

of godliness"; "a mystery of God, and of the father, and of Christ."[112] And as Christianity has its mysteries, so have these mysteries a direct and great influence upon Christian morals. For instance, what can give us so great a detestation of sin, and so effectually deliver us from the power of it, as the mystery of the incarnation of the son of God? When we learn that God could not, or would not (which is one and the same when we speak of God, who always does what most becomes Him; and can, that is, will do nothing but what is best, and therefore would not) pardon sin, without such a propitiatory sacrifice,[113] such a full satisfaction to His justice, as the passion and death of His only and well-beloved son! Did we always keep a lively sense of this in our minds, we might sin if we could; it would be morally impossible, I mean, for any the greatest temptation to prevail upon us.

65. *They who object against mysteries most unintelligible themselves.* Indeed I have always observed, that those men who talk the most against mysteries, are of all others the most mysterious and unintelligible. Give me leave to ask you, Madam, if you have not a clearer notion of God and his goodness from those words of scripture, which inform us, that in "Him we live, and move, and have our being,"[114] than from that "most lively manner," as the *Lady's Religion* tells us, in which "the divine nature is set forth by" Pythagoras?[115] Should I say to your Ladyship, that "deity is the vital spirit of the universe"; "that God is the temperament of all ages," "the principle of all things individual, and so on,"[116] I'm afraid you would think it jargon; and tell me I would never have made use of such expressions, if I had not affected to be "dark"

---

112. Astell's marginal note: 1 Tm 3:9, 16; Col 2:2.

113. propitiatory sacrifice] an atoning sacrifice.

114. Acts 17:28.

115. *Lady's Religion*, 53.

116. Astell paraphrases the author's summary of Pythagoras's views about the divine nature: "God is surely one, nor is He resident ... without the structure of the universe, but is entire within Himself: surveying all generations in a complete circle. He is the temperament of all ages, the agent of His own powers and works: the principle of all things individual ... the vital spirit of the universe" (*Lady's Religion*, 53–54). Astell repeats these words in order to mock the obscurity and unintelligibility of the author's concept of God.

and "mysterious."[117] I was indeed almost afraid that our divine had forsaken his "easy and familiar way of instruction,"[118] and was returned to his old "by-paths of obscure and unintelligible doctrines, which can have no effect upon us besides unprofitable amusements,"[119] when I read his pages 60, 61, and 64.[120] But then I began to consider, that in this learned age of ours, it is to be supposed that ladies understand not only Latin and Greek, but even Hebrew and Persian criticisms!

66. *The truth of Christian mysteries evident, though the philosophy difficult. Instances.* In a word, though the *philosophy* of the mysteries of the Christian religion is above our reach, yet the *truth* of them is plainly laid down in holy scripture. And I entirely agree with our divine,[121] that the Christian institution which was designed for all sorts of men, the poor in particular, who don't use to be the most learned, is "easily intelligible."[122] His brevity it's like would not allow him to give instances and therefore I shall offer one in each of his four general heads.[123]

"First" then, matters of "fact" are "plainly related."[124] Thus it is very plain from the whole tenor of the gospel, that "the believing that Jesus was the messiah, the giving credit to the miracles He did, and

---

117. See *Lady's Religion*, 10. Astell turns the author's criticism of "dark" and "mysterious" conversation against his own work.

118. Astell's marginal note (first edition only): *Lady's Religion*, 112. [This is a mistaken reference. The correct page numbers are *Lady's Religion*, 10–11, where the author says that "all instruction must of necessity be plain: since it is by things easy and familiar ... whereby we can be led on to the knowledge of matters more remote and difficult."]

119. See *Lady's Religion*, 2, 11. Astell sarcastically invokes the author's reference to "those by-paths, in which I have sometimes walked" while neglecting his religious duties.

120. In these pages of *A Lady's Religion*, the author refers to ancient conceptions of God, providing the Hebrew, Egyptian, Greek, Roman, and Persian names for the two coordinate powers of deity, one for good and one for evil (60–61). He also provides various Latin translations of the word "devils" (64).

121. The author of *A Lady's Religion* calls himself "a divine of the Church of England."

122. See *Lady's Religion*, 14.

123. In *A Lady's Religion*, the author outlines four parts of the Christian institution that are conducive to moral improvement: a narration of matters of fact, a declaration of moral laws, a revelation of motives to obey those laws, and exhortations to remind us of our duty (11–13).

124. *Lady's Religion*, 12.

the profession He made of Himself,"[125] and upon this ground giving up themselves to His conduct, and to the rule of life proposed by that God into whose name they were baptized, was that which made men Christians. It is also as plain, that it was the faith of the Jewish church that the messiah was "the son of God";[126] that He "was to be without sin," which God only is;[127] according to what our savior said to the young man, "Why callest thou me good?" Doest thou believe me to be God the messiah? For "there is none good but one, that is God."[128] Nor can anything be plainer than that Jesus took upon Him to be God equal with the father, when He said to the Jews, "I and my father are one";[129] that the common people as well as other Jews understood Him so; and that He did not go about to remove this opinion, but confirmed them in it. And it is also plain, that in the opinion of the Jews, and indeed of all mankind, whoever takes upon him to be God, and is not God, is a blasphemer. And we may observe, that the Jews upon this occasion, were ready to execute the punishment of law inflicted for blasphemy.[130] So that anyone who had made an "attentive and unbiased search," might have "found another law" besides "that against false prophets, Deuteronomy 18:20, whereby" our savior's "making himself the son of God deserved death," in the opinion of the unbelieving Jews.[131]

"Secondly, all laws must be plain because they are directions. And laws which are difficult and dubious to be understood are snares

---

125. Astell's marginal note (first edition only): Locke, *Reasonableness of Christianity*, second edition, 26 [23], and so on. [Astell refers to the 1696 second edition of Locke's *Reasonableness of Christianity*. The work was first published anonymously in 1695, but following his death in 1704 Locke's authorship was made public.]

126. Astell's marginal note (first edition only): See Locke, *Reasonableness of Christianity*, 25 [22], and so on, 49, 50, 96 [34, 60].

127. Astell's marginal note (first edition only): Locke, *Reasonableness of Christianity*, 33 [27].

128. Mt 19:17; Mk 10:18; Lk 18:19.

129. Astell's marginal note: See Jn 10:30, and so on.

130. Astell's marginal note: Lv 24:16.

131. Astell's marginal note (first edition only): Locke, *Reasonableness of Christianity*, 152 [87]. [Astell also alludes to "The Preface" of the *Reasonableness of Christianity*, where Locke indicates he has made an "attentive and unbiased search" of the scriptures (A2r [3]).]

and traps."[132] Therefore when Jesus commanded His disciples to "teach all nations, baptizing them in the name of the father, son, and holy ghost,"[133] making this the very form of admission into His religion, it's plain that He neither makes, nor supposes, any difference in the nature of the father, son, and holy ghost, but places them in an equality, which had certainly been a "snare" and a "trap," and apt to lead men into idolatry, had there been any essential difference in the nature of the divine three; and had men been obliged to believe that "pretended deep speculation" of an inferior, a created, or made God, that "unintelligible mystery," set on foot by "profound men."[134]

"Thirdly, it is necessary that moral motives should be very intelligible."[135] Therefore when St. Paul goes to convince the Philippians, that they ought to be humble, because of that wonderful example of humility set before them by Jesus Christ, he tells them plainly, that Christ who was in the "form of God," and "equal with God," did not disdain to "humble Himself," and "to be made in the likeness of man."[136] Now this had been nothing extraordinary, and consequently no motive, but rather an "abstruse and mysterious" jargon, had Jesus been *only* a mere man, how "extraordinary" so ever.[137]

"Fourthly, mystical and unintelligible exhortations are ridiculous";[138] so that when St. Paul exhorted the bishops of Asia "to feed the church of God which He has purchased with His own blood";[139] he must mean that the church of God was purchased or redeemed by blood, and that this blood was the blood of God; or else

132. *Lady's Religion*, 12–13. The exact wording is: "Secondly, all laws *must* be plain, because they are directions. Now, obscure directions are but delusions. And laws which are dubious and difficult to be understood, are *traps* and *snares*" (12–13).

133. Astell's marginal note: Mt 28:19.

134. *Lady's Religion*, 15.

135. *Lady's Religion*, 13.

136. Astell's marginal note: Phil 2:5, and so on. [Astell also refers to Phil 2:6–8].

137. Astell's marginal note (first edition only): Locke, *Reasonableness of Christianity*, 36, 55 [28, 37].

138. *Lady's Religion*, 13.

139. Astell's marginal note: Acts 10:28. [The reference should be to Acts 20:28.]

it is plain that the apostle speaks in an unknown tongue, uses an "obscure and unintelligible" language,[140] and means nothing.

67. *How our Lord Jesus Christ saves us from our sins.* And because the holy scriptures do frequently tell us of "remission of sin," and that this remission and "redemption" is purchased for us by the "blood of Christ," which is a "propitiation" for all them who with hearty repentance and true faith turn unto Him;[141] I dare not say that our savior's "only design" was to "save us from the prevailing power of sin, and those miseries it would involve us in";[142] if by this power no more be meant than what we usually call the dominion of sin. Christ indeed came to save us from our sins in all senses; to save us from the guilt, and thereby from the punishment of sin,[143] from which we could never have delivered ourselves, the most perfect mortal being liable to this guilt, since "there is not a man upon earth that doth good and sinneth not."[144]

68. *He was our expiatory sacrifice.* And as the "expiatory sacrifices"[145] practiced by the heathens throughout the world,[146] showed it to be the commonsense of mankind, that "without shedding of blood there is no remission."[147] So God Himself expressed His approbation of this natural notion, by rectifying the abuses crept into it, and giving several laws to the Jewish church concerning expiations. But then as the apostle argues, since "it is not possible that the blood of bulls and goats should take away sin," these must be typical of something else that could, even of the "precious blood of Christ, as of a lamb without blemish, and without spot."[148] Who offered "one sacrifice for sins," and "by that one offering, has perfected forever them that are sanctified," has "purged our sins," and given us "redemption

---

140. *Lady's Religion*, 11.

141. Astell's marginal note: Mt 26:28; Acts 2:38; Rom 3:24–25.

142. Astell's marginal note (first edition only): *Lady's Religion*, 4.

143. The statement "and thereby from the punishment" is not in the first edition.

144. Eccl 7:20.

145. expiatory sacrifices] sacrifices serving to make amends for an offense.

146. Astell's marginal note (first edition only): Locke, *Reasonableness of Christianity*, 267 [147].

147. Astell's marginal note: Heb 9:22.

148. Astell's marginal note: Heb 10:4; 1 Pt 1:19.

through his blood."[149] And being thus purified from the guilt and stain, we are then, and not otherwise, capable of making use of God's grace to save us from the "power" and "dominion," and consequently from the "evil effects of sin." For all "being sinners and transgressors of the law, and so unjust; are all liable to condemnation, unless they believe" in the messiah,[150] who "by His own blood has obtained eternal redemption for us," "putting away sin by the sacrifice of Himself." And as the messiah "was once offered to bear the sins of many, so unto them that look for Him shall He appear the second time without sin unto salvation."[151] Which with many other discourses, some of them in the gospel and Acts, as well as in the epistles, not only "sounds something like," but plainly declares "Christ's purchasing life for us by His death; laying down His life for another, and restoring life to mankind."[152]

69. *The occasion of making creeds.* Supposing then, but not granting[153] that we are "not to learn the fundamental articles of faith in the epistles";[154] yet they to whom we make this concession cannot deny, that the epistles are the best expositions of those fundamental articles taught in the gospel. For when men through ignorance or ill-design, had put a false gloss on the Christian doctrines, the apostles took care

---

149. Astell's marginal note: Heb 10:10, 12, 14; Heb 1:3; Col 1:14.

150. Astell's marginal note (first edition only): Locke, *Reasonableness of Christianity*, 245 [134].

151. Astell's marginal note: Heb 9:12. See the whole chapter 5:26, 28. [This last reference should be Heb 9:26, 28.]

152. Astell's marginal note (first edition only): Locke, *Vindication*, 5, 6 [10]. [Astell refers to Locke's *Vindication of the Reasonableness of Christianity* (1695). This work was appended to the 1696 second edition of Locke's *Reasonableness of Christianity*, in response to John Edwards's *Some Thoughts Concerning the Several Causes and Occasions of Atheism* (1695). For a modern edition of the *Vindication*, see John Locke, *Vindications of the Reasonableness of Christianity*, ed. Victor Nuovo (Oxford: Clarendon Press, 2012). Henceforth, whenever I provide Astell's original references to the *Vindication*, I also provide page references to this modern edition in square brackets. For details on Edwards's criticisms of Locke, see the "Historical-Intellectual Context" section of the introduction to the present volume.]

153. In the first edition, this sentence begins "Let it then be allowed" instead of "Supposing then, but not granting."

154. Astell's marginal note (first edition only): Locke, *Reasonableness of Christianity*, 295, 298 [165], and so on.

to "resolve doubts, reform mistakes,"[155] "and explain fundamentals,"[156] for the "expounding, clearing and confirming the Christian doctrine," and with "regard to the state and exigencies of those times."[157] Upon the same occasion arose the creeds of the catholic church, who did not "enlarge" her articles by adding to them, but only explain them; whence the "spirit" of a certain author's "creed-making" took its rise, let him declare.[158] For as for the Christian religion, upon the most "attentive" and "unbiased search,"[159] I find it conveyed to us in the following manner.

70. *A summary of Christ's religion.* The messiah, the wisdom of the father, did by His own and His disciples' preaching, instruct mankind in a religion which the truly "wise" and "learned" may be satisfied with, as well as the "laboring and illiterate man may comprehend."[160] He taught men to worship the one true God, father, son, and holy ghost, by whom the world was made, and who in the fullness of time spoke to us by the son, "God manifest in the flesh,"[161] who was conceived and born without sin, that He might be crucified, dead, and buried, for the remission of our sins, and who rose again and ascended

155. Astell's marginal note (first edition only): Locke, *Reasonableness of Christianity*, 298 [165].

156. Astell's marginal note (first edition only): Locke, *Reasonableness of Christianity*, 299 [166].

157. Astell's marginal note (first edition only): Locke, *Reasonableness of Christianity*, 300 [167].

158. Astell's marginal note (first edition only): Locke, *Vindication*, 17, 18 [16]. [Astell drily alludes to Locke's statement that "the spirit of creed-making" always arises "from a heat of zeal for our own opinions, and warm endeavors" (Locke, *Vindication*, 18 [16]).]

159. See Locke, preface to *Reasonableness of Christianity*, A2r [3].

160. Astell seemingly agrees with Locke's view that scripture offers "articles that the laboring and illiterate man may comprehend" and was not written merely for the "learned scribe" or the "wise of this world" (Locke, *Reasonableness of Christianity*, 305, 306 [169, 170]). He goes on to say that "The bulk of mankind have not leisure for learning and logic, and superfine distinctions of the schools. Where the hand is used to the plough, and the spade, the head is seldom elevated to sublime notions, or exercised in mysterious reasonings. It is well if men of that rank (to say nothing of the other sex) can comprehend plain propositions, and a short reasoning about things familiar to their minds" (Locke, *Reasonableness of Christianity*, 305 [170]).

161. 1 Tm 3:16.

into heaven, in earnest of our resurrection, and to obtain for us eternal life, "through sanctification of the spirit," whom He sent "to guide His church into all truth," and belief of the gospel.[162] These were the plain and simple truths that were everywhere preached and believed by all who were admitted into the communion of saints; as is evident to anyone who reads the gospels and the Acts with singleness of heart, nor needs there a pompous enumeration of texts to prove it. The "several texts" of scripture may be "put" and made to "consist together" in this sense,[163] very easily and naturally, and without any force, by him who uses "fair endeavors, who comes with a docility and disposition prepared to embrace and assent to all truths coming from God," with "submission of mind."[164] Nor *can* he who brings such a disposition of mind be "ignorant" of them,[165] so far as one can conclude from the reason of things, and without seeing "deeply into the heart," the heart of man which is unsearchable by human eyes.[166]

71. *How it was corrupted.* But when the enemy of souls, according to our Lord's prediction, began to sow his tares by the hands of men, "who because when they knew God they glorified Him not as God, neither were thankful, but being vain in their imaginations," and "professing themselves to be wise," above what is written, "became fools";[167] when some began to corrupt the Christian doctrine by either openly maintaining, or covertly insinuating, that the object of the Christian worship, was no more than an "extraordinary man," or a made God at best;[168] that he was a quality, or mode, or manifestation,

---

162. 2 Thes 2:13; Jn 16:13.

163. Astell's marginal note (first edition only): Locke, *Reasonableness of Christianity*, 304 [169].

164. Astell's marginal note (first edition only): Locke, *Reasonableness of Christianity*, 302 [169]. [The correct page reference should be 303; there is a typesetting error in the second edition.]

165. Locke, *Reasonableness of Christianity*, 302 [169].

166. Astell presumably alludes to Locke's *Vindication*, in which he sarcastically accuses Edwards of being "so much better acquainted with me than I am with myself" and of seeing "so deeply into my heart" (14 [15]).

167. Astell's marginal note: Rom 1:21–22.

168. Locke, *Reasonableness of Christianity*, 36, 55 [28, 37].

and not a subsistence, or in the plainest language, not a real being:[169] it was then absolutely necessary for the church to explain her fundamental articles, according to the "form of sound words," which she had heard of Christ and His apostles, and in opposition to those "false teachers who privily brought in damnable heresies, even denying the Lord who bought them"; and who by "good words and fair speeches, deceived the hearts of the simple."[170]

72. *Who are the most dangerous seducers.* Indeed the most dangerous sort of seducers, are they who with "cunning craftiness lie in wait to deceive,"[171] men who do not speak out, and declare in words at length, what they too plainly insinuate, for then one could know what to say to them. But by mixing truth with error, and delivering their propositions in such doubtful expressions, as are true in one sense, though false in another, they secure themselves a retreat in the "sincerity" of their "thoughts," and their "single denial," if you press them with that sense they do not care to own; for who can "pretend to know other men's thoughts and reasons, better than they themselves?"[172] How far this agrees with that ingenuity and sincerity that always accompanies truth, I leave the world to judge.

73. *Wherein the reasonableness of Christianity consists.* But though our savior thought fit to decline declaring Himself to be the

---

169. Astell alludes to commonplace philosophical distinctions of the time. A substance (or a "subsistence") is an independently existing thing, while qualities, modes, and manifestations exist only insofar as they inhere in a substance. According to a Cartesian (a follower of Descartes), for example, "being round" is a mode or a way of being an extended substance, while "doubting" is a way of thinking or a mode of a thinking thing. Here Astell reacts to the suggestion that Christ was a mere mode or way of being God and not an independently existing being in his own right.

170. Astell's marginal note: 2 Tm 1:13; 2 Pt 2:1. [Astell also refers to Rom 16:18: "For they that are such serve not our Lord Jesus Christ, but their own belly; and by good words and fair speeches deceive the hearts of the simple."]

171. Eph 4:14.

172. Astell invokes Locke's responses to Edwards's accusations of Socinianism (see Locke, *Vindication*, 4, 10, 13 [10, 13, 14]). In the early modern period, Socinianism is a religious movement characterized by a strong reverence for reason, the reduction of Christianity to bare fundamentals, the denial of the trinity (the doctrine that three persons—the father, son, and holy ghost—constitute one God), and denial of the divinity of Christ. For further details, see the "Historical-Intellectual Context" section of the introduction to this present volume.

messiah in express words, and that for very good reasons, according to the account of a late author,[173] that is to say, to avoid all occasions of sedition, or the least "suspicion" of it; that he might "not die as a criminal and a traitor," or do "anything that might be offensive, or give the least umbrage to the Roman government."[174] Yet we find His apostles declared this and all other truths with *boldness*, being neither ashamed nor afraid to own them without reserve. Thus St. Paul assures his Asian converts, that he "had kept back nothing that was profitable unto them," and "had not shunned to declare all the counsel of God."[175] Though a prisoner at the bar, he "urged such points to Felix," as made him tremble, "persuading him to be a Christian," not by concealing, but by inculcating such truths, as he was most averse to.[176] And whether or not we are to "blame" the "prudence" of some men, such as the missionaries in China, who "mention" no more of Christianity than will give them "access to those men" they would "prevail upon," I am not now to examine.[177] But, as appears to me, the reasonableness of Christianity does not consist in avoiding such "arguments as men object against,"[178] but in these two great truths, namely: 1. That there is not anything so reasonable as to believe all that God has revealed, and to practice all that He has commanded. 2. That God has given such proofs and evidences as are sufficient to satisfy any reasonable person, that the Christian religion is a divine revelation.

74. *What gospel articles of faith required by Christ and His apostles.* The business then is to enquire, what are those "propositions which are required to be actually believed to make us Christians."[179] And I shall not scruple to say with a certain author,[180] that the "believing Jesus of Nazareth to be the messiah, was the only gospel article of faith, preached by Christ and his apostles, upon their assent to which

173. i.e., John Locke.

174. Astell's marginal note (first edition only): Locke, *Reasonableness of Christianity*, see 137, 147 [79, 85], and so on; 134, 154 [78, 88].

175. Astell's marginal note: Acts 20:20, 27.

176. Astell's marginal note: Acts 24:24, and so on. [Astell also refers to Acts 24:25.]

177. Astell's marginal note (first edition only): Locke, *Vindication*, 7 [11].

178. Astell paraphrases Locke, *Vindication*, 7 [11].

179. Astell's marginal note (first edition only): Locke, *Vindication*, 16 [15–16].

180. i.e., John Locke.

men were received into the Christian church,"[181] provided, that this be understood, not as excluding, but as it includes, all those propositions or articles of faith that are summed up in what is commonly called the Apostles' Creed; and that it does include them see the appendix.[182]

75. *Eternal misery the sanction of the Christian law.* We have already proved[183] that there is a God; consequently we who are His creatures and who depend upon Him entirely, owe Him the utmost duty and service. It has also been proved, that God has revealed His will to us, hence it follows, that it is our duty and wisdom to pay the most exact obedience to His revealed will, even though there were no sanctions annexed to it. But since it is plain from scripture, that there are such great and dreadful ones as become the divine majesty, it is our highest interest to be obedient, and we can't transgress without the greatest folly and madness, as well as the most notorious injustice, ingratitude, and wickedness.

76. *And why.* Eternal misery being the penalty annexed in the gospel to willful disobedience and impenitency, is for this reason highly equitable, since everything that God does is holy, just, and good. But we need not rest in this general account; God's "ways are equal,"[184] they will bear the test of the severest reason, to which with amazing condescension He sometimes appeals. And though He is absolute sovereign of all things, so that none may "say unto Him, what doest thou"?[185] Yet He not only allows, but requires us to judge of the reasonableness and equity of His proceedings.

77. *The equity of this.* Tell me then, "oh ye potsherds[186] of the earth," who take upon you to "contend with your maker"![187] Why God who is the fountain of being and perfection, may not communicate these in what manner, and by what measures, is most agreeable to His

---

181. Astell's marginal note (first edition only): Locke, *Vindication*, 16, 27 [15, 20–21]; *Reasonableness of Christianity*, 194, 195 [108, 109], and throughout.

182. The first edition reads "will appear presently" instead of "see the appendix." In that edition, this paragraph is followed by §§356–69 of the present volume.

183. "seen" in first edition.

184. Ez 18:25, 29.

185. Jb 9:12.

186. potsherds] broken pieces of pottery.

187. Is 45:9.

own infinite wisdom? We know that the excellency of a work appears by that variety of beauties that are in it: what makes the universe so beautiful but its innumerable varieties? And you who are such lovers of variety can have nothing to say against it. Was it then unfit for God to adorn His creation with all imaginable ranks and degrees of being, consequently with free agents which is a very noble order?

78. *Some actions naturally tend to happiness and other to misery.* Now the difference between a free and a necessary agent consists in this, that the actions of the former, or more properly the motions of his mind, are in his own power. He has ability, as everyone of us is sensible, to determine them this way or that, according to his own pleasure, and as he is affected by the supposed agreeableness of the objects he pursues. This power or faculty is what we call liberty, which distinguishes a free from a necessary agent; for this last does not determine itself, has no command over its own motions, but is absolutely governed by a foreign cause. But in whatever degree of being a creature is placed, whether it be a free or a necessary agent, there must be a certain measure of perfection belonging to its rank, which it cannot attain but by some certain and stated progressions or methods, suitable to the nature that God has given it, and in the same manner as a seed becomes a plant, or a plant a tree. Some actions therefore do naturally and necessarily tend to the perfection of mankind, and others as naturally and necessarily drag us down into misery.

79. *God has done all that can be done for free agents.* If then you will allow that God may create free agents, and where I pray is the injustice of it? Since it can't be supposed that He lays irresistible restraints upon them, or gives them irresistible impulses, which were to destroy the nature He has made, and to contradict Himself, consequently all that can be done for them, even by infinite power and goodness, conducted by infinite wisdom, is to allure them to good by the vastness of the pleasure proposed, and to deter them from evil by the dread of the pain that is threatened. God can neither be hurt by our wickedness, nor benefited by our obedience, His promises and threatenings therefore are purely for our advantage. And since we find in fact that the severest threatening, even inconceivable and eternal misery, does not deter mankind from sinning, from doing that which naturally and necessarily tends to their own hurt, it is not to

be imagined that lower motives would have any effect upon them. So that God has appointed a hell for the wicked in mere goodness to mankind, since this or nothing will work upon the most disingenuous tempers, and stir them up to qualify themselves for that heaven which He is desirous to bestow on them.

80. *The sanction suitable to the dignity of the legislator.* This argument sure may weigh with us because it is drawn from our own interest, though we have the insolence to overlook another not less reasonable in itself. We take no notice how indecent and every way unfit it is, that the divine authority should be violated, as it will certainly be, unless God's laws are asserted by a sanction someway suitable to the dignity of the legislator. But though our great pretenders[188] to wit and reason are often guilty of the grossest follies and absurdities, yet they ought to know that the wisest and the best of beings can never contradict Himself. He will for certain do what is fit, though through our own ill management it may happen to be to our infinite damage. For the essential rectitude of His nature, does as much oblige Him to punish the wicked, as to reward the obedient.

81. *Absurdity of libertines in denying a God.* Atheism is not tenable, the shrewdest wits among our libertines, who are most desirous to throw off the fear of God, and of a *future life*, that they may indulge themselves as they please in *this*, are not able to maintain it. Much less can the little fry defend it with their noise and confidence, which can't silence the convictions of their own minds, though the violence of their appetites may overrule them. They are therefore forced to confess a God to solve the appearances of nature, and to avoid a world of absurdities arising from their Epicurean systems,[189] and they find that a future state is a necessary consequence of the former truth, and therefore can't absolutely be denied.

82. *Or forming a wrong notion of Him.* But then lest they should be disturbed in their vices, the purity of the Christian moral being the true objection against the truth of the revelation, they take up with

188. pretenders] aspirers.

189. Astell refers to Epicurean atomism, an ancient natural philosophy revived in the mid-seventeenth century by thinkers such as Pierre Gassendi, Walter Charleton, and (in her early works, at least) Margaret Cavendish. "Epicurean systems" are worlds composed entirely of material atoms and the void.

certain loose notions, not less extravagant and absurd than downright atheism; but which they force themselves to be content with, since they can have no better. There is a God they say, but if you put them to explain their notion of Him, you'll find them so intent upon His self-sufficiency and mercy, as to forget all His other attributes. So that the God of this sort of people, is not that great and all-perfect being, who is the creator and lord of all things, but an idol of their own invention. They do Him no hurt they cry, therefore His goodness won't permit Him to hurt them. And while they pretend to think very greatly of the divine nature, they describe His mercy and goodness not like the attributes of a God, a being infinite in all perfections and consequently essentially just and holy, but like that foolish pity and softness which we usually despise in those we call easy and good-natured people.

83. *Mere reason reproves their folly.* But does not our natural notion of God, that which mere reason will help us to, if we don't neglect to use it, convince us, that God is absolute lord and sovereign of all His creatures; that He has more right in us than we have in ourselves, since we subsist only by His power, depending upon Him for every moment of our being? Therefore all the homage we can possibly pay Him is indispensably due; justice and order which are essential to the divine nature require it, so that it must necessarily, and according to the reason of things, either be paid in kind or by an equivalent.

84. *God's commands an effect of His goodness.* The same natural notions do also assure us, that the essential rectitude of the divine nature, will not permit Him to use His power and lawful authority otherwise than is just and fit, so that when of His free bounty He gave us being, He did not intend to make us miserable but happy. But then if we confess that God is infinitely wise, we must needs allow Him to know wherein our happiness consists, and to be best able to prescribe us the proper methods of attaining it. His very goodness will determine Him to give us rules, and our own interest as well as duty will incline us to observe them.

85. *Impossible to be happy unless obedient.* So then, happiness is to be obtained not by following our own will, but by observing His. For sure we don't pretend to treat[190] with God, and to tell Him we will have none of His happiness, none of that which is suitable to the

190. treat] negotiate.

nature He has given us; but a happiness after our own wild fancies, such as is[191] contrary to all the rules of order and right reason; so that God cannot gratify us in our folly but by denying Himself, that is, by acting contrary to the essential perfections of His own nature!

86. *God has put happiness in our power.* If God had not given us sufficient light to discern between the evil and the good, nor motives strong enough to incline us to pursue the one, and to avoid the other; if He had not put happiness in our own choice, but had inevitably determined us to destruction, this indeed had been a want of mercy and goodness, if not a want of justice towards His creatures.[192] But none of all this is our case, to be sure we who live in a Christian, in a reformed country, can't with any face complain of it. Shall we pretend ignorance? We who pride ourselves so much upon the refinements of our wit, and the improvements of our knowledge? Or are we only ignorant of the noblest and most important truths, though they are daily taught[193] in our churches? And though many of them may be discovered only by retiring into ourselves, and humbly and attentively consulting the eternal reason of things? Nor can we pretend to want motives, for what can be greater than eternal happiness and eternal misery? The last it seems is too strong[194] for us, and therefore we object against it, pretending it is not reconcilable with the goodness of God, according to the usual absurdity of people of libertine inclinations. For were not the reasonings of such, as corrupt and vicious as their practices, and both of them all over folly and inconsistency, they might easily discern that the divine excellencies will not suffer it to be less. Because the very goodness and mercy as well as the wisdom of God require Him, if He is pleased to propose *any* motive, to propose *such* a one as is most like to be effectual.

87. *We lose it because we will.* Where God has given but little light, no doubt He makes great allowances; this we may be sure of, that

191. The first edition reads "though it be" instead of "such as is."

192. Astell agrees with Locke's claim that if God had condemned human beings to misery "without any fault or demerit of their own," then this would be "hard to reconcile with the notion we have of justice, and much more with the goodness and other attributes of the supreme being" (Locke, *Reasonableness of Christianity*, 8 [10]).

193. "read" in first edition.

194. "big" in first edition.

He is no hard master, nor requires an increase beyond the talents He has given us. But though the light shine ever so bright about us, we can have no vision unless we open our eyes. Though the motives are ever so strong and powerful, yet they are *but* motives; they are most proper to persuade, but they neither can nor ought to compel.

88. *A senseless objection made by men of wit.* Oh but, say some, why should God thrust me into being whether I would or no, imposing such conditions on me, that had it been left to my choice, I would have refused being rather than have consented to them? Such are the wise sentences men[195] utter when they forsake reason to follow their vain imaginations! It is a wonder they do not quarrel with their fathers for making them heirs to great estates: for why may not one conclude that these noble spirits if it had been put to their choice, would have thought it better to have had no claim to their fathers' estates and titles, than to have been the offspring of such misers and unpolite persons,[196] as these elevated genii[197] may, it's like, suppose them!

89. *No condition on which eternal happiness is offered can be hard.* And were it not that such mighty wits as these are much beyond the reach of my poor understanding, I would humbly beg leave to ask them, whether any imaginable restraint or difficulty how great so ever, that is to continue but for a certain time, and much more if it can't exceed a hundred years, and very probably will be over in half that time, bears any manner of proportion to eternal happiness? Certainly their nature and mine are of a very different make, if they don't find an incessant desire after happiness, even endless happiness. And our understandings are as opposite, and so I can't argue with them, if they will not allow that we are very graciously dealt with, by being admitted to receive endless happiness upon *any*, even the hardest conditions. Nor can any conditions be called hard, that are to take place no longer than this very short life of ours.

195. In the first edition, this sentence begins "Such stuff do men" instead of "Such are the wise sentences men."

196. The first edition reads "blockheads" instead of "unpolite persons."

197. genii] plural of genie, "a tutelary spirit" (*OED*).

90. *He who has his choice is not hardly dealt with.* But if the "beasts of the people,"[198] it is a scripture phrase and a very apposite one, will be so sottish[199] as to part with a glorious reversion, an everlasting felicity for a mess of pottage,[200] there's no more to be said, they must have their wise choice! And since this and all the consequences of it is their *choice*, let them not for shame say they are hardly dealt with. For in a word, all the pretenses that are made for infidelity and immorality, resolve into love of the *present* pleasure whatever it be. We *will not* use our reason to compare what we get with what we lose, but are hurried on by a *present* brutal appetite, though to the loss of pleasures unspeakable and eternal.

91. *Eternal misery the natural effect of impenitency.* This is then the sum of the matter; God who is infinite in all perfections, in justice and holiness, as well as in goodness and mercy, always does what is best and most becoming His perfections, and cannot act but according to the nature and reason of things;[201] nor is it possible that our wishes or actions should make any alteration in the immutable rectitude of His conduct. He has made us free agents, which is an inestimable benefit unless we willfully abuse it. There can't be a more outrageous violation of the sacred law of order, than disobedience to the sovereign lord of all things; our great and liberal benefactor, our creator and the best being; to Him who would have all men to be saved; who has designed us an endless felicity, which nothing but our own willful obstinacy can deprive us of. Hence it follows, that since God has made us immortal, and it does not become Him to annihilate His own work, the eternal misery of an obstinate sinner, is necessary and unavoidable. Such a willful perseverance in sin, notwithstanding all the convictions of reason, and all that God has done to call him to repentance, resolving finally into a contempt and hatred of God. A temper so utterly incapable of happiness, that (as must be acknowledged by the greatest

---

198. The phrase "beasts of the people" appears in Psalm 68:30 of the Psalter of the Church of England, *Book of Common Prayer*, "Day 13. Morning Prayer," 410. In the King James version of the Bible, Psalm 68:30 simply reads "the calves of the people."

199. sottish] foolish.

200. pottage] thick soup or stew.

201. The first edition reads "according to the *essential* nature and reason of things" (my italics).

libertine) unless God should give him a new nature, he cannot *possibly* be happy. And sure men have not confidence to expect this from the divine goodness, how easy and soft so ever they may fancy it, after so ill a use of God's former favors! Neither would a new act of grace be of any advantage to them, unless God should deprive them of liberty and make them necessary agents, that is, make them other creatures and not men. Otherwise he who is at present unaffected with the infinite "goodness and long-suffering of God," which ought to "lead him to repentance," would continue in his impenitency; "he who is unjust, would be unjust still"; and "he who is filthy, would be filthy still."[202] Leaving these men therefore in their own mire, and to be corrected by their own folly, let us consider the practical duties of Christianity, that we may practice as well as believe, all that is required of us in order to our salvation.

---

202. Rom 2:4; Rv 22:11.

Section II

Of Christian practice; and of our duty to God more immediately[1]

92. Religion not arbitrary but founded in nature. Whoever considers religion as he ought, will find that it is not an arbitrary thing, much less an invention of men, or as some think fit to call it, priestcraft;[2] but that it has its foundation in nature, being derived from the two principal powers of the mind, the understanding and will.[3] For I hope it has been already shown, that reason brings us to the knowledge of God, and to a belief of all His revelations; and I shall now add, that our desire of happiness exacts from us a strict conformity to His will. So that it would be no ill definition of mankind to term them, *a race of religious creatures inhabiting this earth, whose nature leads them to adore God, and to desire incessantly to enjoy Him*; they of our race who do not come within this definition, being monsters rather than men.

93. *The desire of happiness teaches us obedience to God.* That we always thirst after happiness needs no proof; and I should think it needs as little, that He who gave us being, neither wants power nor goodness to give us well-being, without which the other would be no favor, and that He is best able to show us the way to happiness. Consequently the Christian religion which comes from God, as has been already proved, must be the *certain*, and at present, at least to them to whom it is preached, the *only* way to felicity. However I shall

1. This subheading is not in the first edition.

2. priestcraft] a common derogatory term for the maintenance or extension of priestly power and influence, "priestly scheming, guile or deceit" (*OED*). In the *Letter concerning Church Communion*, the author blames "priestcraft" for the fact that the "primitive simplicity" of the gospel "grew up into such a mystery, as is not only *above*, but *contrary* to all sense and reason" (9). In her *Discourse*, Damaris Masham also refers to "the superstitions of priestcraft" (124); and in his *Reasonableness of Christianity*, Locke likewise alludes to the "priestcraft" of those who would keep men to their "superstitious and idolatrous rites" (289 [162]).

3. Astell uses a commonplace philosophical distinction of the time. The understanding is that faculty of mind which is capable of receiving ideas, and the will is that which is capable of affirming or denying, accepting or rejecting ideas. For further details on these faculties and their role in the avoidance of error, see Astell, *Proposal II*, 205.

take it for granted here, hoping by God's assistance to make it out more fully presently;[4] and shall lay it down for a maxim, that the law of God is not only most just and fit, and most excellent in itself, but even most desirable to us. As everyone who makes a due use of his reason, will be forced to confess.

94. *Whose commands are necessary in order to happiness.* For what is it that God requires of us? No very hard task one would think, for it is only a sincere and constant endeavor after our own perfection. God has made us rational and free agents, capable of paying a reasonable and voluntary homage to His majesty, and of enjoying the happy effects of it. He has set before us good and evil, life and death, and conjures us by all the duty we owe to Him, by all the gratitude we ought to pay for the most stupendous instance of His love in our redemption, and by all the kindness we have for ourselves, to do what becomes us, and to avoid the necessary and intolerable effects of degenerating from the dignity of our nature. Since therefore we desire our own happiness, and God desires it also, and has done so much, even beyond our modest hopes, in order to it, what can hinder it? What, but that we ourselves do not know the way to happiness, and yet are so sottish that we will not follow God's directions. "This is the will of God, even your sanctification," says the apostle, there being no way to be happy but by being perfect, and no way to perfection but by being "holy as God is holy," according to our proportion, and so far as we are capable of imitating His glorious example.[5] And sure we are mightily hurt by being commanded to be godlike! For whatever we may think of holiness, mere heathens could say, that God is not more happy than mortals but by how much He is more just and holy.

95. *The glory of God is His end, and must be ours.* Could there have been a more excellent end than the glory of God, *that* had been the end of the creation. But the glory of God (which is not a mere empty show and noise like human glory, but which consists in the beauty and perfection of His works and ways) being the best design, all things were created for this purpose. And as it is God's end, so it must be ours, our great and last end, preferable even to our own happiness, could they be supposed to come in competition, as indeed

4. In the first edition, this sentence reads "in another place" instead of "presently."

5. Astell's marginal note: 1 Thes 4:3; 1 Pt 1:15–16.

they never can, the goodness of God being such, that we infallibly find our own felicity in doing what is best, that is, in conforming ourselves to His will; and in every case preferring His honor and service.[6] The world was made for the church, the church for Christ its head, the great high priest, the glorious architect of a spiritual temple, to the honor of the father, wherein God shall be worshipped with pure and holy worship to all eternity. Christ has been pleased to form the materials of this building, the members of this church, in diverse manners, and by diverse methods, that so every spiritual beauty may shine forth in it. The tempers and talents of mankind are various, and so are the exercises of their graces, their trials, and their conquests. Yet all the works of God are perfect in their kind, though all of them do not possess the same degree of perfection, for this would not consist with the perfection of the whole, which arises from the order and symmetry of the several parts; among which there would be little or no beauty if there were no distinctions, no different degrees of glory. And therefore, as we learn from that apostle who had been in heaven, and had seen its unutterable excellencies, "one star differs from another star in glory," even where all are glorious.[7]

96. *Perfection the business of a Christian.* But yet perfection was and must still be the business of God's church, from its infancy to its consummation in glory. Thus God instructed the patriarchs, "walk before me and be perfect."[8] The law of God, whether the moral or mosaical, each of them were "perfect" in their kind, and so far as they went.[9] These were excellent preparations for the gospel, which is the last method God thinks fit to take with us in this world, to raise us to perfection. And happy is it for us that we are born into its light, if we duly improve this advantage: as it will be most miserable if we "receive the grace of God in vain," and "neglect so great salvation."[10] He who is least under the gospel dispensation, is greater than the greatest under the other economies:[11] and that degree of virtue which rendered

6. This sentence is not in the first edition.

7. 1 Cor 15:41. The apostle is St. Paul.

8. Astell's marginal note: Gn 17:1.

9. Astell's marginal note: Pss 19 and 119.

10. Astell's marginal note: 2 Cor 6:1; Heb 2:3.

11. Astell's marginal note: Mt 11:11.

David a man after God's own heart, will not be sufficient to raise a Christian to that most glorious title. The scribes and Pharisees were very punctual in observing the law, and though too many of them were mere outsides,[12] yet we have no reason to conclude that they were all hypocrites. Saul to be sure was none, but though he was a mistaken zealot, yet as he tells us, he "served God with a good conscience" and in sincerity.[13] And yet our Lord assures us, that "unless our righteousness exceeds the righteousness of the scribes and Pharisees," we are not Christians.[14]

97. *Christianity the most perfect, and therefore most difficult institution.* To be a Christian is a greater thing, and a more honorable character than most of us imagine. But as all real honor is attended with difficulty and dangers, so they must not expect to be exempt from combats who engage in the Christian warfare, and list themselves under the banner of a crucified savior. "The disciple is not above his master, nor the servant above his lord." What greater honor can the disciple expect than to "be as his master"? Or the "servant" than "to be made like unto his lord"?[15] There is no quarter[16] to be had in this war, we must conquer or die; nor any victory to be obtained but by following "the captain of our salvation," "who for the joy that was set before Him endured the cross, despising the shame," and "was made perfect by sufferings."[17]

98. *Courage necessary; and not misbecoming a woman.* Your Ladyship sees I have pursued a warlike metaphor, which we frequently meet with in holy writ. But "the weapons of our warfare are not carnal," they enable us indeed to conquer the world, and which is more, ourselves, but all this without doing violence to any person.[18] A woman may "put on the whole armor of God" without degenerating into a masculine temper; she may "take the shield of faith," "the sword of the spirit," "the helmet of salvation," and "the breast-plate of

12. outsides] likenesses or effigies.

13. Astell's marginal note: Acts 23:1.

14. Astell's marginal note: Mt 5:20.

15. Astell's marginal note: Mt 10:24–25.

16. no quarter] no mercy.

17. Astell's marginal note: Heb 12:2 and 5:8–9.

18. Astell's marginal note: 2 Cor 10:4.

righteousness" without any offense to the men, and they become her as well as they do the greatest hero.[19] I could never understand why we are bred cowards; sure it can never be because our masters are afraid we should rebel, for courage would enable us to endure their injuries, to forgive, and to despise them! It is indeed so necessary a virtue that we can't be good Christians without it; for till we are got above the fear of death, it is in anybody's power to make us renounce our hopes of heaven. And it can't be supposed that men envy us our portion there; since however desirous they are to engross *this* world, they do not seem so covetous of *the other.*

99. *What hinders our perfection.* But let us leave them to their conquests while we push on in ours; and with undaunted bravery pursue the great design of Christianity, by advancing to the utmost degree of perfection of which human nature is capable. There may be difficulties indeed, but what do they signify, considering the present assistance, and the future reward? If it be enquired whence these difficulties arise, we shall find that it is "the corruptible body that presseth down the soul";[20] and that the objects of sense are the cause of our imperfection, and the exercise of our virtue. Human nature always desires happiness, and places its happiness in that which pleases; sensible pleasures being present, intrude upon us and will be attended: whereas spiritual pleasures though unspeakably greater, are more remote, they must be sought after and waited for. Therefore the main business of those who aspire to perfection, a very laudable and necessary ambition, is to throw off the prejudices of sense, which have nothing to plead but the prepossessions of childhood; to free themselves of the distempered[21] relish of present pleasures; to raise their affections above "the things that are seen," and which are but vain and "temporal," that they may fix them upon "things which" though at present they "are not seen, are" yet certain, infinitely satisfying, and "eternal": in a word, to live *by faith and not by sense.*[22]

19. Astell's marginal note: Eph 6:11, and so on. [Astell also refers to Eph 6:14, 16–17.]

20. Astell quotes from an apocryphal book of the Old Testament, Wisdom (or Wisdom of Solomon): Ws 9:15.

21. distempered] immoderate. The first edition reads "false" instead of "distempered."

22. Astell's marginal note: 2 Cor 4:18.

100. *Christianity teaches us to surmount it.* Now what can be so admirably well fitted to this divine end, as the precepts and example of our great master? Which express the greatest contempt of all that worldly minds prize and dote on, and which despise and trample on all that they fear. At least if I understand the gospel, this is what it teaches us, whatever we may be taught by one another. As might be easily shown from the whole tenor of the New Testament, and particularly from our Lord's divine sermon on the mount, which is not a collection of a few scattered precepts, but which with admirable order, beauty, and a divine force of reasoning, tends to disengage our thoughts from *this* world, and to inspire us with a noble ardor in the pursuit of the glories and felicities of the *next*. How come we then to frame another gospel? And to take to ourselves the honorable name of Christians, though we mind little else but what we renounced at our baptism? Christ came to raise us above these little and low pursuits, but we are sunk and lost in them! And if anything, by the grace of God, revives the life and vigor of Christianity, it must be that which some are pleased, though very unjustly, to call pride; even a generous neglect of all worldly enjoyments, which are given us for our use and exercise, but ought not to be considered as our good or our reward.

101. *Instances.* To instance only in the beatitudes,[23] we find, that our Lord pronounces them "blessed," whose actions and sense of things are directly opposite to worldly-minded men. For thus, like Job's friends we "call the rich happy," and "laugh the poor upright person to scorn";[24] whereas they who don't value themselves upon what worldlings esteem, are by our Lord pronounced "blessed," as being inheritors of the true riches, "theirs is the kingdom of heaven."[25] We will not be persuaded that the "house of mourning is better than the house of laughter," but would always live in mirth and jollity;[26] our Lord tells us, that "they who sow in tears shall reap in joy";[27] that they who "mourn" and whom we reckon afflicted, are indeed the happy

23. Mt 5:3–11.

24. Jb 12:4.

25. Mt 5:3.

26. Eccl 7:4.

27. Ps 126:5.

people, "for they shall receive *solid* comfort."[28] We imagine the world will trample on us unless we resent injuries; but the lamb of God assures us, that the way to be happy, even in this world, is to be "meek"; that revenge will continue and increase injuries, and that he who passes them by, both possesses his own soul in patience, whereby he is in an impregnable fortress, and even secures to himself an "inheritance in the earth."[29] We have eager appetites after sensible objects, and place our felicity in gratifying them; but our Lord informs us, that an "earnest desire after righteousness" is the only way to happiness, for in this only we shall receive no disappointment.[30] We generally look no further than ourselves, and so we are at ease and secure, we consider not what others suffer; our Lord would have us know, that the "same measure we mete,"[31] shall be measured to us,"[32] and that the only way to "obtain mercy" is to be "merciful."[33] Sensual pleasure possesses our hearts, we fancy ourselves undone without it; whereas our Lord declares that "purity" makes us "blessed," qualifying us for the highest transport of delight, the vision of God.[34] Animosities, contentions, and victories pass with us for mighty matters, and he has the loudest fame who has done most mischief to mankind; but the son of God, the fountain of true honor, bestows the highest title on the contrary temper, pronounces the "peace-makers blessed," and calls them the "children of God."[35] Nothing frights us so much as persecution, flesh and blood we think is not able to endure it, and what would we not do rather than take up the cross of Christ! But our divine master is very plain with us, as He assures us of His assistance, which will render us blessed even under our persecutors' hands, so He lets us know that He promises no crown without a cross, if we refuse to "suffer with Him"

28. Mt 5:4.

29. Mt 5:5.

30. Mt 5:6.

31. mete] allot.

32. Mt 7:2.

33. Mt 5:7.

34. Mt 5:8.

35. Mt 5:9.

in this world, we must not expect to "reign with Him" in His heavenly kingdom.[36]

102. *The great design of Christianity.* So different are the morals and views of our Lord from those of modern Christians, that while these abhor nothing so much as "suffering for righteousness sake,"[37] and had rather *do* the greatest evil than *endure* the least; our blessed savior commands us to "rejoice and be exceeding glad" when we are persecuted; and would not have us look upon persecutions as a calamity or matter of grief, but as an opportunity of obtaining the "greatest blessing."[38] In a word, what can pour a greater contempt upon this world and all its enjoyments, what can be a fuller or more sensible proof that all its offers are very despicable, than the manifestation of the son of God in the flesh, and the circumstances of His appearing among us? A proof that strikes even the meanest and grossest capacities, a proof that condescends to our very senses.

103. *Prosperity insufficient to happiness, and dangerous.* It is not improbable that among many other wise reasons for which God was pleased to establish the Jewish economy, one was to convince mankind experimentally, this being the only way of convincing most people, how little temporal enjoyments contribute to human happiness, and that the mind can't be satisfied with any good but what is spiritual and eternal; cannot indeed but be miserable in the midst of all outward affluence, unless it has some relish and enjoyment of such a good. The Jews enjoyed the greatest worldly felicity, and yet they were far from being a happy, an easy, or contented people; no nation more apt to murmur, or to fall into the grossest follies. Even Solomon who is represented as at the very top of worldly bliss, and who amidst all this prosperity, had "great experience of wisdom and knowledge,"[39] which is more than can be said of most people in his circumstances; yet even this great, this wise, this happy king, if anything in this world could have made him so, pronounces all to be "vanity"! And not only vanity which is bad enough, but which is yet worse, "vexation of spirit"![40] Nor

36. 2 Tm 2:12.

37. 1 Pt 3:14.

38. Mt 5:12.

39. Eccl 1:16.

40. Eccl 2:11.

could all his wisdom great as it was, and much above our pretensions, defend him from the poison and mischiefs of prosperity; none having acted more foolishly, with reverence to His majesty and to the sacred text be it spoken, than this wise and mighty man! Which is a lasting evidence that prosperity, how apt so ever we may be to presume on our own skill in managing it, is of infinite danger, even to the wisest and the best, and can't be tasted by them who have no mind to be ruined by it, but with great caution and fear, and a continual watch over themselves, which is enough, one would think, to spoil its relish.

104. *The gospel sets us right as to the world.* But prosperity and those sensible pleasures which it affords, are what mankind run madding[41] after. And though reason, if duly attended, offers motives enough to check this wild career, yet nothing but the grace of God can effectually restrain it. The Jews indeed were under great difficulties, temporal blessings were promised them, and consequently they were allowed to desire and pursue them. And yet even under *their* dispensation it is observable, that the favorites of God, the men "of whom the world was not worthy, were destitute" of all worldly comfort, "afflicted, tormented," and "received not the promise in this life."[42] But God has been more gracious to us Christians than He was to the Jews, and has done all that is consistent with the nature He has given us, to set us right in this matter. We have in the New Testament, "precept upon precept, line upon line,"[43] to disengage us from the "love of the world" and "the things that are in it," which are said to be inconsistent with the "love of the father."[44] But which is above all, and one would think is an irresistible argument, we have the example of the son of God, who could as easily have been born in the court of Augustus[45] as in a stable, and who could have commanded all the pleasures and grandeurs this world affords, without being hurt by them, had prosperity been either best in itself, or best for us.

41. madding] frenzied.

42. Astell's marginal note: Heb 11. [Astell refers to Heb 11:37–39 in particular.]

43. Is 28:10, 13.

44. Astell's marginal note: 1 Jn 2:15.

45. Augustus (or Octavian, as he was also known) reigned as the first emperor of Rome from 31 BCE to the year 14 CE.

105. *Benefit of living above the world.* To recount all the benefits we receive by "setting our affections on things above, and not on things on the earth," were to enumerate all the felicity that mankind is capable of in this life, and all the glorious hopes of the next. We shall be dead to the world it's true, but then we shall live an infinitely better life; for "our life is hid with Christ in God."[46] Nor can we be sure that our "treasure is in heaven," any other way than by having our "hearts there," and by being thus dead to all other things.[47] Which will give us a foretaste and earnest[48] of that blessed life, without the hopes of which this present life and all it can afford, is not so much as tolerable. A truth which I am sure they will witness, who have so much resolution and nobleness of mind as to make the experiment, nor will they ever repent the trial; in the meantime let them take your Ladyship's word for it, if they have no confidence in mine.

106. *Folly of mankind in this matter.* But too justly did our Lord reproach us with the "children of this world's being wiser in their generations than the children of light."[49] For no time, no care, no pains, is thought too much for the acquisition of honor, or pleasure, or riches, though we may be taken from them very soon, and are sure we cannot long possess them. The making their fortune as men call it; or with us women the setting ours to sale, and the dressing forth ourselves to purchase a master; and when we have got one, that which we very improperly term our business, the economy of his and our own vanity and luxury, or covetousness, as the humor happens, has all the application of our minds; we watch all advantages, improve all accidents, and let no opportunity slip us.[50] But the other world is out of sight, and for this reason out of mind; it is enough if we think of it hereafter, when we are at leisure, and have dispatched all the other worthy and grand affairs! The people with whom we transact won't stay for us; the

---

46. Astell's marginal note: Col 3:2–3.

47. Astell's marginal note: Mt 6:19, and so on. [Astell also refers to Mt 6:20–21.]

48. earnest] token.

49. Lk 16:8.

50. Astell expresses a similar sentiment in her *Reflections upon Marriage.* She describes marriage as literally "a caring for the things of the world, a caring not only to please, but to maintain a husband" (53), a state in which a woman makes it "her business, her very ambition" to content her husband (51).

present occasion if lost can't be retrieved; God will have patience, at least He must, if He means us any favor; and though perhaps we have a little more reverence than to say "let Him wait," yet we make no scruple to proclaim it without a blush, by our actions.[51]

107. *The Christian's business.* I conclude therefore, that the main thing in order to a Christian life, is to look upon the service of God and the salvation of our souls, as our *only business.* All other things, except as they relate to this, being mere impertinencies;[52] too frequently a sinful, often a vain, and at best but an innocent amusement. For it can never be supposed that God created us, that is our minds, after His own image, for no better purpose than to wait upon the body, while it eats, drinks, and sleeps, and saunters away a *useless life*; or to forget themselves so far as to be plunged into the cares of a *busy* one.[53] God, whose works are all in number, weight, and measure, could never form a rational being for so trivial a purpose; since a little more mechanism than what He has bestowed upon some brutes, would qualify us sufficiently for those employments, even for the very best affairs that this world, separate from the next and without any relation to it, is capable of.

51. Astell voices a common complaint of Anglican advice manuals for women in her time. See, for example, Allestree, *The Ladies' Calling*: "But, what is yet worse, how vile a contumely is offered to the majesty of God, who is used as they do their dunning [i.e., importuning] creditors, posted off with an excuse of no leisure yet to speak with him; whilst in the meantime, all the factors for their vanity can have ready access and full audience. God must wait till their tailor, their shoemaker please to dismiss them, and at best, can be allowed only to bring up the rear of a whole shoal [i.e., crowd] of artificers" (121–22).

52. impertinencies] irrelevancies.

53. Astell's words recall those of Bathsua Makin in her *Essay To Revive the Antient Education of Gentlewomen, In Religion, Manners, Arts & Tongues. With An Answer to the Objections against this Way of Education* (London: J.D., 1673): "We cannot be so stupid as to imagine, that God gives ladies great estates, merely that they may eat, drink, sleep, and rise up to play" (26). Like Astell in her *Proposal*, in her *Essay* Makin calls for the establishment of an academy for women in early modern England. Makin (née Reginald, 1600–c. 1675) was herself highly educated and an active participant in the mid-seventeenth-century republic of letters (most notably, in correspondence with Anna Maria van Schurman). See Frances Teague's biography in *ODNB*, s.v. "Makin, Bathsua," http://www.oxforddnb.com/view/article/17849 (accessed November 8, 2012). For a modern edition of Makin's *Essay*, see Frances Teague, *Bathsua Makin, Woman of Learning* (Lewisburg, PA: Bucknell University Press; London: Associated Presses, 1998), 109–50.

108. *To be ambitious of perfection, good and necessary.* Shall I then receive the bounty of God in vain? God forbid! And therefore did I know or could find out, a nobler employment than the making my calling and election sure, woman though I am, I would employ all my thoughts and industry to compass it. For if to pursue the best design, to strive to be as perfect as I can, is pride and ambition, it is what I must never correct, but rather pray for its continuance. And I know not a more melancholy consideration, than that one meets with so few of these proud and ambitious spirits (if this must be the character by which the world distinguishes them) who might provoke us to push onward in our Christian race, not by pulling them back, which nothing but the envy of a devil would attempt, but by assisting them to the utmost of one's power to obtain their crown.

109. *Indifferency not excusable.* Having thus considered the excellence and importance of the Christian profession, computed the expenses of this work, and weighed the difficulties of this warfare; difficulties which be they as great as they may, bear no proportion to the assistance afforded, or the magnificent reward that attends the overcoming of them. The next thing to be done, is to fix on the best method of pursuing this glorious design, to adhere to it with an immovable resolution, and to pursue it with an unwearied vigor; for sure none can content themselves with taking such a course as may or may not do, and which can give them no comfortable and well-grounded hope, at that awful day when all other consolations fail them!

110. *Distinct ideas of what is commanded and forbid necessary.* Now in order to this, I make it my business to get as clear and exact a knowledge of the whole will of God revealed to us, as possibly I can, and of the best way and manner of performing it; endeavoring to fix in my mind clear, distinct,[54] and just notions of all those sins He has forbid, and all those duties He has commanded, and all this not for

---

54. Astell alludes once again to the Cartesian criteria of truth and certainty, "clarity" and "distinctness." Following Descartes in his *Principles*, in her second *Proposal* Astell defines an idea as clear when it is immediately present to the mind, and distinct when "it is both clear and contains not anything in itself which appears not manifestly to him who considers it as he ought" (Astell, *Proposal II*, 172). Like Descartes, she holds that true knowledge consists "in a firm assent to conclusions rightly drawn from premises of which we have clear and distinct ideas" (Astell, *Proposal II*, 149).

speculation but practice. For as the knowledge of God's will won't at all avail me, but only increase my condemnation unless I do it; so neither can I do God's will unless I know it; nor am I like to know it by loose and confused ideas. Your Ladyship must needs have observed pretty often, that many persons who seem to profess the Christian religion in sincerity, do yet indulge themselves in practices which sure they would not dare to continue in did they believe them sins; and omit many acts of virtue, which sure they would not dispense with did they believe them duties. Hence it is that the best of us are afraid to die, for though we have performed our duty in some measure, yet we are conscious of having done it very carelessly and after a sorry manner. And by this also appears the mischief of being engaged in the follies and cares of this present life, for it is from this engagement that we want leisure to examine the precepts of the gospel so nicely and accurately, and to imprint them in our minds, as we ought.

111. *This attempted.* I must not pretend to consider this subject at large, and according to its merit, but shall only give a definition or short description of the principal, and the most neglected, Christian duties, or of the opposite sins. Taking my accounts from scripture only, as I understand it, though perhaps I may not always fall in with the opinions of some, and seldomer with the practice of the greatest number of Christians. And having constantly in view the design of our holy religion, which, as was said above, is to withdraw our hearts as much as possible from temporal things, and hereby to advance us to the utmost degree of perfection that we are able to attain.

112. *What a duty is, and what a sin.* A *duty* is much the same as a debt; it is that which in reason and justice we are obliged to pay, and by the neglect of which we shall incur a penalty. *Sin,*[55] as the apostle defines it, "is the transgression of the law,"[56] that is of any law of God, whether natural or revealed. And this may be either directly or indirectly, against the plain and obvious letter of the law, or the just and necessary consequence. Hence disobedience to any command of a lawful superior which is not contrary to the commands of God, is indeed a breach of God's law which enjoins obedience to just authority, and in this respect it is a sin, as well as it is a crime with relation

55. In the first edition, this sentence begins "*Sin* is the reverse of this, or."
56. Astell's marginal note: 1 Jn 3:4; Rom 4:15 and 2:14.

to human sanctions. Unless the human law proposes a mulct[57] as an equivalent to obedience, in which case upon payment of the mulct the conscience is discharged from the sin, as well as the person from the crime. But it must be observed, that when the penalty is not proposed by human laws as an equivalent to obedience, but as a punishment for the neglect of it, in this case, our having suffered the punishment does not excuse us from the guilt, or the sin. But until we have repented we are obnoxious[58] to God's vengeance, even though we have satisfied man's.

113. *Connection of Christian duties.* We usually distinguish our duties into such as are due to God, to our neighbors, and to ourselves; but this is only for order's sake. For the obligation arising from God's authority[59] is the same in all, since we can be obliged in conscience only by the sanctions of the divine law; and the duties themselves are so happily linked, that he who would perform any of them as he ought, must needs perform them all. Abstractions how useful so ever in speculation, because we can't have just and accurate notions of things without them, are yet very dangerous in practical divinity, where to abstract and divide is to destroy. They don't effectually or to any purpose believe who don't practice, and they can never practice as they ought who don't believe. He who does not discharge the duties of a rational and sociable creature, in obedience to the commands of the divine lawgiver, will discharge them no longer than suits with his own humor and serves his own turn. As on the other hand, we can neither serve God nor ourselves by injuring our neighbor; nor can we violate our duty to God and to our neighbor, without doing the highest injury to ourselves.

114. *Universal obedience.* Hence are those general expressions or summaries of our duty, which we meet with in holy scripture, where sometimes faith, sometimes faith and repentance, or the love of God, or the love of our neighbor, or any other particular duty, is put for the whole of religion, and made the terms[60] of salvation. It being certain, that no person who does *indeed* believe the great truths of

57. mulct] fine.

58. obnoxious] liable or subject.

59. The words "arising from God's authority" are not in the first edition.

60. In the first edition, this sentence reads "or the terms" instead of "and made the terms."

the gospel, but will set himself in earnest to perform those conditions upon which eternal happiness is to be obtained, and eternal misery to be avoided. He can't be said to be truly sorry for past faults, who does not use his utmost endeavors to be guilty of them no more. It is a jest to talk of loving God while we willfully offend Him, or do not strive to please, and long to enjoy Him. And as they who truly love God will love their neighbor for God's sake, this being one of the principal evidences of our love to Him: so whatever pretenses may be made to friendship or public-spiritedness, it is certain, and he who tries them long enough will find, that except upon a religious principle and out of love to God, men will not love their neighbor. They will not do to mankind all the good that is in their power, which is the only true love of our neighbor. That which they call doing good, and which may be so far good as to be a service to them who receive it, being only done to have a hank[61] upon them, or for the doer's humor, or interest, or to serve his party, to be rid of importunity, or out of shame to do less than other men have done, or for ostentation, or perhaps by chance, or some such motive which will not hold universally, nor carry him to the performance of this duty in its true and utmost extent. So that he can't truly be said to love his neighbors, any more than he can be said to love God, whatever he may profess, or whatever passions he may feel, who lives in the violation of *any of* God's laws. According to that of St. James, "whosoever shall keep the whole law and yet offend in one point, he is guilty of all."[62] He has not the true vital principle of obedience, but is ready to break all the rest, as soon as ever an apposite temptation is thrown in his way. So then, though for method's sake our duties must be distinguished, they can't be so separated but that the one will very often include, and will always have an influence on the other.

115. *Wherein Christianity is distinguished from natural and Jewish religion.* It must also be observed, that the Christian religion is not opposite to natural and mosaical religion, but is an improvement of both. Of the former by setting its precepts in a clearer light, discovering them to the meanest understanding, enforcing them with stronger motives, and in a word, supplying whatever was wanting to

61. hank] restraining hold.

62. Astell's marginal note: Jas 2:10.

raise human nature to the highest perfection of which it is capable: of the other, by bringing the substance into the place of shadows.[63] But that which is peculiar to the Christian religion is, the explicit knowledge of the mediator Jesus Christ, and the worshipping of God by and through Him. Christianity sets before us as the object of our worship the son of God in the nature of man, the mediator of a new and excellent covenant; and the holy spirit of God the principle of a new and spiritual life, by whose assistance we have access to the father, for the merits and sake of Christ. And it being the declared will of God that He will be thus worshipped, they to whom the Christian law is promulged, can't worship Him acceptably any other way. Nor can they expect salvation without an explicit faith in the mediator, and in the sanctifier of the human race. As is plain from the New Testament, a great part of which would be transcribed did I bring all the proof it affords, and therefore I shall leave it to your Ladyship's own observation as you read the holy scripture.

116. *Of our duty to God more immediately.* The duty which we owe more immediately to God, does in general consist in having worthy thoughts of Him, and in a demeanor suitable to those thoughts; in serving Him with that purity and simplicity of mind, that entire and constant obedience and zeal, that is due to the searcher and judge of hearts, to the sovereign lord of all things, to Him upon whom we entirely depend for all we have or are, for every moment of our being. But I shall not consider our duty to God as He is our creator and preserver, for this is a relation that all other creatures have to Him as well as we; I shall rather derive our duty from His being our redeemer, and from the purchase Christ has made of us by His blood, which is the principle, and the foundation of the Christian religion; is a motive of the tenderest endearment, requiring a return of the greatest love and the most entire devotion to His service. So that the sum of our duty

---

63. The words "discovering them to the meanest understanding" are not in the first edition. Instead this sentence reads: "Of the former by setting its precepts in a clearer light, enforcing them with stronger motives, raising them to higher degrees of perfection, and in a word, filling up whatever was wanting: of the other, by bringing the substance into the place of shadows." Astell's reference to substances and shadows evokes the well-known moral of Aesop's fable about the dog and his shadow: "Beware lest you lose the substance by grasping at the shadow." This may also be a reference to Colossians 2:17, "Which are a shadow of things to come; but the body *is* of Christ."

is faith, such as the apostle[64] defines it, "a faith working by love"; and this love what our Lord describes, a love that shows itself by obedience; and this obedience so uniform, so constant, so zealous, as the belief and love of God, "God manifested in the flesh," requires.[65] Faith sets before us an object worthy of our love, love stirs us up to obedience and endears it to us. Without obedience we must not pretend to love God, and without love it is certain we can never serve Him as we ought; nor can we either obey or love unless we believe. Disobedience proceeds from a want of love, as this does from a want of faith. So that faith will be found to be more necessary in order to good morals, and to the delivering us from the "prevailing power of sin," than some are pleased to make it.[66]

117. *Of faith.* Now faith is here taken for a belief that "God is, and that He is the rewarder of them that diligently seek Him";[67] and for a firm persuasion of the truth of all that is revealed in the holy scripture. More especially of that which is the great fundamental of Christianity, that "God has sent His only begotten son into the world that we might live through Him."[68] To believe that there is a God is to believe that He is the *best* being, infinite in all perfections, our true and only good. To think worthily of God, is to think of Him according to that perception of Himself which He always exhibits to those minds that reverently and attentively turn towards Him; and according to what He has declared of Himself in His holy word, not according to any devices or wishes of our own. And if we thus believe and often consider the necessary consequences of this faith, affecting our minds therewith, it will engage us in all other duties. For it will convince us that our all ought to be dedicated to God's service; that it is not only most becoming, and our just and bounden[69] duty, but even our

---

64. St. Paul.

65. Astell's marginal note: Gal 5:6; Jn 14:15, 21; Rom 14:7, and so on; Eph 2; 1 Tm 3:16. [The reference to Romans should probably be Rom 13:7, and the reference to Ephesians should probably be Eph 5.]

66. Astell refers to the author of *A Lady's Religion*, who notes that Christ's "only design was to save us from the prevailing power of sin" (4).

67. Astell's marginal note: Heb 11:6.

68. Astell's marginal note: 1 Jn 4:9.

69. bounden] "under obligation on account of favors received" (*OED*).

greatest interest, to pay the utmost submission to His will and obedience to all His commands. And this not only formally and outwardly, but sincerely and affectionately, with an entire devoting of our understandings and wills, and all our powers and faculties to His service.

118. *The influence that faith in the son of God has upon practice.* Especially since to endear our duty and render it most easy and delightful, God has been pleased to manifest His love to us in a most amazing manner, by the incarnation and death of His son: assuring us hereby that we are allowed to love Him; that our love will be acceptable to Him; and that as He only *is*, He only *can be* our felicity, so we may assure ourselves that He is not only willing, but even desirous to impart Himself to us. The manifestation of the son of God in the flesh, as it is the greatest evidence that could be given, both of the evil of sin and God's infinite hatred of it; and also of His infinite love to mankind and readiness to pardon them: so it is a "sensible" argument, and what the most "simple" and "illiterate" may understand.[70]

119. Such a neglect both of the terrors and allurements of this mortal life, such a contempt of this world and all its glory; and which is more, such a willing and cheerful enduring of the cross, the cross which Christians nowadays, to their shame be it spoken, are so much afraid of; such an abstraction from sensual pleasure, such an elevation of mind towards our true and only good, as is indeed the perfection of human nature, was not expected from mankind till life and immortality were brought to light by the gospel, and that the son of God in the form of man, had by His own most illustrious example, directed our steps and plained the way. But if Jesus had been only a mere man, how wise and good so ever, it had been no great matter for one in those poor and mean circumstances He was pleased to appear in, to suffer what He endured.

120. *The difference between faith and knowledge.* Strictly speaking, we do not *believe* there is a God, but we *know* there is one, though I am here speaking of our acknowledgment of God as a matter of faith, in compliance with common usage, and because faith is the most

---

70. Astell refers with irony to the "Preface to the French Translation" of *A Lady's Religion*: "the Christian religion ought to be for the use of the simple and illiterate" (A4v). She may also be alluding to that part of *A Lady's Religion* where the author says that by following the rule of reason, religion can be rendered a matter "*sensible* unto us" (16).

comprehensive term, taking in all that we are to acknowledge concerning God. For though faith is ultimately founded upon reason, it being most reasonable[71] to believe what God declares, yet such truths as we could not have come at by the common methods of meditation and discourse, nor otherwise than by God's particular revelation, are very properly said to be believed, not in contradiction to reason, but by way of difference and distinction. Nor is this any more than what daily happens in common affairs, there being some truths which are demonstrated to us, such as mathematical propositions; others, such as matters of fact, which we must either be ignorant of, or receive them upon the credit of the relator. Nay, even mathematical truths, though capable of demonstration, can only be said to be believed, and are not known, by him who does not acquaint himself with the demonstration. And perhaps all people are not capable of a demonstration, to be sure there are too many who will not take the pains to know. Though to speak my thoughts freely, I take God to be the same to the mind that light is to the eyes, with this difference, that the intellectual sun never sets. And as he who has the organs of sight[72] and will use them, cannot but perceive the light, so he who uses his reason can't but perceive the existence of God, which is so bright and obvious a truth that it manifests itself to all understandings. The very meanest among them who are capable of any sort of employment may come at this great truth, if they will but apply themselves to it as they do to their worldly business, and may deduce all other necessary truths from this. In a word, all that we discover concerning God by natural reason, is knowledge; and all that we learn of Him from holy scripture and receive upon its authority, is faith. Nor is faith less certain, that is less credible, or a more insufficient ground of assent, than knowledge. For I am not less certain of that which, as I learn from revelation, God knows to be true, than I am of that which I myself know to be true; nay rather more certain, provided I know the truth of the revelation. Because God can't be deceived, He Himself is *the truth*, and He thoroughly understands it, whereas I have not a full and comprehensive view of ideas, my view is often attended with obscurity, so that many times I cannot clearly, and seldom fully, perceive their agreement or disagreement.

71. "rational" in first edition.

72. "seeing" in first edition.

121. *What we are to acknowledge concerning God.* Scripture and our natural notions of God, do each of them inform us, that as He can't be deceived Himself, so it is not possible for Him to deceive His creatures; as He can't be hurt, so He neither can nor will do them injury; that He gives without our desert, but He never chastises but for our demerit; that He rewards purely because it is His good pleasure, but He punishes because He must, that is, because the eternal reason of things requires His vengeance. Our sins are in some respect the natural as well as the meritorious cause of our misery, but the goodness of God is the only reason why He does us good. For creatures who depend upon their creator in the most absolute manner can't possibly deserve anything from His bounty, much less can sinners, whose iniquities set them at a distance from their God. All our good, both what we do and what we enjoy, is entirely from Him; all the evil that we do is absolutely and entirely from ourselves, and by consequence we draw upon our own heads all the evil that we suffer. It follows therefore that we assent to all God's declarations and revelations as true, that we receive His promises as faithful, His threatenings as just, and His commands as holy, wise, and good, and conform ourselves to them in all things.

122. *The love of God an effect of faith.* Which considered simply in itself is no hard matter, for it is no more than the doing what is fit, much less can it be difficult to those who love. Now love is the natural effect of faith, for whoever is acquainted with so amiable a being as the Lord our God, must needs be enamored of Him. And whether love be considered as the motion of the soul towards good,[73] or as a passion,[74] or as that delight we take in reflecting on that which

73. Astell echoes John Norris's definitions of love in his *Theory and Regulation of Love. A Moral Essay* (1688), in John Norris, *Philosophical and Theological Writings*, ed. Richard Acworth, 8 vols. (Bristol, UK: Thoemmes Press, 2001): "the most general and comprehensive notion of love will be found to be, *a motion of the soul towards God*" (2:12) and "the motion of love may be considered either barely as a *tendency* towards good, or as a *willing* this good to some person or being" (2:14).

74. The view that love is a passion of the soul is commonplace in seventeenth-century literature. See, for example, Descartes, *Passions of the Soul*, in *Philosophical Writings of Descartes*, 1:350.

pleases,[75] it is certain that love will be the effect of true faith, and will produce obedience. So thought our Lord and His apostle, "if any love God," says St. Paul, the "same is known of Him"; there needs no more than knowledge to excite love, and love to increase knowledge; and our savior makes obedience the test of love, "if ye love me," says He, "keep my commandments."[76] You do not indeed love unless you obey; and obedience will be but a forced and ungrateful task, neither easy to ourselves nor acceptable to God, unless it proceeds from love.[77]

123. *How we may try our love to God.* And[78] since the persons we love are ever in our thoughts, since we endeavor to recommend ourselves to them by resembling their manners, and take great satisfaction in their conversation, we need but try our love to God in these three instances, to find whether it be genuine.[79] It is certain we can have no real affection whatever we may pretend, for those whom we seldom think of, or think of very coldly; whom we take no care to please, and whose ways are not agreeable to us; whose company is irksome, and whom we would entertain as seldom and as late as is possible. If then we love God He will be ever in our thoughts with pleasure, we shall imitate all His imitable perfections; His worship and our addresses to Him whether in our closets or in the place where His honor dwells, will be the pleasantest not the heaviest part of our lives; we shall be sorry not glad to defer this conversation upon any pretense of company or business. But to be sure, we shall have longing, if not impatient desires after the perfect enjoyment of God in glory. For human nature is so formed, that it incessantly pants[80] after that which it takes to be its true good. And if we do not thus pant after God, desir-

---

75. Astell echoes Masham's definition of love in her *Discourse concerning the Love of God.* Love, Masham says, is "that disposition, or act of mind, we find in ourselves towards anything we are pleased with" (18). In his *Essay,* Locke likewise states that "anyone reflecting upon the thought he has of the delight, which any present, or absent thing is apt to produce in him, has the *idea* we call *love*" (II.xx.4).

76. Astell's marginal note: 1 Cor 8:3; Jn 14:15.

77. Astell's marginal note (second edition only): See the appendix, 370 [i.e., §370], and so on. [In the first edition, this paragraph is followed by §§370–85 of the present volume.]

78. In the first edition, this sentence begins "In sum."

79. The words "to find whether it be genuine" are not in the first edition.

80. pants] longs or yearns.

ing to be dissolved and to be with Christ, it is, it can be ultimately, for
no other reason but want of love to Him. Other things please us better,
so that we desire to enjoy them as long as we can, and to go to God
only when of necessity we must. Whereas a true love to God, though
it keeps us content to live so long as He thinks fit, yet it gives us such
an indifferency to this world, that we are but *barely content*; and this in
pure obedience to God's will, not because of any relish of this present
life, or fondness for it. And even while it is His pleasure to have us
tarry in this state of absence and infelicity, our thoughts will fix on
the object of our love. We shall contemplate God with all that veneration and desire that is due (or rather the *due* that we are able to pay)
to His excellencies; shall find no good that can come in competition
with Him, indeed no good besides Him. And while we thus constantly
think of God, it is hardly possible to disobey Him. We may fail in our
duty sometimes, through mere ignorance, mistake, or inadvertency,
but we can never willfully transgress, any more than human nature
can refuse good and choose evil, purely as such.

124. *Love of God makes the world tolerable.* For the irregularity of our wills proceeds from the error of our understandings, from
calling good evil, and evil good. How we come to do thus is too
large an enquiry for this letter, which has already grown too much
upon my hands. But the best way to avoid it, is to keep our true good
continually in view. We may live a contemplative life without being
recluse, and as this will be very much for the good of society, so I
know not anything else can render society in its present degenerate
condition, tolerable to an honest mind. The Christians of our days
being no better than Jeremiah's contemporary Jews, that "assembly of
treacherous men," who made the prophet sigh after "a lodging place
in the wilderness."[81] Esteeming it better to live in deserts among wild
beasts, open and declared enemies, than in cities among pretended
and deceitful friends, who will do nothing but "for a reward," as another prophet[82] complains, or out of some sinister and base design;
unless it be "evil," and this they do "with both hands earnestly." "The
best of them being as a brier, and the most upright sharper than a

81. Astell's marginal note: Jer 9:2.

82. Micah, a Judahite seer or prophet, roughly contemporaneous with Isaiah (late eighth
century BCE).

thorn-hedge," so that an innocent and sincere person can't converse among them, without hazard of having his liberty or integrity torn from him.[83] The love of God indeed, and this only, can reconcile him to this burden, which becomes tolerable when endured for God's sake, and in submission to His providence.

125. *We may contemplate God in the midst of crowds.* Everyone knows, that the mind will not be kept from contemplating what it loves, in the midst of crowds and business. Hence come those frequent absences, so observable in conversation; for while the body is confined to the present company, the mind is flown to that which it delights in. If God then be the object of our desires, we shall relieve ourselves in the common uneasinesses of life, by contemplating His beauty. For certainly there cannot be a higher pleasure, than to think that we love and are beloved by the most amiable and best being. Whom the more we contemplate the more we shall desire, and the more we desire the more we shall enjoy. This desire having the preeminence of all other desires, as in every other thing so particularly in this, that it can't be disappointed; no one who brings a sincere heart, being ever rejected by this divine lover. Whose eyes pierce the soul, and as He can't be deceived by an imposture, so He never mistakes or neglects the faithful affection; which too seldom finds ways to make itself understood among mortals, even those who pretend to be the most discerning, but who give themselves up to the flatteries of deceivers, while they treat the plain and honest person with the utmost outrage.

126. *Whence our duties are derived.* It has been said already, that these and all other duties to God, arise from the infinite perfection and supereminency of His nature, and the imperfection and dependence of our own; and from the relation we bear to Him through Christ our head. But because few people are reasonable enough to deduce their duty from its principles, or will give themselves, what they think, the trouble of doing it, though it is in truth one of the noblest and most entertaining pleasures; and because God in great condescension to human infirmity, has given us the precepts and example of His son, for our more particular direction; and further, because all our performances receive their value from that principle of entire obedience from whence they must proceed, and which is better in God's account

83. Astell's marginal note: Mi 7:3–4.

than the most pompous sacrifices and services of our own invention; and that such actions as are not done for God's sake and in obedience to His will, however they may appear to men, are of no value in His sight;[84] I shall therefore consider all the rest as acts of obedience.

127. *Of obedience; and the insolence of disobedience.* Everyone can tell what it is to obey, and how they themselves desire to be obeyed, nor will they endure to have their own commands disputed, how forward so ever they are to dispute the commands of their rulers. And were it not that all sorts of disobedience proceed from the same principle of impiety and pride, one would be less surprised to find men examine and contradict the commands of men like themselves in all respects, except in that sacred character stamped upon them by God, whose authority they bear, and which is a much greater distinction, and ought to receive a greater deference than most of us imagine; even though[85] they are not infallible, nor always so just and good as they ought to be. But what pretense can we have to dispute the commands of God Himself? For setting aside His absolute sovereignty, His wisdom and goodness must render them infinitely desirable! He is indeed pleased to treat us like what He has made us, rational creatures, and allows us to examine the goodness and equity of His precepts. Shall we then abuse His condescension? And instead of inquiring into divine truths with a becoming modesty, humility, and thankfulness, treat God with that insufferable insolence which is too much practiced everywhere, from which even good breeding, the only religion that some people have, should methinks restrain them, if reason and religion do not weigh with them. For if they have no sense of the distance between their maker and themselves, they should at least, in good manners to His servants, keep their impieties and sins as private as they can. For whose heart can choose but burn within them, who can refrain from "answering the fool according to his folly,"[86] when

---

84. The words "and that such actions as are not done for God's sake and in obedience to His will, however they may appear to men, are of no value in His sight" are not in the first edition.

85. The first edition reads "yet this notwithstanding," instead of "even though."

86. Prv 26:5 ("Answer a fool according to his folly, lest he be wise in his own conceit"). The same biblical quotation appears on the title page to Astell's *Bart'lemy Fair*, a work purposefully directed against libertines and atheists.

they see the king of glory affronted by every vile worm, who breathes only by His sufferance?

128. As for the better sort of us, one would think by our way of serving God, that we fancy He's obliged to us for our homage; that our keeping some of His laws, gives us a privilege to break others; and that He ought to humor us in all our desires. And to speak a plain truth, one hardly finds that person who will be content with such an obedience from his servant, as he himself offers to the great lord of heaven and earth!

129. *Of worshipping and honoring God.* To "worship" and "adore" the divine majesty, to "pray" to God and to "give Him thanks," both as a homage to His perfections, and as a means to supply our own wants, and also to express our gratitude and sense of His bounties, is a natural duty.[87] As it is also to pay "honor" and "veneration" to everything that has a relation to the worship of God, as the time, the place, the persons who officiate, the holy rites that are performed; and in a word, to all that is dedicated to His service, which is for this reason sacred, and not to be touched by profane and common hands. But the circumstances relating to His worship, must be learnt from divine revelation. And since He expects that we pay Him public homage, in a congregation assembled according to His directions, we can't excuse ourselves by paying it at home, or in company of our own choosing. His grace is His own free gift, and is not to be expected but in such methods and by such conveyances as He Himself has ordained. Surely then one would think they had never read the scriptures, who presume to teach the ladies of their acquaintance, that there is nothing in the gospel ordinances, and the solemn assemblies of Christians for religious worship, but what anybody, even "women," may perform,[88] and that the necessity of "communicating at the Lord's table" by the

---

87. Some of these phrases form part of the "Catechism" in the Church of England, *Book of Common Prayer*: "My duty towards God, is to believe in him, to fear him, and to love him with all my heart, with all my mind, with all my soul, and with all my strength; to worship him, to give him thanks, to put my whole trust in him, to call upon him, to honour his holy name and his word; and to serve him truly all the days of my life" (298).

88. See *Letter concerning Church Communion*: "you should farther consider, if there be any part of this primitive church communion which might not have been performed by a Woman as well as a Man" (10).

ministry of a "priest," is only derived from the power of "priest-craft," and is not according to "gospel simplicity."[89] St. Paul for certain was of another mind, or else he would not have bestowed so many directions concerning this sacred ordinance; and so were the first ages of the church, for they looked upon this sacrament as the highest act of religious worship, and cannot be thought to have degenerated so early.

130. *Of devotion and prayer. Devotion* is properly the giving up ourselves entirely to the service of another; and "pure religion and undefiled before God, is" (as St. James tells us) to "visit the fatherless and widows in their affliction, and to keep ourselves unspotted from the world."[90] To *pray* to God is to put ourselves more immediately and expressly into the divine presence, in order to offer up our addresses to Him. And as it is a mockery and profanation, and such as no civil person would be guilty of towards an earthly superior, to repeat so many devout words without an awful[91] sense of the divine majesty, and without those affections our words express: so be our attention and affection what they may, it is in vain to pray unless we endeavor to imitate the holiness we adore, to practice the virtues we ask, and to use the grace we implore. As for such as neglect the devotion and religion above expressed, let them say ever so many prayers, hear ever so many sermons, profess ever so much zeal either for church or conventicle, they are not devout or religious persons: for the one is to be done, and the other is not to be left undone. To "be holy as God is holy" is the main business, but unless we pretend to be wiser that God, we must allow Him to prescribe the means in order to this end.[92] Jordan had in itself no more virtue to cure a leprosy than Abana and Pharpar,[93] till God had said to Naaman, "go wash in Jordan and be clean."[94] But after this command, the waters of Jordan were so absolutely necessary, that he could not be cleansed without them.

89. Astell's marginal note (first edition only): See *Letter concerning Church Communion*, 9, and so on.

90. Astell's marginal note: [Jas] 1:27.

91. awful] reverential.

92. 1 Pt 1:16.

93. Abana and Pharpar are two rivers of Damascus, Syria. The Jordan River flows from western Asia to the Dead Sea.

94. 2 Kgs 5:10.

131. *Of the sacrament of the Lord's supper.* Our blessed savior having set us the brightest pattern of every virtue, the best thing we can do is to form ourselves upon this most perfect example; but this is not the *only* thing to be remembered at His table. He did that for us which no mere man, no nor the whole creation, could possibly perform, He satisfied divine justice for the sins of the whole world, and "having made peace through the blood of His cross," as scripture speaks, "reconciled all things unto the father"; so that we have "redemption through His blood, even the forgiveness of sins."[95] And the "Lord's supper is a sacrament of our redemption by Christ's death":[96] it is not only "a badge or token of our profession, but rather a certain sure witness and effectual sign of grace and God's goodwill towards us, by the which He does work invisibly in us, and does not only quicken, but also strengthen and confirm our faith in Him,"[97] as the church teaches in her articles, which our divine having subscribed, this must needs be his sense, for we may not suspect him of prevarication. He says indeed very truly, that our "preparation for the Lord's table," should not be "accompanied with anxieties."[98] For as one can't well understand why people will take the liberty to do that presently after the holy sacrament, which they would not allow themselves two or three days before; so neither why they make that a task and toil, a sort of penance, which is in itself a most delightful performance, a feast of joy and gladness. Or what can be the meaning of those melancholy looks and airs that are then put on, unless it be that believing it necessary to dismiss our sins at the Lord's table, we are sad and out of humor till we think we may meet again.

132. *Of the fear of God and how to honor Him.* For the *fear* of God does not consist in an uncomfortable dread of Him who is the best, the most lovely, and most desirable being, but in a reverential awe of His majesty and care that we do[99] not offend Him. To *honor*

95. Astell's marginal note: Col 1:14, 20.

96. Astell's marginal note: Article 28. [Here Astell cites from the "Thirty-Nine Articles," the authoritative statement of Anglican doctrine in her day. See Church of England, *Book of Common Prayer*, 571.]

97. Astell's marginal note: Article 25. [See Church of England, *Book of Common Prayer*, 569.]

98. *Lady's Religion*, 33.

99. "may" in first edition.

God, is to give Him the preference that is due to His excellency. But we do nothing like it, if we run the risk of His displeasure upon any consideration, any gain or loss, any pleasure or pain whatever; or if we can be much uneasy when we are not under it, be our lot what it may in other respects. I therefore reproach myself with want of veneration for God, when I find I am concerned for anything besides His favor. For if He smiles, it matters not who frowns, nor how the world goes if we have peace with Him. As on the other hand, we are truly miserable, how prosperous so ever our neighbors may reckon us, or we may call ourselves, unless God approves both the design, whose success we are so much pleased with, and our method of obtaining it.

133. *The heinousness of doing wickedly under pretense of serving God.* In truth, the "speaking," or doing "wickedly for God," or rather ourselves, for ourselves are always at the bottom of it, is such a complicated wickedness, that I know not to what sin I should refer it.[100] Our more immediate duty to God, consists in those several acts of acknowledgment, worship, or homage that we owe to each of His divine attributes. The doing evil that good may come,[101] is a sin that affronts them all, and in the most provoking manner, for it affronts God under pretense of honoring Him. Faith acknowledges God's being and veracity; but this is a practical atheism[102] and disbelief of providence, whose conduct it does not like, and therefore will follow its own. Obedience confesses God's sovereignty and authority; whereas this is a rebellion and direct disobedience to many plain commands. Love declares God's goodness, and follows Him in all things; this expects felicity somewhere else, forsaking His methods to go after its own inventions.[103] Hope relies upon His bounty and faithfulness, and trust refers itself to His wisdom and power; but this questions His wisdom, slights His power, and has no regard to anything but its own sufficiency. We proclaim God's holiness by the purity of our manners, and His justice, by fearing to offend Him; this profanes the one and dares

---

100. Astell's marginal note: Jb 13:7.

101. In the first edition, this sentence begins "The doing wickedly for God" instead of "The doing evil that good may come."

102. practical atheism] the practice of professing belief in the existence of God but acting as though God does not exist.

103. The words "and follows Him in all things" are not in the first edition.

the other; and will take no warning by those severe examples of God's
chastisements of such presumptuous sinners, recorded in holy writ.
We own God's mercy when we repent; whereas this knows no repentance, but "wipes its mouth and says it has done no wickedness";[104] nay,
even accounts its very sins, hallowed by its pretended good design, as
meritorious actions. We pay homage to God's omnipresence by every
act of religious worship, and by flying to Him in our distress; but this,
supposes Him not to be a God at hand; and therefore it "sacrifices to
its own net, and burns incense to its own drag."[105] By all the abovementioned acts of duty, by that superlative honor and veneration we
pay to God, and by resigning ourselves to His conduct, we adore His
infinite perfections, glorify them in the world, and express our awful[106] sense of His omniscience, omnipotence, eternity, and other attributes, without which He could not observe and reward our duty;
whereas this, instead of seeking God's glory as it pretends, does only
seek to carve out to itself a *present* reward; though hereby it offers God
the greatest dishonor,[107] that creatures can show to their creator, laying
one of the most dangerous stumbling blocks in the way to heaven. For
how can mankind distinguish in this case between the servants of the
only Lord God, and the slaves of the "God of this world,"[108] who can do
no more than depend upon their own cunning and strength, and stick
at no measures to accomplish their designs? We ought therefore to
have the same abhorrence of this detestable sin that St. Paul had; and
when we are tempted by the plausible harangues[109] and pretenses of
crafty and designing men, who dare not take God's word, nor depend
on Him alone,[110] let us set before our eyes the sentence that apostle
pronounces upon such as "do evil that good may come," namely, that
their "damnation is just."[111]

104. Prv 30:20.

105. Hb 1:16.

106. awful] reverential.

107. In the first edition, this reads "the greatest dishonor *among men*" (my italics).

108. 2 Cor 4:4.

109. harangues] speeches.

110. The words "who dare not take God's word, nor depend on Him alone," are not in the first edition.

111. Astell's marginal note: Rom 3:8. [The apostle is St. Paul.]

134. *Of hope, trust, submission, and resignation.* Hope and *trust* in God are of so near affinity, that they are put promiscuously[112] one for the other in holy scripture; for they cannot in reality be separated, hope regarding the end we aim at, and trust the way to this end. For a Christian hope is the firm expectation of that future good which Christ has promised in His gospel. And trust is a dependence upon the divine conduct, a referring ourselves entirely to God's method and way of obtaining all that we can hope or desire. Trust does not otherwise differ from obedience, than in that sweet repose it gives to every obedient mind. And *submission* and *resignation* are nothing else but the highest acts of obedience and trust, the giving up our understandings and wills entirely to God's precepts and providence, acquiescing in all His orders with a firm persuasion that they are best.

135. *Particularly of hope and despair.* The glorious promises of the gospel excite our natural passion of hope, and this hope secures our duty, keeping us firm and steady in the way to obtain them.[113] It makes us "not ashamed" to confess the faith of Christ whatever we may suffer by this confession.[114] And thus it is that we are "saved by hope," that is, we are kept from falling off from our duty, and are carried through all present difficulties in expectation of a future recompense.[115] Therefore *patience* is commonly joined with *hope*: and be our present pressures what they may, we are "filled with all joy and peace in believing," and in depending on "the God of hope."[116] But then it is to be remembered, that we don't hope in God, whatever else we hope in, if we expect salvation, of any sort, by any other ways and means than what God has appointed. It is not despair to conclude that there is no mercy for impenitent sinners, it is a just and sound judgment: the sin against hope, is neglecting "to purify ourselves as God is pure."[117] Nor is there any great difference whether this neglect proceeds from a groundless despair of God's mercy, when His covenant and promises encourage us to depend upon it; or as groundless a presuming beyond

112. promiscuously] indiscriminately.

113. Astell's marginal note: Rom 15:4; Heb 6:19.

114. Astell's marginal note: Rom 5:5.

115. Astell's marginal note: Rom 8:24–25; Rom 15:4, 13; Lam 3:26.

116. Astell's marginal note (first edition only): Rom 15:13.

117. Astell's marginal note: 1 Jn 3:3.

what He has promised and covenanted; since both center in the same point, and have the same fatal conclusion.

136. *Of trust in God and resignation.* We can never obtain the end that hope has in view, without depending on the conduct of our guide, nor is there the least reason to doubt that He who invites and leads us on, will be wanting in affording us all necessary assistance and refreshments in the way. But we do not trust God if we expect success by any method but obedience; or if we do not firmly adhere to His commands, even when there is no human prospect, no probability of obtaining our innocent, or most laudable designs by such a method. And whatever we may talk of resignation, we do nothing like it, if we are solicitous any further than for the doing of our duty which is our part, and do not leave the event which is God's, entirely to Him, with perfect satisfaction in His wisdom in discerning, and goodness in dispensing, what is best for us; being not only pleased with all His dispensations, but even cheerful under them.

137. *How little it appears among men.* But now, if the noble theory and practice of these duties as recorded in holy writ, be compared with our modern attainments, one shall be apt to conclude, that either we do not serve the same God whom the primitive Christians trusted in; or else that He has given us new measures of dependence. For nowadays we put more confidence in our own craft and the assistance of our rich and great patron who seldom if ever answers our most reasonable and just expectations; we rely more upon an arm of flesh, upon worldly, not to say wicked, arts and contrivances, than on the promises and protection of the almighty, who neither does nor can disappoint them who put their trust in Him. Though if God does not govern the world, it is not worthwhile to stay in it; and if He does govern it, every event, however unlikely, shall tend to the good of His faithful servants. And I dare appeal to the experience of mankind, that the things we have been most fond of, and as we may think innocently so, have done us the greatest mischief. Whereas the being disappointed has been much to our advantage, not only with regard to our future happiness, but even after the first struggle, to our present pleasure and satisfaction.

138. *The folly of solicitude.*[118] Well then, if I "seek the kingdom of God and His righteousness,"[119] and don't carelessly squander the provision His providence has made for me, or which my own industry may obtain, in a just, an honorable, and moderate way, what occasion for complaints, *solicitude*, and fears, or any the least uneasiness about worldly matters? These being evident signs of distrust, let us call them by what names we please. But though there were no sin in it, there can't be a more ridiculous folly than this solicitude; a folly our Lord has most divinely exposed in His sermon on the mount. For what more absurd than to be full of thought and concern about trifles? Things, that God the best judge, makes so little account of, that He bestows them indifferently on the good and on the evil. Things we can enjoy but a very short while, and which though possessed ever so long would not satisfy. Things which the providence of God furnishes without our care, and which all our care cannot secure! To see a man tormenting himself and his neighbors to no better purpose than to make a fortune, in which he's either defeated by somebody more cunning than himself, when it is just in reach; or if he obtains it, either death takes him off in the height of his delight, and then all his thoughts perish, or he only lives to taste the bitter draught of a declining fortune. And be it how it may, the fine scene continues but thirty or forty years at most, though generally not half so long. Thus we see the utmost that's to be got by solicitude, but who considers what's to be lost? Our reasonable hopes of a kingdom that can't be shaken! An eternal crown of glory! Pleasures that never cease, and that always satisfy! It being certain, that the mind is too narrow to attend two things at once to any great purpose, even though there be no contrariety in them, so that if we are full of this world and make it our business, there's little or no place for the concerns of the next.

139. *What is not pride. Pride* is a sin that is generally complained of, and it may be not without cause. Though I can't say, that the true reason of the complaint is always told; or that the assigned reason of the accusation is always a just one. There are so many in the world who will do any mean thing to get into favor and office, or to put a little money in their purse, that he's usually counted proud whose

118. solicitude] disquietude or anxiety.
119. Mt 6:33.

soul is not as base as theirs. He who will not fall into all the opinions and measures of such as are richer and greater, not better, than himself, overvalues his own judgment in their account. Another is proud, because he knows the worth of time too well to throw it away upon every impertinence. To have but few wants when most people have so many; to bear those one has without complaint; is not prudence, temperance, and fortitude, but insufferable pride in their esteem. To refuse an obligation from an unworthy person, and they are not the least unworthy who would barter their favors for your liberty and virtue, is an insolence not to be endured. And in a word, to remember the dignity of a member of Christ when others forget it, and to attempt to be wiser and better than your neighbors, is that sort of assuming which they least forgive. But while we are correcting these and other sorts of pride, more truly so called, which offend us in our fellow creatures, who is there that regards the daily pride and insolence that all of us show to our creator?

140. *Wherein humility consists.* I do not deny but that we may behave ourselves proudly, and hereby unjustly, towards our neighbors; but then it must be granted, that this pride reflects upon God Himself, and is a contempt of our creator. So the wise king informs us when he says, "he that mocketh the poor, reproacheth his maker";[120] and the apostle assures us, that "he who despiseth, despiseth not man but God."[121] *Humility* according to St. Paul's account of it, consists in "not thinking of ourselves more highly than we ought to think,"[122] and consequently in actions suitable to these *sober* thoughts; in not assuming to ourselves any honor or advantage that is not our due, nor denying to others what they have a right to. Now all we *have* and all we *are* is so entirely from God and does so absolutely depend on Him, that every sort and every degree of arrogating[123] to ourselves any manner of way, with regard to Him, is in prejudice of His right; and to do thus, or to use any of His gifts contrary to His will and service, is pride; it is an unjust assuming of what does not belong to us. But it is not so with respect to any of our neighbors, for there are certain rights belonging

120. Prv 17:5. The wise king is Solomon.

121. 1 Thes 4:8.

122. Astell's marginal note: Rom 12:3.

123. arrogating] unduly assuming.

to mankind in general, and others that are justly appropriated to particular persons, and he who pretends no further than he has a just claim, can't fairly be accused of pride.

141. *Several sorts of pride.* There's a reverence due to human nature, because of God's image, which all of us in some measure[124] bear. We are brethren, not only by nature, but after a more excellent manner, in Christ our elder brother; nay we are yet more nearly related, being members of the same body. And therefore owe respect and civil usage, and all the offices of humanity and Christian charity to each other, to the meanest and most despicable; from which, even the sins of the wicked can't wholly exclude them, though sin is of all other things the most dishonorable and degrading. There is also a more peculiar *outward* respect and honor due to *some*, according to the laws and customs of the place we live in; and an *inward* esteem to *others*, in proportion to their real worth. Nor is he less guilty of pride and folly, who refuses to pay his neighbors that honor and value which is due to their wisdom and virtue, than he is who denies them that precedence which belongs to their birth and quality: nay, his pride is more unreasonable, and his folly more ridiculous, by how much he is injurious to a greater excellency. He who has not so much money as his neighbors, is foolishly proud if he vies with them in expenses and way of living: but he is not less ridiculous, who fancies he has better sense than another, because he has more money; or that they ought to submit to his judgment, because he ought to go before them;[125] or that he knows more than another only because he is older; or lastly, and which is as reasonable a conclusion as any of the rest, that a man is wiser than a woman merely because he is a man! For he who has no more understanding than to argue at this rate, must not take it amiss if he is esteemed accordingly, it being very hard to keep one's self from despising those who are so weak as to discover such ridiculous pretensions.

142. *Humility how taught by St. Peter.* As for that *humility* which consists in resignation and the giving up ourselves to another's disposal, this can be due to none but God. It is arrogance in any mortal to

124. "sense" in first edition.

125. Astell refers to the right of precedence, "the right of preceding others in ceremonies and social formalities" (*OED*), often bestowed upon persons of rank.

assume such a power over another, any further than as he can show by divine commission, that God has delegated a part of His own authority to him. The pride then is not in them who refuse to pay, but in them who pretend to receive such a subjection. "All of you be subject one to another and be clothed with humility," is indeed a divine precept;[126] but this can't oblige me to subject myself to any private person whoever, since this precept does as much require him to pay subjection, as it gives him a right to claim it. But, as appears by the context, the subjection and deference required by that text, is to be paid to those whom God has set over us in His church. Who as they are not to take upon them that weighty office for the sake of "filthy lucre," or of "dominion"; nor to exercise it in a lordly manner, but to imitate the great shepherd who gave Himself for His sheep, in prospect of that "crown" of glory that fades not away: so the "younger," or inferior ministers, are to submit themselves to the "elder," that is, to the bishops and governors; and the people to be "subject" to their lawful pastors, whatever their own gifts and graces may be.[127] For this being the divine institution, whoever takes upon him to transgress it, under pretense of greater purity, greater edification, or his own wondrous abilities, will find that "God resisteth" such "proud" assuming, and such disorderly walking; whereas "He giveth grace to the humble," to those who dutifully maintain the station wherein God has placed them, and carefully preserve the order that He Himself has established.[128]

143. *Who is the proud person.* He then is the proud person, who forgetting the giver of all good things, looks on himself as proprietor of that which he has only received, and for which he must strictly account; or who uses and boasts of it, as if it were absolutely his own.[129] He who thinks he has gifts which he has not; who fancies himself to be "something" when indeed "he is nothing";[130] or who rates what he possesses above its real worth, valuing himself upon that which is not truly valuable; who upon *this* account exalts himself above, or upon *any* account despises his neighbor. He who foolishly imagines himself

126. Astell's marginal note: 1 Pt 5:5.

127. 1 Pt 5:1–5.

128. Jas 4:6.

129. Astell's marginal note: 1 Cor 4:7.

130. Astell's marginal note: Gal 6:3.

too great or too good to perform any office of humanity, or charity, to any the meanest of his brethren; if any can be mean who are the work of God's hands, the price of Christ's blood, and "heirs of the glorious inheritance of the saints in light":[131] such a one "deceiveth himself, he is proud and knoweth nothing," he knows not that his neighbors partake in the most valuable privileges, and that the things whereby he is distinguished are very inconsiderable.[132]

144. *What sort of pride the holy scripture chiefly reproves.* All sorts of *pride* are "an abomination to the Lord," and "he who exalteth himself" in any other manner than by pursuing the perfection of his nature, "shall surely be abased";[133] yet that which we least observe, though we are most frequently admonished in holy writ to avoid it, and that which God does in an especial manner, set Himself against, is, the "lifting up ourselves against the Lord of heaven," the being "proud against the holy one of Israel."[134] For the holy scripture joins humility with the "fear of God," commands us to "humble ourselves in His sight," and "under His mighty hand."[135] And God is pleased to tell us, that He "dwells with the humble and contrite heart," those who "tremble at His word," and pay Him an awful and constant obedience.[136]

145. *And this we take least notice of.* But among all the complaints against pride, when do we hear anyone blamed for being proud against God, or for treating the divine authority contemptuously, unless when we ourselves have a share in it, and by this means partake in the affront? Otherwise we leave the divine majesty to assert its own rights, while we take care of ours! And though we stand so much upon our own punctilios,[137] and are ready to take fire upon the least seeming neglect, which we hardly if ever forgive; yet we make nothing of behaving ourselves with the most audacious arrogance towards our great and sovereign Lord.

131. Eph 1:18.

132. Gal 6:3.

133. Astell's marginal note: Prv 16:5 and 8:13; Lk 14:11.

134. Astell's marginal note: Dn 5:20, 23, and so on; Is 2:11, and so on; Ps 75:5, and so on; Jer 50:29; Ez 28.

135. Astell's marginal note: Prv 22:4; Jas 4:10; and 1 Pt 5:6.

136. Astell's marginal note: Is 57:15 and 66:2.

137. punctilios] petty formalities.

146. *Ways of being proud against God.* By violating His laws; by profaning His awful name; by a contempt, or at best a neglect of His service; by careless and irreverent addresses; by murmuring at His providence and finding fault with His ways, or which is the same thing, by refining on them;[138] by not suffering Him, I mean, so far as we can hinder, to govern the world that He has made, and to bring about His glorious designs by His own most upright methods; but pretending to assist His providence by our little and indirect arts, and our unrighteous actions; by "doing evil that good may come,"[139] which is the vilest pride, and contempt of God, for it is a supposing ourselves wiser than Him, and that "He stands in need of the sinful man";[140] by assuming the divine prerogative while we take upon us to humble our neighbors; it being as much God's peculiar,[141] and that which He has reserved in His own hand, to bring down the proud as to take vengeance upon the injurious. For we are as improper judges of our neighbor's pride, as of what's a just recompense for our own wrongs. Daily experience showing, that they are the proudest people who take upon them to correct their neighbor's haughtiness; and that we never go about to humble the supposed or real pride of another, but that we manifestly declare a greater pride and insolence of our own.

147. *Schism*[142] *and sedition.* It were endless to trace all the ways of the children of pride, I shall mention but two more, one of which strikes at God's authority, the other at His very being. The first is that seditious and schismatical spirit, derived from the devil the first pattern of pride, which prompts us to "despise dominions, and to speak evil of dignities";[143] to behave ourselves irreverently, and as often as we can with impunity, disobediently to our lawful governors in church and state. For rebellion and disobedience, besides the hurt they do to society, the injustice, confusion, and irreparable injuries that attend them; are highly aggravated, and become sins of the deepest dye, by

138. refining on them] employing overly subtle reasoning about them.

139. Rom 3:8.

140. Astell alludes to the apocryphal text Ecclus 15:12: "Say not thou, He hath caused me to err: for He hath no need of the sinful man."

141. God's peculiar] God's exclusive or special concern.

142. schism] division or disunity in the church.

143. Astell's marginal note: Jude 8.

that open contempt of God from whence they spring, and which they loudly proclaim, whatever may be the pretense, even though it be that which is the furthest in the world from allowing such practices, religion.

148. Our Lord has told us, that whoever "despiseth" His ministers "despiseth Him," and God "who sent Him."[144] And since it is by God's appointment that "kings reign," and that "princes" have authority to "decree justice";[145] and that "there is no lawful power but of God";[146] he who will not "submit himself for the Lord's sake, to every ordinance of man,"[147] that is, to every lawfully constituted form of government (for I hope nobody will say, that banditti[148] and pirates, though they have a constitution and laws among themselves, act by God's authority) but who takes upon him any pretense whatsoever, to resist the supreme power, such an one "resisteth the ordinance of God," is a rebel against the divine majesty, and must expect the terrible punishment due to such resistance.[149]

149. *Nonresistance.* A doctrine as plainly delivered in holy scripture, as "thou shalt not kill," "thou shalt not steal," and we may as well distinguish away murder and theft, and seek for plausible colors to justify or excuse our making bold with the properties and lives of our neighbors, as suppose that any expositions or facts of ours, can "null" the divine "establishments," or make any "mutations" in the laws of God,[150] by which Christians are under the strictest obligation to render active obedience to just authority, in all instances that are not contrary[151] to God's commands, and to submit quietly to the penalty where they cannot actually obey.[152] There are so many plain precepts to this purpose that it is unnecessary to collect them, and to put the doctrine past doubt, they have been exemplified in the most

144. Astell's marginal note: Lk 10:16.

145. Astell's marginal note: Prv 8:15.

146. Astell's marginal note: Rom 13[:1].

147. 1 Pt 2:13.

148. banditti] bandits.

149. Rom 13:2.

150. Astell's marginal note (first edition only): *Letter concerning Church Communion*, 17.

151. "contradictory" in first edition.

152. Astell articulates the Anglican royalist doctrine of passive obedience.

lively manner by the primitive and best Christians, whatever some modern teachers may say,[153] who take upon them to the scandal of the age, to call the doctrine of the cross "pernicious," with as good divinity as they do with law and sense call "nonresistance a traitorous doctrine here in" England.[154] And as it can't be denied that the church teaches this doctrine in her *Homilies*,[155] as she has received it from the word of God, and therefore they might have spared their proofs; so, whatever else she may be ashamed of, she has no reason to be ashamed of her doctrines.

150. *Why mentioned here.* Your Ladyship it's like will wonder why I say so much in a matter wherein women are supposed to be unconcerned. My reason is because the "divines" who write "letters," and "explain principles" to "ladies," insist upon this among the rest.[156] And because a little practice of the world will convince us, that ladies are as grand politicians, and every whit as intriguing as any patriot of the good old cause.[157] Perhaps because the gentleness of their temper makes them fitter to insinuate and gain proselytes; or that being less suspected they may be apter to get and to convey intelligence, and are therefore made the tools of crafty and designing demagogues.[158] This made me think it not improper to take notice of the plain and genuine sense of Christianity in this matter, that if ladies will needs be politicians they may not build upon a rotten and unchristian foundation. A foundation destructive of all kinds of government,[159] leaving no sort settled and quiet any longer than till a party can be formed strong enough to overthrow it. How busy looks and grand concern about that bill and the other promotion, how whispers and cabals, eternal

---

153. Astell refers to the anonymous author of the *Letter concerning Church Communion.*

154. Astell's marginal note (first edition only): *Letter concerning Church Communion*, 16, 17.

155. The sixteenth-century *Books of Homilies* contain sermons expressing the fundamental doctrines of the reformed Church of England.

156. Astell refers to the authors of both *A Lady's Religion* and the *Letter concerning Church Communion.*

157. patriot of the good old cause] broadly speaking, a supporter of the republican cause in England during the years 1640 and 1660.

158. demagogues] political agitators.

159. In the first edition, this reads "all government in general" instead of "all kinds of government."

disputes and restless solicitations, with all the equipage of modern politicians, become the ladies, I have not skill to determine.[160] But if there be anything ridiculous in it, I had rather leave the observation to the men, as being both more proper for their wit, and more agreeable to their inclinations.

151. *Atheism, and so on, spring from pride.* The other contempt of God which I was to take notice of, is what ladies I hope are but little, if at all concerned in, that is, those bold discourses about the nature and attributes of God, wherein men take upon them to deny not only what He has declared of Himself in His word, but even what natural reason teaches; which plainly proves, that if there be a God, He must needs be infinitely wise and good, just and holy; and that to deny Him to be infinite in all perfections, either directly or by consequence, is in some respects worse than to deny His existence.[161] In a word, atheism, impiety, and immorality, schism and rebellion, have commonly one and the same original; they come from pride, which will not suffer us to submit our understandings to God's word, nor our wills to His authority.

152. *Of envy.* But pride is not the only sin which we copy from the enemy of mankind, there's another for which he is not less remarkable that we too much imitate. "Through envy of the devil sin came

160. Astell is being rather disingenuous here, given that she herself wrote political pamphlets on "that bill," the Occasional Conformity Bill of 1704. See Astell, *Moderation truly Stated*; Astell, *An Impartial Enquiry*; and Astell, *Fair Way with the Dissenters*, in Astell: *Political Writings*. In these pamphlets, Astell takes the Tory nontolerationist position on the practice of those Protestant dissenters who would attend Anglican services solely in order to qualify for public office. For further details, see the "Historical-Intellectual Context" section of the introduction to the present volume.

161. I am unable to pinpoint Astell's exact targets here. It is possible that she has in mind Samuel Clarke, *A Demonstration of the Being and Attributes of God* (1705), first delivered as the Boyle Lecture in 1704. In this work, Clarke argues that the certainty of God's existence cannot be grounded on an idea or definition of God as "a being of all possible perfections," but rather must be based on a cosmological argument for a self-existent being, "the supposition of whose not existing plainly implies a contradiction." See Samuel Clarke, *A Demonstration of the Being and Attributes of God, and Other Writings*, ed. Ezio Vailati, Cambridge Texts in the History of Philosophy (Cambridge: Cambridge University Press, 1998), 16. This work first appeared in print in November 1704 (Arber, *Term Catalogues*, 3:424). Astell might also be referring to Samuel Bold's defense of Locke's *Reasonableness of Christianity*, titled *A Short Discourse of the True Knowledge of Christ Jesus* (1697), i.e., a "bold discourse."

into the world," says a wise observer;[162] and we may add, that through the *envy* of mankind a great deal of good is kept out of the world, if not very much evil introduced. It is a duty no doubt which we owe to God, to use our utmost endeavors that His name may be glorified, and that all possible good may be done and received by mankind; and in short, to promote the cause of truth and virtue. But who among us has any concern for either, except it be to serve our own temporal interest or party, or out of some such petty aim? We are as afraid of imparting truth, unless to gain an admirer or disciple, as if truth were like worldly possessions, lost by being communicated. Sloth and a base ignoble spirit which is the natural effect of every indulged sin, especially of voluptuousness,[163] won't suffer us to do anything that's excellent ourselves, and envy won't endure that it should be done by another, lest this reproach our negligence. Envy, which is so injurious to God, to our neighbor, and to ourselves, so black in its own nature, that were we saints in all other respects, this alone would transform us into devils, so very detestable, that though it is a plague that most of us are dying with, yet none will own that they are infected!

153. *Signs of envy.* But not to judge others I judge thus for myself; since a good understanding, with a noble because a virtuous ambition to improve it, together with an honest and sincere disposition of mind to do the greatest good, are beautiful and valuable qualities; since they are the gift of God and benefits to mankind, for when God is pleased to send such an excellent spirit into the world, He designs it as a blessing to the age it appears in; if I do not find a joy at heart whenever I discern these qualifications, and an earnest desire to do all the good offices in my power to the persons who possess them, whoever they be, I conclude I am infected with envy, and that the plague is begun. For in God's name, what but envy can hinder me from admiring what is beautiful, from esteeming what is valuable, and from

---

162. The saying is a variation on the apocryphal text Ws 2:24: "through the devil's envy death entered the world." The "wise observer" is possibly King Solomon, who was thought to be the author of the book of Wisdom. John Norris uses the same variation of the text in his "Discourse Concerning Religious Singularity," in *Practical Discourses upon Several Divine Subjects* (London: S. Manship, 1691), 74.

163. voluptuousness] indulgence in sensuous pleasure.

giving all the assistance I am able, with due praise and encouragement to what is useful and beneficent?

154. *Wherein it differs from emulation. And of detraction.* If I find an honest *emulation* to do as well as they do, this ought not to be checked but encouraged, because it is a spur both to their virtue and my own. But then this emulation must always be attended with a value for, and love to their persons, and must render them all the praise and service they can any way pretend to. For *detraction*, or the lessening our neighbor's merit and reputation, by concealing or misrepresenting his honorable actions, which is indeed a detracting from virtue, and a robbing God of the glory that is due to His grace, is a necessary effect and certain sign of envy. And since the effect is observable everywhere, we may well conclude that the cause how much so ever it be concealed, is as epidemical.

155. *Effects of envy.* But if instead of showing gratitude to God, goodwill and esteem to His servants, and assisting them in their generous designs, I do all that in me lies to frustrate the divine favor; if it is come to that pass that my neighbor's virtue grows an eyesore and galls me at heart; if from not assisting, I go on to lay traps to destroy it, or openly oppose it, as the progress of sin, and of this particularly, is very easy and quick; if I first try to work them after my own fashion, and to make them my property; or if failing in this I contrive their fall, rejoice in it; am pleased to see virtue lost for want of encouragement, and with a devilish joy erect a glaring trophy on its ruins; if like those professed opposers of God and true goodness, whom the wise Jew speaks of, "I examine the *virtuous person* with despitefulness and torture, that I may know his meekness and prove his patience, because he is not for *my* turn, he was made to reprove *my* thoughts, his life is not like other men's, his ways are of another, *and better* fashion, his example upbraids *me* with *my* offending the law, and objecteth to *my* infamy, *my* transgressions";[164] if this is my progress, it is to be feared that the poison has seized my heart, and my case is in a manner desperate.

---

164. Astell partly paraphrases Ws 2:12, 19 ("Therefore let us lie in wait for the righteous; because he is not for our turn, and he is clean contrary to our doings: he upbraideth us with our offending the law, and objecteth to our infamy the transgressings of our education," and "Let us examine him with despitefulness and torture, that we may know his meekness, and prove his patience").

156. *Envy hard to be cured.* For who shall admonish their neighbor of so detestable a sin as envy, were anyone honest and kind enough to undertake that very friendly but very thankless office? Since to suppose them guilty of it is to lash them with the severest satire;[165] and since envy is a sin that lies lurking in the heart; a sin which we not only industriously conceal from others, but even from ourselves; because though it often appears in them who are fullest of their own sufficiency, and is an inseparable attendant on the proudest spirits, yet it proceeds from a consciousness of our own infirmities and weakness. For how much so ever the envious person may be above the envied in outward appearance, yet his own mind reproaches him with the real superiority of those whom he envies, making him sensible whether he will or no, that they are his betters: which is the true reason of his ill will to them, whatever the pretense may be.

157. *Wherein it differs from a generous indignation.* Not but that it is possible that the displeasure we feel at the good our neighbor receives, may proceed from covetousness, as well as from envy, or from better reasons, as justice, and that laudable indignation that arises in every generous breast, when an unworthy person goes away with the recompense that is due to merit; and under these disguises we endeavor to conceal our envy. But then if we pretend to this *generous indignation*, we must be sure to feel[166] it, not only upon our own disappointment, but rather, and chiefly, upon the ill usage of others, whose merits we may be allowed to value without being partial. And whatever fault we find with men's partiality in bestowing their favors, there can be none to be sure in God's distribution of His graces. So that every degree of indignation at those gifts which are derived from His bounty only, and are not misapplied, is no better than envy, whose "eye is evil because God is good," disputing His right to "do what He will with His own," and insolently taxing Him of injustice.[167]

158. *Envy a contempt of God.* For, to pass over the injury we do to our neighbor himself by *envying* and opposing, instead of promoting "every right work,"[168] which injury is at once a flagrant injustice

165. satire] censure.

166. "have" in first edition.

167. Mt 20:15.

168. Astell's marginal note: Eccl 4:4.

and the height of uncharitableness: to say nothing of the damage the world sustains, which would not be so bad as it is, were everyone's talent observed, and were they assisted in the work for which God has fitted them; especially persons[169] of a superior genius, of activity and resolution, who are qualified for the highest attainments; and are the only persons that can give check to that torrent of corruption that breaks in upon mankind in all ages; and who *will* exert themselves, if not in doing good, in doing of mischief, unless their virtue be as great as their other qualifications, enabling them to overcome, I had almost said their just resentments, at an ungrateful world, for checking them in their generous and best endeavors to serve it. Besides all this, the laying such a temptation in our brother's way, as it's like we ourselves would not conquer, and depriving mankind of the benefit of his virtues; we rob God of the glory of His graces by this malignant envy; are ungrateful to Him, "from whom every good and perfect gift cometh,"[170] and who bestows it for the common good; we affront His majesty by our spite to them whom He favors, and by hating them for that very reason for which we ought to love them. And in fine, we express our contempt of God by standing out against His pleasure, and by opposing, or at least slighting His commission, that is, those abilities which He bestows, and which give a right to the persons who possess them, to receive all that assistance and furtherance we are able to afford them, in the execution of that work, to which God, by giving them those talents, has plainly designed them.

159. *How to be avoided.* If therefore we desire to clear ourselves of this vile sin, and to be indeed *public-spirited*, let us help everyone forward in the best way; let us inquire after the masterly genius, rejoice when we have found it, and instead of our former poor little artifices to curb it, let us set it in the best light, and no more endeavor to form it by our model, or work it to be our tool. If we find it has too much virtue and honor to make so poor a figure, and too much sense of God's bounty to employ His talents to no better purpose; let us not try to defeat its hopes by diverting it from its proper employment to some attempts it is not fit for, and so not like to succeed in. But if it is so discerning as to avoid this trap, if it is above temptation,

169. "those" in first edition.

170. Jas 1:17.

and defended with a virtue that cannot be corrupted, let us not for shame, miscall its integrity obstinacy. Let us not say they are proud whose spirits we cannot break; or rash, whose noble ardor is not to be stopped; or full of themselves who only follow sincerely the best light they can attain; or that they attempt things too high for them, who do no more than labor after that perfection to which God at least invites them, if He does not command them to pursue it. Instead of thinking it reason enough to oppose, or at best to afford no assistance to a laudable undertaking, because our advice was not asked, or it is not pursued by our direction; by which it is evident, that the good we may sometimes do, does not proceed from a love to God and to true goodness, but is performed merely to aggrandize ourselves, and to set forth our own abilities; instead of racking our invention to raise objections, displaying our wit in detracting from it, and using all our artifices to lay rubs[171] in its way; instead of bare commendation and doing nothing further, though this as the world goes is a mighty matter; and what but few come up to; let us, even for our own sakes (that most powerful persuasive!) henceforth heartily espouse and vigorously promote every good work, since by this means we ourselves will be sharers in the benefit and honor.

160. *When disappointed.* All sin is folly, but envy is more particularly so, because it brings no pleasure but pain to him who harbors it. The indifferent or middling genii[172] may perhaps be taken off, they may leave the way of honor through want of due encouragement; and therefore God has graciously allowed us reputation, and little, present recompenses, to spur us on in a virtuous course. But the poor-spirited envious will find, to their great mortification, that if a genius is rightly turned, nothing animates and improves it so much, as that ungenerous and unchristian enmity it meets with, as has been observed in all ages. This makes it exert itself and find its own strength, this is a theater to its prudence, and exercises its fortitude. And by doing the best things constantly and vigorously, notwithstanding all the opposition and evil return it meets with for doing so; by going forward with no other encouragement but the sense of duty, and the consciousness of doing nobly (that divine pleasure!), and without any other prospect

171. rubs] impediments.

172. middling genii] mediocre intelligences.

but the expectation of a future reward; it obtains the most illustrious character, and arrives at the highest degree of heroic virtue.

161. *Of rejoicing in God.* I know not whether I should call "rejoicing in God" a duty, or the result of all other duties; but I know it is unaccountable why we pursue so many foolish pleasures, and neglect this divine one. The good Christian only has reason, and he always ought, to be cheerful. For, considering the goodness of our master, the excellency of our work, and the grandeur of that reward we have in view, our hearts must needs leap for joy at all times, except when we reflect upon our offenses against so great a goodness, and the danger of falling short of so excellent a reward.

162. *Consistent with religious mourning.* It is true our Lord pronounces the "mourners blessed"; but it is also true, that we are commanded to "rejoice evermore"; so that Christian mourning and Christian rejoicing are not inconsistent, *comfort* being the beatitude promised to these religious mourners.[173] The mourning our Lord enjoins being only opposed to sensual and worldly mirth, to which spiritual joy is also so opposite, that the one always drives away the other. Therefore God in His goodness tries to wean us from that carnal and vain jollity, which cannot last, and does not profit, that we may be capable of those solid joys, which the world can neither give nor take away. They injure both themselves and religion who make all its joys future, for it has the "promise *even* of this life," it enjoys its "hundred fold" in tranquility of mind, and substantial pleasure, in the midst of persecutions.[174] So that a true Christian "rejoices evermore," in all circumstances; he gives "thanks always for all things"; for *all things* that God sends without exception, for poverty, afflictions, persecutions, and what men account most calamitous.[175] And good reason, since these are only exercises of his virtue, and opportunities to increase his reward; since they deprive him of no real good, but bring him much, fortifying his mind with such a "joy as no man can take from him."[176]

163. *Sin and holiness the only just cause of sorrow and joy.* Sin alone is the just cause of sorrow, therefore the lessons of mourning

---

173. Astell's marginal note: Mt 5:4; 1 Thes 5:16.

174. Astell's marginal note: 1 Tm 4:8; Mk 10:30.

175. Astell's marginal note: 1 Thes 5:16; Eph 5:20.

176. Astell's marginal note: Jn 16:22.

are read only to the jolly sinner; to the "rich men," to those who "have lived in pleasure on the earth and been wanton," who are exhorted to "weep and howl for the miseries that shall come upon them."[177] But there's scarce a more unseemly sight than dejected looks and melancholy airs in a Christian; who sincerely endeavors to approve himself to God, though he does it with much imperfection, being sensible of the weakness of human nature in general, and very particularly affected with his own. He who does not think that "the lot is fallen unto him in a fair place, and that he has a goodly heritage," well worth his joy, when he can say, "the Lord is my portion," even though it be his *only* portion, is a most ungrateful person, and unworthy of so great a blessing.[178] And I very much fear it is not, or will not long be his, since he knows so little how to value it. Let every sincere Christian therefore, as much as natural temper will admit, "rejoice in the Lord always, and again I say, rejoice"; for this holy joy is at once the cure of foolish mirth, and of as foolish sorrow.[179]

164. *What obedience will bring us to heaven.* To close this head; I neither believe in God, nor love, nor honor, nor fear, nor worship, nor pay Him any sort of duty which is indispensably due from a creature to the great creator, unless I obey Him. Nor is my obedience what God requires unless I avoid every known, willful sin, do not allow myself in the habit of any infirmity, nor indulge any noted ignorance or imperfection whatsoever. It is very fashionable[180] indeed to forget both God and myself, and to spend more thought, time, and pains, in the affairs and pleasures of this present life, than in working out my salvation; the corruptions of the age give us but too many instances. But then this is in reality a loving the world more than God, how loath so ever we are to call it so; nor can I see how such a course of life is consistent with our hopes of heaven.

165. *The dangers we are exposed to.* It is also possible, after we have begun well, and made some progress, "to grow weary in well-doing," otherwise we had not been cautioned against it.[181] It is that

177. Astell's marginal note: Jas 5:1, 5.

178. Ps 16:5–6.

179. Astell's marginal note: Phil 4:4.

180. "possible" in first edition.

181. Gal 6:9; 1 Thes 3:13.

to which our own sloth, and the ill air of the world too much dispose us.[182] We may by a vain presumption on our own strength, by a forgetfulness of God, or an imprudent security and carelessness, expose ourselves to temptations that may prove too hard for us. Or though we are for the most part watchful, the devil and his instruments may sometimes take advantage of our temper, or indisposition, of some unforeseen accident, or great surprise, or ill-grounded principle, and place a temptation in such circumstances as that it may overcome us.

166. *Self-confidence.* Thus St. Peter, whose love to his master was very sincere, and who doubtless was resolved to die with Him rather than deny Him when he made this profession, did notwithstanding fall very deplorably. Either because the fear of suffering prevailed and his courage left him (though I do not think this was the reason, since he was of an undaunted temper), or else the confusion he was in to see his dearest Lord so vilely used, and his own hopes defeated, made him no longer master of himself; or rather (and which I take to be the true reason), because God left him to himself to correct his confidence, to make him sensible of his own weakness, and to teach him an entire dependence on God the giver of all grace. But had he instead of a speedy, a very particular, a bitter, and lasting repentance, persuaded himself that there was no great hurt in what he had done, and (as some did afterwards) that it was enough to believe with the heart, and that one needs not expose himself to dangers by open confession; that he only yielded to the infirmity of nature, and to a violent temptation, so that he might refer himself to God's mercy, without being much concerned about the matter: or had he on the other side gone over to the unbelieving Jews, in order to stifle his remorse; had he thrown off, as much as he could, all sense of his savior, and hardened himself in wickedness, which is the true desperation; we should never have had St. Peter in the catalogue of saints, but his "latter end had been worse than" his "beginning."[183]

167. *How repentance and godly sorrow differ. Repentance* then is somewhat else besides a solemn sorrow, returning at certain seasons set apart for the purpose. *Godly sorrow* which arises from a full conviction and lively sense of the goodness of God and the evil of sin,

182. This sentence is not in the first edition.
183. 2 Pt 2:20.

will indeed work a "repentance not to be repented of";[184] that is, it will produce a thorough change of life, more especially in that particular we have lately offended in, and "a carefulness" and "zeal" to "approve ourselves" to God in all things for the future, "by patient continuance in well-doing."[185] But sorrow, even godly sorrow, and repentance are two distinct things, as is plain from St. Paul's discourse, 2 Corinthians 7. For let our sorrow be what it will, unless it "brings forth fruits meet for repentance," even universal obedience, so far as we have life and power, though it may perhaps deceive *us*, it can never reconcile us to *our maker*.[186]

184. Astell's marginal note: 2 Cor 7:10.

185. 2 Cor 7:11; Rom 2:7.

186. Astell's marginal note: Mt 3:8. ["Meet for repentance" means suitable or fit for repentance.]

Section III

Of our duty to our neighbor

168. *Who is our neighbor and the extent of our duty towards him.* Our *neighbor* is everyone to whom we can do any manner of service, enemies as well as friends.[1] And among all those duties we owe to God, there are not any enforced with greater earnestness, than those which for His sake are due to our neighbor. They are preferred sometimes to those immediate acts of worship that we owe to His own majesty; so little reason have we to fancy, that we do God service by any rigorous usage of mankind. And that we may never be at a loss in our conduct towards them, we are commanded to do to others, as we, supposing we judge according to right reason, desire to be treated ourselves. But how depraved so ever our judgments may be, the not doing to another that which if we were in his case, and he in ours, we would not have him do to us, is a rule of equity of perpetual obligation; so that a *little* share of sense, with *any* degree of honesty may direct us in this matter. Nor can we ever be absolved from any duty to our neighbor that is in our power by his ingratitude, because being due for God's sake, the duty must still be paid, whatever returns may be made us by our neighbor.

169. *Whence the obligation to this duty arises.* He who has never heard of Christianity, is obliged to love his neighbors because they partake of the same nature. But Christians are under a further and higher obligation, the duty they owe to one another being founded on their mutual relation to Christ their head. And therefore, since everyone is, or may be a member of Christ, he is to be treated with brotherly affection. It is as unnatural for Christians to disobey those whom Christ has substituted to "have the rule over them," as it is for the inferior members of the body to rebel against the superior.[2] As well may the stomach refuse to distribute into every part of the body the nourishment it receives, as Christians refuse to "do good unto all

1. Astell's marginal note: Lk 10:30, and so on. [Astell alludes to the tale of the Good Samaritan, Jesus's response to the question "who is my neighbor?" (Lk 10:29).]

2. Astell's marginal note: Heb 13:7.

men, especially to them who are of the household of faith":[3] which by
the way, instructs us, when all other circumstances are equal,[4] to give
the preference to the best Christian in all our acts of kindness and
beneficence. Injuriousness among the members of Christ, is the same
thing as for one member of the body to wound and destroy another.
And it will be as fatal in one case as in the other, for the members to
transgress their several duties.

170. *A general rule.* I consider myself therefore as a part of one
great whole, in the welfare of which my own happiness is included.
And without regarding any particular or separate interest, endeavor
always to pursue that which in itself and absolutely speaking, is the
most public, universal, and greatest good; and to avoid that which
absolutely and in itself is the greatest evil. Which principle rightly
understood and strictly pursued, will at once fill up all the offices of
justice and charity, and every other obligation. Let us then enquire
what are the measures and degrees of good and evil.

171. *Of the measures of good and evil.* Now not to be too metaphysical, or tedious in this enquiry, I take the glory of God to be the
greatest good, and the offending of God to be the greatest evil; everything being more or less good or evil, according as it conduces more
or less to these. By the glory of God, I understand the manifestation of
the divine attributes, according to the eternal reason of things; which
some call the rule of order. Now this rule is nothing else, but that way
which the wisdom and perfection of the divine nature oblige God to
act, whenever He thinks fit to exert His power and show forth His
glory. And because His goodness is over all His works, He is pleased
to take the greatest glory in the display of this attribute. And therefore,
by offending God, I understand those hindrances which rational and
free agents put in their own, and in each other's way, towards the attainment of that happiness which the wisdom and goodness of God
originally designed them. It must also be observed, that there can
be no comparison among evils of the greatest kind, for all offenses
against God are at all times and in all circumstances utterly to be
avoided. And though some of them may be more heinous than others,
on account of certain aggravations, yet none of them can ever be the

3. Astell's marginal note: Gal 6:10.

4. The qualification "when all other circumstances are equal" is not in the first edition.

object of choice, because being of the same evil nature, they are in this respect equally evil: so that when we speak of greater or lesser evils, of which the one may be chosen to avoid the other, it must always be understood that the evil to be chosen is in no respect sinful. Or as the learned distinguish, it must be such an evil as is barely a pain or punishment, not such an evil as is in any manner a guilt or sin.[5]

172. *Thence our duty deduced.* Upon the principles of reason, the good of *many* is preferable to the good of a *few,* much more of *one;*[6] a lasting good is to be preferred before a temporary; the public before the private. And upon Christian principles, which I shall here take for granted, having as I think already proved the authority of holy scripture, the good of the mind is infinitely preferable to the good of the body; spiritual advantages to temporal; and temporal are to be valued among themselves, in proportion as they contribute to spiritual and eternal. Christians are members one of another, and therefore the good of my neighbor is not to be separated from my own good, but to be estimated with it.

173. *First, to superiors.* From all which it follows, first, in reference to superiors, it is better that I endure the unreasonableness, injustice, or oppression of a parent, a master, and so forth, than that the established rules of order and good government should be superseded on my account. It is better that my just pretensions should be thrown out, and my merit, if I have any, should be disregarded, than that I or any other private person should be our own carvers,[7] and force rewards from our superiors. It is better that I should submit to an unjust sentence, than that there should be no end of strife; and that some private persons though ever so innocent should suffer, than that the majesty of government, and herein the divine authority should be violated, and the public should be disturbed.

174. *Second, to inferiors.* In regard to inferiors, I consider, that since the good of many is a greater good than the good of one, it is therefore to be preferred, even though I be that one. That all authority being derived from God's absolute dominion, which dominion in its

---

5. Astell discusses this definition of lesser evil as "pain" and not "sin" in her correspondence with John Norris. See Astell and Norris, *Letters,* 87–90.

6. In the first edition, this sentence reads "*few,* or of *one*" instead of "*few,* much more of *one.*"

7. be our own carvers] choose for ourselves at our own discretion.

last resort arises from the excellency of His nature, by which He is our creator, preserver, and constant benefactor; consequently the reason and ground of superiority is the supposed excellency of the superior. But because order and government must be maintained, which could not be, considering the corruption and partiality of mankind, were everyone left to be judge in this matter, therefore we must submit to him, who by the laws and usages of the place, or by prescription when there is not a better title, has a claim to superiority, even though he be not really better than his neighbors. However the superior ought to consider, that though for order sake his will must take place in all cases wherein God, and under God his proper superior if he has any, have not determined; yet since this is only upon supposition that his will is most agreeable to right reason, that is, to God's will, in conformity to which our true excellency consists, if the will of an inferior be more reasonable than the will of his superior, then according to the reason of things, *that* is preferable to *this*.

175. *Third, to equals.* As to mankind in general, among whom there is no natural inequality, but what arises from their different participation of those divine excellencies which God is pleased to communicate to them; of which excellencies, authority and dominion, though not best in itself, is to be most observed and respected by us, because government depends upon it, and without government mankind cannot subsist: I consider, that it is not only inhuman, but even devilish, to hurt or vex my neighbors, for no other advantage to myself but the unnatural pleasure of seeing them suffer; that their greater good is preferable to my lesser good; and that a less evil suffered by me, is not so bad in itself as a greater suffered by my neighbor. Therefore it is not reasonable, and consequently not best, that my neighbor should endure an evil to procure me a good not equal in degree to that evil; or that I should refuse pain or loss to procure for another a good that outweighs it. Much more am I obliged to deny myself a little good, in order to obtain a great one for my neighbor; and also to suffer a less evil, to keep him from a greater. Nor shall I in the main, and taking the *future* into the computation, be a loser by giving my neighbor in these cases, and for the *present*, the preference. For to act thus is in reality to pursue my own greatest good, which they, and they only provide for, who conform themselves in all things to the will of God, who is

no respecter of persons, and therefore does not, absolutely speaking, will a good to any one of His creatures that tends to the greater evil of another; but who by the prerogative of His nature, always wills, what upon the whole, all circumstances considered, is the greatest good.[8]

176. *The rule of justice.* To descend to particulars: since everyone has a just claim to certain rights and properties from the laws of God, or man, it is fit that my appetite should give place to his rights, and that it should never be gratified to their prejudice. For justice is preferable to inclination, nay, even to necessities; it being better I should suffer some real wants, than that by invading my neighbor's property, the laws of society and good government should be broken. And besides, it is a fundamental rule, that among corrupt mortals no man shall be his own carver, or judge in his own case to his neighbor's damage.

177. *Of charity.* It is much better that I should want some of the conveniences of life, than that any of my neighbors should want the necessaries; nay, that I should abridge myself in what I may reckon necessaries, rather than that they should be driven to violent necessities and grievous wants. For unless this be the duty of everyone who loves God and hopes for His love, I know not how to make sense of that scripture, "who so hath this world's good, and seeth his brother have need, and shutteth up his bowels of compassion from him, how dwelleth the love of God in him?"[9] And surely a well-tempered mind, will make us look with greater joy on the covering we have put upon our neighbor's back, than on the gaudery[10] lavished on our own. Every morsel the hungry soul swallows so savorily, will afford us a higher *goust*,[11] than all that cost and luxury can furnish for our own tables. And we shall find a much greater pleasure in making our neighbor's heart rejoice, than in gratifying any of our own appetites.

178. *Superfluity due to the indigent.* Nor is it only charity but justice, that requires our superfluities should be laid out upon our indigent brethren. All that which in the opinion of the soberest and

8. The qualification "what upon the whole, all circumstances considered, is" is not in the first edition.

9. Astell's marginal note: 1 Jn 3:17.

10. gaudery] finery.

11. *goust*] from the French *goût*, "liking, relish, zest, fondness" (*OED*).

wisest persons, exceeds the necessities and moderate conveniences of life, according to that rank which providence has placed us in, not according to what we can compass, or to the extravagancies of other people, is a superfluity in God's account, whatever it may be in ours. So that though we may not be unjust to this or that particular person, it is certainly an injustice with respect to God, to waste upon ourselves those goods of His, which He committed to our stewardship to no other end or purpose, but that they should be spent in supplying our neighbor's wants. This disposal of them being our present honor, and title to a future reward.[12]

179. *Unobserved instances of pride.* Therefore all that which we *cannot use*, is due to our neighbors; but I could never understand upon what just ground we presume to give them that which we *will not use*, because not good enough for ourselves, as we suppose: unless it is upon account of a public character, and to maintain that dignity and station God's providence[13] has placed us in; splendor and show being the trappings of authority, which it must put on to raise a veneration in the vulgar, who won't be moved by better reasons. Or else by stipulation and agreement, since it is not unbecoming to give another that which he has sought and submitted to. Or if neither of these, then the real, not pretended necessities that education and custom have brought upon us, may be the excuse. For these do sometimes produce wants, that can't so readily be provided for, as the simple and natural necessities of others, whose way of living has been less delicate, may: but this is far from being an advantage, it is indeed the contrary, he being furthest removed from unhappiness, who has the fewest wants, and such as are most easily supplied. In the last place, we may make some allowances to ourselves to avoid singularity and affectation, and in compliance with the decent, not the extravagant customs of those among whom we live. But excepting these reasons, there's no manner of ground, why I, or any other person, should conclude that to be good enough for another which we don't think good enough for ourselves. And it is without dispute a greater pride in us to proffer our offals[14] to our neighbor, than it can be in him to refuse or despise them.

12. This sentence is not in the first edition.

13. In the first edition, "the government" replaces "God's providence."

14. offals] leftovers.

180. *Intriguing.* If our neighbor is more capable of serving the public, that is, if wise and unprejudiced persons, or our governors, whom we are to suppose wise and impartial out of the respect we owe them, think so, it is much the best to give way quietly to his pretensions, for to oppose, were not only an injury to him but even to the public.

181. *Inquisitiveness into the affairs of others.* It is not only unmannerly and rude, but even unchristian, and a certain effect of pride and assuming, whatever show of humility they may put on, who take upon them to interrogate their neighbor concerning himself, and much more concerning others, when they have no authority to ask such questions, and there is no manner of reason they should be satisfied in their inquisitiveness. For this is not only a proud and unjust encroachment upon another's rights and liberties, who though he is obliged to communicate all useful truths, yet may lawfully keep his own affairs to himself, should do it in prudence, and ought in faithfulness or charity, to conceal what he knows concerning the affairs of others: but these questioners do also tempt their neighbor to lie, when they leave this the only way to prevent such discoveries as they ought not to make, and which against all right, and justice, and good breeding, they will draw from his silence; they force him to rudeness or disrespect to themselves, or to other inconveniencies which he desires not to fall into.

182. *Truth not to be extorted.* However it is better to suffer these than to lie, or which is the same thing to equivocate, or to betray a trust, or to speak an uncharitable truth; and the best way is to get as much out of the reach of such inquisitors, as charity and civility will allow. For truth is due to our neighbor, because as the apostle argues, "we are members one of another," and to put off lies in its stead, is to destroy conversation and civil society.[15] But it is also a great injustice and insufferable tyranny, to pump and rack him for truths that don't belong to us. Lawful authority, justice, or charity may, but impertinent curiosity can never justify such pretensions.

183. *Of injuries.* As to injuries, it is better that I put them up even from equals and inferiors, letting things rest as they are, than that

---

15. Eph 4:25. The apostle is St. Paul.

I multiply injuries by returning them.[16] It is better to make my enemy my friend by forgiveness and noble beneficence, than to continue him my enemy by revenge. It is better that I suffer some light injury, such as I can well enough bear in my fortune or person, than that by seeking legal reparation, I bring an intolerable, or very great damage on my neighbor. For nothing but a just authority derived from God, and a pure intention to use it for His honor and the benefit of His subjects, in the reformation of the guilty, or to put a stop to their wickedness for the benefit of the innocent; or lastly, as a warning to others, that they may hear and fear, and avoid the like iniquity; nothing else can justify the inflicting severities and punishments on our fellow creatures.

184. *Regard to our neighbor's reputation.* It is better that I suffer in my estate or conveniencies, than that another suffer in his reputation, which is not to be exposed on any account unless the greater good of a third, or more persons. A knave may be detected, but not barely because he is a knave, but because his concealed knavery may be injurious to honest and unsuspecting people. But I am not to expose my neighbor on any other prospect, for it is possible he may repent, and so the reason of his discredit ceases, when the ill effects of my needless exposing him, remain and are irreparable. Nay, if I should go further, and add, that upon the same ground I am to prefer my neighbor's reputation before my own, supposing him a person of greater consideration, and whose fair character may do more good, I should not exceed the truth, nor it may be what some have practiced.

185. *Our duty to our neighbor's soul.* To be sure, no temporal interest of mine how great so ever, be it estate or life itself, or what in my reckoning is more than either, a clear reputation, quiet, and health, none of all these, nor all of them together, are to be put in the balance with my neighbor's soul. Whose eternal interest I am to prefer before all considerations whatever, except the salvation of my own, and other souls. For this is truly to seek God's glory, and to pursue my own good in the best manner, and to most purpose.

186. *Of scandal.* Hence it is, that the damage we do to one another's souls, by tempting them to sin, by turning them off from a virtuous course, or stopping and hindering them in it, and in a word,

---

16. Astell's marginal note: Mt 5:38, and so on. [Astell refers to the gospel passages advising Christians to "turn the other cheek" (Mt 5:39).]

by laying any sort of impediment or stumbling block in their way to heaven, is called emphatically in scripture *an offense*, as being a complication of sins, and one of the biggest transgressions. For it is of all other sins most opposite to God's gracious intentions towards mankind, and hurts the body of Christ in its tenderest interests. It offers God the highest dishonor by hazarding at least, if not ruining a soul that is so dear to Him; it robs our Lord of the price of His blood; does our neighbor the greatest and most irreparable injury; and in fine, draws down our own souls in the ruin we bring upon our brother's. A frightful sin, and yet daily, nay hourly committed, even for our sport and entertainment, and so habitual have we made it, that it goes down without any remorse! For not being sensible of the worth of our own souls, we are not affected with a due concern for our neighbor's; exposing those to infinite hazards, the wonder is less that we expose these.

187. *How given.* St. Paul brings everything that is "an occasion to fall in our brother's way, *every*thing whereby he stumbleth, or is offended, or is made weak," within the verge of this heinous sin.[17] The consideration of which is a matter of great importance and vast extent; so that besides my own inability, it is not possible to treat of it in the short bounds of this letter, with that accuracy that it deserves. I shall therefore but barely name the direct and obvious ways of tempting our neighbor to sin, such as a superior's commanding it; or anyone's advising, or persuading and alluring others to be partners in his guilt; or assisting, encouraging, excusing, or justifying them in sin; or setting them an ill example; or bringing up an evil report upon a Christian life, these being so happily observed by the excellent author of *The Whole Duty of Man*.[18] A book to which I beg leave to refer your Ladyship for a more perfect account of what in many places I have only hinted at, and which women have a peculiar claim to, because

17. Astell's marginal note: Rom 14:13, 21.

18. See Allestree, *The Whole Duty of Man* in *Works of the Learned and Pious Author*, 80–81. In chapter 10, sections 6–8 of this work, Allestree warns against all the ways in which we might draw our neighbors into sin, including "commanding," "counseling," "alluring," and "assisting" them in sin, as well as setting "an ill pattern" and "bringing up any reproach upon strict and Christian living" (80–81).

there are many probable arguments to back a current report that it was writ by a lady.[19]

188. *In things indifferent or commendable.* That which I mean to take notice of more particularly, is the scandal we may give by what is commonly called innocent liberties; and by our indifferent, or even our good and virtuous words and actions. Because the scandal St. Paul so strictly reproves, Romans 14 and 1 Corinthians 8, was not instanced in anything directly sinful, but in an ill use of Christian liberty in things indifferent. And those "offenses" our Lord so severely threatens and warns us against, arise from something of great use and service, a "foot," a "hand," and an "eye"; yet if even these be occasions of "offense," the one must be "plucked out," and the other "cut off and cast from us."[20]

189. *How negative and affirmative precepts oblige.* Everyone knows that negative precepts always oblige; for it can never be lawful at any time, or in any circumstances or exigencies, or upon any occasion, to do that which God has expressly forbid; unless He should expressly command it, which is a revocation of the former precept; and which seems to me to be the case of the Israelites in spoiling the Egyptians, and of Phineas, Ehud, Sampson, and other zealots under the law, who had express warrant for what they did beyond the stated rule and law. On the other side, affirmative precepts, though of perpetual obligation, don't oblige equally at all times, but take place according to our power and opportunity of performing them.

190. *Of scandal in relation to affirmative precepts.* It is our duty to worship God, and to do acts of charity to mankind, but these are to be performed in their seasons; for were we continually employed in

19. Lady Dorothy Pakington (1623–79) was once thought to be the author of *The Whole Duty of Man*, a work that is now widely attributed to Richard Allestree. See Sara H. Mendelson's biography in *ODNB*, s.v. "Pakington [*née* Coventry], Dorothy," http://www.oxforddnb.com/view/article/21142 (accessed January 16, 2012). Upon reading Astell's *Christian Religion*, a near-contemporary, William Parry, says that "This lady's acute and clear reasoning and surprising abilities in theology, have made me less diffident concerning the very pious and worthy Lady Packington's [*sic*] capacities to write such a book as *The Whole Duty of Man*" (William Parry to George Ballard, February 12, 1743; Bodleian Library, Oxford, Ballard MS 40:158). *The Christian Religion* resembles *The Whole Duty of Man* in its division into the subject matter of our duties to God, to our neighbors, and to our selves.

20. Astell's marginal note: Mt 18. [The references are to Mt 18:7–9.]

the one, we must of necessity omit the other. And the time being left to our discretion, they become unlawful to us at such a time, and in such circumstances, as they are like to be attended with foreseen and certain scandal. Nay, if the scandal be but probable, unless the present occasion be so urgent that it will be sin to omit it, or that the present and certain good, outweighs the danger of the probable scandal, they are to be deferred to a fitter opportunity.

191. *In things indifferent.* Much more do actions barely lawful, because not forbidden, become unlawful when attended with any sort of scandal, if it was in our power to prevent it. Because though our neighbor may be unreasonable in taking occasion to sin from our innocent and indifferent actions; yet we are much more unreasonable, if knowingly and willfully, or even when there is but a probability of such a danger, we hazard our neighbor's soul, and consequently venture dishonoring and offending God, rather than forbear our own pleasure, or profit, it may be only our humor or diversion. Nor are we less guilty before God in offering the scandal, or in want of due care to avoid it, though our neighbor proves so wise, or so good, as not to *take*, or so happy as not to be *hurt* by it; the offense we intended or might have given being the same, though it happens to fall only on our own head.

192. *Of hindering our neighbor's salvation.* Ill principles, vicious inclinations, or carelessness and inadvertency, may exclude us from the kingdom of heaven as well as great and notorious sins. I do not say, that all sorts of ignorance or error, even in fundamental truths will ruin us, for such is the goodness of God that He does not take advantage of our invincible, or next to invincible, mistakes. But willful and indulged ignorance and error are certainly ruinous; and what degree of application, diligence, and caution is necessary to avoid this, is not easily determined. So that the principles of faith and practice, are not such a matter of indifferency as some would insinuate.[21] And since the kingdom of heaven is to be taken by violence; since the foolish virgins, and slothful servant,[22] whose negligence is the only fault we read of,

21. Astell likely has in mind the authors of *A Lady's Religion*, the *Letter concerning Church Communion*, and Locke's *Reasonableness of Christianity*.

22. foolish virgins, and slothful servant] Astell alludes to the cautionary tales of the five virgins who were unprepared to meet their husbands (Matthew 25:1–13), and the

were shut out, and cast into outer darkness, it is not to be doubted, but that we may lose our souls by want of diligence to save them. As for vicious inclinations indulged, or that pravity[23] of will which alienates us from the life of God, this without question excludes us from the enjoyment of Him. We may therefore become guilty of scandal, not only by a direct tempting our neighbor to sin, whereby we become accessory to all the evil effects that this temptation may produce; but also by contributing to his ill principles, vicious inclinations, or supine[24] carelessness any manner of way.

193. *Instances.* It will be necessary then for us to consider, how much of our neighbor's guilt we have to answer for? And how many souls we have exposed to ruin? By venting, or propagating, or by neglecting as much as we can in our several stations, to discourage and suppress atheistical, immoral, and unchristian principles. By our professions of religion, while we show little or nothing of the life and power of it in our conversation; or while amidst all our pretenses to it, we indulge ourselves in some flagrant sin. From whence our neighbors are tempted to conclude, that either all religion is a cheat, or else that it allows *some* transgressions upon *some* occasions; than which there can't be a greater reproach to the holiness of its author.

194. *Tempting him to sin.* How often have our discourses, and how much oftener have our practices degenerated from the purity and severity of the gospel, while the young and the unwary have been tempted to think, and say, and do, according to the pattern that their elders and betters have set them? How many times have we hazarded our neighbor's soul for the sake of our reputation, or estate, our party, or our pleasures, it may be for our sins? What shall we say for ourselves who make it a diversion to stir up in our neighbor any sort of passion? Either out of a foolish vanity and to gain admirers; or that we may have the malicious gratification of finding and triumphing over his weakness, and reducing his virtue to our own poor level; or else in pure spite to vex and torture that virtue we can't overcome. How often have we poured vinegar instead of balm into the wounded spirit, and by our insolence and oppression provoked him to curse us in the

---

unprofitable servant who buried his talent (Matthew 25:14–30).

23. pravity] depravity.

24. supine] inert or indolent.

bitterness of his soul, and to cry to his patron and avenger against us? How many of our diversions, if they are not directly sinful to *us*, but that our heads and hearts are strong enough to bear them, are at least infectious and dangerous to *our neighbors*, who are encouraged in the use of them by our example? Exciting a generous emulation, which the apostle calls "provoking to love and good works,"[25] has in it somewhat noble, and agreeable to the dignity of human nature; but vying in trifles and sins, alas! What is it but the very height of madness and folly?

195. *Several ways of doing it.* I would fain know what good or reasonable end, a woman can propose to herself by all the arts of coquetry? What can be the consequence, but her being at first the admiration, and in a little time the very scorn of fools? How many attacks have we made upon our neighbor's humility and meekness, fortitude, charity, and other virtues? Under pretense (forsooth!) of trying and exercising them, which is God's prerogative, and which we audaciously usurp; we, who neither know our neighbor's strength, nor are able to give him necessary assistance, and are therefore accountable for the damage he may suffer by such presumptuous trials. How many things have been said and done, for no better reason than to expose our neighbor, to lead him into error and folly, and for ought we know into sin, for nobody can tell where a temptation will stop? How little do we regard what jealousies and suspicions our censures, our talebearing and tattles[26] may cause? What a blot they may bring upon our neighbor's good name, and this shadow being gone, how it may tempt him to quit the substance;[27] or to what returns our ill usage may provoke him? What concern do we show for those animosities and feuds our foolish and inconsiderate, our selfish and indiscreet words and actions may create? Such as when we have made the best of them, we can only say, that they are not directly sinful, but which are of ill report, and therefore give just cause of censure, estrange the nearest relations, extinguish, or at least bring a coldness on Christian charity; and which considering our characters and circumstances, are neither

25. Heb 10:24.

26. tattles] gossip.

27. Once again, Astell alludes to Aesop's well-known saying: "Beware lest you lose the substance by grasping at the shadow."

honorable, nor decent in themselves, nor fit for us. Such as not only bring a reproach upon ourselves, but even a scandal and dishonor upon wisdom, virtue, and religion.

196. *A case of ill report.* For instance, nobody can say that generally speaking, it is unlawful for any woman to converse with any man, there may perhaps be some advantage in it, he may assist her in her worldly affairs, may improve her understanding, or be the guide of her soul. But yet, if either the privacy, or frequency, or any other circumstances attending this conversation, is of ill report, or gives occasion of scandal; either by affording those who will make an ill use of such an intimacy, a pretense to encourage themselves in it by her example; or by bringing a suspicion or blemish on her reputation, or any other way; she is obliged in conscience to remove the stumbling block, either by changing those circumstances which gave the scandal; or else by that which is much the best, because the only sure proof of *innocence*, by breaking off the conversation. For she can't well pretend any damage to her soul by this; her soul which is the *only* thing preferable to her reputation, and to be considered before the scandal: or if she makes this pretense, such a wild supposition gives too much reason to conclude, that the censure she suffers is just. If she gives her necessary support, or the prejudice she may suffer in her estate for the reason; besides that a woman of honor prefers an unspotted name before any of these considerations; she owes so much to herself and the world as to give it all the satisfaction in her power, by making this out clearly. And if she is resolved at all hazards to continue the conversation, she should at least converse so openly and in such an unsuspicious manner, as may excuse her in the judgment of all equitable persons, which is very possible, as censorious as the world is, unless she is so imprudent and obstinate, not to say so guilty, as to think to justify one error or folly by another.

197. *The consequences of our actions should be considered.* But where are they who consider all the consequences of an action, before they venture on it? Most of us think ourselves very good Christians if we do nothing that's plainly and directly sinful. For as to the evil effects of our actions, the dangers they may draw upon our own or our neighbor's soul, the scandal whether probable, or evident, we never regard it. But notwithstanding those most severe denunciations in

holy scripture against him "by whom the offense cometh," and that we are assured we shall one day find, it had been better to have parted with what was dearest to us, nay even to have had "a millstone hanged about our neck, and to have been drowned in the depth of the sea," than to have "offended" the "least" and most despicable person; we are forward to say with Cain, "am I my brother's keeper?"[28] What's that to *me* how others take *my* actions, am I accountable to every little body for *my* innocent liberties? Or shall I suffer them to set up to be *my* censors?

198. *Practice of the world contrary to the gospel.* To which I shall reply in the apostle's words, "now walkest thou not charitably: destroy not him with thy meat," your dress, your play, your company and conversation, your way of living—or whatever it be, that grieves him "for whom Christ died."[29] "But take heed, least by any means this liberty of yours become a stumbling block to them that are weak." "For when ye sin so against the brethren, and wound their weak consciences, ye sin against Christ."[30] So that whatever is the opinion of the world, or however wise and great it may seem in our eyes to follow our own humor, or to stand upon what we may call our own right, without any regard to our neighbor, sure I am, it is not Christian. Such an insensibility towards our brethren plainly shows, that we are not living members of the body of Christ, for "if one member suffer, all the rest suffer with it."[31] Nor is it at all agreeable to that strict charge our Lord lays upon us to avoid offenses; or to the direction and example of the charitable apostle, who tells us he would "neither eat flesh nor drink wine," that is, he would forbear the most innocent entertainments, nor would he do "anything," anything that might be omitted without sin, "whereby his brother stumbleth, or is offended, or is made weak."[32]

199. *Of doing good to the soul.* But our duty to our neighbors is not barely negative; it is not enough to do them no hurt, we must do them all the good we are able; as in all other instances so especially to their minds which are truly themselves. Therefore, besides taking

28. Mt 18:7; Lk 17:2; Gn 4:9.

29. Astell's marginal note: Rom 14:15, 21. [The apostle is St. Paul.]

30. Astell's marginal note: 1 Cor 8:9, 12, 13.

31. 1 Cor 12:26.

32. Rom 14:21. The "charitable apostle" is St. Paul.

care to give my neighbor no offense, I must do what in me lies to remove all the stumbling blocks which himself or others may have put in his way to heaven. This duty goes a great way where there is authority and power, such superiors being in great measure answerable for the faults of their inferiors. But I shall consider it no further than as it regards equals, which will also take in inferiors, who are to do the same thing in a manner becoming their station, and so far as they have opportunity, and see any probability of success. Indeed strictly speaking, they only are to be considered as inferiors, who are in subjection to the *authority* of others. For a mere inferiority in rank and worldly circumstances, does not, as some may imagine, take away a Christian equality. It is true, in relation to outward respect, and certain ceremonies that custom and order have introduced, there is a difference which ought to be observed. But yet for all this, the duties of Christians, except in that particular, are equal and reciprocal, and ought to be mutually received and paid (so far as they will bear, and with a due allowance for circumstances) as if there were no such difference. Otherwise a person of riches and title were very miserable, he would be a loser not a gainer by these admired advantages, did they set him above the Christian admonition and advice of those of a lower rank. Unless good sense and virtue increased proportionably to our wealth and honor, which is seldom if ever seen. On the contrary, we commonly find, that he who seemed to be endowed with wisdom and virtue in a low estate, loses both when he is advanced to a high one.

200. *Of Christian admonition.* As for Christian admonition, he best knows how to perform it, who can rightly adjust that divine command given by St. Paul to the Thessalonians, "study to be quiet and to do your own business";[33] with that moral precept given to the Jews, "thou shalt not hate thy brother in thy heart; thou shalt in any wise rebuke thy neighbor, and not suffer sin upon him";[34] which if obligatory to a Jew, is much more so to a Christian. Especially since our Lord has given us particular directions how to endeavor the offender's reformation in sins against ourselves, which are most like to breed ill blood in us, and make us regardless of our neighbor's good.[35]

33. Astell's marginal note: 1 Thes 4:11.

34. Astell's marginal note: Lv 19:17.

35. Astell's marginal note: Mt 18.

201. *How it differs from pragmaticalness.* But the misfortune is, in this as in most other points, we leave undone that which we ought to do, and we do that which ought not to be done. Thus, whenever we are pleased to admonish our neighbor, we take no notice of, or slightingly pass over, evident and indisputable sins, notorious errors, and such things as will certainly be his ruin, such as are offensive to God, or give scandal to the world; but all our zeal and charity (such as it is) is spent in teasing him about disputable points, to bring him over to our party; in censuring his innocent, perhaps commendable, or very often (all things considered) most laudable actions; and in carping at such things in his manners, as do not suit with our humors, nor conform to our models. So that we are not forward to admonish our neighbor of what will hurt him, which is *our business*, because an act of Christian charity; but we pertly correct him for what is displeasing to ourselves, though we can assign no good reason why it is so, and this is meddling with *his business*, and being very troublesome in it, instead of being quiet in our own.[36]

202. *And from inquisitiveness.* What a number do we find of those who are impertinently inquisitive into their neighbor's affairs, when they neither can nor will do them service; but how few who will give themselves any real concern for their neighbor's good? They will scarce endure to be informed of his necessity, unless to insult it, and to indulge a malicious pleasure; or that they may make use of this opportunity to enslave a mind as free as their own. It being too sure, that the greatest pretenders to liberty, are the people that use their evil endeavors to put the vilest chains upon their fellow Christians, while they clandestinely enslave their minds, which are the true seat of liberty. For to judge by the practice of the world, one would think that Christians had no belief of a future reward, there being few, very few, who do anything but what they suppose will turn to present account. We have no taste of the noble pleasure of doing good, nor do we regard its glorious recompense, so seldom is it that we dare refer ourselves to God, though He is the best paymaster!

---

36. Astell alludes once again to 1 Thes 4:11: "study to be quiet and to do your own business."

203. *Admonition makes the difference between a flatterer and a friend.*[37] It is to no purpose to say how the duty of Christian admonition ought to be performed, till people are convinced how it ought to be received. Were mankind as reasonable as they would be thought, I would recommend it upon the same motives that make all of us so fond of flattery. For the flatterer by giving us a little present and silly pleasure, ruins our merit which he seems to applaud. Whereas the faithful wounds of a Christian friend, do only let out our corruption in order to health and beauty. Helping us in reality to those good qualities which the other keeps us from obtaining, by falsely soothing us as if we were possessed of them. Self-love, which is often mistaken, is out in nothing more than in this business; for it is self-love that makes us fond of flattery, whereas if we considered at all, a true love to ourselves would make us abhor it. Nothing being surer, than that he who flatters us only means to *serve himself*; and that he who admonishes and reproves in a Christian manner, has no design but to do *us service*.

204. *How to be given.* It is very true, that an attempt to reform our neighbors ought not to be made, without some probability of success as well as a good intention. Otherwise, this professed zeal for others, will appear nothing else but our own odious pride; and a desire to show how much we are above them in prudence and virtue. We should not take upon us to direct or reprimand others, when we are in passion, and so not masters of ourselves. To correct in public, unless upon very extraordinary occasion, and with the utmost address, shows more of ostentation than kindness. And he who does it with bitterness and raillery, expresses his wit perhaps, or rather his spleen, but not his charity. To aggravate our brother's guilt by admonishing him at a time when he is not like to be better for it, does by adding to his weight sink our own souls. He who corrects in another what he is guilty of himself, who neglects "the beam in his own eye," to have a pull at "the mote in his brother's";[38] and who does not begin his reformation at home, will do no service to his neighbor, but only draw pity or contempt upon

---

37. Astell alludes to a popular theme of the time, epitomized in the Greek thinker Plutarch's highly influential essay "How to Know a Flatterer from a Friend," in his *Morals* (written in the first century). For a modern edition, see Plutarch, *Moralia: Volume I*, trans. Frank Cole Babbitt, Loeb Classical Library No. 197 (Cambridge, MA: Harvard University Press, 1927).

38. Mt 7:4. A "mote" is a tiny particle of dust.

himself. Human nature indeed is full of infirmities, and because we must in *anywise*,[39] without endeavoring to find excuses, and without fear of ill reception, rebuke our neighbor and not suffer sin upon him; and because it is most unseemly and unreasonable to reprove others when we ourselves are guilty, therefore we must for this among other reasons, study and strive to be as perfect as we can.

205. *And how taken.* But it is also true, that be the reprover ever so wise and good, though the admonition is performed with the greatest prudence, kindness, and address, unless the person who receives it understands his own good so well as to take it as he ought, it will not be effectual. How it is to be taken is not hard to learn, for he who truly thirsts after perfection, will be glad of any sort of help, though not always the best, in order to it. He will not discourage, but thank that faithful heart, which neglects its own temporal interests to do him service. Though he should discover more pride, or passion, or malice, than goodwill, he will however make the best of everyone's observation, and know how to use it, though it be not to the admonisher's purpose. And though he may be free from the fault he is charged with, the accusation will at least admonish him, that he has not taken due care to be clear of the appearance.

206. *Of Christian friendship.* Indeed next to the grace of God, and His giving us good sense of our own, together with health and quiet to make use of it, there's not any blessing comparable to this of a prudent and honest adviser. Friend I should say, if I followed my own sense, but I submit to the usage of the world, since we certainly lose what people call their friendship, by presuming to tell them the truth, though ever so kindly and modestly. Yet if there be any such thing as particular friendship under the gospel, which makes us friends to the whole human race, and more especially to the body of Christ, so far as power and opportunity allow; I take friendship to consist in advising, admonishing, and reproving as there is occasion, and in watching over each other's souls for their mutual good.

207. *Wherein it differs from general charity.* Not but that one would serve their friend to the utmost in temporal affairs. If we had two coats we should give one to the friend who wanted it, for so a Christian ought to do to any other Christian whosoever. We would

39. *anywise*] any manner.

not only abridge ourselves of superfluities, to provide for the decent conveniencies of a friend, but even of necessaries, to relieve his greater necessities; for this is no more than what all Christians ought to do for one another. Nay, a truly charitable mind will cast its two mites[40] into the treasury, even though they be all our living.[41] We should not scruple to lay down our very lives for our friend, for this must be done for our Christian brethren, when it can be instrumental to the salvation of a soul, when it can glorify God and edify His church. What remains then to be done for a friend in particular? Nothing that I know of, but to prefer him in our charity, because we are best acquainted with his affairs; and, which is the greatest of all charities, to watch over his soul, and to promote his perfection to the utmost.

208. *How to be expressed.* This indeed is to be done to all mankind so far as we can, as has been shown above, but it will not be done to any great purpose, except where we have an intimate acquaintance and particular endearments. The constant and shining light of a bright example; magnanimously asserting the cause of God and religion in the midst of a crooked and perverse generation;[42] a prudent and gentle insinuation of something useful in conversation; an undaunted and impartial correction of vice where we are superiors; a frank condemning it where we are equals; and the expressing some way or other a modest dislike even where we are inferiors; is all that can be done in the common course of the world, and in general conversation. But we must go further with our friends; be "instant in season," and, as they may think, "out of season";[43] their dislike should not restrain, nor ill success discourage us from such endeavors as may possibly do them good. We should watch all opportunities, attack all avenues, call in all assistances to serve them in their most important interest. To prevent not only their being guilty of a sin, but to secure them from a folly, from the approaches, the very appearance of evil, the remotest dangers and inconveniencies, and to preserve their reputation as well as their innocence. Nor should anything blunt the edge of our charity, but the impossibility of doing service. And if after all our "labor of

---

40. mites] small coins.

41. Mk 12:42.

42. The words "in the midst of a crooked and perverse generation" are not in the first edition.

43. 2 Tm 4:2.

love" the harvest is nothing but hatred for our tenderest goodwill, as we may make "some mourning," though not much, for a dead friend, so we may be allowed to weep bitterly for those who "are dead whilst they live"; to mourn for the "fools" and the sinners "all the days of their life," since "the life of the sinner is worse than death."[44]

209. *False friendship.* I could never understand the meaning of some who call themselves our friends, to be sure I could never comply with them, when they expect to be followed right or wrong in their principles, party, and passions, looking for a blind approbation, or if they are more refined, an artful pretense of being convinced of the reasonableness of all they propose. Who with all their semblance of humility, are so nice and tender, as not to be able to bear the truth that wounds, and which for this reason ought above all others to be considered. Who will never endure you, if you presume to spy a fault, though with the kindest intention, and only in order to mend it. Who will not be helped to be in reality, those excellent persons which everyone must wish to be; but who would be flattered as if they were so already, when alas they are nothing like it. They would be thought wise, and yet by "hating reproof" prove themselves "brutish";[45] are above human nature as they imagine, for they must not be supposed liable to mistakes or infirmities, or obnoxious to the dangers that have undone their neighbors; though at the same time, they are sinking under follies that very indifferent persons would scorn to be guilty of. People who fancy that the little, unseasonable, the awkward and disdainful good offices, they do one (if I may call them good) such as a generous mind would blush to offer a stranger, much less a friend, ties one to them as their slave; not considering that they who do good to the mind are the noblest benefactors.

210. *Beneficence the genius of the gospel.* Indeed, beneficence and goodwill to mankind, even to those who hate us without a cause, are the very spirit and genius of the gospel. Our glorious lawgiver when He conversed among us, "going about doing good, leaving us an example that we should follow His steps,"[46] who though He was perfectly innocent, and therefore most unjustly persecuted, yet "being

44. 1 Thes 1:3; 1 Tm 5:6; Ecclus 22:11–12.

45. Astell's marginal note: Prv 12:1.

46. 1 Pt 2:21.

reviled, He reviled not again, when He suffered He threatened not, but committed Himself and *His cause* to Him who judgeth righteously."[47] It being very plain to everyone who reads the New Testament with an honest heart, that the gospel is to be spread and maintained only by those divine characters it bears. By the excellency of its doctrine, the holy lives of its professors, their generous and unwearied doing of good, and their meek and heroic patience in suffering evil. Thus was it diffused over the face of the earth at its first appearance, nor can it be secured and conveyed to posterity but by the same methods. What defenses may be used to secure our civil properties is another question, but it is certain, that prayers and tears, strong arguments, holy and peaceable lives, the strictest obedience to God, and to all who are in authority under Him, are the only lawful ways of defending our religion; which, thanks be to God we can't be deprived of but by our own fault, it is out of the reach of the greatest tyrant.

211. *Christianity triumphs over persecution.* To say that religion won't suffer us to be "persecutors,"[48] is but a poor and lame account of it, for it enables us to triumph over the rage and power of the most violent persecutors; and where it possesses the heart, preserves us from being either ashamed or afraid of the cross of Christ. So far from this, that it disposes us to "count it all joy,"[49] even the very height of good fortune, when we are called to bear witness to the truth, and to follow "the captain of our salvation," even to the death, since we are "one" with Him; and cannot "be brought unto glory" but by following His steps who was "made perfect through sufferings."[50]

212. *Of quarrels and law.* But if we must not quarrel with our neighbors about religion, that being no fit way to defend the truth, or to convince them of their errors, what is there else worth contending for? St. Paul in a case he speaks of, requires the Corinthians "to take wrong, and to suffer themselves to be defrauded, rather than go to law."[51] One can't say indeed, that all appeals to the sword between nation and nation, or to civil justice between private persons

47. 1 Pt 2:23.

48. Astell's marginal note (first edition only): *Lady's Religion*, 17.

49. Astell's marginal note: Jas 1:2, and so on.

50. Astell's marginal note: Heb 2:10–11.

51. 1 Cor 6:7.

are unchristian, neither of these being absolutely condemned in holy scripture, only some undue circumstances attending them are censured. However, it is evident, that Christians are not to be of a vindictive spirit in any measure; those divine commands that we "resist not evil," and that we "turn the cheek," and so on, having for certain *some* meaning.[52] And how low so ever we reduce it, they can't import less, than that "as much as lies in us, we should live peaceably with all men."[53] That we should prefer Christian charity and peace before all the goods of this present life; and that if after all our forbearance and condescensions, men will needs be our enemies, we are not to think that this gives us any allowance to be theirs.

213. *Christian retaliation what.* Love is all the retaliation our religion allows us; by which esteem can't be meant, since it is neither reasonable nor possible, to esteem anyone for being wicked and injurious. But we are to "do good to them who hate us," as our Lord enjoins, and according to St. Paul's comment, for this very reason because they hate us.[54] And why should we scruple to return good words for evil, hearty prayers for bitter and unjust reproaches, since there are few present pleasures comparable to this of overcoming evil with good? But how transporting will be the joy, when meeting with our enemies in heaven hereafter, they shall be sensible that their admission is in some measure owing to our importunate intercessions for them, even while they persecuted us as Saul did Stephen, with the most implacable and deadly malice. And that how much so ever they have sought our ruin, we have been more industrious in seeking their salvation. This will be no doubt a sweet revenge, but I know not after what fashion those minds are turned that can relish revenge in any other instance.

214. *Vengeance is God's.* For though some may fancy that the command to forgive offenses is a hard precept; upon a just view of the matter it appears, that God has been very gracious to us in reserving vengeance in His own hand. For were it left in ours, we should dart[55] it on our best friends, there being none that we hate more implacably,

52. Astell's marginal note: Mt 5:39.

53. Astell's marginal note: Rom 12:18.

54. Mt 5:44; Lk 6:27.

55. dart] inflict.

than those who have been so honest and so kind as to tell us the truth. Truths which are so much the more necessary, by how much we are the more unwilling to hear them. Truths which will some time or other be cleared up to us for our punishment, if we will not now consider them to our advantage. For nobody does a wicked or foolish action, but sooner or later it recoils upon them; they are lashed with the reproaches of their own minds, and bitterly pursued with the anguish of their folly.

215. *Christian charity very different from what is commonly practiced.* Is there anything more strictly enjoined in the gospel, or more loosely practiced by us who call ourselves Christians, than mutual forbearance and forgiveness? We are so far from forgiving real and great offenses, which yet we are obliged to, as we hope for remission of our own sins, that we retain our resentments for the most trifling and imaginary offense; nay, even for those real good offices which we are pleased to misconstrue injuries. We say we are in charity, and then we think we have done a mighty matter; but this saying is all; our charity never shows itself by its genuine fruits, it has none of those properties by which it is described in the gospel.

216. *God's forgiveness our pattern.* Were our enemy as we call him, low and groveling at our feet, it is like we might with a scornful and supercilious, or perhaps with a pitying air, afford him a scanty relief; such as might upbraid his wants,[56] or display our own generosity, for a little matter will do this nowadays. But we never forgive as God does, though God's charity is proposed as the pattern of ours. We do not wait and long to be gracious; we don't offer reconciliation, but rather fright people from it by our haughty and inhuman usage; and who is there that pursues the offender with the most engaging instances of a noble beneficence?

217. *But we do nothing like it.* We would not cut our neighbor's throat it's true, and this perhaps for fear of our own, but we do all we can to grieve him; we murder his reputation, betray his confidence, misrepresent all he says and does, it may be we slander and revile him. Not the ingenuous acknowledgment of a fault, or of what has been falsely taken for one, can remove the rancor of our hearts, though for fashion's sake it may smooth our brow. Our hatred is rather increased

56. upbraid his wants] insult his needs.

by it, for we can't endure to find our neighbor's charity so much greater than our own. And be the reparation ever so generous and full, it never restores the real or supposed offender to the favor lost, as it certainly ought, if not to greater. For he who can so far overcome the pride of human nature as to ask pardon and make satisfaction, who can submit to anything for the sake of charity and peace, gives such real proofs of a Christian temper, that supposing the rest of his life is any way agreeable to this part of it, we should be highly injurious as well as uncharitable, did we doubt the sincerity of his heart, or refuse to reinstate him in our favor. For this is God's way of forgiving us, and nothing can excuse us from imitating it towards our neighbor, but only our just and reasonable fears of his want of penitence and sincerity.

218. *Virtue reckoned the most unpardonable injury.* But if such a reconciliation ought to attend a real repentance for the greatest injuries, and sure we can neither read the holy scripture, nor say our daily prayers, but we must be sensible that it ought! Shall we pretend to be Christians when we continue our distances and coldnesses, not upon the score of real injuries, but it may be for the highest services; such as are too great to be returned, and therefore as we fancy, not fit to be acknowledged! Services which are not the less though they happen not to be attended with desired success; for the most generous and best concerted designs, are not always the most successful. A mind so large as to form a noble undertaking, being usually too great to stoop to those little and base ways, which as the world goes are the only method of succeeding. It may be it is ignorant of them, which yet is no blemish; or if it knows, yet it disdains to use them. Indeed to act thus nobly is the certain way not to be forgiven, they who hate us for our virtues being our most irreconcilable enemies. Could they deprive us of this crown and glory, it is like we might be very dear to them; but though we would readily give up any other pretension, this is a price we cannot, we must not pay to purchase their favor.

219. *Of doing as we would be done by.* After what has been said, it does not seem necessary to insist on those particular wrongs which Christianity restrains us from offering to our neighbors, or the good offices it obliges us to do them. For if I must make no returns to the greatest injury, by a stronger reason I must not offer the least, nor be

ashamed to make restitution for any I have been guilty of. I must not so much as censure, or judge, or despise my neighbor. For though I may reckon this wit, or by whatever other plausible[57] name I may call it, when done to others, I look upon it as a great injury when offered to myself. If I must do all the good in my power to my most inveterate enemies, much rather to my acquaintance, relations, and friends. And as the *Lady's Religion* well observes, by consulting our own reason we know when we are well or ill used;[58] so that a moderate share of sense with any degree of honesty, will instruct us how we ought to treat others, by showing us how we desire to be treated ourselves.

220. *The springs of injuriousness.* And that I may effectually perform my duty to my neighbor, I endeavor to dry up the springs from whence all injuriousness, whether positive or negative proceeds. Such are fondness for the world and the things thereof, envy and pride, of all which already, only pride in this branch of it has not been so much insisted on. I therefore add, that our ill usage of our fellow mortals often proceeds from our looking down on these our brethren, as creatures of a different species from ourselves, so much beneath us that it matters not how we treat them.

221. *No great inequality among mankind.* Now allowing there is some difference, there can be no great one, since our neighbor is a member of Christ, and a child of God, as well as ourselves. God is no respecter of persons whatever we are;[59] He made us all to be happy, and never intended that some should riot[60] in luxury while others starve with want; that some should be sick even with ease and plenty, while others are overburdened with sorrow and care. But having made us rational and free, he would have us reduce this inequality, and supply the seeming defects that providence has left for the exercise of our virtue. So that those talents of any kind whereby we differ from our neighbor, and which we are apt to look on as great prerogatives and distinctions, are indeed only trusts, for which we are highly accountable if we misemploy them.

57. This word is not in the first edition.

58. *Lady's Religion*: "by consulting your own reason, you know wherein you are justly dealt with, and wherein you receive wrong; when you are kindly used, and when otherwise" (16).

59. Acts 10:34.

60. riot] indulge.

222. *Talents matter of fear rather than of pride.* Perhaps I have five talents,[61] and my neighbor has but two, how do I know but he doubles his talents, whereas I do not make any increase, or but a very small one of mine, he then is by much the better person, and shall have the greater reward. And it generally happens, that the rich and the great stand in much more need of the good poor man's charity and assistance, than he does of theirs. For all that he wants from them is a little food and raiment,[62] whereas they need his help to remove their ignorance, and to cure the raging distempers of their mind. If he will not flatter them to their ruin, and dares tell them the truth, he is indeed the benefactor; nor is it worthwhile for a person of sense and virtue to lose his time among the luxuries and follies of a great fortune, unless he is allowed to observe what's amiss, and to use his honest and prudent endeavors to reform it: for otherwise he could spend his time, both with more profit and more pleasure in the closest retirement.

223. *Humanity and charity our common interest.* In fine, our common interest might teach us to be humane, condescending, and courteous; "to be kindly affectioned one towards another with brotherly love, in honor preferring one another";[63] and not to show all the "respect to him who wears the gay clothing," whereby we become "partial, and judges of evil thoughts," that is, false reasoners;[64] humanity would teach us this, though the gospel had been silent, instead of saying so much, and taking away as it has in good measure all those petty differences, by making us members of one body. So that the most honorable can't say to the less, "we have no need of you," but all of them "should have the same care one for another": for "whether one member suffer all the members suffer with it, or one member be honored all the members rejoice with it."[65]

---

61. talents] ancient units of currency.

62. raiment] clothing.

63. Astell's marginal note: Rom 12:10.

64. Astell's marginal note: Jas 2:3–4.

65. Astell's marginal note: 1 Cor 12:18, 25–26.

Section IV

Of our duty to ourselves[1]

224. *Wherein it consists.* As for the remaining duties, those which we owe to ourselves, one would think that the great fondness we have for ourselves, should keep us mindful of them: but this like all other fondness, is usually wrong expressed. To speak as a mere natural person, our duty to ourselves consists in making the best use of our talents, and hereby aspiring to the highest degree of happiness and perfection of which we are capable. But considering it as a Christian, I place it in doing nothing that misbecomes the relation we bear to Christ as members of His body, and in living suitably to so high a dignity. Thus the sacred text requires us to reverence ourselves; to "glorify God in our bodies and in our spirits which are His"; to "honor Him with our substance," and in everything that is ours.[2] And this upon the matter is all one with what we naturally owe to ourselves; for to be a member of Christ is the very best thing we can be; and by living up to this honor, and by this only, we attain the greatest happiness and the highest perfection of our nature.

225. *Knowledge of ourselves and the world.* Now in order to this we must know ourselves, be acquainted with the weaknesses and the excellencies of human nature, that we may provide against the one and improve the other. We must also understand the true value and use of all that we possess, that so we may esteem and employ it as we ought. For if we know ourselves, we shall know what is our true good, and knowing it we shall pursue it. Because everyone pursues that which seems to them for the present, to conduce to their happiness: nor will they be so senseless as to seek for happiness where they know it is not to be found.

---

1. In accordance with modern style, I have changed all references to "our selves" (two words) to "ourselves" (one word) in the following passages. But the reader should keep in mind that Astell typically regards the self as the immaterial soul, and so "our duty to ourselves" strictly speaking means "our duty to our souls."

2. 1 Cor 6:20; Prv 3:9.

226. *Our immortality.*[3] Not to enter into a physical disquisition of our nature, which though much better performed than I can pretend, must be very imperfect, since we have no idea of the noblest part of us;[4] I shall only consider it with regard to religion, but this will lead me to enquire whether or not the mind is immaterial. Because they who deny it to be so, deny its natural immortality, which is one of its greatest and most distinguishing excellencies, leaving it only a positive and arbitrary immortality,[5] which is no more that what a stock[6] or a stone may have if God thinks fit. And hereby they leave us no way to prove our immortality, to those who don't admit the authority of the holy scripture; and by consequence, they render natural as well as revealed religion a matter of no concern to such persons, by destroying the motive and reason of their enquiry after it. For though no reasonable person can doubt that there is a God, His existence is of no great importance to us if there be no future state, and if we must continue no longer than this short, present life. Whereas if we are of an immortal nature, it is of the highest consequence to provide for a happy eternity, by knowing and doing the will of our maker.

3. In the following six subsections, Astell's argument closely follows the logic and language of John Norris's Cartesian-style argument for the real distinction of mind and body in *An Essay Towards the Theory of the Ideal or Intelligible World. Being the Relative Part of it. Wherein the Intelligible World is considered with relation to Human Understanding. Whereof some Account is here attempted and proposed. Part II* (1704), in Norris, *Philosophical and Theological Writings*, 7:1–57. Norris's argument is Cartesian in the sense that, like Descartes in the Sixth Meditation of his *Meditations*, he draws on the conceivability of the mind's existing apart from the body in order to ground his conclusion that the mind is distinct from the body.

4. The "noblest part of us," according to Astell, is the soul or mind. Here she endorses the Malebranchean view that we can have no clear and distinct idea of our souls, a notion discussed in her correspondence with Norris. In one letter, Astell says, "I do confess to you ingenuously that I have no clear idea of that which is properly the self" (Astell and Norris, *Letters*, 88). Norris agrees that "We do not know our souls here by an idea of them ... but only a consciousness or interior sentiment" (94). He then provides Astell with a translation of relevant passages about the soul in Nicolas Malebranche's *Méditations chrétiennes et métaphysiques (Christian and Metaphysical Meditations)* of 1683.

5. a positive and arbitrary immortality] an immortality bestowed by the positive command and arbitrary will of God.

6. stock] block of wood.

227. *What renders a being naturally immortal.* Immaterial being opposed to material, that is, to extension, or body (which words I mean to use promiscuously[7] as different expressions of the same idea)[8] and consequently an immaterial nature being that which has no parts, and which is therefore indivisible; it is in itself incorruptible and permanent, or in another word, immortal. Because, though this system of bones, flesh, and skin, and so on, which I call my body, shall within this threescore years;[9] and this wood which is now upon the fire, shall in an hour or two; and all other material beings shall in their proper seasons be no more; yet not the least particle of body does totally perish. Not but that He who made all things out of nothing, can as easily reduce them to nothing; but because it does not consist with the wisdom and majesty of the great creator to annihilate His works. For He does nothing in vain, and can't be supposed to make a creature with a design to destroy or unmake it. So that a being is mortal and corruptible, or ceases to be, when those parts of which it consists, and whose particular composition and figure, which denominate it *this* or *that* being, and which distinguish it from all other beings, are no longer thus or thus united, but ceasing to appear under their first texture and figure, are therefore very properly said to be no more.

228. *Indivisibility.* Hence it follows, that a being which is uncompounded, which has no parts, and which is therefore incapable of division and dissolution, is in its own nature incorruptible, it must always be the same individual being, and can never cease to be. For because it is uncompounded and indivisible, it can't be destroyed from any principle in itself, nor indeed from any outward force whatsoever, its creator only excepted; who, as He gave it being, has power to resume this being, if He thinks fit.[10] But then, from the reason already

---

7. promiscuously] indiscriminately.

8. Astell subscribes to the Cartesian idea of matter or body as pure extension (that is, substance geometrically extended in length, breadth, and depth). Descartes's argument for the view that the essence of matter is extension can be found in the Second and Fifth Meditations of his *Meditations*. This view amounts to the idea that material things are in themselves incapable of life, perception, and self-motion.

9. threescore years] sixty (or, three times twenty) years.

10. Astell's marginal note (second edition only): See Mr Boyle's *Christian Vertuoso*, 23, 24, and his *Excellency of Theology*, 57. [Astell refers to Robert Boyle, *The Christian Virtuoso:*

mentioned, it appears, that He will not annihilate it; so that the mutations which creatures are subject to, arise only from the division and
change of the several parts of which they are composed. It also follows,
that whatever is in its own nature incorruptible, can be so for no other
reason because it is indivisible and has no parts. The change and dissolution of the parts, being the only reason why a being is corruptible
and ceases to be. If then the mind be immaterial, it must in its own
nature be immortal, and this comes now to be examined.

229. *Mind and body of different natures.* That we all *think*, needs
no proof; and that body can't think, appears not only from the incongruity between thought and extension, and even from the confession of those who while they contend that God *can* endue body with
thought, do also allow that thought "is not in the essence" of body;[11]
whereby they acknowledge, that no reason can be given why body
should think, and that all they have to say, is barely that it is not impossible: but it likewise appears, because, having no way to judge of
things but by their ideas, or to distinguish *this* from *that*, but by the
distinction and difference of ideas; therefore when two complete ideas
(as complete is opposed to abstraction, or a partial consideration of an
idea)[12] have different properties and affections, and can be considered

---

*Shewing, That by being addicted to Experimental Philosophy, a Man is rather Assisted, than
Indisposed, to be a Good Christian. The First Part* (London: Edw. Jones for John Taylor
and John Wyat, 1690): "the rational soul ... being an immaterial spirit, and consequently
a substance not really divisible, can have no parts expelled or transposed, and so being
exempted from the physical causes of corruption that destroys bodies, she ought always
to last. ... unless it please God to annihilate her; which we have no reason to suppose he
will do" (23–24). See also Robert Boyle, *The Excellency of Theology, Compared with Natural
Philosophy (as both are Objects of Men's Study) Discoursed of In a Letter to a Friend* (London:
T.N. for Henry Herringman, 1674), 57–58. For modern editions, see *The Works of Robert
Boyle*, ed. Michael Hunter and Edward B. Davis, 14 vols. (London: Pickering and Chatto,
2000), 8:34–35 and 11:298. Hereafter I give page references to these modern editions in
square brackets following Astell's original references.]

11. See Locke, *Third Letter*, 397. The emphasis and quotation marks in the main text are
not in the first edition of Astell's *Christian Religion*. In his *Theory of the Ideal World, Part II*,
Norris likewise points out that Locke "exalts the power of God so far as to be able to endue
matter *with* thought," and yet Locke also expressly owns "that thought is not included in the
essence of matter" (Norris, *Philosophical and Theological Writings*, 7:34, 47).

12. In his *Theory of the Ideal World, Part II*, Norris likewise states that "if the ideas are
adequate and complete, and not made distinct only by abstraction and partial consideration,

without any relation to, or dependence on each other, so that we can be sure of the existence of the one, even at the same time we can suppose that the other does not exist, as is indeed the case of a thinking and of an extended being, or of mind and body; here these two ideas, and consequently the things they represent, are truly distinct and of different natures. Now, to be distinct from a thing, is all one as not to be this thing, so that since thought and extension are distinct and different in their own natures, as we have seen, it is evident that a thinking being as such, excludes extension; and an extended being excludes thought. The one is not, cannot be, extended, nor does, or can the other think, any more than a circle can have the properties of a triangle, or a triangle those of a circle.[13]

230. *What is immaterial, is naturally immortal.* For there can't be anything in a being, or at least not anything that we can judge of, or discourse about, but what is contained in the idea of this being. But thought is not contained in the idea of body, the ideas of thought and of extension being as different as the ideas of a triangle and a circle, and those are as little capable of the properties of each other as these are. Therefore body can't think, and because I and all other reasonable creatures think, therefore we are something that is not body. Now all beings whatsoever, are either material or immaterial; therefore since that which thinks is not material, it must be immaterial; and for this reason it is not liable to separation of parts or corruption, as all material beings are; consequently the human mind is in its own nature immortal, as was to be proved.

231. *Body cannot think.* Again, if body can think, then thought must be either the essence, or the mode of body; or in the plainest words, either the thing itself, or its way and manner of being. But though some may dispute (how reasonably I am not now to enquire)

then the things themselves are also really distinct, and we may securely say, that one of them is not the other" (Norris, *Philosophical and Theological Writings*, 7:19).

13. This passage resembles Norris, *Theory of the Ideal World, Part II*: "to suppose thought to be contained in the idea of matter, notwithstanding this ideal diversity between a thinking and an extended being, would be all one as if you should suppose that a circle should have the property of a triangle" (Norris, *Philosophical and Theological Writings*, 7:47).

whether extension be the essence of body,[14] none will pretend that thought is its essence. It remains then, that if body can think, thought must be in it as a mode. But modes do immediately depend upon, and are inseparable from the thing whose modes they are, existing no otherwise but in it. Therefore, if thought be a mode of body, besides all other absurdities, it will follow, that God is an extended being or a body, otherwise upon this supposition He could not think. Unless you make thought to be a mode of both body and of mind, which to me seems a contradiction. Because body and mind, or material and immaterial being directly opposite, and in their own natures inconsistent; to say that the mode of the one may be the mode of the other, amounts to as much as to say, that a thing may be and may not be, at the same time. But we are sure, that God who is all perfection thinks, and that though He be immense and omnipresent, in a way to us incomprehensible, yet He is not extended.[15] For to be extended, and for this reason divisible, at least mentally,[16] is a great imperfection, and not consistent with His eternity. And since the first intelligence, the father of spirits, is not, cannot be extended, this is a strong presumption at least, if it is not a proof, that body is incapable of thought, and that creatures formed after His own image are immaterial, and consequently in their own nature, and not barely by positive institution, immortal. May we not then conclude, that it is as improper and absurd to say, that body is *capable* of thought, as it is to talk of the dimensions of a thought, or of the figure of a thinking being? Or to say that thought can be extended in a strict and proper sense?[17]

232. *Of the weakness and imperfection of human nature.* Having thus considered the bright side of human nature, the immaterial and immortal mind, created in the image of God, and made to contemplate

14. A number of seventeenth-century philosophers challenge the idea that extension is the essence of body. Henry More defines body as essentially passive, divisible, and impenetrable (he allows that extension is a property of both material and immaterial substances), and Locke defines body as "solid extension" but denies that we can have an idea of its real essence.

15. The words "though He be immense and omnipresent, in a way to us incomprehensible, yet" are not in the first edition.

16. The qualification "at least mentally" is not in the first edition.

17. Astell's marginal note (second edition only): See the appendix. [In the first edition, this paragraph is followed by §§386–93 of the present volume.]

and love Him to all eternity; let us now turn our eyes to our weaknesses and imperfections. And alas! They are so many and so great, that the mortifying thoughts they give us, is perhaps the reason why we care so little for this prospect. To find our views so short! Our attention so unsteady! Our resolutions so imperfect, so vain! Our prepossessions and prejudices so inveterate! The bias that education and custom, example and authority have put on our minds so strong! The deep impressions that sensible objects have made upon our imaginations so hard to be wrought off! So lively and affecting, as to disturb us in our closest retirements, and most serious contemplations, raising our passions, and hurrying us in defiance of reason, into wild disorders! The power that the pleasures and pains of sensation have over us, and how little we are affected with such as are spiritual and eternal! Miseries of nature that the most holy persons groan under; to say nothing of the defilements of the wicked and profane. The best of us seldom going further than the government of our words and actions, and this God knows very imperfectly; whereby we only avoid the shame our folly would expose us to in the sight of the world: while the great and holy God, our lord and judge, beholds our shameful disorder and dishonor! And yet alas! What avails it to make a fair appearance before our fellow mortals, since all our passions and every irregular motion of the will is manifest in the sight of God! And He whom we love, and to whom we desire to approve ourselves, knows all our deformities, not a wicked or vain thought being hid from Him!

233. How seldom do we judge conformably to God's judgment, or will as He wills! We can't see but in His light, and yet how much oftener do we consult our own darkness! How rarely do we turn the eyes of our mind towards Him! We are unable to do anything that's good but by His grace, and yet how little do we attend its dispensations, how often do we neglect or resist its motions! We forget God our savior who has done so great things for us; and behave ourselves towards our God, our maker, and sovereign lord on whom we entirely depend, as we would blush to demean ourselves towards an earthly superior. Our God who waits to be gracious, even while we despise the good He offers us! Horrible folly and ingratitude, who can without confusion reflect on it!

234. *Our dependence on God, a great benefit.* But as our weaknesses and wants perpetually remind us that we are poor, dependent beings; *creatures*, whose very nature and existence as such, supposes entire dependence; so they ought to teach us to depend in the right place: it being our privilege and felicity to depend upon God, and upon Him only. For hereby we are out of the reach of the malice of men and devils, who may put us to some small inconveniencies, may unhouse us it's true, by dissolving the union between mind and body; but this is only to send us to a better habitation, "a house not made with hands, eternal in the heavens."[18] God *will not* hurt us, and therefore nothing but our own perverseness *can.*

235. *Our danger from ourselves.* Our danger then is from ourselves, from the ignorance of our *own* weakness, errors, and sins; from depending on our *own* strength, or on any creature, and forgetting God our *only* support, by whose grace *alone* we stand. The world is full of temptations, we are taught to pray against them every day; but they who distrust themselves and put all their confidence in God; who watch diligently over their own infirmities; who humbly and heartily implore His grace and diligently use it, shall not be hurt by those temptations. They shall be enabled to "do all things through Christ who strengthens them";[19] "He who is in" them being "greater than he who is in the world," and therefore if they are not wanting to themselves, they shall be strong enough to overcome it.[20]

236. *We should live up to our dignity.* It is in this confidence that we aspire after perfection; for though we are nothing in ourselves, yet so long as we are conformable to the will of God, and living members of His son, this relation makes us valuable creatures, who both may and ought to have a generous disdain of such things as are beneath us. "How shall I do this great wickedness?"[21] Dishonor myself by breach of trust, ingratitude, and pollution, as well as "sin against God?" said a chaste and holy patriarch.[22] "Shall such a man as I flee?" was no vain

---

18. 2 Cor 5:1.

19. Phil 4:13.

20. 1 Jn 4:4.

21. Astell's marginal note: Gn 39[:9].

22. Joseph in Gn 39:9.

rant, but the just and noble sentiment of a truly great person.[23] And as there is not anything more conducive to our safety, than a constant sense of our weakness and danger, the grace of God always supposed, without which we can neither do any good nor escape any evil: so there is not a stronger inducement to avoid the shame of sin, and to aspire to the perfection of holiness, than a due sense of our dignity as rational creatures, and especially as members of Christ; and of the great and glorious things for which we were created, and of which we are at present capable, through the grace of God and the merits of our redeemer.

237. *Reverence ourselves.* That esteem of human nature, that reverence of ourselves, or rather of the holy spirit of God who dwells in us, which makes us abhor and disdain a vile action, and which spurs us on to the highest attainments, keeping us jealous lest by any means we fall short of them, is one of the most necessary points of wisdom. Though this is plainly what some people mean by pride, when they accuse their neighbor of this sin, not for pretending to any good quality that he has not; or for arrogating to himself, instead of ascribing to God, the glory of what he has. But for laboring to be in reality as good as he can be; for doing what the scripture commands, "coveting earnestly the best gifts";[24] and if this is to be proud, I pray God give us all such a pride as this!

238. *What is beneath us.* It is then our duty to be sensible of our quality, our high alliance even with the king of kings, and noble hopes, the birthright of every the meanest Christian, and to be careful to do nothing that misbecomes us. For if we forget to reverence ourselves, it will not be long before we make as little reckoning of our duty to our neighbors and even to God Himself. A thing may misbecome us either as it is beneath the dignity of our Christian calling, or of human nature in general: or else as it is unsuitable to our character and station in the world, and for this reason, not expedient, nor of good report, and therefore not fit *for us*; though otherwise, and absolutely considered, it might be innocent. This last case shall be taken notice of, when I come to speak of reputation and the circumstances of our actions; at present let it be remembered, that sin, in every instance, or

23. Astell's marginal note: Neh 6:11.

24. Astell's marginal note: 1 Cor 12:33. [The reference should be 1 Cor 12:31.]

whatever may be the fruit of it, even though an empire should be its present income, is dishonorable and base. Every sin being infamous in the sight of God, the true judge of honor, though men have not fixed such a note of infamy upon it, as every civilized nation has upon all sorts of pollutions and dishonesty, lying, breach of faith, and breach of trust; which make us not only to be abhorred of God, but even odious to mankind.

239. *Instances.* As for the flatterer and detractor, everyone professes to detest them, but all of us are fond of the flattery and detraction. Pride is abominable in others, and we believe we see it, both where it is, and where it is not, but who discerns it in himself? Covetousness is a sordid uncreditable[25] vice, and yet we are all slaves to wealth, and he who despises it, is reckoned a vain pretender or a fool. To break a man's house is ignominious, but who thinks it so to ruin his innocent family by gaming; or to seize upon his estate by form of law, though ever so unjustly? There are a sort of men indeed who pretend to moral honesty as they call it, and—wondrous humanity!—who would boggle at this injustice, if you will believe them. But they make no scruple to offer a woman the most irreparable injury, to ruin her virtue, honor, and soul, and to glory in it! He who takes your purse upon the highway, how great so ever his necessities may be, must die for it as a villain; while he who out of wanton ambition robs his neighbor of a territory, or crown, shall be applauded as a hero! To put up the lie[26] is scandalous, even though it be our due; but to carry on a holy cheat for the support of a good cause, or what we resolve to call so; to pursue our designs, by the most tricking and disingenuous methods, especially if they are successful, is a meritorious action! To suffer like a Christian, and to receive the glorious crown of martyrdom for so doing, in some men's reckoning is a slavish tameness; but to die in a silly quarrel, with a sword at his brother's breast, is like a man of honor! So equitable is mankind! But God determines by juster measures.

240. *Dissimulation.* The "knowledge of the world," as we call it, that is, the skill to disguise our own tempers and designs, and to accommodate ourselves to others in such a manner as that they shall not be able to discover our aims, while we penetrate theirs and work

25. uncreditable] disreputable.

26. to put up the lie] to expose the falsehood.

them over to our own ends, is reckoned a great accomplishment, but is in truth a despicable baseness. For simplicity is one of the divine perfections, it is the character of the gospel (which can't be served by anything opposite to its spirit and design) and indeed of a great mind, which endeavors to be, what all desire to appear, and what the gospel aims to make us. A sincere Christian has no end but such as he can, not only own, but glory in; his natural complexion is better than any paint he can put on, to show him as he is, makes the most for his honor; and being conscious of his own integrity, he has no need to dissemble. Whereas the artificial person is self-condemned, his dissimulation shows a conviction of his demerit, and a consciousness of some baseness which he is ashamed to own. And besides, when our actions are evil it does us hurt to conceal and palliate them; we ought to submit to the shame they merit, as a due punishment of our folly, and as that which by the grace of God may bring us to repentance, and so be our cure. Indeed it is not necessary to show ourselves at all times, for if the good were so open, they could not live among the wicked, but whenever we think fit to appear, we're obliged to seem no other than what in reality we are. For though we may sometimes in prudence conceal our sentiments, it is always beneath us to disguise them.

241. *Revenge.* And so it is to take revenge, how just so ever the provocation may be, or however great the injury. For revenge as it usurps God's prerogative and hurts our neighbor, so it degrades and injures ourselves. Because it does but quit scores[27] and set us on a level with our enemy; or at most shows us to be more wicked and injurious than he was. Whereas a generous neglect and forgiveness raises us above him; nor will it suffer people to have the pleasure of vexing us, which is often the chief, or only reason, why they do an ill turn. But the doing good for evil, makes us a sort of gods to our offending brother, and if he has a spark of ingenuity, it will soften and reclaim his obdurate[28] heart.

242. *How to treat the injurious.* But it may be said, suppose we have receded from our just rights and liberties, and even brought ourselves into difficulties, for one who without cause is our enemy, and with no other prospect but to provoke him to love and to good works;

27. quit scores] avenge injuries or "get even with" (*OED*, s.v. "score").

28. obdurate] impenitent.

though we may overlook his stupidity in being unmoved with so great an obligation, and so much the greater, by how much the less we valued and set it out in parade: yet if he only treats us the more inhumanely, the more disinterested and unwearied we are in our kindness; making no other return but the greatest hatred for the greatest goodwill; when the noble sacrifice we have made of our own interests, shall only bring inconveniencies on ourselves; but does not as we hoped, soften the implacable, nor rouse the ungenerous, nor shame the disingenuous and base temper; though our own private wrongs might not move us, yet the affront offered to virtue, and hereby to God Himself, the horrible injustice, uncharity, and indeed complication of crimes in such a villainous return, can't but stir up some resentments in a noble mind; which if in any case, may be allowed to be just ones in this. But shall they proceed to revenge? By no means; that were to wrong ourselves because others have injured us, who may have used us ill, but they have used themselves much worse. They are beneath our anger, for this passion when conducted by reason, does not chasten but in order to amendment, which those people seem past hopes of, since all our generous goodness has been lost upon them; so that they are now only objects of our pity and our prayers.

243. *Worldly mindedness vile.* Further, since the mind is immaterial as we have seen, it is evident, that this world and the things thereof, are not, cannot be its good; they are of a much inferior nature, and their duration is contemptible. Nay, supposing them to be real goods, and ever so fit to be enjoyed, yet how can a material good satisfy or improve a spiritual nature? How can a temporal good render an immortal being happy? And therefore we do very much debase ourselves by supposing, that we are the better for having, or the worse for going without those temporal and transitory things, which add no real value to us; which are so far from being good, that on the contrary they are very hurtful, unless we are so wise as to make a right use of them. But since experience shows that they are more frequently temptations than advantages, and the instruments of sin than the exercise of virtue, there's little reason to desire them; we should rather fear than rejoice when we obtain them, though by the most just and honorable methods.

244. *And placing our happiness in what is out of our power.* Christianity, and even common prudence, which neither contradicts, nor is contradicted by religion, when each of them are rightly understood, requires us to make as sure of felicity as we can; and consequently since God has been so gracious as to place our happiness in our own reach, we should not be so foolish as to disappoint ourselves, by imagining it to be in things out of our power, where indeed it is not. He who judges so ill, and has so mean a thought, gives the world too great hold of him, and shall never want vexation; for besides the instability of all temporal things, he lies at the mercy of every ill-natured person, perhaps the greatest part of mankind. But he who places his happiness only in God and in a good conscience, is out of the reach of all sublunary[29] things, and enjoys a peace that this world can neither give nor take away.[30]

245. *How to value the world.* Innumerable are the advantages we receive by passing a due estimate on the world and the things thereof; that is in truth neglecting it, or considering it only with respect to the life to come, which is the true way of valuing it. Not but that the world considered in itself, and as it is the work of God is good, because all God's works are so, but the shortness and uncertainty of this present life, render it of no worth to us, unless in relation to the next world. And oh what security, what pleasure do they enjoy who regard it no otherwise! They can never be disappointed who expect all from the omnipotent and unchangeable Lord God, and nothing from this poor mutable world. They are engaged in no troublesome affairs, they have no quarrels with their neighbors who are indifferent to money and all its purchases, these being the true cause of contention, whatever the pretense may be. Their passions are never tumultuous, because not placed on wrong objects, nor on lawful ones to excess,[31] and therefore they are the wings, not the clog of the mind. Temptations can't fasten on them, who have neither hopes nor fears for anything this earth affords. Few people, if any, are such very devils as to be wicked for wickedness sake, it is a desire to avoid some present pain, or to

29. sublunary] earthly or terrestrial.

30. In the first edition, this sentence ends with "nor deprive him of" instead of "nor take away."

31. The words "nor on lawful ones to excess," are not in the first edition.

obtain some present pleasure, which inclines them to evil. Therefore they who apprehend no pain that's considerable but from an evil conscience, nor any pleasure but from a good one, are not "obnoxious"[32] to the "fiery darts of the wicked," whether it be the devil, or his instruments in human shape.[33]

246. *Foolish love.* One may remember a time perhaps, when they have thought they could not be happy unless another was so; but this was venturing too much on an uncertain bottom,[34] it was besides the command, and therefore so far from being excellent, that it was not prudent. For we are commanded only to love our neighbors *as* ourselves, and to wish them all the good we wish to our own souls, but we are not to make ourselves uneasy because they *will* be unhappy. God Himself who is the great lover of souls, does not think fit to compel us to be happy whether we will or no, why then should any mortal pretend to force another to be wise and good, or to drag them out of that misery which they resolve to plunge into?

247. *A just cause of grief.* Indeed, if among all the chances and changes of this mortal life that are out of our power, there be any one worth our concern, it is "when the righteous man turns from his righteousness," when there appears any "folly" whether great or "little in such as are in reputation for wisdom and honor," in which case I had almost said we do well to be grieved.[35] For besides our charity to our neighbor, the joy a Christian mind receives from the good actions of others as well as from its own, and that being members of one body, we ought to be affected with all its sufferings: besides this, virtue itself, and the honor of God are concerned, and religion, however unjustly, is disparaged by the faults of those who profess it. A consideration that ought to weigh very much with them who are eminent upon any account; and should prevail with us either to lay aside all pretensions to religion, wisdom, and honor, or else to take care to live up to them. And whatever our haste may be when we are spurred on by our passions, we should do well to take this heavy aggravation of our guilt into consideration; if when we are in such circumstances we are fit

32. obnoxious] exposed.

33. Eph 6:16.

34. bottom] foundation.

35. Ez 3:20, 18:26; Eccl 10:1.

to consider, and not rather fit for Bedlam to which place in charity and to remove the scandal of so ill an example, our friends ought to confine us.

248. *How we come to forget God and ourselves.* One can hardly think it possible for any person in cool blood, and with eyes open, to forget God and himself so much as to fall into sin and folly, unless his very understanding is perverted by evil habits. Because we always will our own good, and if we do at all consider like reasonable creatures, the way that God has prescribed us will appear to be the only way to obtain it. Hence I conclude that we are hurried on to sin and folly, by rash judgments arising from our passions,[36] or from an ill use of our understandings, or from disusing them.

249. *Of rash judgments and passions; liberty and slavery.* I call a judgment or conclusion rash and precipitate, how much time so ever we spend in making it, if we do not hold the balance even, by reducing ourselves to an indifferency to either side of the question, so that we are no longer solicitous whether *this* or *that* be true or good, but only that we may find what is so. If we are not thus impartial, it is plain we are not led by the holy spirit of God, and by consequence, are not living members of His son; but are slaves to our passions, and under the bondage of sense and corrupt inclinations. For "where the spirit of the Lord is, there is liberty";[37] true liberty, which consists not in a power to do what we will, but in making a right use of our reason, in preserving our judgments free, and our integrity unspotted, which sets us out of the reach of the most absolute tyrant.[38] Neither is a petulant censuring and judging our governors liberty, but licentiousness, whereby seducers make us the instruments of their passions, under appearance of indulging our own. But subjection to our passions is of all slaveries the most grievous and ignominious; because the mind itself puts on its own shameful yoke, and we are willing slaves to the vilest masters.

36. In the first edition, this sentence reads "that rash judgments hurry us on to folly, and these arise from our passions" instead of "that we are hurried on to sin and folly, by rash judgments arising from our passions."

37. 2 Cor 3:17.

38. In the first edition, Astell writes that "true liberty ... consists in making a right use of our reason, in preserving our judgments free, and our integrity unspotted (which sets us out of the reach of the most absolute tyrant) not in a *bare* power to do what we will" (my italics).

Whereas in other cases, our bodies only are slaves by constraint, and perhaps to an honorable person, while the mind may be freer than his whose chain we wear. And therefore did not compassion restrain one, who could help laughing to hear a vicious man exclaim against slavery, and harangue for liberty,[39] he himself being all the while, the most contemptible slave! He and he only is a freeman who acts according to right reason, and obeys the commands of the sovereign Lord of all, who has not put the liberty of His creatures in anyone's power but in their own. And as prejudice and the dominion of passion is a sign that we are not led by the spirit of God, so does it also deprive us of His influence and assistance, preventing the good He would otherwise do us. For if we are not disposed to do God's will except in our own way, if we are not indifferent to the methods He chooses for us, it is plain we mean to serve ourselves and not Him, whatever pretenses we make to His service, and are like to be left to the folly of our own conduct.[40]

250. *Prepossession and prejudice.* There are some, though one would hope not many, who plainly own that they love their prejudices, and are resolved not to part with them, at least not yet, because they give them present pleasure, which everyone is greedy of. And these people are not to be reasoned with, for they have deposed reason and set up instinct in its place; nor are they to be reclaimed without the extraordinary grace of God, or some bitter affliction, which shall spoil their relish of the pleasures of sense.[41] But mankind does generally declare against prepossession and prejudice, and though few of us but are subject to it more or less, we will not be brought to own it. So that in charity one is to believe, that to convince people of their partiality were to cure them of it. And because few of us are humble enough to submit the diseases of our minds to anyone's cure but our own, it may not be amiss to consider the symptoms of that disease.

251. *Signs of them.* We may conclude then, that we are not indifferent, but prepossessed and liable to rash judgments, when we adhere to principles which we never examined, which are only recommended

39. Astell partly alludes to the popular slogans of the Whig political party: "No Popery, No Slavery" and "Liberty and Property."

40. The first edition reads "the conduct we make choice of" instead of "the folly of our own conduct."

41. The first edition reads "sensible pleasures" instead of "the pleasures of sense."

by education and custom, or by authority and interest; and which we dare not examine because it would be a temporal loss to part with them. When we have no principles, that is when through ignorance or carelessness we are altogether unacquainted with the measures of truth and falsehood, good and evil, and so lie at the mercy of our own and other people's humors and passions as it happens; and when our principles are not fixed, but are so flexible as to bend to every present occasion. When we have diverse weights and measures, and allow that in our own case which we will not allow in another's; and without any change of circumstances, or any sufficient reason, like or dislike that today, of which we had contrary sentiments the other day; or act by some certain rules upon some occasions, and oppose or neglect them in a parallel case. If our imaginations are agitated, and our passions inflamed when we speak or think of a particular subject; if it takes up our thoughts, and they pursue it with pleasure and quit it with regret; it is plain that we have lost so much of our indifferency and liberty as this amounts to. For excepting matters of salvation, there's not anything worth great application and zeal, and if our concern for heaven shows itself in some affairs and not in all, it is certain that not God's glory, but our own passions and prepossessions move us.

252. *Mistaken zeal.* It is to me a strong presumption that people are in the wrong, I had almost said, and know, or at least suspect themselves to be so, when they are earnest and violent in making proselytes[42] to their persuasion in lesser and disputable points. An honest and impartial heart may well be warmed, nay, it ought to be so, in spreading and defending the great truths of the gospel and Christian morals. But fervor in other cases shows that we have either some by-end[43] to serve under a fair pretense, or else that we suspect our cause, and by a weakness incident to human nature, think to fortify ourselves in it by drawing in company. Truth and virtue are open and ingenuous, they neither need nor seek reserves; they do not fear the light, for they will bear examination. And provided our heads are not weak, nor our hearts corrupted, their adversaries' arguments do only strengthen their cause. Error and vice can never carry their point, but by a partial consideration; and what but a willingness to be deceived

42. proselytes] converts.
43. by-end] secret purpose.

by our passions, and a loss of our liberty, can keep us from a readiness to view an object on all sides, so far as we are able? And since it is certain that education and received opinions, passion, and worldly advantages, the approbation and authority of men, especially men of note for wisdom and learning;[44] give our minds a bias, we should allow for this, and by suspecting them put as much weight into the other scale. Being fully convinced that there is not anything so much for our true interest as to receive the truth in the love thereof, and we should always act up to this conviction. Not supposing there's any necessity that such a proposition should be true, or such a thing be good, but that it is absolutely necessary for us if we would be wise and happy, to find out truth, and to pursue good, though ever so contrary to our present opinions, practices, and inclinations.

253. *Christianity the only cure of sin and error.* In a word, we judge and choose amiss, because our judgments are hasty and partial; it is our passions for the most part that make our judgments thus precipitate and defective, we suffer passion to lead when it ought to follow; and sensible things, the love of this world, and present pleasure, is that which moves our passions. Wise men in all ages have exclaimed against prejudices and prepossessions, and advised us to get rid of them, but they have not informed us how, nor enabled us to do it, Christianity only does this. And it does it by stripping sensible things of their deceitful appearances, and finding us nobler objects of our passions than any this world affords.

254. *By governing our passions.*[45] It shows us the "great things of God's law," the glorious reward of obedience, and "His wondrous

44. The words "the approbation and authority of men, especially men of note for wisdom and learning" are not in the first edition.

45. In this subsection, Astell refers to the passions as they are enumerated in the English translation of René Descartes's *Les passions de l'âme* (1649), titled *The Passions of the Soule In three Books. The first, Treating of the Passions in Generall, and occasionally of the whole nature of man. The second, Of the Number, and order of the Passions, and the explication of the six Primitive ones. The third, of Particular Passions. By R. des Cartes. And Translated out of French into English* (London: A.C., 1650). The Cartesian passions are admiration (article 53), estimation, contempt, generosity, pride, humility, dejection (54), veneration, disdain (55), love, hatred (56), desire (57), hope, fear, jealousy, security, despair (58), irresolution, courage, boldness, cowardice, affright (59), remorse (60), joy, sadness (61), derision, envy, pity (62), satisfaction, repentance (63), goodwill, gratitude (64), indignation, wrath (65),

works towards the children of men,"[46] which are truly worthy of our *admiration*. It proposes to us the *love* of God, an infinite good; and the *hatred* of sin, the greatest of all evils. It convinces us that our *desires* will not labor in vain, when they put us upon pursuing the one, and avoiding the other. So that *despair*, whose business is by the pain it gives, to admonish us that felicity is not in worldly enjoyments, is superseded here, for whatever our lot may be in this world, we are carried on by an active and vigorous *hope* of the next. Which is not disturbed, but only poised by *fear*, and kept from *presumption* and *security*. And while we fear to offend God, we are above the fear of any other thing. A good conscience will, and nothing else *can* unless by accident, inspire us with true *courage*, render us *firm* and *bold* in difficulties, and intrepid in the greatest dangers. It is that which arms us with a just *indignation* against *wickedness*, even though it be "in high places,"[47] in persons of power and greatness, and excites us to do our endeavor to pull the prey out of their teeth. It turns our *anger* chiefly against our own sins, which makes it a minister of justice, not an instrument of revenge. The law of God shows vice to be the most *despicable* thing; and inclines us to *pity* every unhappy person, among whom they are the most so, who are under the dominion of sin. It teaches us to bestow our *favor* and place our *delight* "upon the saints that are in the earth, and such as excel in virtue."[48] To whom, as to the great benefactors to mankind, the Christian pays his greatest *esteem* and *gratitude*; and is *thankful* in proportion, to everyone who does any sort of good to himself or to his neighbors. If he has any *regret* or *envy*, it is only when vice goes away with the recompense of virtue; and how prosperous so ever the

---

glory, shame (66), distaste, sorrow, and light-heartedness (67). See also Descartes, *Passions of the Soul*, in *Philosophical Writings of Descartes*, 1:350–52. Astell supplements this list with some of those mentioned in Henry More, *An Account of Virtue: Or, Dr. Henry More's Abridgment of Morals, Put into English* (1690), trans. Edward Southwell (Bristol, UK: Thoemmes Press, 1997), 43–54. Generally speaking, More follows Descartes's taxonomy but adds a few extra passions, including presumption, firmness, despising, favor, delight, thankfulness, regret, emulation, rashness, caution, and grief. In her *Proposal II*, Astell cites Descartes's *Passions* and More's *Account* together in the lead-in to a passage remarkably similar to this one (*Proposal II*, 218, 219–20).

46. Hos 8:12; Ps 107:8, 15, 21, 31.

47. Eph 6:12.

48. Ps 16:3.

wicked may be, all they obtain from him is *disdain*. It is the good person only whom we are taught to *venerate*; and while we kindly *emulate* his excellencies, to bear him the greatest goodwill. The word of God instructs us how to be *humble* without *baseness*, and to have a great and *generous* mind without *pride*, by showing us what is valuable and what contemptible; that all rational creatures[49] may make a due use of their liberty as well as we, by which and not by outward circumstances, they are truly distinguished;[50] and that being nothing in ourselves, all our merit consists in our union with our redeemer. It convinces us, that nothing is *shameful* but the living unworthy of this honor; and that God's approbation, and the honor that comes from Him, is the only *glory*. And lest we fall short of this, the gospel instructs us to be watchful over ourselves and others with a *godly jealousy*.[51] Which prevents *rashness*, and gives us all necessary *caution*, at the same time that by convincing us that our happiness depends only upon God and ourselves, it banishes *irresolution*, a passion that puts a stop to all excellent and praiseworthy actions, and whose only use is to check ill minds in their career after evil; as *remorse* is designed to correct them when they have done amiss. But while according to the precepts of the gospel, we "exercise ourselves to keep always a conscience void of offense towards God and towards men," there's no place for remorse that bitterest pain.[52] We only wash off by a daily repentance, the daily stains we contract by living in a corrupted world. And because mortal man as such, is liable to pain and *grief*, therefore as winds and storms purge the air, so *godly sorrow*[53] purifies the Christian's mind, and renders it more healthy. And how can a life thus led but abound with *self-satisfaction*? Which as a great man[54] who had thoroughly considered this subject tells us, is "the sweetest of all the passions."[55] None indeed

49. The first edition reads "all men" instead of "all rational creatures."

50. In the first edition, this sentence reads "which is that which distinguishes them" instead of "by which and not by outward circumstances, they are truly distinguished."

51. 2 Cor 11:2.

52. Acts 24:16.

53. 2 Cor 7:10.

54. i.e., René Descartes.

55. In the 1650 English translation of *Les passions de l'âme*, Descartes defines self-satisfaction as "an inward satisfaction, which is the sweetest of all the passions" (*Passions of the Soule*,

but the good Christian can have it, or enjoy that *tranquility of mind* which is his portion, both in the nature of things, and by his great master's promise. Which tranquility he enjoys in the midst of all outward troubles, and which is much beyond an equivalent, for it makes up his losses even in this world, a hundredfold. For the favor and love of God on which the Christian's heart is fixed, is a fund of *joy* that never fails, but after it has made him as happy in this life as mortality can be, secures him an unspeakable happiness to all eternity.

255. *How to judge of our passions.* In fine, we can never be sure of ourselves, nor have a comfortable prospect of our perseverance, till religion becomes our pleasure, and it will never be our pleasure till our passions as well as our reason, and under the direction of reason, are engaged in it. For passions are the great scene of temptation; and we may take it for a rule, that whatever varnish they use, no action or passion can be good or innocent, which we are afraid or ashamed to own; which we blush at by ourselves, and are provoked[56] when others remind us of it. For virtuous actions and dispositions, though they should happen to be discountenanced[57] in a wicked world, do yet support the mind, rendering it cheerful, fearless, and undaunted in owning them. Whereas those which put us in disorder, which cover us with shame, and sting us with inward reproaches, are self-condemned. But our passions have always excuses ready till they have entangled us, and then they leave us in the snare, to the reproach and derision of the world, and to the bitter regret and confusion of our own minds.

256. *Of the improvement of our understandings.* As to our understandings, I consider, that God did not give us any talent to lay up in a napkin,[58] we must therefore improve in our intellectuals as well as in our morals. There is no heed to be given to those eternal disputers who perplex the clearest case, and bring colors[59] for some of the foulest sins; and who either to show their wit, or to exert their pretended

---

art. 63, 52). See also Descartes, *Passions of the Soul*, in *Philosophical Writings of Descartes*, 1:351–52.

56. The first edition reads "in fury" instead of "provoked."

57. discountenanced] discouraged.

58. Astell refers to the parable of the wicked servant who hid his money in a napkin instead of investing it (Lk 19:20).

59. colors] excuses.

authority, take the assurance, though perhaps with the softest and most submissive language, to place themselves in God's stead and judge for us. But though it were the utmost baseness to submit to their usurpation and tyranny, by parting with that most valuable privilege, and indefeasible right, of judging for ourselves where God has left us free to do so; yet far be it from us to pretend to infallibility and self-sufficiency; to despise anyone's lights,[60] or to reject their advice, with whatever spirit it may be offered. For as I placed Christian friendship in giving frank advice, so I now reckon the taking it among the duties we owe to ourselves. Nor can we be more unkind to our own souls, or guilty of a greater folly, than by supposing we are too great, or too wise, or too good, to be advised.

257. *Wherein it consists.* And yet after all, we must judge finally for ourselves, as was said in the beginning, because if we determine amiss *we* must answer for it. Hence it becomes necessary to improve our understandings to the utmost, that so they may serve us to all those purposes for which God designed them. Nor is it so difficult as sloth and the envy of those who would have nobody wiser than themselves, endeavor to represent it. The business of the understanding is to contemplate truth, and it is so much the more excellent in proportion as it is enlarged, and more able to take in, to consider and compare, the greater number of truths. And being we are at present in a state of probation, the best use we can make of our mind consists in furnishing it with such qualities and dispositions as may enable it to judge according to the eternal reason of things, especially in such matters as are of greatest consequence to us.

258. *Connection between holiness and wisdom.* So that though moral and intellectual improvements may be considered apart, they can't really be separated, at least not in a Christian sense. There is a natural connection between purity of manners, and soundness of judgment; "if any man will do God's will," says our Lord, "he shall know of the doctrine whether it be of God."[61] For every sin, and more particularly, impurity, pride, and worldly interest, is a prejudice that shuts out the light of truth, keeps men obstinate in error, and hardens their minds against conviction. And therefore having Solomon on my

60. lights] suggestions or instruction.

61. Jn 7:17.

side, and which is more, that divine spirit by which he wrote, I shall not scruple to call "the sinner a fool," though he be ever so learned, so witty, so ingenious, or what passes with the most for the top of wisdom, so cunning and so worldly wise.[62] For since wisdom consists in pursuing a worthy end by proper means, he whose end is to be despised and abhorred, can't be a wise man, but is only the more foolish, by how much he is the more artful and industrious in pursuit of it. But the Christian whatever his understanding may be in other matters, is wise in respect of his end, which is the main point of wisdom; and according to his capacity he will be wise with regard to the means of obtaining it. Indeed I heartily wish that we were all better instructed in this part of wisdom, and more diligent in the practice.

259. *All understandings should be improved.* All understandings are not of equal reach and brightness, but all may and ought to be improved; the most excellent because they are most capable of improvement, and the meaner because they need it most. But whether the having too high or too low an opinion of our own abilities is the greater hindrance, is not easily determined; for they who think they *can't* improve, will no more attempt it than they who think they *need not.* Experience shows, that people often act in this case just contrary to what they ought; it being easier to make some ladies understand everything, than to persuade them that they are capable of understanding anything. On the other hand, they are usually most confident of themselves, who have least reason to be so. I would never advise a woman to study to improve her mind, if I did not think her capable; and few things mortify me more than the not being able to persuade her to make a trial. For could we but once excite in each other's breast a noble thirst after perfection, placing our perfection in that wherein it truly consists, the greatest difficulty were past, we might go on with pleasure, and prosper in our attempt.

260. *Women's spoiled.* But to what study shall we apply ourselves? Some men say that heraldry is a pretty study for a woman, for this reason, I suppose, that she may know how to blazon her lord and master's great achievements! They allow us poetry, plays, and romances, to divert us and themselves; and when they would express

62. Astell possibly alludes to those biblical passages on the fool thought to be by Solomon, such as Prv 1:7–10, Prv 10–22:16, Prv 26:1–12, and Eccl 10.

a particular esteem for a woman's sense, they recommend history: though with submission, unless we take a greater compass than they allow us language and leisure to reach, that we may trace divine providence, and admire it in the government of the world, and conduct of the church, history can only serve us for amusement and a subject of discourse.[63] For though it may be of use to the men who govern affairs, to know how their forefathers acted, yet what is this to us, who have nothing to do with such business? Some good examples indeed are to be found in history, though generally the bad are ten for one; but how will this help our conduct, or excite in us a generous emulation? Since the men being the historians, they seldom condescend to record the great and good actions of women; and when they take notice of them, it is with this wise remark, that such women "acted above their sex."[64] By which one must suppose they would have their readers understand, that they were not women who did those great actions, but that they were men in petticoats!

261. *End of study.* Speculation is one of the most refined and delicious pleasures, but it is not to be followed only as a pleasure, but as an exercise and duty. There is as great variety in understandings as in faces, they have not all the same beauties nor the same defects, but every genius has its particular turn, and therefore the same course of study is not equally fit for everyone. The business is, to learn the weakness and strength of our minds; to form our judgments, and to render them always just; to know how to discover false reasonings, and to disentangle truth from those mazes of error into which men have hunted her; and whatever method tends to this end ought to be pursued.

262. *What sort of truths most proper for contemplation.* True knowledge, and not science falsely so called, is a "divine thing," as an

---

63. The qualification "unless we take a greater compass than they allow us language and leisure to reach, that we may trace divine providence, and admire it in the government of the world, and conduct of the church," is not in the first edition.

64. Astell refers to Charles Davenant's *Essays upon Peace at Home, and War Abroad. In Two Parts*, 2nd ed. (London: James Knapton, 1704). In that work, Davenant observes that Queen Elizabeth I of England had "a mind above her sex" (180). Astell addresses his remark both here and in the "Prefatory Discourse" to her *Moderation truly Stated*, where she complains directly against Davenant that "if women do anything well, nay should a hundred thousand women do the greatest and most glorious actions, presently it must be 'with a mind (forsooth) above their sex'!" (*Moderation Truly Stated*, lii).

excellent pen has proved it.[65] For to know is to perceive truth, and the perception of truth is a participation of God Himself who is *the truth*, and the participation of God is the perfection of the mind: but yet all truths, even among necessary truths, are not equally perfective. Were we created only for contemplation, or were this the only business of our present state, there might be no great difference to what sort of necessary truths we applied ourselves. But being made for action also, and at present in a state of probation; and truth being infinite, and therefore not to be exhausted by a finite understanding, we are chiefly, and in the first place, to consider such truths as are not only *necessary* in their own nature, as *necessary* is opposed to *contingent*, but such as are also most *necessary for us* to know, because of greatest importance, as helping us to regulate our actions according to the will of our creator.

263. Pure speculations of any kind, do us service by withdrawing our minds from sense, whereby they moderate our passions, and bring them into subjection to reason, which those speculations enlarge and fortify. But yet it seems to me, that the contemplation of extension, even though it be intelligible extension,[66] is not so perfective as metaphysical, moral, and divine contemplations.

264. *The benefit of speculation.* It is the misery of our depraved nature to be too fast tied to sensible things, to be strongly, and in a manner wholly affected with them; and whatever loosens this tie and weans us from them, does us a very considerable service. But we are not apt to think so, and have ways to frustrate the advantage might be

65. Astell refers to John Norris and Nicolas Malebranche's theory of vision in God, the hypothesis that the immediate objects of our thoughts, including all the representative ideas of material things in our minds, are "seen" in the mind of God. In the second part of his *Theory of the Ideal or Intelligible World*, Norris says that since "truth is of a divine extraction, and has a real divinity in its nature, what a divine thing must all *true* science be" (Norris, *Philosophical and Theological Writings*, 7:485–86). He also writes that "the truth which we see is divine, and … the knowledge which we have of truth, is, in some degree, a participation of the divine nature, and a kind of possession of God Himself" (7:485). According to this hypothesis, every idea in our minds partakes of an essence or an eternal archetype in the divine mind.

66. Astell refers to John Norris and Nicolas Malebranche's concept of intelligible extension, the pure nonsensory idea of matter in the mind of God. See Norris, *Theory of the Ideal World*, in *Philosophical and Theological Writings*, 6:251, 295; 7:12, 32.

reaped by speculation. Most men are so sensualized, that they take nothing to be real but what they can hear and see, or which is some way or other the object of their senses. Others who would seem the most refined, make sensation the fund of their ideas, carrying their contemplations no further than these, and the reflections they make upon the operations of their minds when thus employed.[67] Men speculate what will be of use to human life, what will get them a name in the world, and raise them to the posts they covet. But the contemplation of immaterial beings and abstracted truths, which are the noblest objects of the mind, is looked on as chimerical and a sort of madness; and the studying to live up to the pure morals of the gospel, is in their account visionary.[68]

265. *Study the women's province.* Except in the duties of our Christian calling, and the little economy of a house, women's lives are not active, consequently they ought to be contemplative; for I hope our Christian brethren are not of the Turks' opinion, that women have no souls;[69] I heartily wish indeed, that we made more use of them. And since it is allowed on all hands, that the men's business is without doors, and that theirs is an active life; women who ought to be retired, are for this reason designed by providence for speculation: providence, which allots everyone an employment, and never intended that reasonable creatures[70] should give themselves up to idleness and unprofitable amusements. And I make no question but great improvements might be made in the sciences, were not women enviously excluded from this their proper business. Quickness and penetration our masters vouchsafe to allow us, while they deny us judgment, and I own it is too true, that too many of us have given them just reason,

67. Astell alludes to John Locke's empiricist theory that all our ideas are gained from sensation and reflection alone. In his *Essay*, Locke says that "external, material things, as the objects of *sensation*; and the operations of our own minds within, as the objects of *reflection*, are, to me, the only originals, from whence all our *ideas* take their beginnings" (Locke, *Essay*, II.i.4).

68. Astell possibly alludes to Masham's denunciation of the Malebranchean theory of vision in God as "too visionary" (see Masham, the preface to *Discourse*, A2v).

69. Astell refers to a common (but mistaken) view in her time that the Islamic or "Mahometan" religion denied souls to women.

70. The first edition reads "anyone" instead of "reasonable creatures."

gratitude apart. For it is no great sign of prudence to choose a service when we are free; or if a service must be taken, not to stay till we are offered one that's creditable. But this case excepted, I am at a loss to find those instances in which men in general judge better than women, even without abatement for the advantages of their education, which yet in reason ought to be allowed. Indeed if they can prove that they give more diligence to make sure of heaven, this will put the superiority of their wisdom past all peradventure.[71]

266. *Christianity at least is as much our business as men's.* However, not to contest whether learning be their prerogative or our privilege; not to deny their self-evident principle, and therefore what they do not attempt to prove, "that women's understandings are inferior to men's,"[72] though my blind soul can't discern it: since the duties of a Christian are as much our business as theirs, all I shall contend for, is only that we may be suffered to improve our minds so far as this may influence our duty. And had I any interest with my sex, I would humbly entreat them to learn the measures of their duty from the word of God and right reason, not by hearsay. I beg the ladies for their own sakes, not to like me the worse, or at least to forgive me, for persisting in this desire, though it be even against hope, and some years' experience.[73] For though it would not be so easy for some people to make their markets[74] on occasion, by making fools of us, were we so wise as we may and ought to be; yet I'm fully persuaded, it is but

71. past all peradventure] beyond question or without doubt.

72. I am unable to locate this reference. It is possible that Astell simply summarizes the prejudicial opinions expressed in the preface to the French translation of *A Lady's Religion* and *The Reasonableness of Christianity*. Both Locke and Coste (the "French Prefacer") suggest that the Christian religion is fitted to the "meanest capacities," and they list women among the inferior sort. Alternatively, she might be paraphrasing Allestree's remarks on women's understandings in *A Ladies' Calling*, that "it will be a little hard to pronounce, that they are naturally inferior to men, when it is considered how much of extrinsic weight is put in the balance to turn it on the men's side" (b2r).

73. In the first edition, this sentence is addressed to a single female (presumably Catherine Jones): "Your Ladyship I know does not like me the worse, and I hope all other ladies will at least forgive me, for persisting in this desire."

74. to make their markets] "to make their profits" (*OED*, s.v. "market").

a very little time, before we heartily repent of permitting ourselves to be made their properties.[75]

267. *To depend on God, and not on man, the way to wisdom.* The more entirely we depend on God, we are so much the wiser and happier, but the less we depend on men so much the better. If a woman takes them for the only oracles of wisdom, I give her up for lost, it being certain that she will find them so crafty, for I can't call that wise which is not just and honorable, as to serve their own ends whatever becomes of her. Excellent is the advice of the wise Jew, "let reason go before every enterprise, and counsel before every action," and "let the counsel of thine own heart stand, for there is no man more faithful unto thee than it"; and "above all things pray to the most high, and He will direct thy way in truth."[76]

268. *What knowledge perfective.* As it is the "blessing of the Lord that makes rich, and He addeth no sorrow," the natural effect of riches, "with it";[77] so it is the blessing of the Lord that makes wise, and preserves us from being puffed up with a vain opinion of our wisdom. That knowledge of God which none can miss of, who will at all employ their thoughts about so divine a subject, is sufficient to convince them that He is worthy of all their love. And the "love of God surpasses all things for illumination," because it keeps the mind in the deepest humility, and most entire dependence on its beloved.[78] By the knowledge of God and of ourselves, which I take to be the proper aim of all our contemplations, I do not mean a curious research into the divine nature, which being hid from us in inaccessible light, we should humbly adore and not subtly dispute about; nor a physical disquisition of our own nature, since God by denying us an idea of our souls, signifies that this is not our present business. But I understand a knowledge of the relation we stand in to our God, and of the obligations arising from it. This is the study of greatest consequence, and though we fail of certainty in other enquiries we may obtain it here: and that wisdom

75. "*dupes*" (Astell's italics) in first edition.

76. Ecclus 37:16, 13, 15. The "wise Jew" is Ben Sira, author of the apocryphal text Ecclesiasticus, known for his great wisdom.

77. Prv 10:22.

78. Ecclus 25:11. Astell quotes the same biblical passage in a letter to Norris (see Astell and Norris, *Letters*, 111).

and integrity which this knowledge produces, is the true and the only perfection of human nature.

269. *None want ability and opportunity to endeavor after perfection.* An endeavor after which is, an employment neither "difficult nor tedious,"[79] for the yoke of Christ is "easy" and His "burden light," and the "way" of wisdom is a "pleasant path":[80] yet, considering the dignity and importance of the work, it is certain we ought to attend it more that the most of us do. The "spinsters and dairy maids," as one author speaks;[81] and as our "divine" observes, the "poor day-laborers have ability and opportunity sufficient to instruct themselves therein, without hindering the constant work of their calling."[82] And certainly they who are of a higher rank can't want it, provided their care hurries them no further than the making necessary and reasonable provisions for their families, as suitable to their conditions; they are obliged. But where is the necessity, or what tolerable pretense to "rise early and sit up late," and "to eat the bread of carefulness,"[83] only to leave an overgrown estate to their heirs, that these may perk up[84] among a higher rank, with no other merit or title than what their money purchases? Should day laborers, or mechanics,[85] or people of better fashion take this fancy in their heads, what they call their particular calling, will I fear allow them little time for their general calling as Christians. I need not say they had been *better* employed in endeavoring to be "rich in faith and good works,"[86] for it is certainly matter of *duty*, both as it is the most proper and worthy employment of a rational nature, and because a happy or miserable eternity depends upon it; so that unless we duly improve this short and uncertain life, we are undone forever.

79. *Lady's Religion*: "the greatest part of mankind ... cannot attend to any religious institution which is either difficult or tedious" (19).

80. Mt 11:30; Prv 4:11.

81. Locke, *Reasonableness of Christianity*, 282 [157].

82. Astell's marginal note (first edition only): *Lady's Religion*, 20.

83. Ps 127:2; Ez 12:19.

84. perk up] rise up.

85. mechanics] manual workers or tradespersons.

86. 1 Tm 6:18; Jas 2:5.

270. *Christian moderation.*[87] Ought we not therefore in mere kindness to ourselves, where everyone tells us our charity should begin, to make those "daily provisions for ourselves and families" which "necessarily employ us,"[88] subservient to those grand provisions we are to make for eternity? Nor can they have any excuse who do not in the first place, and with the greatest solicitude, "seek the kingdom of God and His righteousness";[89] who do not discharge the "common offices of life" in such a manner as is most for the good of their minds; setting very short bounds to their daily wants and provisions, which is the scripture "moderation";[90] a word that so many have in their mouths and so few practice. For our holy religion *moderates* our desires after sensual enjoyments, teaching us to live according to nature whose wants are few, and even to deny ourselves, and to despise the world. So that our worldly affairs, that is, those which reason and religion make *necessary*, though perhaps not what most of us think so, go in a little room. All the rest of our time being allotted by God for our real business, our "merchandize," our "race," our "warfare," the "pearl of great price," which all considerate persons strive to purchase, though at the expense of all besides; the "one thing needful, the good part that shall not be taken away from us."[91] Nor will the preference we give to heaven, hinder any of our just and lawful worldly affairs, for besides all other advantages, it will entitle us to the particular care of divine providence, which is all in all.

271. *Improvement of time necessary.* But if he whose present wants are greatest, must not for this reason be slack in his provision for eternity, what shall be said for them to whom the bounty of God has left no other necessities, no other business but the improvement of their minds? Happy people, if they make a right use of these advantages, but so much the more miserable for being allowed them, if they are abused or neglected! I can never read the parable of the talents[92]

---

87. Here Astell revisits the theme of her 1704 pamphlet on occasional conformity, *Moderation truly Stated*, a response to James Owen's *Moderation a Virtue* (1703).

88. Astell's marginal note (first edition only): *Lady's Religion*, 19.

89. Mt 6:33.

90. Astell's marginal note: See Phil 4:5, and so on.

91. Astell's marginal note: 1 Cor 9:24; 2 Cor 10:4; Mt 13:45–46; Lk 10:42.

92. Mt 25:14–30; Lk 19:12–28.

without fear and trembling; for if he who made no improvement of his master's talent, though he did not waste it, was cast into outer darkness; what shall become of us who have so grievously wasted ours! May the time past suffice to have been foolish and wicked, vain and trifling, slothful and useless, and let us now, even this minute, for this only is ours, begin to exert ourselves. And disregarding the example, or scoffs and persecutions, of those who at best only eat, drink, and sleep, flutter, or loll, or prate away an insignificant life, "let us run with patience the race that is set before us," and if we have opportunity, "endure the cross, despising the shame," after the example of our glorious leader.[93] Being fully assured, that we very much dishonor both our Lord and ourselves, if we who were created for the noble employment of contemplating and loving God, and preparing our souls by His assistance for the endless enjoyment of Him in glory, should take up with the base and contemptible office of making provision for the flesh, whether to fulfill its irregular appetites, or to supply its pretended necessities.

272. *Duty to our persons.* Human nature is indeed a composition of mind and body, which are two distinct substances having different properties, and yet make but one person. The certainty of this union is not to be disputed, for everyone perceives it in himself; but we can't attain a clear and distinct knowledge of it, from our present ideas.[94] No authority but His who made this union can justly dissolve it; for no person has a right over his own or his neighbor's life, or liberty, to dispose of either, any further than as he can show a warrant and commission from God. But I am not at present concerned with the magistrate's right, I am only to consider my own.

273. *How far life to be preserved.* The laws of men allow me to defend my life against an unjust assault, though it be at the peril of my neighbor's. But as appears to me, not only some particular texts

93. Heb 12:1–2.

94. Astell refers to the Cartesian notion that the mind-body union can be known through interior sentiment or sensation alone, and not by clear and distinct ideas. For details on Descartes's views, see Princess Elisabeth of Bohemia and René Descartes, *The Correspondence between Princess Elisabeth of Bohemia and René Descartes*, ed. and trans. Lisa Shapiro, Other Voice in Early Modern Europe (Chicago: University of Chicago Press, 2007), esp. 69–70.

literally taken, as this, "I say unto you that ye resist not evil," and so on,[95] but even the whole current of the gospel, requires me to hazard my own life rather than my neighbor's even upon such an occasion, except my soul, or any other person's, be endangered by this hazard. For the gospel teaches us to make very little reckoning of what is temporal and perishing, but to set the highest value on the immortal mind, whether it be our own or our neighbor's. So that it can be nothing else but the regard I have to my own soul and its preparation for eternity, that can justly acquit me from what I ought otherwise to have to the soul of the unjust aggressor, which is in the way to ruin, if to save my own life, I take his in the midst of his sin. And it ought to be remembered, that he is the purchase of Christ's blood, and therefore should not be lost upon any temporal consideration; he is a member of Christ though a corrupt one, and ought to be treated with tenderness. So that however valuable life may be, they rate it too high who prefer it to the soul of the vilest person, or their greatest enemy.

274. *Wherein self-preservation consists.* What then is *self-preservation*, that fundamental law of nature, as some call it,[96] to which all other laws, divine as well as human, are made to do homage? And how shall it be provided for? Very well; for it does not consist in the preservation of the person or "composite,"[97] but in preserving the mind from evil, the mind which is truly the self, and which ought to be secured at all hazards. It is this "self-preservation" and no other, that is "a fundamental sacred and unalterable law,"[98] as might easily be proved were this a proper place; which law he obeys, and he only, who will do or suffer anything rather than sin. "No man having a power to deliver up *this* preservation, or consequently the means of it, to the absolute will and arbitrary dominion of another," but "has always a right to preserve what he has not a power to part with," as a certain author says in another case where it will not hold.[99]

95. Astell's marginal note: Mt 5:39.

96. Astell refers to John Locke. In his *Two Treatises*, Locke defines self-preservation as "this fundamental, sacred, and unalterable law" (II.149). My references to the *Two Treatises* are to treatise and section number.

97. "composite"] i.e., the human being, a substantial union of both mind and body.

98. Locke, *Two Treatises*, II.149.

99. Astell's marginal note (first edition only): Locke, *Two Treatises*, II.149. [See also II.23.]

275. *Self-murder cowardice*. Yet *life* is to be preserved where innocently it may, nor should we dare to quit the post in which our sovereign Lord has placed us, till He is pleased to call us off. Self-murder, that heroic action with the heathen, being indeed neither virtue nor courage, but a want of spirit to bear up against the miseries of human life, and therefore through cowardice they fled for relief they knew not where. On the other hand, it is want of judgment, or want of heart, to be solicitous for life, for the bare sake of living. But to receive death, or life with all its miseries, with an equal mind as God sees fit to dispense them, and in submission to His will, is true Christian fortitude. So that they are much mistaken who fancy we would part with life unnecessarily, only because we talk of it with indifferency. We do not value it the less, but the more, for being ready to quit it when God requires it, for nothing but what is valuable ought to be sacrificed to Him. But the current of the world running so strongly to a mistaken love and fondness for life; one may reasonably use a vigorous expression, to reduce[100] it to a better course.

276. *Christian fortitude wisely parts with life*. Life then must be preserved till God calls for it; and He calls for it, when by being laid down to bear witness to truth, to give example of patience, constancy, and other virtues, it can glorify His name, and edify His church.[101] St. John argues from Christ's laying down His life for us, to the necessity of our laying down our lives for the brethren.[102] And the rest of the apostles thought it became them and every other member, to imitate the sufferings of the head, and to be in this as well as in other respects conformable to Him, whenever they were so happy as to be called to it.[103] For this is indeed the truest kindness to ourselves, "our short affliction" for Christ's sake, "which is but for a moment, working for us a far more exceeding and eternal weight of glory."[104]

---

100. "divert" in first edition.

101. Astell's marginal note: See Mt 10:38, and so on, and the parallel texts. Also Mt 16:24, and so on; Jn 15:20; 2 Tm 2:10, and so on. Also [Tm] chapter 4:6.

102. Astell's marginal note: 1 Jn 3:16.

103. Astell's marginal note: 1 Pt 2:19, and so on. Also [1 Pt] chapter 3:14, and 4:1, 12, and so on; Jas 1:12; 2 Cor 4:10–11.

104. Astell's marginal note: 2 Cor 4:17; [see also] Rom 8:18.

277. *Wherein reputation consists.* Next to life *reputation* is preferred and would take place in all generous minds, were life at their disposal. It may be taken in general for the approbation and praise of those among whom we live; and *fame* is nothing else but a louder and more extended reputation. But since reputation may be over, as well as undervalued; since mankind neither are, nor ever will be all of a mind; we ought to know with what part of them our good name is lodged, and how far their good word is to be sought and valued; lest in reality we lose our reputation, or what is better, by a foolish and improper way of preserving it. The judgment of God is without controversy the only true measure of what is praiseworthy, or blamable, and a reputation not conformable to God's judgment is not honorable, or whatever it be it is not valuable. Thus we find the praise of men opposed to the praise of God in holy scripture; though it is certain that a good Christian may lawfully receive, nay, he is in conscience obliged to provide for it. But if men are disposed to praise what God condemns, in this case there is not anything more pernicious, nor more to be avoided than such applause.

278. *A Christian's duty in regard to it.* And therefore since we must live so that "no man" may "despise us";[105] must "provide things honest" or honorable "in the sight of all men";[106] must "give no offense in anything," "neither to the Jew nor gentile, nor to the church of God";[107] must "cut off occasion" of censure and evil speaking, "from them that desire" and seek "occasion";[108] and "whatsoever things are lovely and of good report, if there be any virtue, any praise" must "think on these things";[109] since our Lord commands us to "let our light so shine before men, that they may see our good works, and glorify our father which is in heaven";[110] and yet we must "not be desirous of vainglory,"[111] nor "seek glory of men,"[112] nor "do our works" like the

105. Astell's marginal note: Ti 2:15.

106. Astell's marginal note: Rom 12:17.

107. Astell's marginal note: 2 Cor 6:3; 1 Cor 10:32.

108. Astell's marginal note: 2 Cor 11:12.

109. Astell's marginal note: Phil 4:8.

110. Astell's marginal note: Mt 5:16.

111. Astell's marginal note: Gal 5:26.

112. Astell's marginal note: 1 Thes 2:6.

Pharisees "to be seen of men,"[113] unless we mean to lose all "reward" from our heavenly father,[114] and to incur the woes denounced against such hypocrisy; and therefore St. Paul tells us, that he thought it a "very small thing to be judged of man's judgment";[115] and our Lord Himself imputes the unbelief of the Jews to their "receiving honor one of another," and "not seeking the honor that comes from God";[116] since all God's commands are consistent, and the scripture reconcilable to itself; it is evident, that though by "keeping consciences void of offense towards God and towards men";[117] by "abstaining from the very appearance of evil,"[118] and doing "nothing but what is of good report,"[119] so far as it is in our power, and as we can without omitting any necessary or greater duty; we are to preserve ourselves "blameless" as well as "harmless," the children "of God without rebuke, in the midst of a crooked and perverse nation, among whom we" are to "shine as lights in the world,"[120] and by this means to "commend ourselves to every man's conscience in the sight of God";[121] yet we must not desire the praise of men for itself, or for our own exaltation, nor seek it on any other account than as it is a means to glorify God, and to edify our neighbor; and hereby to procure to ourselves the honor that comes from God, the searcher of hearts and rewarder of everyone according to his works.

279. *What must not be done to acquire it.* But if after all this care to gain the esteem and approbation of men to ourselves, and to excite their thankfulness to God for His grace in us, if any or all of them are so unjust and wicked, as not to discern the gifts and graces of God, and bless Him for them; or if they enviously conceal the esteem they have at heart; if they will give no "praise" without receiving it from us by our "forsaking the law," and becoming partners with them in

113. Astell's marginal note: Mt 23:5–6.

114. Astell's marginal note: Mt 6:1.

115. Astell's marginal note: 1 Cor 4:3.

116. Astell's marginal note: Jn 5:44.

117. Astell's marginal note: Acts 24:16.

118. Astell's marginal note: 1 Thes 5:22.

119. Astell's marginal note: Phil 4:8.

120. Astell's marginal note: Phil 2:15.

121. Astell's marginal note: 2 Cor 4:2.

their wickedness;[122] if we can neither get nor keep their good word, but by sinful, servile, and unreasonable compliances; we must not be so foolish and so unkind to ourselves, as to "love the praise of men more than the praise of God."[123] For applause so unjustly acquired, will neither be of use to others nor to ourselves, bating[124] a present turn, and much less can it glorify God, whose service is never promoted by evil methods. And indeed, by approving ourselves to Him we are most like to preserve our character with the wise and good, who are the true dispensers of reputation; which does not receive its value from the numbers, but from the worth of them who praise. The multitude being almost ever in the wrong, so that they who enjoy the loudest fame, have seldom, at least not in a Christian sense, the best.

280. *How to bear the loss.* However, "though all who see" us should "laugh us to scorn," though "we should be a reproach of men, and despised of the people," as was the "author and finisher of our faith," yet like Him we must "endure" this "cross, despising the shame," and by "patient continuance in well-doing seek for glory, honor, and immortality."[125] For "so is the will of God, that with well-doing," and with this only, we should "put to silence the ignorance of foolish men."[126] And if we take any other method besides this to "please men," we shall "not be" able to approve ourselves "the servants of Christ."[127]

281. *Glory belongs to God, not to sinners.* After what has been said of reputation, one needs not be told what end is to be proposed in seeking it, how it is to be valued and preserved, and how to be used. Glory is a reward, and as such not due to sinners till God shall purify us, and crown His own work in us. So that if there be any sense and meaning in what men say when they commend us, it is only this, that the gifts and graces of God being manifested in us, He is to be glorified, and we are to be encouraged in the good use we make of them. Our master's talents must be employed for His service, to whom all glory is due; and to make this to be remembered, we have upon record

122. Astell's marginal note: Prv 28:4.

123. Astell's marginal note: Jn 12:43.

124. bating] excepting.

125. Astell's marginal note: Ps 22:6–7; Heb 12:2; Rom 2:7.

126. Astell's marginal note: 1 Pt 2:15.

127. Astell's marginal note: Gal 1:10; 1 Thes 2:4.

a dreadful and exemplary punishment, inflicted on him who "gave not God the glory" of his eloquence.[128] But we may lawfully be God's stewards, or receivers of the increase of those talents committed to our trust, provided we transfer the gain to the rightful owner. Thus did St. Paul, "I labored more abundantly," said he, "than all the" apostles, "yet not I, but the grace of God which was with me."[129]

282. *The value of reputation.* As for the value of reputation, it best appears by the care that God Himself commands us to take to obtain and to preserve it. He promises it as a blessing, and proposes it as a reward to the just, while the wicked are threatened with the want of it. We are told in scripture, that it is preferable to "great riches";[130] and that of all perfumes a good name is the most precious, for it spreads its odor far and near;[131] our own hearts are cheered, and our spirits refreshed by it, and so are our neighbors', who are encouraged to labor after that which procures so great a pleasure to all ingenuous minds. To be lavish of it unnecessarily, is a dishonor to God as well as to ourselves; nor do they value their innocence and virtue as they ought, who do not by all fair and lawful ways secure a good reputation. Not to be sensible of it argues a mean and base spirit; women especially ought to have the nicest sense of honor. For men have twenty ways of retrieving their characters, whereas if ours is once sullied by any sort of folly, by the appearance, or suspicion of it, there's no way to recover its first luster, but though we may have preserved our innocence, our reputation is lost forever, and all the good might have been done by it. And therefore though the holy apostle does in general advise us to prefer that state of life which in "his judgment," who "had the spirit of God," is the more "comely, best" in itself, as being freest from the "distractions" of this present life, and more devoted to the service of God, and in all respects the "happier" state;[132] yet he commands us

128. Astell's marginal note: Acts 12:21, and so on. [Astell refers to King Herod's divine punishment for an oration that "gave not God the glory" (Acts 12:23).]

129. Astell's marginal note: 1 Cor 15:10.

130. Astell's marginal note: Prv 22:1.

131. Astell's marginal note: Eccl 7:1.

132. Astell's marginal note: 1 Cor 7:34, and so on. [See 1 Cor 7:34–40. In this passage, widows are advised that they may marry again, but that they will be happier if they remain unmarried. Astell includes citations from 1 Cor 7:28, 39–40 on the title page of the 1706

to abate of this perfection, and to condescend to a less excellent way, rather than give "occasion to the adversary to speak reproachfully."[133]

283. *Our foolish conduct with regard to reputation.* But alas! How unequal is our conduct! We are humble and unaspiring in some cases where we ought not to be so, and therefore are indeed not humble but base; and upon other occasions our vanity has no bounds. We value our reputations, or more properly our vanity, so much sometimes as to sacrifice even our innocence to it, never regarding how many unjust, uncharitable, and malicious things we do or say, upon a mistaken point of honor. At other times we easily give it up to our humor and folly; we have no regard to the opinion of the world in cases where we ought to prefer it to our own, it governs us only where it ought not to be considered. For instance, tell a woman of improving her talent, of being eminently wise and good in her generation, of doing such things as God approves, and which ought to have the approbation of mankind, whether or no they obtain it, she is the poorest, humble, unpretending[134] thing! Alas she has no ambition! She's afraid of censure, and dares not cross the vogue of the world, nor by doing what is unfashionable, hazard her character though to improve it! But if she takes a fancy to play the fool ever so notoriously; to put herself in the power of she knows not who; to do what all the world, but those mercenary spirits who get by it, condemns; to fall under the pity of the wise and good, and the contempt and laughter of those whom she most despised; why in this case who so stout[135] and so exalted as she is! She has no caution, no fear, she tramples upon your best and kindest advice, and hates you for it. She is got above censure in a trice,[136] and is carried away in her own lofty thoughts one knows not where, but to a fool's paradise you may be sure!

---

third edition of her *Reflections upon Marriage.* These citations are omitted in Springborg's modern edition of the work.]

133. Astell's marginal note: 1 Tm 5:14. [This passage reads "I will therefore that the younger women marry, bear children, guide the house, give none occasion to the adversary to speak reproachfully."]

134. unpretending] unaspiring.

135. stout] proud.

136. in a trice] in an instant.

284. *Uniform virtue the best way to reputation.* The best and the only way to get a reputation worth having, is to do such things as deserve it. For perfumes can't be concealed; and if we have light it will shine forth and discover itself, in spite of the malice of God's enemies and ours, provided it is "burning" like St. John Baptist's bright and flagrant;[137] but your twinkling and half-lighted tapers are soon extinguished. It is but by accident and the evil dispositions of mankind, that virtue is not followed with praise; for being beautiful in itself, and beneficial to the world, reputation is its natural effect. But sometimes our lives are too much clouded, they do not shine enough; and sometimes they are too bright and dazzling; in the first case we do not deserve, in the latter the envy of men won't allow us reputation. Nothing so lovely nor consequently so reputable, as a life that's all of a piece; the same even thread running through it from the beginning to the end. When our words correspond with our thoughts, and our actions with both, and all these with each other; so that we are entirely consistent with ourselves, and with the precepts of the gospel, which never interfere. Nor is there anything sinks our reputation more, or renders us more despicable than an unsteady conduct, which today would represent us saints, and tomorrow shows us to be no little sinners, zealous for some precepts, and scandalously loose in others. For what can this be but hypocrisy, that most abominable sin! And a concealing some secular design under the veil of religion! Which brings more disreputation on ourselves when it is discovered, as it generally is, and even upon religion, than open profaneness.

285. *Reputable virtues. (1) Simplicity and sincerity.* And as a uniform virtue does naturally produce esteem, so more especially if among its circle of graces, any of those which have a peculiar aptness to attract commendation, shine forth with a particular luster. Such is simplicity of manners in the first place, as St. Paul thought who opposes "the hidden things of dishonesty," and "walking in craftiness," to the "commending ourselves to every man's conscience in the sight of God."[138] For the good opinion men have of their own understandings, though it inclines them to use artifices and disguise *themselves*, gives them a great abhorrence of it in others, as supposing it put on

137. Jn 5:35.

138. Astell's marginal note: 2 Cor 4:2.

to overreach[139] them, which they cannot bear. And the reason why there is so much professed sincerity, and so little in effect, is because everyone is sensible that they lose all credit with their neighbor when he suspects them of falsehood and doubling.[140] And one finds by the conduct of your cunning people, that the greatest of all artifices is to appear open and plain when they are not so.

286. *(2) Disinterestedness.*[141] Try them then before you trust them, and particularly by disinterestedness, for they would not be at the pains to act artificially but that they have their aim, which is something in this world, since the interests of the next are not served by such methods, nor would men give themselves the trouble on this account. There may be other designs besides getting of money; however this is called being interested, because money generally purchases every other thing except wisdom and virtue, and he who has it seldom finds his want of these. For in most men's reckoning, riches stand for all other good qualities, and the rich man shall be cried up and followed more than anybody, but I cannot say he shall be more esteemed; for when the carcass is devoured the vultures leave him.[142] And because a contempt of money sets us above many dirty temptations, and is an uncommon virtue, few things give a clearer or more lasting fame. This the Stoics were sensible of, whose vainglory was their predominant passion, and therefore they despised riches in their words and writings though they had their hundred thousands out at use.[143]

287. *(3) Liberality.* Yet money rightly used may procure esteem; and it is rightly employed if it be neither penuriously hoarded, nor lavished out profusely, but bestowed generously. For liberality is a beautiful quality, but it does not consist in squandering wealth without distinction of things or persons, and in wasting it in vanity and luxury:

139. overreach] deceive.

140. doubling] deceit.

141. *Disinterestedness*] impartiality.

142. Astell possibly evokes Matthew 24:28 ("For wheresoever the carcase is, there will the eagles be gathered together.")

143. Astell probably has the Stoic philosopher Seneca specifically in mind. Throughout the ages, Seneca has been criticized for the apparent inconsistency between his theory (namely, the idea that material goods are valueless) and his practice (his accumulation of great personal wealth).

but in laying it out on worthy designs and worthy persons, with a free and plentiful hand, and in a handsome and engaging manner. The same reason for which men love money, disposes them to speak well of him who gives them what they love; and yet all people don't gain a reputation by giving, at least not among those who judge rightly. And the reason is, because they plainly show, that they do not *do a benefit*, which is something done for the sake of the receiver, but they *make a bargain* for their own sakes; they would purchase one's liberty, honor, or conscience. In which case he with whom they traffic thinks he has a right to be upon his guard, and so perhaps may disappoint them of their purchase; nor can I see where that ingratitude lies against which they so much exclaim. It is indeed a hopeless undertaking to oblige him with money who despises it. If the way and manner of giving be such as expresses the judgment and kindness of the giver, he accepts it for the giver's sake; otherwise he disdains the gift.

288. *(4) Good nature, that is Christian charity, and (5) good breeding.* Good nature truly so called, not that foolish easiness which makes us mere properties, without any rule or judgment of our own, carried on by what our company, or any assuming person has the assurance to impose: but good nature, or rather Christian charity grafted on the stock of a sweet, obliging, affable temper, which makes our access easy and agreeable, suitable to our own character and station without offense to others, goes a great way towards reputation. When neither our fortune, quality, or wit sit hard on our neighbors, but are employed to do them good, and we know how to preserve our own dignity without shocking or lessening those who approach us; when we are free from selfish narrowness, humane and compassionate to all who need our help, and offensive to none. This is to be the delight of mankind, especially if a good fashion and polite address attend it. For good breeding is the ape of good nature and charity, and since there is so little of the last among us, there would be no living in the world, did not the former in some measure check the fierceness and brutality of mankind, especially men of power. Now, though charity and good nature are in effect and substantially, and excepting some formalities, what good breeding is in appearance, yet because outside takes with the most, who are but superficial judges, the greatest merit and best temper are often disliked for want of it. As on the other side, when

our good manners is upon trial found to be no more than a formality, people learn to use it so far as it will go, and know how to resent the cheat it has put upon them.

289. *(6) Decency and decorum.* But though our actions are innocent, or even useful, if they are not suitable to our persons and character, they lose their beauty, they merit blame and not praise. It is not the quantity and oddness, but the fitness and proportion that renders things valuable; where this is wanting in the works of nature we call them monstrous; and art is nothing else but a result of due proportions. When the apostle commands us to think on such things as are "lovely," or becoming, he means this suitableness if I am not mistaken.[144] And they who have the judgment to discern wherein it consists, and the felicity to express it, must needs shine in every condition of life. There are ways of getting money very lawful and commendable in some people, that would be highly disreputable in others. Abraham and Ephron understood themselves too well to barter for the field of Machpelah, they treated each other like men of quality.[145] But churlish Nabal who knew not what was fit, too late repented his ill-mannered folly.[146] And as some sort of marriages are not honorable, but must be condemned for several good reasons, so they are particularly scandalous and of ill report because of the indecency, the woman being supposed to make the address.

290. *(7) Humility. (8) Modesty. (9) Magnanimity.* Humility and modesty do also help to gain reputation, for they are decent and amiable virtues. A great mind which is not opposite to humility but to its counterfeit, and which is the only soil wherein true humility thrives, has so large a view and so lofty an aim, that when it has done its utmost, and what everyone does or ought to value, that idea of excellency and perfection which it always keeps in view, so far exceeds its performances, that it is rather mortified through consideration of what it wants, than exalted with any attainment. It still presses forward looking upon the most excellent patterns, and can't be so mean as to compare itself with any who are beneath it. And being most sensible of its own defects, and very diligent in the cure of them, it is not at leisure

144. Astell refers to St. Paul in Phil 4:8.

145. Astell's marginal note: Gn 23.

146. Astell's marginal note: 1 Sm 25. [The word "ill-mannered" is not in the first edition.]

to observe its neighbors. It endeavors to deserve well, and takes for granted that others do, till they give it demonstration to the contrary, and then its love to virtue makes it pity, not insult them who have lost their glory. And to make the best use of this melancholy subject, it turns its thoughts to the apostle's advice, "be not high-minded but fear," "considering thyself lest thou also be tempted."[147] If it despises anything, it is those evil arts which under the specious name of humility and kindness, are used to stop its progress in well-doing. And though it is too modest to prescribe to others, to pry into their actions, or to worry them with its importunities, yet it is sufficiently resolute to guard itself; nor will it be so tame as to deliver up either its virtue or its judgment, to every bold imposer. So exactly well does magnanimity agree with humility and modesty, so reputable, and so lovely are they; but their apes, and their opposites are most contemptible.

291. *(10) Public-spiritedness.* I say nothing of public-spiritedness, for besides that we have almost lost the very notion of this virtue, it being too certain that men have projects for themselves afoot, when they cry out for the public; and the public is ruined under pretense of serving it; besides this, the sphere allotted to us women who are subjects, allows us no room to serve our country either with our counsel or our lives. We have no authority to preach virtue, or to punish vice. As we have not the guilt of establishing iniquity by law, so neither can we execute judgment and justice: and since we are not allowed a share in the honorable offices in the commonwealth, we ought to be ashamed, and scorn, to drudge in the mean trade of faction and sedition.

292. *Some good actions to be concealed, and why.* Some good actions are private in their own nature, and some are so by the command of Christ, so that to publish them does not make for our reputation but disgrace. The reason of things requires that a benefit should be concealed by the doer, and published by the receiver; for he who "proclaims his own goodness" or "bounty" as the margin reads (and who is opposed by the wise king to "a faithful man," or a friend) pays himself, and has no title to the gratitude of him who received it, nor to

147. Rom 11:20; Gal 6:1.

the esteem of other men.[148] And therefore to "let another man praise thee and not thy own mouth, a stranger and not thy own lips," is in no case more necessary than in this.[149] Our Lord has particularly commanded us to conceal our "prayers," "fastings," and "alms" from the eyes of men, lest we should be as the "hypocrites," and lose the "reward of our father who is in heaven"; and the divine authority of the lawgiver is the best and most undeniable reason of His laws.[150] But since He condescends to give us leave to enquire further, we may with all humility presume that prayer and fasting being transactions between God and our own souls, and such as do no benefit to mankind, nor are of any use unless they are sincere, which none but God alone can know; being also easily counterfeited, and apt to attract the eyes of the common sort, as instances of great religion, for which reason they do it the greatest injury when they are discovered to be but counterfeits: therefore our Lord who knows our frailty, to remove these stumbling blocks out of our way, requires our light to shine forth in instances not so easily dissembled, and which whether sincere or no, may be useful to mankind. Alms indeed are of this nature, and therefore it is for some other reason, which shall be accounted for in its proper place,[151] that our Lord enjoins us to do them with so great secrecy, that if it were possible we ourselves should not be witnesses of our own charity.

293. *Yet without affectation.* In the meantime we may observe, that the true Christian seeks a reputation from virtues of a public, not of a private nature. One's circumstances it is confessed may be such, as that they can't distribute their alms with their own hands, nor conceal themselves from the receiver: the family will know of their fasts, and others suspect them of devotion in their retirements. But

---

148. Astell's marginal note: Prv 20:6. [Astell's point about "bounty" corresponds to the marginalia for Proverbs 20:6 in a contemporary version of the King James Bible, *The Holy Bible, Containing the Old Testament and the New: Newly translated out of the Original Tongues and with the former Translations diligently Compared and Revised. By his Majesties Special Command. Here are added to the former Notes in the Margin* (Edinburgh: Heirs and Successors of Andrew Anderson, 1696). The margin for this text reads "*Or, bounty." The "wise king" is Solomon.]

149. Astell's marginal note: Prv 27:2.

150. Astell's marginal note: Mt 6.

151. Astell's marginal note: See §316.

provided these duties are not neglected, the less occasion is given for observation, and the more industriously, but not with an *affected* industry, they are concealed, they are so much the more excellent. And whenever they shall break out, as it is like they may even in this world, by the disposition of divine providence, God Himself taking care of our honor, when we are only solicitous for His, they will be the more exemplary, and shine with the brighter luster.

294. *Virtues of a public nature.* But supposing they should not be disclosed till the great day of recompense, there are opportunities enough for a Christian to "let his light shine before men,"[152] in instances that can't be concealed from them, and in which if he does not behave himself reputably, he brings a reproach on his Christian profession and glorious master, as well as on himself. For there is not anything more injurious to religion than to handle it with treacherous, rapacious, or dirty fingers. There are certain virtues which don't much heighten anyone's character because they are expected from all, but it is a very great infamy to neglect them, and so much the worse if he who offends against these common duties, pretends to higher attainments. Many things pass without observation in common and unnoted people, which are scandalous in those who have a name for wisdom and virtue. Some men's employment makes that an abomination in them, which in others is no more than the way of the world; and though he is a base person who deceives and overreaches anyone, yet he is the basest traitor who betrays where he is entrusted, and has been obliged. For men[153] whose proper business it is to guide us into the way of truth, instead of this to lead and hurry us into the road of perdition, is the most outrageous of all villainies; and so much the worse by how much the better they pay themselves for doing it.

295. *Public confession of Christianity.* I know not how it comes not to be infamous in a Christian country to speak irreverently of God, of our savior, and the sacred mysteries and doctrines of our holy religion: but whether it be fashionable or no, it is for certain our duty "not to be ashamed to confess the faith of Christ crucified" openly to

152. Mt 5:16.

153. "those" in first edition.

all the world.[154] Our holy mother the church requires this of us when she receives us into her bosom,[155] and it is like this is one of her principal faults with our modern wise reformers! But they may please to remember, that the apostle tells us, that it is not enough to "believe with the heart," unless "confession be" made "with the mouth"; for our "faith" should be spoken of as that of the Romans was, "throughout the whole world."[156] Our Lord Himself having assured us, that if anyone is "ashamed" of any Christian doctrine or practice "in this adulterous and sinful generation, of him shall the son of man be ashamed when He cometh in the glory of His father with the holy angels."[157]

296. *Other virtues wherein our light must shine.* All the world should be witnesses of our exact and nice justice and generous disinterestedness; should know so well our contempt of money, as to blush more at offering us a bribe or any clandestine gain, than most people do to receive it. Moderation and a temperate use of prosperity should appear to all, though fasting and mortification must not. Our alms must be secret in regard to the modesty of human nature, and lest we should increase our brother's affliction by exposing it: but when the necessity of God's church calls for public charities, our "zeal" should be such "as to provoke" others.[158] And we ought to be as regular and open in our public devotions, as our private ought to be stolen and concealed. Our veracity and faithfulness should be so remarkable, that they may be as securely depended on, as the strongest bonds and most solemn obligations. Our purity and loyalty of all kinds must be unspotted, and free from the least suspicion; they have lost their luster if they come to be attacked, for their brightness ought to confound the presumptuous, and keep temptation at an awful distance.

297. *Particularly restitution and repentance.* Restitution and penitence are public virtues, he who has been so unhappy as to do wrong, and to give scandal, must not be less open in his repentance

---

154. Church of England, "Public Baptism of Infants" in *Book of Common Prayer*: "We receive this child into the congregation of Christ's flock, and do sign him with the sign of the cross, in token that hereafter he shall not be ashamed to confess the faith of Christ crucified" (285).

155. i.e., upon baptism.

156. Astell's marginal note: Rom 10:10; Rom 1:8.

157. Astell's marginal note: Mk 8:38.

158. Heb 10:24.

than he has been in his sin. For it is not enough to sin no more, without making reparation for the injury and scandal; and if the heart is truly contrite, and desirous to be rid of its guilt, it will not scruple to give glory to God, and to take shame to itself, as a due punishment for its transgressions. In which case, wherever these are mentioned, the repentance attending them will also be remembered for an atonement and memorial. Whereas people who are so tender as to suffer nothing, may be weary of their sin perhaps, or want opportunity to commit it, but they give the world no evidence that they abhor it. When our sins have been great and notorious, the most profound abjection and lowliness of mind becomes us. For it is the being "precious in God's sight" that makes us "honorable,"[159] and if we have unhappily made ourselves "abominable" in His eyes,[160] we ought to be abundantly more so in our own; for in this case especially, "before honor is humility."[161]

298. *Relative duties, and so on.* Further, we may be very exemplary in the discharge of our duties to our several relations, and whatever our employment or circumstances are, it is in our power to make them shine by filling our sphere. Christians ought to have no enemies, that is, they ought to give no occasion or just pretense to anyone's enmity: but if people will hate and persecute us without a cause, everyone who knows of their malice, should also be acquainted with our readiness to forgive, and our charity towards them. For whoever resolves to live a Christian life, will meet with provocations more than enough, to give continual exercise to his meekness and long-suffering. And the calamities of life are so many, that our patient resignation, and cheerful submission to the will of God, and our fortitude in bearing afflictions without murmuring or complaint, may be very conspicuous.

299. *Suffering for righteousness sake.* But if we are "reproached, for the name of Christ,"[162] and "persecuted for righteousness sake,"[163] "happy are we, for the spirit of glory and of God rests upon us."[164] The noble army of martyrs obtained a lasting "fame" in this world, as well

159. Astell's marginal note: Is 43:3–4.

160. Astell's marginal note: Ti 1:16.

161. Astell's marginal note: Prv 15:33.

162. Astell's marginal note: 1 Pt 4:14, and so on.

163. Astell's marginal note: Mt 5:10–11.

164. 1 Pt 4:14.

as the brightest crowns in the next, by laying down their lives for the glory of God, and the edification of His church, and to bear witness to the truth among unbelievers. "Let none of you suffer as an evil doer," says the apostle, "or as a busy body in other men's matters," that is, as a factious, seditious, or rebellious person; "but if any man suffer as a Christian let him not be ashamed, but let him glorify God on this behalf."[165] It being the highest honor a Christian can attain, to lay down his life rather than break any of God's commands, among which the being "subject" to, and the not "resisting" the lawful "power" that God has set over us, is none of the least.[166]

300. *How vainglory differs from letting our light shine before men.* In a word, a Christian endeavor to obtain a good reputation is distinguished from vainglory, by the *motive*, which in the former is obedience to God, in the latter the mere pleasing of ourselves; by the *method*, which is only good and upright actions in the one, and in the other any arts and ways that will take with men; by the *value* set upon our reputation, the vainglorious preferring it before a good conscience, to which the Christian makes it always give place; by the *end* proposed, and the *use* that is made of it, the vain man seeking nothing but his own exaltation and temporal interests; while the Christian proposes only the honor of God at present, expecting hereafter that real glory which God will bestow upon all His faithful servants. For praise considered in itself, and separate from its use, is but a vain thing; because God alone knows the heart, and therefore He only can pronounce concerning the merit of an action. And further, since every good and perfect gift is from above, since the use of it is ours, but not the property, all praise that is not chiefly and ultimately referred to God must needs be vain. A great fondness for reputation being I confess, no good symptom of integrity: the sincere Christian regarding God alone, and being very indifferent to everything besides His approbation.[167]

301. *The use and benefit of reputation.* As for the use of reputation, it powerfully restrains us from evil, and encourages us in well-doing, increasing our future reward by the good it enables us to do

---

165. 1 Pt 4:15–16.

166. Astell's marginal note: Rom 13. [The citations are from Rom 13:1–2.]

167. This sentence is not in the first edition.

to others. For by showing them that virtue is practicable, and that no more is required of them than what has been done before, by those of like infirmities, it excites the generous mind, and renders the slothful and wicked without excuse. And by raising the admiration of mankind, and working a veneration in their hearts, it disposes them to attend to what we say and do, and to be persuaded by it. And therefore upon this account, "a good name is rather to be chosen than great riches, and loving favor rather than silver and gold";[168] because it gives us an interest with those, whom riches as powerful as they are, can't influence.

302. *The ground of it.* For the mind of man however corrupt, perceives it to be just to esteem and praise actions conformable to the will of God, and that because for the most part, it finds its own account in them; obedience to the law of God tending to the common good, and therefore it is generally reputable even among the worst of men. It happens indeed sometimes, that a holy life, especially the most generous and heroic acts of holiness, disturbs them in their sins, and upbraids them with their iniquities, and for this reason procures their ill will. Thus we find that virtues of the middle rank are most commended, but the greatest and most excellent are not understood, being too frequently miscalled by the names of vice. And this happens sometimes through mere ignorance, and sometimes through the malice of men, who misrepresent virtue that they may with the better grace decry it, few or none being so impudent as to blame a good action as such.

303. *How to distinguish some resembling virtues and vices.* Some virtues and some vices bear a great resemblance in the mere outward act, so that they are not to be distinguished but by the intention, the reason, and the end of the action. Thus he who lets his light shine before men in obedience to God's commands, and he who does his good works only to be seen of men, do the same thing as to outward appearance, though the one only seeks a good report for his master's honor, and the other is vainglorious. He who firmly adheres to truth, and he who will not be convinced of his error, are equally fixed and immovable, though the one is virtuously constant, and the other viciously obstinate. He who values himself *only*, and despises his fellow

168. Astell's marginal note: Prv 22:1.

creatures, is proud; but he who esteems human nature in general, and is sensible of the dignity of a Christian, and values both himself and others for this reason, has a truly great and generous mind. Our neighbor's necessities are equally relieved, whether we give him money with an intention to help him for God's sake, or meaning to buy him over to our party; though the one is charity, and the other corruption. To refuse an obliging compliance with our reputed benefactors, to contradict their will, and oppose their measures, passes for ingratitude, and is really so when their desires are just and reasonable, or even innocent and indifferent; and if we make unkind and evil returns to the good they endeavor to do to our minds, this is the vilest ingratitude. But if they expect submission right or wrong, if they would have us stifle, or act contrary to the sentiments of a well-informed judgment, and expect a tame compliance where honor and conscience oblige us to oppose them, in this case opposition is integrity. There is a zeal that is set on fire of hell, and a zeal according to knowledge; and it is not so much the warmth of the pursuit, as the goodness and consequence of the matter, and the regular methods of pursuing it, that give the distinction.

304. *The way of calumniating*[169] *good actions.* And therefore, since we can't demonstrate the goodness of our actions, but only make it probable, because we don't view each other's hearts, and in all probable truths there is something to be offered on the other side; since few men's judgments as they manage them, are so correct as to distinguish nicely between good and evil, praiseworthy and blamable; few judge rightly for themselves much less for their neighbor, whose principles and circumstances they know but in part, and whose heart they can't penetrate; and since a failure in any circumstance spoils the goodness and beauty of the action; when men are disposed to decry what is not for their turn, and can find people to spread, or countenance, or listen to their calumnies,[170] and such are seldom wanting, it is no hard matter to give the best action an ill representation. Either the motives are not good, the circumstances faulty, the end is not the best, or the method improper, or if all other detractions fail, the intention which they know nothing of, shall be suspected and arraigned, nay the very

169. *calumniating*] falsely representing.

170. calumnies] slanders.

consequences, events which no human wisdom or power can provide for, shall be objected. And by such wise reasonings, the very worst actions when they succeed are generally applauded, and the best designs decried when they are unsuccessful!

305. *What regard due to our bodies.* I am next to consider what regard is due to our bodies, which some of us are so concerned about as if they were our all. And yet we seem to forget their greatest excellency, which is the being "members of Christ,"[171] and "temples of His holy spirit."[172] Upon this account, and this only we ought to value and reverence them, it being sacrilegious to desecrate what is "holy," and what was devoted to God's service at our baptism. And the punishment of such a profanation is proportionable to the guilt, for "he who defiles a temple, shall God destroy."[173] All the works of our great creator are in number, weight, and measure, and therefore without controversy, it is for very good reasons that He has *so* united a corruptible body to an immortal mind, that the impressions which are made on the former, shall be perceived and attended with certain sensations in the other, and this by ways altogether mysterious and incomprehensible, and only to be resolved into the efficacy[174] of the divine will. The body then may be of great service to us, if we know how to employ it according to the design of our maker. And not to enquire what our bodies would have been, had we preserved our innocence, the restorer of our nature has shown us, that they are capable of glorifying God by being offered up "a living sacrifice, holy and acceptable to Him, which is our reasonable service."[175] The meaning of which is, that whereas under the former economies beasts were slain and offered on God's altar; under the Christian, the appetites arising from the union of the body with the mind, are to be sacrificed all the days of our life, than which there is not anything more reasonable.

306. *A Christian's is a life of sobriety and severity.* For it is evident from many texts of holy scripture, which command us to "mortify the body," to be "dead" to it, and to "be crucified with Christ,"

171. 1 Cor 6:15.

172. Astell's marginal note: 2 Cor 6:16; 1 Cor 6:19.

173. Astell's marginal note: 1 Cor 3:17.

174. efficacy] causal power.

175. Astell's marginal note: Rom 12:1.

if we desire to "live with Him," that the life of a Christian is a life of sobriety and severity, in opposition to voluptuousness and the pleasures of sense, to which we are so prone by the corrupt nature we bring into the world with us, and yet more by the evil manners and customs we learn in it.[176] And therefore upon our admission into the church of Christ, we are required and strictly engaged, to renounce all these, as much as the necessities of life permit. And that this is highly reasonable is also evident, not only by reason of God's sovereignty, who may set His servants and creatures what task He pleases; but also because this present life is but a state of probation, and a very short passage to eternity, and God only knows what dispositions are necessary to qualify and prepare us for that kingdom and bliss He has provided for us; nor is there any manner of proportion between the short work enjoined, and the endless reward with which it is His good pleasure to recompense our honest endeavors.

307. *What to be understood by mortification.* The *mortification* of a Christian is not a transient act, it is a living above the pleasures of sense, and the low concerns of the body. And it is not to be wondered that our holy religion requires this, for even reason will inform us, that an all-wise God could never design an immortal mind so contemptible an employment, as the busying itself about a corruptible body. Nor is the subjecting of the body to the mind in reality a pain; on the contrary it is a pleasure, as being most agreeable to the nature and reason of things. But it is called mortification, because most of us being educated in a sensual life, it becomes painful to deny our once indulged desires and to reduce them to reason, and the doing of this is all the difficulty of a Christian life. A life that abounds with pleasure, and has no pain, but what is accidental, arising from our indisposition and the ill habits we have needlessly contracted, or else from the malice of men, who are resolved that "all who will live godly in Christ Jesus shall suffer persecution."[177]

308. *A sensual, opposite to, and less pleasant than a Christian life.* To live a *sensual life*, by which I mean not only those gross liberties and intemperances of any kind, which everyone owns to be sins, but even an indulgence to the innocent pleasures of sense as we call them,

176. Astell's marginal note: Rom 8:13 and 6:6.
177. 2 Tm 3:12.

is to be "alienated from the life of God";[178] for if sense has dominion over us, it is no great difference after what manner, or to which of our senses we are enslaved. And it is very remarkable, that the rich man of whom we have so terrible an account in the gospel, is not blamed for any notorious sin.[179] We don't read that he got his estate by fraud or injustice, or that he was a drunkard, a glutton, or an unclean person. He only "lived well," and indulged himself in the free use of such sensible pleasures as a great fortune afforded. And as a natural consequence of this, being well and at ease, he looked no further than himself, and had no regard to his indigent brother. But though the gospel condemns such a life as this, it does not follow that the life of a Christian is not a life of pleasure in reality and in a true sense. So far is Christianity from depriving us of anything desirable, that it affords us the only solid, satisfying, and durable pleasures. For our creator is too good to give us appetites and desires merely to torture us, and having planted in our nature a desire of pleasure, He designs without doubt to satisfy it. But then having given us reason and liberty, and set before us great variety of pleasures, He expects we should choose the best; and by forbearing the other, exercise our virtue and so prepare ourselves in this short time of trial, for pleasures infinite and eternal.

309. *Of bodily austerities.* As for bodily austerities, I neither commend nor blame them, "let everyone do" as he is "persuaded in his own mind."[180] The apostle tells us, that they "profit" a "little," but that "godliness is profitable unto all things";[181] a Christian disposition and temper of mind being the business, to which all the actions of our lives must tend. If austerities make us more holy, just, and good, let us use them in God's name: but if we place our religion chiefly in these, neglecting "the weightier matters";[182] if they render us supercilious and sour, opinionated and censorious, it is hard to say whether such a severity as this, or indulgence to the body is more pernicious, for both are contrary to the spirit of Christianity. For to be rigid to others is an excess and disorder of mind, and not less an intemperance than to be

178. Eph 4:18.
179. Astell's marginal note: Lk 16.
180. Rom 14:5.
181. 1 Tm 4:8.
182. Mt 23:23.

indulgent to the body; it is indeed an indulgence to ourselves only in another instance. Nor does anything bring a greater reproach upon a strict and regular life, than that undue liberty which some who pretend to it take, to censure and judge such as don't come up to their measures.

310. *Of fasting and its use.* Yet fasting is a duty, for the church enjoins it, whose injunctions are not superseded because they are too much neglected. And unless we have spoiled our constitution, moderate fasting and abstinence is the most wholesome physic, and on this account useful even to the body. But if the church's authority is not sufficient, though she derives it from her Lord, we have that of our Lord Himself,[183] who had not given directions about fasting, if He had not judged it requisite and expedient. For though it is superstition or weakness of judgment, and not reason, that prompts us to such a rigorous usage of the body as to disable it from serving the mind; yet reason may use a discreet authority over it, if for no other end, yet to preserve its dominion, and to make the inferior appetites pliable to the mind. Such self-denials do also dispose us to compassion, by making us feel sometimes what our poor brother often suffers, and which we too seldom consider, unless it comes home to ourselves. A day of fasting is also a good opportunity for recollection, especially if we live in the hurry of the world; but I am at a loss to find how bare fasting makes us more capable of devotion. For they who eat and drink till they are unfit to meditate and pray, ought to be taught daily temperance, rather than prescribed a weekly or monthly fast.

311. *Not to judge others, nor indulge ourselves.* And therefore, though I will not say my neighbor sins when he indulges the reputed innocent pleasures of sense, because I am not a judge of his circumstances and necessities, and "to his own master he stands or falls,"[184] yet I may reasonably conclude, that such an indulgence were a sin in me. As the example of others does not authorize me to allow myself the pleasures they take; so neither am I to blame them for taking those allowances I think fit to deny myself. Everyone is best acquainted with his own temper and necessities, he best knows what pleasures refresh and what bewitch him; what gives him new vigor in the works of his calling and the offices of religion, and what engrosses his thoughts

183. Astell's marginal note: Mt 6. [Astell refers to Mt 6:16–18 in particular.]
184. Rom 14:4.

and time, making his addresses to heaven a mere verbal and tasteless employment. Unless he has spoiled his relish, he is able to distinguish between a transient *goust*,[185] a short commotion of the passions, and striking of the fancy, which goes off in weariness, trouble, or satiety; and those calm, but yet satisfying joys which sweetly charm the mind, leaving no sting, no uneasiness behind them, and which being reviewed by the severest reason, afford a new and lasting entertainment. In fine, he is best able to compute for himself the difference between little momentary pleasures, and such as are of an endless duration; and when this is done, a reasonable person I should think, needs not be told where to fix, his very love of pleasure is sufficient to determine him. For a Christian's mortification is no hard task upon the main, it is only a little physic[186] to carry off his distempers, an exercise to strengthen his constitution, and by this means to prepare him for the greatest delights, such as never end, and always satisfy.

312. *The body to be subjected to the mind, even for pleasure's sake.* I conclude then, that we have at once most effectually mortified our bodies, and also taken the most reasonable care of them, when they are reduced to be most obedient servants to the mind; when we have brought them to stand in need of no great observance, but to be ready to accommodate themselves to all conditions and circumstances, so that they know how "to be full and to be hungry, to abound and to suffer need."[187] When we neither surfeit[188] in plenty, nor repine[189] in want, nor are disordered by either; but can thank God for both, correcting the former with fear, and supplying the latter with cheerfulness. When our bodies never call away the mind from its proper pleasures, to supply their imaginary wants, or to humor their appetites, but are healthy and satisfied with what reason assigns them. And this I take to be the best way to keep the body in good tune, to avoid pain, and to be always easy. I only fear there is too much Epicurism in it;[190]

185. *goust*] from the French *goût*, "liking, relish, zest, fondness" (*OED*).

186. physic] medicine.

187. Phil 4:12.

188. surfeit] experience nausea.

189. repine] complain.

190. Epicurism] generally speaking, the pursuit of pleasure. More specifically, Astell may have in mind the ancient Epicurean idea of happiness as the highest form of pleasure

for by living thus according to nature, the simplest refreshments and such as are in almost everyone's power, have a greater relish than the most studied delicacies to an indulged and a disordered appetite, that is always longing after what it has not and surfeiting with what it has. And further, though acute distempers arise from some real disorder in the body or machine, and therefore are not to be cured by mere thinking, or so much as diverted when the pain is violent, yet it must be confessed, that our little uneasinesses and daily complaints, are mostly, if not always, in the imagination only, so that to withdraw the mind from these fancies, and to think *rightly*, is their proper cure. Or suppose they be not wholly in the fancy, a diversion to those noble entertainments which are properly the pleasures of the mind, as arising from its peculiar objects, and not at all from sensation, would take us off from attending to the little complaints of sense, and by this means remove them.

313. *Our duty with regard to our estates. Our estates* are another talent which God has committed to our trust, and our duty in relation to these, is to be *content* with what His providence has allotted us, thankful for it, and careful to dispose of it to His honor and service. For the goods of this world are indeed advantages when "they are found in the way of righteousness."[191] And he who possesses and uses them rightly, is to be highly esteemed, because he gives evidence of an uncommon virtue, showing that he is not to be overcome by that which corrupts the most. There are ladies, I hope, who have so just a sense of this, and distinguish so rightly between solid and superficial advantages, that they will not account it unmannerly to repeat the son of Sirach's words; that "whether he be rich, noble, or poor, their glory is the fear of the Lord";[192] and that "a mean estate is not always to be contemned,[193] nor the rich that is foolish to be had in admiration."[194]

(*ataraxia*), which consists in the body's health and the soul's freedom from vexation or disturbance. She makes a similar point in her *Proposal I* and *II*, 86, 221.

191. Prv 16:31.

192. Ecclus 10:22.

193. contemned] treated with contempt.

194. Ecclus 22:23. In the first edition, this sentence directly addresses a single female (most likely Catherine Jones): "But your Ladyship has so just a sense of this, that I know you would not forgive me if I did not add, that 'whether he be rich, noble, or poor ….'"

314. *The proper object of contentment. Contentment* is properly an acquiescence in our present condition without further desires, and in this sense its only object are the goods of this present life; for it would be a fault and not a virtue to be content with the true goods of the mind, so as to sit down without any further desires after them. We shall it's true be content, if by this is meant *satisfied*, with our portion in the blessed life to come, because everyone will see that the distribution is most equitable, and will be so reasonable himself as not to desire it should be otherwise. But in this present state of improvement, I can hardly call it less than a sin to be content with lower attainments when we are invited and encouraged, nay even commanded to come up higher. And when we have made the most plausible apologies for this inglorious sloth that it will bear, it can't be excused of proceeding from an evil principle. But though we are to be content in whatsoever state God has placed us in this world, without any uneasy desire of change, yet it is neither unlawful nor unseemly to increase our estate as well as other talents, when it comes fairly in our way. When we can do it honestly and honorably, without putting ourselves to much trouble and care, or neglecting a more important business and better improvements. Getting an estate indeed is not a woman's business, and therefore for the most part we are free[195] from the solicitude of "laying house to house, and land to land,"[196] so uncomely in a Christian, who is but a "stranger and pilgrim upon earth,"[197] who "has no abiding city here," but "who seeks one to come":[198] it were well if we knew how to keep and use what our relations have provided for us, and did not put it out of our own power, into hands that seldom or never dispose of it as they ought.

315. It has been already observed,[199] that we are not proprietors, but "stewards of the manifold gifts of God," and of riches among the rest;[200] that our poor brother derives a right from God the lord of

195. The first edition reads "she is free" instead of "we are free."

196. Is 5:8.

197. Heb 11:13.

198. Heb 13:14.

199. Astell's marginal note: See §§143 and 178.

200. 1 Pt 4:10: "As every man hath received the gift, *even so* minister the same one to another, as good stewards of the manifold grace of God."

all, to what exceeds a reasonable provision for ourselves and families, according to that station which God has placed us in;[201] and that this provision is to be estimated by the measures of the gospel, by right reason, and the judgment of prudent and sober persons, not by our supposed and imaginary occasions. I might also add, that alms is the best way of improving our estates, and is a laying of them out to our own greatest advantage; but there has so much been said upon this subject by better pens,[202] that I need not further insist on it. I shall therefore only tell your Ladyship, what sort of distribution of our money that is which I take to be alms, and what not. For they who will not be persuaded to put their money to this most secure and advantageous *use* by the precepts and promises of the holy scripture, by the present pleasure and profit as well as the future, will never be prevailed on by anything that I can say.

316. *What is, and what is not, Christian almsgiving.* A *Christian almsgiving* is a secret and cheerful distribution of our goods to our necessitous neighbor, for God's sake, and with no other prospect but of a reward from Him. They must be *our goods*, we must have a just title to them, and should have discharged all our obligations of justice before we pretend to give alms. Otherwise we only make restitution, or pay our debts; or we give what's none of our own, and so are unjust, or oppressive, but are not charitable. It must be *for God's sake*, for if it is for our own, and to appease the yearnings of our bowels,[203] that pain we can't help feeling when we see or hear of a calamitous person, it is *compassion*: if it be for our neighbor's sake, it is *friendship*, or *humanity*. We must propose no "reward but what God's promises offer us."[204] For if we give our favors to gain the affection of the receiver it is *liberality*, the very name of which virtue shows (by the way) that a scanty and improper gift, where the desire of the giver does not supply it by speaking his kindness, has no claim to the reward of a grateful affection. If we lay out our money to purchase a dependent we drive a bargain, which is so much the better or worse, according to the use we make of it; but *still it is a bargain*, and neither an *alms nor a benefit*.

201. Astell's marginal note: Prv 3:27–28.

202. Astell's marginal note: Mt 25; 1 Tm 6:17, and so on; Is 58; Prv 19:17; Ps 41; Heb 13:16.

203. bowels] "heart" (*OED*, s.v. "bowel").

204. Astell appeals to sentiments expressed in Mt 6:1, 4.

For the scripture enjoins him that "giveth to do it with simplicity,"[205] that is, with a pure intention, and without any sinister ends and low designs. For if it is for ostentation, or to receive the praise of men, this is *vainglory*, and this poor praise is all the recompense we must expect. Since by proposing this we discharge God of the debt, who otherwise has graciously condescended to make the almsgiver His creditor. Our alms must also be done *in secret*, for God who "has made of one blood all nations of men," and who "is no respecter of persons," having allowed us ability to give, "which is more blessed than to receive";[206] expects that we should have some regard to our afflicted brother, and to the modesty of human nature at least in gratitude to Him. And that our poor neighbors may not be despicable in our eyes, as seeming to be neglected by providence, God is pleased to show an extraordinary regard to them, to constitute them His own representatives, to reckon what we do to them as done to Himself, and has promised not only an ample reward, but even a peculiar honor, to him who relieves his neighbor's modesty as well as his want.[207] But to publish our alms by any sort of artifices, to gaze upon his miseries, and to lay them open to the bleak air of an ill-natured world, which is apt to reckon poverty the greatest crime, or to make him more miserable by endeavoring to render him mercenary, may be *vanity*, *pride*, or *insolence*, or even *cruelty*, but is not Christian almsgiving.[208] Which in the last place, must be a *cheerful* distribution, cheerfulness including the readiness and plentifulness of the relief; so far as we are able. For a niggardly alms rather upbraids[209] our neighbor's necessities than relieves them; and if it comes forced from us by importunity, he has paid a valuable consideration for it. "God loveth a secret and cheerful giver,"[210] and so do men; and the most compassionate Jesus who felt all our innocent infirmities, by that very strict charge He lays upon Christians in this matter,[211] has provided for the relief of His poor members without

205. Rom 12:8.

206. Astell's marginal note: Acts 17:26, 10:34, and 20:35.

207. Astell's marginal note: Prv 14:31; Mt 25:34, and so on; Prv 19:17.

208. Astell's marginal note: Mt 6:1, and so on.

209. upbraids] insults.

210. Astell's marginal note: 2 Cor 9:7.

211. Astell's marginal note: Mt 6.

exposing them to the insults of the rich, or increasing their necessities by the pain of disclosing them needlessly.

317. *Of honor, and the use we are to make of it.* Real *honor* is the same thing with virtue, and even *titular honor* considered in itself, I take to be a nobler talent than wealth. Because riches may be acquired by mean and vile methods, whereas titular honor ought, and therefore is supposed, to be the reward of real honor or virtue. And they who are born of noble and generous parents, are presumed to have the best education, and to be fired to great actions by the examples of their predecessors. Honor by placing us on higher ground sets us more in view, and so renders our light more conspicuous, and our evil example more pernicious; and we ought to remember, that as we are accountable for the evil we do, so for the good we omit. It is a dangerous thing to be placed above others, unless our heads are so steady as to discern, that the cringes of the most are for their own sakes, that by seeming our slaves, they may flatter us into being theirs: and that the respect and observance of the wise and good, rest not in us but in God, whose superiority is honored in us. But honor being a sort of reputation, and to be acquired and used after the same manner, needs not be further insisted on.

318. *Of power and authority.* The course of the world does not often lodge *power and authority* in women's hands, though by the use is made of them, when providence has placed them there, one may reasonably conclude, that as it does not show the justice, so neither is it for the interest of men to withhold them. For besides that glorious example we all have in view, which is the delight of English hearts, and on which the eyes of all Europe are fixed with admiration,[212] we have many ancient precedents to show how power and greatness *ought* to be, and how they *have* been used by ladies. To go no further than holy writ, the character of Deborah seems to me much greater than that of any of the mighty men who went before her.[213] Esther employed her interest, and even exposed her life with heroic fortitude for the church of God, for she considered that He who defends it as the apple of His eye, would cause "enlargement and deliverance to arise" some way or other, and if she "altogether held her peace at that time," and

212. Astell's marginal note: n.b., This book was first published in the reign of Queen Anne.
213. Deborah is the strong female political leader of the Book of Judges.

slipped the opportunity of being the glorious instrument, she should only deprive herself of that honor and reward which God designed her, it being highly probable that she "was come to the kingdom for such a time as this."[214]

319. *Of the use and abuse of time; and diversion.* Among all our talents[215] there's not any more valuable than *time*, nor can the other be improved if this is wasted. But we are generally a contradiction to ourselves in this particular, for we seem to have at once both too much and too little of it. The shortness of life is a common complaint, and yet they who complain the loudest, are the people in the world who are most at a loss to get rid of their time, that is, their life. Few have leisure as they tell us, to improve their minds, and to prepare themselves for heaven, they are cumbered[216] with many things, greater affairs one would think, because the other is deferred for their sakes. And yet these same people have twenty impertinent inventions to dispose of their time, which would otherwise be a burden to them. Diversion, or a relaxation of our spirits, when we are wearied with any employment of body or mind, is very requisite. But what can be more ridiculous than for them to seek diversion who have no business, but are only weary of their idleness? Business being the only proper diversion for such as these. And indeed, were we as prudent managers as we ought to be, we might make one useful employment be a diversion to another. For it is the dwelling long upon any one thing that tires us, and we find ourselves as weary of our sports as of our business when we have been long about them. Variety gives the relief, and there is enough to be found among useful things, so that we need not fly to impertinencies.[217]

320. *Conversation, its end and abuse.* Conversation is one way of passing off our time, and were it what it should be, a very useful as well as entertaining one. But alas! Among all the talk that is in the world, where shall we find the conversation? For the end of speech is to communicate our thoughts for mutual advantage; but where is he who speaks his thoughts? Or who thinks so as to deserve attention?

214. Astell's marginal note: Esther 4. [The quotations are from Esther 4:14.]

215. talents] riches.

216. cumbered] encumbered.

217. impertinencies] irrelevancies.

The Jews were commanded to "talk" of God's precepts "sitting in the house," and "walking by the way," when "they lay down, and when they rose up";[218] and particularly of that great commandment, "thou shalt love the Lord thy God with all thine heart, and with all thy soul, and with all thy might."[219] But we who are called Christians, to whom "life and immortality is brought to light by the gospel";[220] we who are to "have our conversation in heaven," we who have been told by our judge, that we must give "account for every idle word at the day of judgment,"[221] and according to the apostle, those are idle words, or "corrupt communications" "which do not tend to edifying";[222] yet for all this, we Christians conclude, that religion is a business to be transacted in our closets only, it must not appear in the world to spoil conversation, and we choose to talk of anything rather than of the best, and most sublime, as well as the most useful and most necessary subject!

321. *Topics.* St. Paul would not have "filthiness, nor foolish talkings; nor jestings which are not convenient so much as once named among Christians, but rather giving of thanks."[223] As much as to say, mirth and the refreshment of the spirits are the usual pretense for frothy[224] talk; but a Christian can cheer his heart a much better way, even by remembering the infinite and innumerable mercies of God, which call for our continual acknowledgments and loudest praises. But few of us take up the son of Sirach's grateful resolution, "the Lord hath given me a tongue and I will praise Him therewith,"[225] we seldom remember that "in the multitude of words there wanteth not sin," and that "he who refraineth his lips is wise."[226] And that "if any man offend not in word, the same is a perfect man, and able also to bridle the

218. Dt 11:19.
219. Dt 6:5.
220. 2 Tm 1:10.
221. Astell's marginal note: Mt 12:36–37.
222. Astell's marginal note: Eph 4:29.
223. Astell's marginal note: Eph 5:3–4.
224. frothy] trifling.
225. Ecclus 51:22.
226. Prv 10:19.

whole body."[227] But the vices of the tongue are too many to be enlarged on here, and when we have cut off all profane and unseemly, censorious and detracting, slanderous and false, ill-natured and scurrilous, boasting and vain, rude and flattering, pragmatical and impertinent talk, there will not much remain I fear to keep up the common way of conversation. Even the best and the most innocent one meets with, does only give us stronger impressions of sensible things, withdrawing our minds from what is spiritual and eternal; tying us more and more to this present world, whereas our perfection and happiness consists in being loose to it: and I make no doubt that our "evil communications" have contributed more than anything to the general "corruption of our manners."[228]

322. *Censoriousness and rash judging.* It may look affected to place the *not judging* others among the duties owing to ourselves, rather than among those that are due to our neighbor, yet I shall venture to do it. Because *censure*[229] may sometimes be of use to others, but can never be so to us, who discerning only the appearances of things, and this very imperfectly, can't but be ignorant of the merits of the cause; and were we ever so well informed, yet wanting authority, our judgment must needs be rash and unjust, and as such is condemned and forbid by our Lord, and therefore whatever injury our neighbors may suffer by it, we ourselves incur a greater, by drawing upon our heads His severe and righteous judgment. Censure may do good to the world in that it is a check upon vice and carelessness; it may discover and convict the guilty; may admonish the innocent to walk with more circumspection; and by showing everyone what they are to expect unless they watch over their actions, it may remove the occasion of censure from such as idly or maliciously seek it. But this does no way justify the censorious, who always do mischief to themselves, whatever good may accidentally happen to others. Nor can it be supposed that they exercise their talent out of public-spiritedness; for it tends as much to the public good to praise and encourage virtue, as to blame and discountenance vice.

227. Jas 3:2.

228. 1 Cor 15:33.

229. *censure*] critical judgment.

323. *Charity to be guarded with prudence.* *Charity* indeed is unsuspicious, it "thinks no evil," it "believeth all things, hopeth all things," taking every action by the best handle, making all allowances that the matter will bear.[230] And what's the consequence of this? Why generally speaking the charitable person will think, or at least speak better of most men than they deserve. And if he does not make use of the "prudence of the serpent" in standing on his own guard, as well as of the "innocency of the dove" by inoffensiveness to others, it is like he may be overreached, and without the special providence and protection of God, may some way or other suffer by it.[231] And therefore when mankind are generally corrupt, so that charity itself can hardly think or speak well of them, St. Peter's advice is certainly to take place, "save yourselves from this untoward generation."[232] "Beware of men" as our Lord directed,[233] keep as much out of their way as innocently you can, not only by reason of the injury you may suffer in your temporal affairs, but chiefly because of the damage that may happen to your mind. Too frequent and sad experience showing, that the manners of the good are more easily corrupted by the contagion of the wicked, than these are reclaimed by the good example and advice of the former. And if no other mischief falls out, a "righteous soul" will at least be "vexed" with the "daily conversation" of the ungodly;[234] it will not without great difficulty be able to "possess itself in patience," and to preserve that meek and charitable temper which the gospel requires.[235] Nor ought anyone so far to presume on their own virtues, as to put them to an unnecessary trial.

324. *We ought to avoid temptations.* For one of the subtlest temptations that the enemies of our virtue and honor can lay in our way, and which in all probability will ruin us if hearkened to, is the supposing that our virtues are not perfect, or so much as sincere, unless they have stood a trial, and that therefore we ought to expose them. Now it is very true that God never calls us to a trial, that is, He

---

230. Astell's marginal note: 1 Cor 13. [The citations are from 1 Cor 13:5, 7.]

231. Astell's marginal note: Mt 10:16–17.

232. Astell's marginal note: Acts 2:40.

233. Mt 10:17.

234. 2 Pt 2:8.

235. Lk 21:19.

never disposes of us by His providence in such a manner as that we can't avoid a temptation, but He also gives us strength to overcome it, if we are not wanting to ourselves, so that if we fall by this temptation, it is too sure a sign that our virtue was either not sincere, or very weak and defective. But it is also too true, that we never voluntarily expose ourselves, but either through such a vain presumption as provokes God to leave us to our own ill conduct, in due correction of our folly; or else when the temptation has got possession of our hearts, and we want some pretense to say it was too strong for us. To be sure, we can have no well-grounded confidence in God's assistance, when we thus foolishly and wickedly tempt Him, by running into dangers which He Himself has taught us to pray against. And they are bold people who, considering the sad wrecks of human nature, will venture anywhere upon their own strength. A hardiness that does not at all become us women, the stronger sex as they call themselves, may show it if they please. For it is certain, that if we mean in good earnest to keep ourselves from sin and folly, we must not parley[236] with our enemy, but must carefully avoid the first beginnings, the occasions, all the approaches, and every appearance of, or tendency to evil. If we do thus, it is not hard to come off conquerors by the grace which God affords us: but it is the height of folly, and contempt of God, to give up our strength, to open the gates to our enemy, and then complain that we are overcome.

325. *Of meekness.* As for *meekness* it may be considered either by itself as it is opposed to rash anger, or else as a part of *patience*;[237] but consider them as we will, these two virtues are absolutely necessary in order to tranquility of mind, which is the heaven of this world. No unreasonableness in others can excuse us from behaving ourselves meekly towards them, because we are commanded to "show all meekness unto all men."[238] Nor do the contentions and furious "disputes of this world," tend at all to the service of religion.[239] For the "word of God" "which is able to save our souls," is to be "received with

236. parley] converse.
237. Astell's marginal note: Lk 21:19.
238. Astell's marginal note: Ti 3:2.
239. Astell's marginal note: 1 Cor 1:20.

meekness";[240] with a humble disposition and readiness to admit of truth upon a fair examination, without captious cavils, or blending it with our interests or humors. "A good conversation and the meekness of wisdom," as it is the best evidence of "a wise man," and one "endued with *real* knowledge," so it is the most probable way to convince the gainsayers.[241] For he is by no means fit to instruct and direct others, who has not first learnt to govern his own tongue and to regulate his passions.

326. *Of patience and perseverance.* But this branch of *patience* which has an affinity with meekness, goes somewhat further; for it not only suppresses our anger, and makes us show "gentleness to all men" so often as we think fit to treat with them, but it also enables us to bear with their stupidity and perverseness, and is that "long-suffering," that "beareth all things, and hopeth all things," whereby the charitable Christian continues his endeavors to reduce his neighbors to reason and to their true interest, notwithstanding all discouragements, which is indeed a godlike temper, and the only patience that the divine nature is capable of.[242] But besides this, our infirmity and mortality make other sorts of patience necessary for us. The calamities of this present life, whether they be sickness and pain, or whatever else, are not only to be sustained with fortitude, but submitted to with humility, meekness, and patience; thus we are commanded to be "patient in tribulation," and "tribulation is said to work patience."[243] There is also another sort of patience or *perseverance*, in opposition to that hastiness of spirit which prompts us to snatch at the fruit before its proper season, expect to compass our end, without taking due measures towards it; and either through an imprudent eagerness, or inconstancy, or weariness, give out in our Christian race before we have received our crown. And therefore we are bid to "bring forth fruit with patience" or perseverance,[244] are told the "necessity" of this virtue, and are assured that without it we cannot "inherit the promises."[245] For

240. Astell's marginal note: Jas 1:21.

241. Astell's marginal note: Jas 3:13.

242. Astell's marginal note: 2 Tm 2:24; 1 Thes 5:14; Col 3:12; 1 Cor 13[:7].

243. Astell's marginal note: Rom 12:12 and 5:3.

244. Astell's marginal note: Lk 8:15.

245. Astell's marginal note: Heb 10:36; Rom 2:7.

"when the righteous turneth away from his righteousness, and committeth iniquity, and dieth in it, all his righteousness that he hath done shall not be mentioned, for his iniquity that he hath done shall he die."[246] In short, patience is such a sedateness of mind, as preserves us from being ruffled or discomposed with the unreasonableness of men, or the miseries of human life, keeping us always ready to do and suffer the will of God with constancy unto the end.

327. *What necessary to render our actions truly Christian.* To say all at once: to act without any principles is to live by chance; and whatever it be it is not a Christian action that is not lawful in itself, and in all its circumstances, and also performed upon a Christian principle, that is, for such an end, with such an intention, and in such a manner, as becomes a Christian. If I am sober or meek by temper and inclination; if I abstain from scandalous sins lest I hazard my reputation; if I am not guilty of murder or theft out of fear of the law; the advantage of good laws, of a sense of honor, and of a happy constitution appears, but there's nothing of religion in the matter. If *passion*, and not reason "kindles our zeal" it is to be feared that it will be without "knowledge," and the same may be said of every other virtue.[247] For Christianity is a reasonable service, nor will the "mind" ever be well "formed," or "brought" to a truly "virtuous religious life," where reason conducted by grace does not drive the "chariot," and manage the "passions and affections."[248] And as our virtues are not true, so neither will they be lasting unless they proceed from a right principle, are done for the honor of God, and in obedience to His commands. For he who

---

246. Astell's marginal note: Ez 18:24, 26.

247. Rom 10:2.

248. Astell refers without acknowledgement to Charles Hickman, *Fourteen Sermons Preached, at St James's Church in Westminster* (London: James Orme, 1700), "Sermon Ninth": "Our reason has but little to do in the forming of our minds, and bringing us to a virtuous religious life; it is our passions and affections that must do the work, for till they begin to move, our reason is but like a chariot when the wheels are off, that is never like to perform the journey" (272). Hickman (1648–1713) was the Church of Ireland bishop of Derry and a well-known spokesperson for the High Church party in Ireland. See S. J. Connolly's biography in *ODNB*, s.v. "Hickman, Charles," http://www.oxforddnb.com/view/article/13210 (accessed January 20, 2012).

recommends *temperance* (as some do)[249] because it "promotes our health,"[250] says nothing to the purpose to people who tell one a debauch does them no hurt, or who pretend it does them good, and who use it by way of physic. If we have no better motive of *justice* than that it "prevents the revenges of the injured," and "gains us trust";[251] he who can conveniently betray a trust without being discovered, and who is too cunning or too powerful to be awed by the fear of revenge, will allow himself to be as unjust as he can be with impunity. And he who is *charitable* to others, only "to draw back their love and affection to himself," will never practice the noblest charity of doing good to those from whom we can't hope for anything again.[252] If we are *patient* only for our own "quiet," and not in obedience to God, we have our present reward, and must not look for a recompense from Him hereafter.[253] If *self-denial* goes no further than the "establishing the power of reason over us";[254] according to some men's account of reason, "self-denial" will never carry us on to take up our cross and follow Christ, and yet without a readiness to do this, we can't be His disciples.[255]

328. *How to secure our principles and intentions.* And therefore if we would secure our virtue, and render it acceptable to God, by uniting it to the merits of Christ our head, whereby it becomes truly valuable, we must act upon the same principle, and with the same design by which our Lord acted, who tells us, He "sought not His own will, but the will of the father who sent Him."[256] For God's will is steady and invariable, it allows no manner of dispensation for iniquity of any kind, or upon any occasion; it forbids secret as well as open sins; those which are profitable and in vogue, as well as such as are at present hurtful and decried; it lays restraints upon the motions of the will as well as upon the words and actions; our very thoughts must be pure

---

249. The first edition reads "(as our divine does)" instead of "(as some do)." The divine in question is the anonymous author of *A Lady's Religion*.

250. Astell's marginal note (first edition only): *Lady's Religion*, 5.

251. Astell quotes from *Lady's Religion*, 5.

252. *Lady's Religion*, 5.

253. *Lady's Religion*, 5.

254. *Lady's Religion*, 5.

255. Astell's marginal note: Mt 16:24.

256. Astell's marginal note: Jn 5:30.

and innocent, because they are "manifest in His sight"[257] who is of "purer eyes than to behold iniquity," without condemning it.[258] And if we thus desire and endeavor to approve ourselves to the searcher of hearts, whatever is done out of reverence to God, though it be ever so small and indifferent in itself, it becomes a religious action; for "a cup of cold water" given to a disciple in "the name of a disciple, shall not lose its reward."[259]

329. *No good intention can excuse an evil action.* But though a pious intention will give value to an indifferent action, yet no intention how good so ever can justify, or so much as excuse a wicked one, an excellent and judicious prelate[260] lays it down for a rule (with what degree of evidence let the reader, upon consulting the place, judge)[261] that we must not do the least sin, that of a "harmless officious lie," "no not for the *glory of God*, and then certainly not for any other inferior end, not for the saving of a life, the conversion of a soul, the peace of the church, and (if even that were possible too) not for the redemption of the world."[262] With what detestation think you would he look down from his bliss, were he sensible of the loose morals of modern guides! Indeed we take such pains to hide our intentions from others, that often they become hid from ourselves; and being accustomed to say we designed all for God's glory, we come at last to believe that we are in earnest. Though one would think the fallacy of these pretenses is so evident, that they could not impose even upon our partial selves. For does not God govern the world? And is He not infinitely jealous of His

257. Astell's marginal note: Heb 4:13.

258. Hb 1:13.

259. Astell's marginal note: Mt 10:42.

260. Robert Sanderson (1587–1663), bishop of Lincoln and author of a popular book of sermons. See J. Sears McGee's biography in *ODNB*, s.v. "Sanderson, Robert," http://www.oxforddnb.com/view/article/24627 (accessed January 20, 2012).

261. In the first edition, the wording is less circumspect: this sentence reads "an excellent and judicious prelate has proved to us" instead of "an excellent and judicious prelate lays it down for a rule (with what degree of evidence let the reader, upon consulting the place, judge)."

262. Astell's marginal note: Bishop Sanderson, Sermon 2, 30. Fifth edition. [Astell refers to Robert Sanderson, *XXXIV Sermons. Viz., XVI. Ad Aulam. IV. Clerum. VI. Magistratum. VIII. Populum. By the Right Reverend Father in God, Robert Sanderson, Late Lord Bishop of Lincoln*, 5th ed. (London: A. Seil, 1671), "Ad Clerum" (The Second Sermon), 30.]

own glory? Which therefore must and will be provided for, in spite of the opposition of men and devils. What is it then that puts us in such fury or despair when our designs miscarry? It can't be a zeal for God's glory, because this will be taken care of whatever becomes of us and our projects: but that which in reality disquiets us, is the disappointment of our own little private aims.

330. *What renders an action good.* As for the circumstances and the manner of acting, they have in part been considered already. And doubtless if we take care of the innocency, and much more if we have regard to the beauty of our actions, we must remember our characters, the rank and station God has placed us in, the gifts He has bestowed upon us, the reputation and esteem we have acquired. For to do anything that misbecomes us, by being contrary to what is justly expected from us on any of these accounts, though otherwise, and simply considered, it were not unlawful, is however unlawful to us, because of its inexpediency and ill report, and for this reason it is a sin against God as well as a dishonor and injury to ourselves. And when we have thus secured the matter and the circumstances of our actions, that is, when upon an impartial and full examination they are found to be both lawful and expedient, we are then to take care that we do not pollute them by an evil intention; nor lessen and sully them by a low and unworthy one; nor disgrace them by our vicious and uncomely manner of performance.

331. *It should be also honorable.* Some gains and worldly advantages though they may be lawful, should however be let alone because they are not honorable, or because we can't convince the world that they are. For selfish designs, and private interest are such disgraceful motives, such contemptible aims, and so much beneath a Christian, that though we don't indeed propose them, yet if we can't so clear ourselves, but that they appear to be the reason of our actions, it is better to forbear these actions if they are not matter of precept, and therefore necessary, even though we may flatter ourselves with specious pretenses of future good from them. It being certain that a false step at first will spoil our race; and he for instance, who gets an estate unjustly, or dishonorably, by any tricking, indirect, or unhandsome ways, will never be able, I had almost said shall never be *willing*, to do the good he seemed to propose by his acquirements. Those plausible

pretenses and designs we form, being nothing else but the deceit and corruption of our hearts, to blind others, and to quiet the reproaches of our own minds.

332. *The measures of duty.* And therefore, we are in the first place to observe the laws of God strictly so called, that is the positive and direct commands and prohibitions laid down in holy writ. For in a latitude[263] all that follows may be called God's laws, as being referred to, and taking their obligation from them. In the next place the commands of our lawful governors are to be actually obeyed, if they are not inconsistent with the laws of God; or if they can't be obeyed they must be patiently submitted to.[264] After this we must take care that we avoid giving scandal; we must consider and observe the laws of reputation; together with all the other rules of decency and expediency, which do not fall under the former particulars. And in the last place, if self-denial, at all times so proper for a Christian, does not restrain us,[265] we are at liberty to comply with our own inclinations, which may lawfully be followed when all the rest are provided for, but not otherwise.

333. *Inclination to be suspected.* For when there are probabilities on each side, as to the lawfulness or unlawfulness, the expediency or inexpediency, the scandal and disreputation, or the innocency and indifferency of the action, I take it for a good rule to determine against that side to which humor and inclination would carry me. Because the heart is deceitful above all things, and there can be no hurt in denying myself, or restraining my liberty, either to secure my obedience to God or to just authority, or for the greater safety and advantage of my own or my neighbor's soul, or even for the sake of a good reputation, or to keep my desires under command. To be sure, we can never warrantably venture on that action to the scandal and disreputableness of which we have nothing to oppose, but its bare innocency, or indifferency, and the supposed future opportunities of doing some good by it, together with a present strong inclination, which last is indeed the weight that turns the scale, and almost always to our prejudice.

263. latitude] great extent.

264. Astell articulates the Anglican royalist doctrine of passive obedience.

265. The qualification "if self-denial, at all times so proper for a Christian, does not restrain us," is not in the first edition.

334. *Mistaken notions of passions and infirmities corrected.* By all that has hitherto been said it appears, that the "frailties" and "infirmities of the best proficients in grace," are not the same with those which the mere "disciples of nature" fall into.[266] "If we say that we have no sin we deceive ourselves"; and to pretend to virtues which we have not, or to appear better than we really are, is hypocrisy; but to endeavor to be "perfect," is to do what God commands.[267] Who "has instituted a holy religion *not* on purpose to pull us down," but to lead "us on unto perfection,"[268] and to "make us perfect in every good work to do His will";[269] not to upbraid the "vileness of our nature," but to *cure* it. Nor does any man who truly knows himself, even though he be the greatest saint, stand in need of the "malignity of his sins, to teach him to give God the glory, and to take shame unto himself"; for his entire dependence upon God will teach him "better manners" than any those "messengers of Satan can buffet him into," and be the best "demonstration that he is but man."[270] There is no necessity therefore to be vicious that we may be humble, they who find no other way to humble us than by proclaiming how "subject we are to passions and infirmities,"[271] do not indeed preach up more humility than their neighbors, but only more "vileness." And by all that appears from the practice of mankind, the men[272] who so little "affect to be counted godlike,"[273] that they own themselves not yet "escaped from the common pollutions of the

---

266. Astell quotes from Hickman, *Fourteen Sermons*, "Sermon Ninth," 257, 247.

267. Astell's marginal note: Mt 5:48; 2 Cor 13:11.

268. Astell's marginal note: Heb 6:1.

269. Astell's marginal note: Heb 13:21.

270. Again, Astell cites phrases from Hickman, *Fourteen Sermons*, "Sermon Ninth": "We are too apt of ourselves to be puffed up, and therefore God instituted a holy religion on purpose to pull us down; to show us the vileness of our nature, and to convince us of the malignity of our sins, and to teach us to give God the glory, and to take the shame unto ourselves. We are too ready to call ourselves God's, but that 'these messengers of Satan are sent to buffet us' into better manners, and our passions are a demonstration that 'we are but men'" (262).

271. Hickman, *Fourteen Sermons*, "Sermon Ninth," 249.

272. "people" in first edition.

273. Hickman, *Fourteen Sermons*, "Sermon Ninth," 260, 264.

world,"[274] are so far from being more humble or modest than others, that too many of them glory in their shame.

335. *With regard to scruples.* Scarce anything is more mistaken than sins of infirmity, or does more hurt both ways, by too much scruple, I mean, on one hand, and too much indulgence on the other. Where there is an honest heart, and but a weak understanding, the sincere Christian's true love to God, and consequently his utter abhorrence of all sin, and of all approaches towards it, which thus far is very right and good, makes him afflict himself unreasonably at such mere human and unindulged infirmities, as are the spots of the best children; as if these would deprive him of God's favor, in which he is much mistaken. And this is one of the last temptations whereby the enemy of our souls assaults us; who when he finds us so well resolved as not to be tempted to sin, tries to disturb us and to stop our progress in holiness; to rob us of our comfort, when he can't deprive us of our integrity.

336. *To unreasonable indulgence.* But it is not too much scruple but too much indulgence that is the common fault, and of most dangerous consequence. It is the taking of our notions of sin and duty from popular opinions and practices, not from the pure light of holy scripture and right reason. It is the making those infirmities which good people always strive against and endeavor to conquer, the measure of our conduct and the utmost of our aim. We are content to serve God in some things, such as don't cross our inclinations and worldly interests, in hopes He will connive at us in others. And then we cry, everyone, even the best, have their "passions," their "frailties," and "infirmities," and we have ours.[275] By which we don't mean the unavoidable weaknesses of human nature, which will stick to us as long as mortality does, but our willful and indulged transgressions, that "right hand" and "right eye" which our Lord commands us "to cast from us,"[276] the "sin that so easily besets us,"[277] and which indeed "has dominion over us."[278] Though whether we will consider it or no,

274. 2 Pt 2:20.

275. Astell refers sarcastically to Hickman, *Fourteen Sermons*, "Sermon Ninth," 249, 257.

276. Astell's marginal note: Mt 18:8–9.

277. Astell's marginal note: Heb 12:1.

278. Astell's marginal note: Rom 6:14.

it is plain from the tenor of the gospel, that such an infirmity as this is not consistent with our duty to God and our hopes of heaven. The very design of our savior's coming into the world, being "to purify to Himself a peculiar people zealous of good works."[279] And this being a matter of great importance, and not always duly represented, it may not be amiss to set it in a right light; for though there is a great respect due to superiors, and to those of a certain rank more particularly, yet the greatest is due to truth.

337. *Christians must subdue their passions.* That "God commandeth all men everywhere to repent,"[280] and has promised that upon true repentance (which is a change of life) they shall find mercy, is indeed "the fundamental notion of the gospel."[281] And it is also true, that "God has not bid a man put off all his passions,"[282] taking passion in a strict and proper sense, exclusive of those vices into which our natural passions too often hurry us; for Christianity does not extirpate the passions, it only teaches us to place them upon their proper objects, as has been already said. But if anyone by passions will needs understand sins, such as *pride, anger, hatred,* and *overwhelming sorrow*, and so on, it is very certain that the gospel commands us "to put off all these" of what kind so ever,[283] assuring us that such sinful "flesh and blood can't inherit the kingdom of God."[284] Nor is this at all "inconsistent with humanity, or impracticable,"[285] there being "so great a cloud of witnesses,"[286] who "through the spirit have mortified the deeds of the body."[287] And therefore far be it from any Christian to say, that God "has made us subject unto sin" any otherwise than by giving

279. Astell's marginal note: Ti 2:14.

280. Astell's marginal note: Acts 17:30.

281. Astell quotes from Hickman, *Fourteen Sermons*, "Sermon Ninth," 257.

282. Hickman, *Fourteen Sermons*, "Sermon Ninth," 263.

283. Astell's marginal note: Col 3:8.

284. Astell's marginal note: 1 Cor 15:50.

285. Astell paraphrases Hickman, *Fourteen Sermons*, "Sermon Ninth": "All men must needs despise a religion that is not consistent with humanity, and when they find its precepts are not practicable, they will believe its author is not true" (263).

286. Astell's marginal note: Heb 12:1.

287. Astell's marginal note: See Rom 8. [Astell refers to Rom 8:13.]

us liberty which we make an ill use of.[288] For the gospel is express, that "sin shall not have dominion over us";[289] and "let no man say when he is tempted, I am tempted of God, for God cannot be tempted with evil, neither tempteth He any man."[290]

338. *Of sin.* Sin, that at least for which God will judge and condemn us, unless we repent,[291] being an opposition to the will of God, an opposing our wills to His (whereby we are deprived of union with Him, and consequently of happiness), it is no great difference whether this opposition proceeds from ignorance, infirmity, or malice; only malice is so much the worse, as it expresses a greater contempt of God, and is more hard to be reclaimed, as having more of the will in it.[292] But our ignorances and infirmities are not wholly free from willfulness, for if there were no irregularity of the will in them they could not properly and strictly be sins, but rather wants and infelicities,[293] for all sin is voluntary. Our opinions and consciences may make that a sin to us which in itself is lawful and indifferent, because the will is as much in fault and in opposition to God's will, when we do that which we take to be a sin, though really and in itself it is none, as if it were indeed unlawful: but no opinion of ours or of other people's, no example, no custom, no authority, can make that lawful to us which is in itself a sin. And through the satisfaction and intercession of Christ all sin is so far pardonable, that upon sincere repentance, which implies a sorrow in some sort proportionable to the degree of our guilt, a sorrow proceeding from the love of God, and a forsaking our evil ways, and returning to Him, we shall be received to mercy.

339. *What are not sins of infirmity.* Hence I conclude, that if by *infirmities* and *frailties* are meant such a daily imperfection and falling short of our duty and desires, as is incident to the best Christians, such as is not inconsistent with the favor of God, but which shall be

288. Hickman, *Fourteen Sermons*, "Sermon Ninth": "it must be confessed withall, that God has made us subject unto sin" (252).

289. Astell's marginal note: Rom 6:14.

290. Astell's marginal note: Jas 1:13.

291. The qualification "that at least for which God will judge and condemn us, unless we repent" is not in the first edition.

292. The words "as having more of the will in it" are not in the first edition.

293. The words "but rather wants and infelicities" are not in the first edition.

pardoned upon a general repentance, through the grace of the new covenant, and which would not be imputed to us though we should be surprised by sudden death: then affected ignorance that shuns instruction refusing to make use of the means of "knowledge," that "hates the light, and will not come unto it lest its deeds should be reproved," and all the effects of this ignorance are so far from being harmless or pitiable infirmities, that such pretended ignorance is indeed a great aggravation of guilt.[294] Because it is voluntary, and not so much a fault in the understanding, as a perverseness in the will, which "despises knowledge and does not choose the fear of the Lord," and therefore is not reconcilable with His love.[295] Again, no surprise or passion how violent and great so ever, can wholly excuse our doing of anything that God has expressly forbid, or render it an infirmity consistent with His favor. For whoever is in a state of love to God, is always on his guard against great and manifest sins; if he sins like David, or like St. Peter, he can't be restored but by their solemn, and bitter, and lasting repentance. It matters not whether they be "sins to which our constitution leads us,"[296] that overcome us, or whether we "sin against the current of our nature,"[297] this may have more willfulness, but both are "unpardonable"[298] without repentance, which is a "ceasing to do evil, and learning to do well,"[299] and is the conditional cause why "the gospel does not condemn us for every vice."[300] Further, such a proneness to sin as carries us to commit it unwittingly, must not be called an infirmity, it is an habitual guilt, arising from many evil actions willfully repeated. And in the last place, though a good Christian may be surprised once or twice, he can't be surprised often in the same instance; for he is not to live loosely and without examination; he is to be acquainted with his own temper and weakness; to consider and

294. Astell's marginal note: Jn 3:20.

295. Astell's marginal note: Prv 1:29.

296. Hickman, *Fourteen Sermons*, "Sermon Ninth," 255.

297. Hickman, *Fourteen Sermons*, "Sermon Ninth," 255–56.

298. Hickman, *Fourteen Sermons*, "Sermon Ninth," 256.

299. Is 1:16–17.

300. Hickman, *Fourteen Sermons*, "Sermon Ninth": "we cannot but admire the excellent constitution of the gospel … it gives us the best encouragement to be virtuous; and yet does not condemn us for every vice" (256).

guard against the temptations to which he is most exposed; to "grow in grace," to know his faults and to reform them.[301]

340. *And what are.* It must be confessed, that our understandings being finite, we can't consider many things at once, nor always view an object on all its sides, and may happen to be under a necessity of acting, before we have fully considered how we ought to act, whereby we may mistake and transgress the righteous law of God. But He is merciful to this infirmity, if in the general course of our lives we take care to fence against it. If we furnish our mind with a stock of good principles, which will serve like way-marks[302] to direct our steps. If we have in general a good intention, singly aiming at the glory of God, and the salvation of our souls. If we maintain reason in her throne, by keeping our passions cool, and our affections disengaged from worldly things, preserving hereby a constant presence of mind, neither overwhelmed with cares, nor dissipated by vain mirth, or diverted by any trifling amusement. If we are thus prepared, by the grace of God, which is never wanting to them who are not wanting to themselves, we shall be more than conquerors. For God would not have shown us "the true way to subdue our passions,"[303] if He had not expected that we should subdue them. And to suppose, that "our savior's coming upon earth and dying for us, is a plain intimation that there are such vicious principles within us as cannot be subdued"; and to conclude from so "extraordinary a redemption," that "we lie under a moral impossibility of avoiding sin," notwithstanding those succors of grace which the spirit of Christ dispenses to all His members, is the most slanderous report that can be brought upon the gospel.[304] Because the son of God took upon Him our "nature" that He might "cure" our sinful passions, as well as make atonement for them. And they who will not be "cured" are the persons who "bring a reproach

301. 2 Pt 3:18.

302. way-marks] objects that guide the traveler.

303. Hickman, *Fourteen Sermons,* "Sermon Ninth," 256.

304. Astell refers with disapproval to Hickman, *Fourteen Sermons,* "Sermon Ninth": "Indeed, our savior's coming upon the earth, and dying for us, is a plain intimation, that there are such vicious principles within us, as cannot be subdued: for if we did not lie under a moral impossibility of avoiding sin, there had been no need of so extraordinary a redemption" (256).

upon His divine art"; for how is it that "religion improves nature," but by teaching us to "subdue" those "passions" it does not "extinguish"?[305]

341. *Wherein the passions, frailties, and infirmities of a good Christian chiefly appear.* In fine, doing what ought not to be done, is very rarely the infirmity of a good Christian, whose daily *frailties* are omissions of duty, and this not total omissions neither, but defects in some circumstances, so that they are upon the whole, imperfections rather than sins. Thus an unforeseen accident may occasion the omission or shortening of our daily offices of devotion, but this can't be often without a faulty negligence. We are too frequently unaffected and wandering in our prayers, and not so attent[306] and devout as we ought to be; yet this is to be provided against, it must not be indulged or neglected, lest it conclude in an indevout and formal temper, and so be no longer a pitiable infirmity. For the frailties of a true Christian are offenses against the rules of expediency, but seldom if ever against the plain and positive commands and prohibitions of the divine law. They arise from want of ability or leisure to compare things as we ought, whereby we happen to prefer a lesser good to a greater; or it may be now and then without any fault of the will, at least any direct one, to take evil for good, or good for evil in some obscure or difficult cases; and this seems to me the utmost latitude that can be given to our unavoidable "passions, frailties, and infirmities,"[307] which ought not to be confounded with our vices.[308]

342. *Passions and natural infirmities not to be confounded with sins.* A Christian therefore is not a "man of like passions with" other men, if by passions be meant vices. He is mortal it is true, and must not be adored as a god, which was all that the apostles meant when they told the Lycaonians, "we also are men of like passions with you."[309] So that in charity it is to be supposed that whoever attempts to prove, that "the most sanctified professors of religion are yet subject to passions

305. Hickman, *Fourteen Sermons*, "Sermon Ninth," 262, 250.

306. attent] full of attention.

307. Hickman, *Fourteen Sermons*, "Sermon Ninth."

308. The words "which ought not to be confounded with our vices" are not in the first edition.

309. Astell's marginal note: Acts 14:15. [This biblical citation is the opening quotation of Hickman's "Sermon Ninth."]

as well as other men,"[310] takes it for granted that all Christian people distinguish rightly between the pitiable infirmities of human nature, such as bodily indisposition, pain, and sickness, want of recollection, surprise, and shortness of view; and excessive "anger" and "hatred," "pride," and "overwhelming sorrow," indulgence to sensuality, and the like.[311] For these last are not in truth their "passions," "frailties," or "infirmities," but their willful sins; and to apply holy scripture to excuse such transgressions as these, is to burlesque rather than to expound it.

343. *St. Paul's sentiments and practice in this matter.* St. Paul I am sure gives no countenance to such doctrines; he was what he exhorts his successors to be, an "example to believers," and in what? But "in charity, in faith, in purity, in spirit," as this is opposed to sense. It was upon these things he meditated, to these he "wholly applied himself, that his profiting might appear to all." He "watched" both over "himself and his doctrine," knowing that loose morality is not less pernicious than erroneous articles of faith.[312] He tells his Thessalonians, that "they themselves know how they ought to follow him, for he behaved not himself disorderly among them";[313] now disorders usually attend upon passions, especially vicious ones. The works of the flesh as he enumerates them, Galatians 5:19, and so on, were none of his passions, for he assures us, that "they who do such things shall not inherit the kingdom of God";[314] and that they who are Christ's have "crucified the flesh with the affections," or passions as the margin reads, and "lusts."[315] And therefore it is evident, that St. Paul and the holy apostles, were not men of such passions as get the dominion over the generality of Christians nowadays, and which we are too apt to indulge under any fig-leaf[316] pretenses.

310. Hickman, *Fourteen Sermons*, "Sermon Ninth," 248.

311. See Hickman, *Fourteen Sermons*, "Sermon Ninth," 250.

312. Astell's marginal note: 1 Tm 4:12, and so on.

313. Astell's marginal note: 2 Thes 3:7.

314. Gal 5:21.

315. Gal 5:24. Astell's point about "passions" corresponds to the marginalia for Galatians 5:24 in a 1696 version of the King James Bible, *The Holy Bible ... [with] Notes in the Margin*: "Or, *passion*."

316. fig-leaf] flimsy.

344. *Why the infirmities of the saints are upon record.* The "fruits of the spirit, love, joy, peace, long-suffering, gentleness, goodness, faith, meekness, temperance, against which there is no law," these were St. Paul's passions.[317] The "infirmities he took pleasure in were reproaches, necessities, persecutions, distresses for Christ's sake."[318] He bids us "be followers of him," but only as "he is of Christ," who was a man like unto us, subject to all the innocent passions of human nature, but to none of the criminal.[319] He was "a man of sorrow, and acquainted with grief," passions I doubt we don't care to follow him in.[320] Many of the ancient Christians indeed "became followers of the Lord and of us," says St. Paul, to cite him once more in his own vindication. For though they lived in persecuting times, so that "they received the gospel in much affliction," yet they also "received it with joy of the holy ghost," and in these passions, and in these only, can we fairly allege the examples of holy men, or will they justify us.[321] For that their faults "are noted in God's book," is not so much to show us, "that there is nothing perfect upon earth,"[322] as to admonish us to be ever upon our guard, since the best of men have been so apt to slip: and to let the greatest sinners know,[323] that they ought not to despair, but should "turn from their transgressions" as those holy men did, and then "iniquity will not be their ruin."[324] It is the "piety" and "religion," not the "failings of the saints" that are "upon record" for our example;[325] nor must we imagine that "if we could but come to be men of like virtues,"

317. Gal 5:22–23.

318. Astell's marginal note: 2 Cor 12:10.

319. Astell's marginal note: 1 Cor 11:1.

320. Astell's marginal note: Is 53:3.

321. Astell's marginal note: 1 Thes 1:6.

322. Hickman, *Fourteen Sermons*, "Sermon Ninth," 258.

323. Astell's marginal note: Thus Mr Boyle in his *Excellency of Theology*, 11–12 [17]: "We may learn with comfort, both that the performance of such an obedience as *God will accept*, is a thing really *practicable by man*; and that even great sins and misdemeanors are not (if seasonably repented of) certain evidences, that a man shall never be happy in the future life. And it seems to be for such a use of consolation to frail men (but not at all to encourage licentious ones) that the lapses of holy persons are so frequently recorded in the scriptures."

324. Ez 18:30.

325. Hickman, *Fourteen Sermons*, "Sermon Ninth," 253.

we need "make no matter of being men of like passions," unless it be the innocent passions abovementioned.[326] Otherwise we may indulge our vicious passions to our destruction, but are never like to imitate their virtues in order to our salvation.

345. *The deplorable practice of modern Christians.* But alas! Though the happiness of the next world is so infinitely desirable, and the misery of losing it so intolerable, that we are extremely wanting to ourselves, if we neglect to make a diligent enquiry, not only into all those methods which may secure it to us, but even into such as will qualify us for the highest degrees of bliss; yet who considers further than to do just so much as may quiet his conscience, and keep him, as he thinks, out of the pit of destruction? We ask how little will suffice, not how much may be attained; and are not solicitous to conquer our infirmities, but how to indulge them with impunity. We fancy all is well, or well enough, if no crying sin stares us in the face; if we speak of religion decently; say our prayers in public and private; give some alms; and at certain times condemn ourselves and purpose[327] to do better, and approach the Lord's table in this sort of wedding garment.[328] We reckon upon the good we wish, or design to do, supposing we continue long enough in this mind, that nothing hinder, that we remember it, and that no business, company, diversion, or any temptation come in our way. We think ourselves saints if we are zealots for a party; and that we do God great service when we labor to make proselytes, not to religion but to our faction. If we do but abhor idols, we conclude this gives allowance to commit sacrilege; and if we preserve our reputation, we take it for granted that this invests us with authority to dispose of other people's, and to censure them rigidly. With the Pharisee,[329] we put it among the catalogue of our virtues, that we are not so bad as other men are, though possibly this betterness, is nothing else but our pride or our hypocrisy!

346. *These terms of salvation not represented too rigidly.* If anyone thinks I have made the terms of salvation too strict, they may

326. Hickman, *Fourteen Sermons,* "Sermon Ninth," 258–59.

327. purpose] propose.

328. Astell alludes to the biblical story of a guest who is ejected from a wedding for wearing inappropriate clothes (Matthew 22:11–14).

329. Pharisee] self-righteous person.

please to remember "that strait is the gate, and narrow is the way that leads to life, and few there be that find it."[330] Not but that Christianity in itself is an "easy yoke" and "a light burden,"[331] the "way" to heaven "is pleasantness, and all its paths are peace."[332] It is only become strait and thorny to us (as has been already hinted) through those evil dispositions we have willfully contracted. We must not think to pass it, with all the luggage of this world about us; they who give us such hopes, who "sew pillows to our elbows,"[333] and "prophesy smooth things," do only "prophesy deceit."[334] Truth itself having assured us, that we can't "serve God and Mammon";[335] nor can we possibly at one and the same time, walk in the broad road of the world that leads to destruction, and in the narrow path that leads to life everlasting. For how can we in conscience and with all our partiality, expect heaven and infinite felicity, when we do less to obtain it than we do for an estate, a place, or something yet more inconsiderable!

347. *A careless life makes an uncomfortable deathbed.* It is easy and fatal to do too little, impossible to do too much, and unspeakably advantageous to do all that we can. What can be so dreadful and tormenting on this side of hell, as the being unable when we come to die, to pass a favorable judgment on our final state, according to the true importance of the gospel covenant! Our attendants and friends, the pleasures we have formerly enjoyed, the riches and honors we leave behind us, will afford no consolation; they will rather afflict and gall us with stinging remorse for the sins they have occasioned. The having "fought a good fight and finished our course," in prospect of "that crown of glory" which attends us, will be the only cordial in this great necessity.[336] For it is somewhat of the latest to begin to live when we are about to die; and supposing us ever so sincere at this time, and that we are as real penitents as the contrite thief was upon the cross,

---

330. Astell's marginal note: Mt 7:13–14.

331. Astell's marginal note: Mt 11:30.

332. Astell's marginal note: Prv 3:17.

333. sew pillows to our elbows] give a false sense of security (*OED*, s.v. "pillow").

334. Astell's marginal note: Is 30:10.

335. Astell's marginal note: Mt 6:24. ["Mammon" refers to "wealth, profit, possessions" (*OED*).]

336. 2 Tm 4:7–8.

though by the way, his circumstances and ours are not at all alike; yet supposing God will indeed out of His superabundant and uncovenanted grace, have mercy on us, this is more than we can justly or reasonably promise ourselves, and therefore it is no just allay of our fears, nor can afford us any true consolation.

348. *Which is a horror no worldly enjoyments can compensate.* For unless we have in the time of health prepared ourselves for the divine mercy, according to the terms of salvation offered in the gospel, and before the strong fears of a deathbed seize us, we have no proof of our own sincerity, no solid ground of hope, but must go out of this world into an irreversible state for eternity, in all that fear and agony, which must needs torment them who have so important a stake depending on the utmost hazard. And I would fain[337] know whether all that this world affords can be an equivalent for these most miserable circumstances. Surely I would not endure this horror, even though it should end well, for all that this present life has to flatter or threaten me with!

349. *How to avoid it.* But what way to avoid it? None that I know of, except by "working while it is day," for "when the night cometh none can work."[338] And let it not be said, that after all our endeavors we can't be sure of our final state; for though it is very true, that when we "have done all that is commanded we are but unprofitable servants, having done no more than was our duty to do":[339] yet such a saying has but an ill grace in the mouths of them who are so far from doing their utmost, that they scarce do anything at all. It is true, that considering the difficulty because the excellency of the work, the greatness of the reward, the infinite distance between God and us, the holiness of His majesty, and the deceitfulness of our own hearts; it will become us to humble ourselves with the lowest prostration of spirit before His judgment seat, to approach His presence with holy awe and reverential fear, and without any confidence in ourselves, though much in our redeemer. But to say that God has not plainly told us what He requires of us, is to charge Him foolishly: and to suppose that we are not, or can't be conscious of our own sincerity, is to destroy the faculties of

337. fain] gladly.
338. Jn 9:4.
339. Lk 17:10.

the mind and is contrary to reason and experience. The premises indeed from whence the conclusion is drawn are not equally evident; for the first depends upon God's infallible testimony, the other only upon our own fallible judgment. And therefore, though it is infallibly true, that if I have performed what God requires I shall be saved through the merits of Christ, yet it is not equally certain that I have done this. But there is a way to remove this troublesome uncertainty in great measure, and that is by "giving all diligence to make our calling and election sure,"[340] and one would think we have lost our reason as well as our religion, if we suffer anything to divert us from this our most important and only necessary *business.*[341]

350. *This discourse submitted to lawful authority and even private admonition.* Thus madam, I have given your Ladyship an account of my principles, and of what I am convinced I ought, and which therefore I desire and endeavor to practice; submitting it to the censure of my proper superiors in the "church of God, the pillar and ground of truth."[342] If any private Christian will take the trouble to show me where I am in the wrong, I shall hold myself obliged to him, and shall neither be ashamed to retract an error, to reform a fault, or to pay my thankful acknowledgments to anyone who will be so kind as to admonish me. It is like I might have brought my thoughts into a shorter compass, but some reigning offenses are so little considered, I was going to say so much excused and justified, that it seemed not improper to attack them on all sides, and to remind us often of what we constantly forget.

351. *Apology for the manners.* Some perhaps will think there's too much of the woman in it, too much of my particular manner and thoughts. It may be so; but as an affectation of other people's ways is generally ridiculous, so the keeping up to our own character is that which best becomes us. And there is this advantage in it, that if these papers shall survive me, by speaking truths which no *man* would say, they will appear to be genuine, and *no man* will be blamed for their imperfections. I am sensible that by giving this account of Christianity according to its truth and purity, I have made a sort of satire on myself

---

340. 2 Pt 1:10.

341. In the first edition, the end of this paragraph signals the end of section IV.

342. 1 Tm 3:15.

and others, whose practice falls so very short of our profession. But if any who read their faults in this letter, shall think themselves aimed at, and be offended at it, they will be unjust to me by rash judgment, and by depriving me of the only way I have to do them service; and also unkind to themselves, by raising a prejudice against the truth, instead of being convinced and amended by it. For moral discourses unless they are very particular do no good upon a reader, everyone being apt to justify or excuse his own conduct, and to believe he is unconcerned. So that a book is only so many words to no manner of purpose, except the reader, even him whom the author never so much as heard of, finds his own picture in it, and is forced to say to himself, "I am the man." I design indeed to do all the good I can, which seems to me to be a Christian's duty, and they who won't suffer us to do it one way, must be content to receive it another. If any are offended at my manner of doing it, let them be pleased to show me a better, and I shall thankfully follow it.

352. *Concealed grudges should give place to Christian admonition.* For happy would it be for us, we should be truly Christians (whereas without it we are only so in name) if instead of those resentments and concealed grudges, those animosities and bitter envyings, those detractions and revilings, and that—I can't say, never forgiving, for this in strictness supposes an injury, whereas the greatest service perhaps is that which offends—but that never ceasing malice so common among us, and which arises too often, rather from our neighbor's virtues and our own vices, than from any real injury he has done us: but happy would it be, if instead of this temper which absolutely excludes us from the divine mercy, we would observe our Lord's command, which is generally dispensed with by one knows not what authority, and with Christian simplicity and goodwill, go and tell our neighbor himself what it was we took amiss from him. We should indeed be ashamed to say, that his merit hurt our eyes, and that his virtue is the injury we know not how to forgive. We should blush to confess, that because we had once done an injury and were ashamed to own it, therefore we resolve to pursue our injustice, and as we imagine, to cover and justify it by doing more. But then if we have any remains of ingenuity this would shame away our uncharity, and

show us how little of human nature, much less of a Christian, and how much of the devil, there is in such a temper.

353. *The freedom of this discourse no real fault.* As it happens, I have said nothing that the nicest breeding can except against with regard to your Ladyship, unless they will reckon me unmannerly, for writing so disrespectfully of worldly advantages, to a lady whose Christian conversation does them so much honor. All I have to say for myself is only this, that though the readers may be displeased with the freedom I have taken with their grand prerogatives, yet it's like I am not much in the wrong, since, whatever they do at other times, in their sober moods and wisest hours, in Lent, against Christmas, and in all their preparations for the holy sacrament, they think and say just as I do. If these good thoughts go off and they forget themselves, I am sorry for it; but truth is constant and self-consistent, it is the "same yesterday, today, and forever."[343] And if truth shall pierce their hearts, the present remedy I know will be to lay the book aside, and to think no more of it, till the next periodical return of a fit of devotion. A remedy for whose success I can't answer; for a time will certainly come when no diversions will be found to silence, nor indeed any way whatever left to ward off their convictions.

354. *What is the truest instance of respect, though not the most agreeable.* Did I know of a darling fault in those I love the most, though it were a right hand or right eye, I should not spare it for this reason; though supposing them governed by the common principles of the world, this were an infallible way to lose their favor. But I had much rather lose it than deserve to lose it, and therefore they should not rest till the darling were thrown out, or at least till they had convinced me they were resolved not to part with it. For if this were the case, one must give over with the sad thought, that the idea one had formed of them, and what one loved and valued, was only the image of one's own fancy. They would then be no more what one had taken them for, no more what one could esteem and love, but what must be always pitied and deplored![344]

---

343. Heb 13:8: "Jesus Christ is the same yesterday, and today, and forever."

344. In the first edition, this paragraph is followed by §§394–408 of the present volume.

355. *Conclusion.*[345] But not to be further tedious, I shall close all with the words of our dearest Lord, "Whosoever shall break one of the least of God's commandments, and shall teach men so, he shall be called the least in the kingdom of heaven; but whosoever shall do and teach them, the same shall be great in the kingdom of heaven."[346] With the ambition of which true grandeur may God inspire us all; to whom let us ascribe the "glory of every right work," and "in His due time He will give us our reward."[347]

345. This paragraph (§408 in the first edition) concludes the main text of both editions.

346. Mt 5:19.

347. Ecclus 51:30: "in his time he will give you your reward."

Section V

Appendix[1]

356. *What Mr. Locke's Reasonableness of Christianity pretends to drive at.* The author of *The Reasonableness of Christianity as delivered in the Scriptures*, very wisely informs us, that to find out the "true meaning, and mind of a writer," we must "look into the drift of the discourse," consider the "occasion" of writing, the "argument in hand," and what "is principally aimed at."[2] Now setting aside "conjectures," and prying into folk's hearts, our author tells us, that "justification is the subject of his treatise."[3] And addressing himself to the "makers of systems" for the "dissenting congregations and to their followers,"[4] he says that his design is to teach them a "plain intelligible" religion, "that they may not be deceived by mistaking the doctrine of faith, grace, free grace," and so on, nor "scruple to call obedience a condition of the new covenant."[5] To this purpose he largely shows the true meaning of faith, that it does not exclude works, nor will be sufficient without them, and that the belief of the messiah, and what necessarily follows from this belief, "a strict and holy life" according to the rules of Christian morality, whether it be called an "historical faith," or by whatever other name, is indeed that faith "our savior and His apostles" preached, and "declared to be a justifying and saving faith."[6] The "priestcraft" therefore which he exposes, is theirs who make it "their business" to get "all the custom," and "not to teach men virtue," and who "distinguish religion from, and prefer it to virtue, making it dangerous heresy and

---

1. The following subsections (§§356–408) correspond to §§75–88, 137–52, 262–69, and 393–407 of the first edition.

2. Astell's marginal note: Locke, *Reasonableness of Christianity*, 294 [164–65].

3. Astell's marginal note: Locke, *Reasonableness of Christianity*, 306 [170].

4. Astell's marginal note: Locke, *Reasonableness of Christianity*, 194 [108]. [Astell is being disingenuous here: Locke does not address himself to makers of systems "for the dissenting congregations" in this section, though he does refer to such congregations in passing later in the work (306 [170]). In short, she misrepresents Locke's intentions.]

5. Astell's marginal note: Locke, *Reasonableness of Christianity*, 304 [169], and so on; 241, 236 [133, 130].

6. Astell's marginal note: Locke, *Reasonableness of Christianity*, 214, 194 [119, 108].

profaneness to think the contrary."[7] All the address he uses being designed to convince the dissenters if possible, how unreasonable it is to "divide communion and separate upon points" which though they reckon "of so great weight, so material, so fundamental in religion," yet are either so abstruse or so unnecessary, that even "some of their teachers" whom "he talked with, confess themselves not to understand the difference in debate."[8]

357. *His management.* But had our author's "argument" been concerning the holy trinity, the divinity or satisfaction of Christ, we should have found how he would have taken the Socinians to task upon this "occasion"! For he "repeats it again," that "there is not a word of Socinianism in his book."[9] Though I do not remember where he had said it before, unless where he makes this quaint answer to his adversary's charge upon the score of his omissions: "but what" (says he) "if I should say I set down as much as my argument required, and yet am no Socinian?"[10] Readers we know are charitable, or at least ought to be so; and it agrees better with some men's "logic and grammar"[11] to "ask themselves the question, what if I should say I am no Socinian?" than to say in plain terms, that they are not Socinians.

358. For as for a man's speaking slightingly of "expiatory sacrifices" and having a fling at "the priest's" good "pennyworths,"[12] at

7. Astell's marginal note: Locke, *Reasonableness of Christianity*, 267, 268 [147].

8. Astell's marginal note: Locke, *Reasonableness of Christianity*, 306 [170]. It is also worth observation, that (as if by the spirit of prophecy) our author [i.e., Locke] lays down a principle to determine the great "controversy" about occasional conformity, "at this time so warmly managed among us" (Locke, *Reasonableness of Christianity*, 306 [170]). For justifying God's conduct towards Adam, in return to the common objection, "how does it consist with the justice and goodness of God that the posterity of Adam should suffer for his sin?" He answers, "very well, if keeping one from what he has no right to be called a punishment. Immortality was not due to Adam, and so on" (Locke, *Reasonableness of Christianity*, 7 [10]). It appears then by the arguing of this great master of reason and friend to moderation, that keeping men from what they have no right to, can't be called a "punishment," how much less a persecution? [On the occasional conformity debate in early eighteenth-century England, see the "Historical-Intellectual Context" section of the introduction to the present volume.]

9. Astell's marginal note: Locke, *Vindication*, 13 [14].

10. Astell's marginal note: Locke, *Vindication*, 4 [10].

11. Astell possibly alludes to Masham, *Discourse*, 38.

12. Astell's marginal note: Locke, *Reasonableness of Christianity*, 267 [147].

"orthodoxy," "creed-making," and "articles not yet" understood;[13] though he expresses himself in the very same terms when he speaks of Adam's being "the son of God," and "of the likeness and image" he had "of his father," as he does when he speaks of "that son of God,"[14] whom the scripture calls "the only begotten of the father,"[15] making no manner of distinction in their "son-ship"; nor between Him "for whom are all things, and by whom are all things,"[16] and those whom out of infinite condescension "He is not ashamed to call *His* brethren," any further than that these are by "adoption," and Christ "is by birth the son of God";[17] "by birth" meaning no more, so far as he lets us into his meaning, than that He had "no other father," which was Adam's privilege as well as Christ's; though he tells us "the great evidence, that Jesus was the son of God, was his resurrection,"[18] intimating at least, and so far as great letters will go, that our resurrection will be the like evidence of our son-ship; though when he speaks of that divine person, "in whom dwelleth all the fullness of the godhead bodily,"[19] he calls Him no more than an "extraordinary man," an "extraordinary person,"[20] making these two expressions, and "messiah," and "son of God," to be all of them synonymous, ascribing to Christ only an "unparalleled wisdom," not an infinite;[21] although the scripture tells us, that in Him "are hid all the treasures of wisdom and knowledge";[22] and also that He has "washed us from our sins in His own blood,"[23] whereas our author says no more than that the messiah "was to suffer death for the testimony of the truth,"[24] and from passages in his treatise collects what "methinks sounds something like

13. Astell's marginal note: Locke, *Vindication*, 17, 18, 32, 35 [16, 22, 23].

14. Astell's marginal note: Locke, *Reasonableness of Christianity*, 202, 203, 204 [112, 113].

15. Astell's marginal note: Jn 1:14.

16. Astell's marginal note: Locke, *Reasonableness of Christianity*, 207 [115]. Heb 2:10–11.

17. Astell's marginal note: Locke, *Reasonableness of Christianity*, 203 [113].

18. Astell's marginal note: Locke, *Reasonableness of Christianity*, 207 [115].

19. Astell's marginal note: Col 2:9.

20. Astell's marginal note: Locke, *Reasonableness of Christianity*, 55, 36 [37, 28].

21. Astell's marginal note: Locke, *Reasonableness of Christianity*, 66 [43].

22. Astell's marginal note: Col 2:3.

23. Astell's marginal note: Rv 1:5; 1 Jn 1:7.

24. Astell's marginal note: Locke, *Reasonableness of Christianity*, 61 [40].

Christ's purchasing life for us by His death";[25] though he insists so largely on the belief and worship of one God, without any the least mention of the adorable persons in the godhead;[26] and though he tells us "we must ascribe the Mahometans owning and professing of one God to that light the messiah brought into the world";[27] whereby we are left to believe if we please, that there is no difference between the Christian and Mahometan belief of that fundamental article: yet this notwithstanding, who can see into "his heart"? Who can "charge him with Socinianism," or say there is anything in his "book against the religion contained in the gospel"?[28] Since he flatly denies it, and that "surmises may be overturned by a single denial"?[29]

359. *An endeavor to reconcile him to himself.* I shall not put him to the expense of one, having no design to accuse him, his meaning and motives be to himself: nor shall I accept his "challenge," page 195.[30] Not out of fear of his strength, since that uncreated and incarnate truth whom I adore, and upon whose assistance only I depend, "is strong and will prevail," and has "chosen the foolish things of the world to confound the wise, and the weak and despised to confound the mighty, that no flesh should glory in His presence";[31] but because I love to be a peacemaker, and had rather reconcile our author to himself. For supposing one might "cull out" of his discourse any "aphorisms" contrary to the "Christian faith,"[32] I will not however, say he has "mistaken or slandered Christianity," which he says he "hoped to serve." Since he tells us he knows the "sincerity of his thoughts," and is "satisfied" with this "assurance, that if there is anything in his book against what anyone calls religion, it is not against the religion contained in the gospel; and for this he appeals to all mankind."[33]

25. Astell's marginal note: Locke, *Vindication*, 5 [10].

26. Astell's marginal note: Locke, *Reasonableness of Christianity*, 261 [144], and so on.

27. Astell's marginal note: Locke, *Reasonableness of Christianity*, 264 [145].

28. Astell's marginal note: Locke, *Vindication*, 14, 12, 10 [15, 14, 13].

29. Astell's marginal note: Locke, *Vindication*, 4 [10].

30. Locke, *Reasonableness of Christianity*, 195 [109].

31. 1 Cor 1:27.

32. Astell's marginal note: Locke, *Reasonableness of Christianity*, 295 [165].

33. Astell's marginal note: Locke, *Vindication*, 10 [13].

360. *Two propositions laid down in order to it.* Come we then to the merits of the cause, and "in the spirit of the gospel, which is that of charity, and in the words of sobriety,"[34] endeavor to show: 1. That the *bare belief that Jesus was the promised messiah*, was not the only article of faith preached by Christ and his apostles to those who acknowledged the one true God. And, 2. What are those other articles, "an explicit belief of which, is absolutely required of all those to whom the gospel of Jesus Christ is preached, and salvation through his name proposed."[35]

361. *First proposition.* The first proposition might be proved by several arguments, I shall only insist on one, which being full and to the point, is as good as twenty. Our author tells us, that "the coming of the messiah, the kingdom of heaven, and the kingdom of God are the same," and was what "John the Baptist preached": and that this "same doctrine and nothing else was preached by the apostles afterwards."[36] The former part of this assertion we shall allow him, the latter is the point in question. If then it can be proved, that either Christ or any of His apostles (for there was uniformity in the church of God at that time, whatever may have been since) did not think the belief of that article into which John baptized sufficient for a Christian believer, or all that was absolutely necessary to be believed; it undeniably follows, that the belief that "Jesus is the messiah," exclusive of all other articles, is not the "one great point"[37] or "gospel-article of faith"[38] requisite to make a Christian believer.

362. *Proved from St. Paul's practice.* Now that St. Paul preached some other "articles of faith," is evident from what we read of the twelve disciples he found at Ephesus.[39] They believed the "messiah,"[40]

---

34. Astell responds to Locke's challenge in the preface to his *Reasonableness of Christianity*: "If upon a fair and unprejudiced examination, you find I have mistaken the sense and tenor of the gospel, I beseech you, as a true Christian, in the spirit of the gospel (which is that of charity) and in the words of sobriety, set me right in the doctrine of salvation" (A2v [3]).

35. Astell's marginal note: Locke, *Reasonableness of Christianity*, 301–302 [168].

36. Astell's marginal note: Locke, *Reasonableness of Christianity*, 52, 53 [35, 36].

37. Astell's marginal note: Locke, *Reasonableness of Christianity*, 186 [104].

38. Astell's marginal note: Locke, *Reasonableness of Christianity*, 195 [109].

39. Astell's marginal note: See Acts 19.

40. Astell's marginal note: Locke, *Reasonableness of Christianity*, 53 [36].

for they had been "baptized into John's baptism,"[41] which was that "men should repent and believe the glad tidings"[42] of the "messiah,"[43] as St. Paul acknowledges. But yet the apostle did not think "this same doctrine and nothing else" sufficient,[44] "this was not the sum and substance of the gospel which he preached," nor "all that he knew necessary to salvation," though our author affirms it was.[45] He therefore baptizes them "in the name of the Lord Jesus," that is in the name of the "father, son, and holy ghost," which was the faith into which our savior commanded His apostles to "evangelize all nations."[46] For St. Paul did not baptize in his own name, nor by any form of his own invention. Now unless the apostle had instructed them in the doctrine of the holy trinity, they would have continued to say to him, "we have not so much as heard whether there be any holy ghost," into whose name you baptize us.[47] And by this whole narration it appears, that the doctrine concerning this divine person was so plainly a part of the Christian faith, that the apostle could not suppose any "disciple" or "believer" was ignorant of it. So that in St. Paul's judgment, who understood the "Christian religion" as well at least as our author, to "be baptized in the name of Jesus Christ," was indeed "that solemn visible act whereby mankind were admitted as subjects into His kingdom," but it signified somewhat more than the bare "believing Him to be the messiah, the receiving Him as their king, and professing obedience to Him."[48] This was not sufficient to make men "members of His church,"

---

41. King, *History of the Apostles Creed*, 318.

42. Astell's marginal note: Locke, *Reasonableness of Christianity*, 198 [110].

43. Astell's marginal note: Locke, *Reasonableness of Christianity*, 42 [30].

44. Locke, *Reasonableness of Christianity*, 53 [36].

45. Astell's marginal note: Locke, *Reasonableness of Christianity*, 239 [132].

46. Astell's marginal note: Mt 28:19.

47. Astell's marginal note (second edition only): It is the observation of St. Jerome, that those persons mentioned in the nineteenth of the Acts, "who were baptized with John's baptism, and believed in God the father, and Christ Jesus, because they knew not the holy ghost, were again baptized, yea then received the true baptism, for without the holy ghost, the mystery of the trinity is imperfect," as he is cited in King's *History of the Creed*, 318.

48. Astell's marginal note: Locke, *Reasonableness of Christianity*, 200 [111].

without an "explicit belief" of other articles;[49] and what they are comes now to be considered.

363. *Second proposition, Mr. L. himself allows other articles.* Our author allows that the "belief of one eternal and invisible God, the maker of heaven and earth," is a fundamental article.[50] And though at the same time he contends, "that salvation or perdition depends upon believing or rejecting this one proposition," "this single truth, that Jesus is the messiah";[51] yet he is more condescending[52] towards the end of his book. For page 294, he takes in "those concomitant articles" of Christ's "resurrection, rule, and coming again to judge the world," making them to be "all the faith required."[53] In page 203, he founds our savior's son-ship, upon his being "conceived of a virgin by the immediate power of God"; and one can't believe that Jesus is the messiah without believing Him to be the "son of" God, for these our author makes to be terms convertible.[54] He is so kind, page 185, as to reckon these particulars, that is, that the messiah "had a kingdom, that He should be put to death, and rise again, and ascend into heaven to His father, and come again in glory to judge the world,"[55] among the things "necessary to be believed," and what Christ "acquainted" His apostles "with," as the "main design of the gospel."[56] And when our author tells us as he does, page 290, that "a perfect complete life of an eternal duration," "was nowhere made an article of faith," "till Jesus Christ came," he would have us understand that then it was.[57] For sure he does not mean to omit a principle that "gives the advantage to piety over all that could tempt or deter men from it"?[58] We have therefore in a manner all the articles of the Christian faith, except those of the holy trinity,

49. Astell's marginal note: Locke, *Reasonableness of Christianity*, 300 [167].

50. Astell's marginal note: Locke, *Reasonableness of Christianity*, 43, 25 [31, 22].

51. Astell's marginal note: Also, Locke, *Reasonableness of Christianity*, 43, 47 [31, 33].

52. condescending] willing to make concessions.

53. Locke, *Reasonableness of Christianity*, 294 [164].

54. Locke, *Reasonableness of Christianity*, 203 [113].

55. Locke, *Reasonableness of Christianity*, 185 [103].

56. Astell's marginal note: Locke, *Reasonableness of Christianity*, 31 [25]. The resurrection of Christ is made a necessary article. See also 40, 41 [30].

57. Locke, *Reasonableness of Christianity*, 290 [162].

58. Locke, *Reasonableness of Christianity*, 290 [162].

the catholic church, and communion of saints; for he makes faith in the messiah to carry with it "remission of sins";[59] and the benefit of the new covenant to consist in "remission or abatement,"[60] and in "that life which Jesus Christ restores to all men at the resurrection":[61] so that we have these articles expressed almost in the very words of the Creed.[62]

364. *But makes no mention of the holy trinity.* I am "perfectly ignorant" of our author's "heart,"[63] and "pretend" not to any knowledge of his "thoughts and reasons,"[64] and therefore I will not presume to "surmise"[65] why he makes no mention of the doctrine of the trinity, since his professed design is to speak of "those truths," and of those "only which are absolutely required to be believed to make anyone a Christian";[66] and he "challenges" the world "to show that there was any other doctrine" than what he mentions, "upon their assent to which, or disbelief of it, men were pronounced believers or unbelievers."[67] It is to be presumed indeed, that Christians can't be ignorant or forgetful of the name into which they were baptized, especially since they either have, or ought to have "ratified and confirmed the same openly before

59. Astell's marginal note: Locke, *Reasonableness of Christianity*, 47 [33].

60. Astell's marginal note: Locke, *Reasonableness of Christianity*, 16, 20 [17, 19].

61. Astell's marginal note: Locke, *Reasonableness of Christianity*, 10 [12].

62. Astell refers to the Apostles' Creed in the Church of England, *Book of Common Prayer*:
    I believe in God the Father Almighty, Maker of heaven and earth:
    And in Jesus Christ his only Son our Lord, Who was conceived by the Holy Ghost, Born of the Virgin Mary, Suffered under Pontius Pilate, Was crucified, dead, and buried, He descended into hell; The third day he rose again from the dead, He ascended into heaven, And sitteth on the right hand of God the Father Almighty; From thence he shall come to judge the quick and the dead.
    I believe in the Holy Ghost, The holy Catholick Church; the Communion of Saints; The Forgiveness of sins; The Resurrection of the body; And the life everlasting. Amen. (43–44, 54–55)

63. Locke, *Vindication*, 14 [15].

64. Locke, *Vindication*, 13 [14].

65. Locke, *Vindication*, 4 [10].

66. Astell's marginal note: Locke, *Vindication*, 30 [21].

67. Astell's marginal note: Locke, *Reasonableness of Christianity*, 195 [109].

the church,"[68] at which time they are blessed, by the successors of our Lord, in the same name.

365. *Though confession of faith in the holy trinity be necessary to our admission into the church of Christ.* But whatever men may say or do, this is certain, that by the very form of admission into His church, the messiah has shut out all those who do not either by themselves or by their sureties, *actually assent* to the faith and worship of father, son, and holy ghost. This is "a fundamental which it is not enough not to disbelieve,"[69] for since "the faith God will accept and account for righteousness, depends wholly on His good pleasure"; since "it is of grace and not of right that this faith is accepted, therefore He alone can set the measure, and what He has so appointed and declared is necessary."[70] Nor could any proposition have been declared necessary, more plainly and universally, than by commanding all men who list themselves in His service and expect the benefit thereof, to make a solemn profession of their belief in father, son, and holy ghost, to whose worship and service they entirely devote themselves. This being the worship of "the one invisible true God, made known to the world"[71] by the messiah. And by this time I hope our author will think fit either to withdraw his "appeal," or else to acknowledge that we have done him no injury by understanding his assertion, "that the belief of the messiah is the only gospel article," not as "exclusive" of all others, but as "including" those already mentioned.[72] To which let me now add, the belief of the "holy catholic church," and the "communion of saints," since we must necessarily believe that there is such a community, when we come to enter ourselves into it. And it is also supposed,

---

68. Astell's marginal note: See the "Order of Confirmation." [Astell refers to the Church of England, "The Order of Confirmation" in *Book of Common Prayer*. This text states that "children, being now come to the years of discretion, and having learned what their godfathers and godmothers promised for them in Baptism, they may themselves, with their own mouth and consent, openly before the Church, ratify and confirm the same" (301).]

69. Astell's marginal note: Locke, *Reasonableness of Christianity*, 302 (it should be 303) [168]. [Astell points to a typesetting error in the pagination of the second edition.]

70. Astell's marginal note: Locke, *Reasonableness of Christianity*, 301 [167–68].

71. Astell's marginal note: Locke, *Reasonableness of Christianity*, 263 [145].

72. See Locke, *Vindication*, 10, 26–27 [13, 20]; *Reasonableness of Christianity*, 195 [109].

that we believe there are advantages to be received in this communion, otherwise we should not desire a fellowship in it.

366. *In what sense Christ is the son of God.* It is then evident,
that the belief that Jesus of Nazareth is the messiah, and the belief
of all the other articles of the Creed,[73] "have so natural a connection
one with the other," that they "may be," and "often are, put" for one
another.[74] For he who believes in the messiah, must believe Him to
be sent into the world to be "our Lord," by God "the father almighty,
the maker of heaven and earth," whose "only son" He is.[75] "That son,"
as St. Peter calls Him by way of emphasis, when in the name of all
the "rest" of the "apostles" he confessed Him to be the messiah; "that
son" (though our author only reads "the son," page 102)[76] in a peculiar
manner different from all other sons, "of the living God,"[77] whether
Adam or any of his posterity,[78] or "those sons of God that shouted for
joy," when *this* son of God, by whom "all things were made" (as we
have it in the gospel as well as in the epistles)[79] "laid the foundations of
the earth."[80] For to which of those other sons did God at any time say,
"thou art my son, this day have I begotten thee: and I will be to Him
a father,"[81] a father before Adam, or anything else was created, before
He "had laid" the foundation "of the earth," or "the heavens" which are
the "work of His hands"? *That son*, who is called the "only begotten
of the father,"[82] "the brightness of His glory, and the express image of
His person," "God's image" in respect of His power as well as of His
"immortality," and that in a manner inconsistent with the nature of

73. the Creed] i.e., the Apostles' Creed.

74. Locke, *Reasonableness of Christianity*, 201 [112].

75. Astell quotes from the Apostles' Creed (see Church of England, *Book of Common Prayer*,
43–44, 54–55).

76. Locke, *Reasonableness of Christianity*, 102 [62].

77. Jn 6:69. Astell seemingly refers to the marginalia for John 6:69 in a 1696 version of the
King James Bible, *The Holy Bible ... [with] Notes in the Margin*: "*Gr, that son."

78. Astell's marginal note: See Locke, *Reasonableness of Christianity*, 202 [113], and so on.

79. Astell's marginal note: Jn 1:3.

80. Astell's marginal note: Jb 38:4, 7.

81. Astell's marginal note: Heb 1:5; Jn 1:14, and so on, 3:16.

82. Jn 1:14.

a creature, for He "upholdeth all things by the word of His power";[83] they depend upon Him, and as a certain author says very well, "God cannot make a being independent on himself";[84] so that this divine person on whom all things depend, must necessarily be God. *That son*, whom the "one supreme invisible God," who is so jealous of His glory as to declare He "will not give it to another," has yet commanded not only all men, but even "all angels to worship."[85] And has Himself said to *this son*, "thy throne oh God is forever and ever"—"sit on my right hand, until I make thine enemies thy footstool."[86] *That son*, who in a most excellent, peculiar, and ineffable manner, such as creatures cannot apprehend nor properly express, is "the only son of the father." The son, not "by birth"[87] as some love to speak, for reasons to themselves best known, but *by nature*. For that this is the meaning of "being in the form of God" is evident from the parallel expression in the next verse, where His appearing in the nature of man, is expressed by His "taking upon Him the form of a servant."[88] To which He condescended when He was pleased to be "born of the Virgin Mary,"[89] after a supernatural manner, as all who believe in the messiah must confess. As also, that this divine person, who as we have seen is God and man (God of the substance of His father, begotten before the worlds, and man of the substance of His mother, born in the world, as the Creed[90] very aptly expresses it) lived such a life, and died such a death, as is recorded in the gospels, and was preached throughout the world by His apostles. That is in short, "He suffered under Pontius Pilate, was crucified dead and buried, descended into hell, the third day He rose

83. Astell's marginal note: Heb 1:3.

84. Astell's marginal note: Masham, *Discourse*, 114.

85. Astell's marginal note: Is 42:8.

86. Astell's marginal note: Heb 1:8, 13.

87. Astell's marginal note: Locke, *Reasonableness of Christianity*, 205, 206 [114, 115].

88. Astell's marginal note: Phil 2:6–7.

89. Astell cites from the Apostles' Creed in the Church of England, *Book of Common Prayer*, 43, 54.

90. Astell quotes from the Athanasian Creed, which states that "we believe and confess: that our Lord Jesus Christ, the Son of God, is God and Man. God, of the Substance of the Father, begotten before the worlds; and Man, of Substance of his Mother, born in the world" (see Church of England, *Book of Common Prayer*, 61).

again from the dead, He ascended into heaven and sitteth on the right hand of God":[91] all which are the evidences of His being the messiah, so that the proof of it was not full and clear without the knowledge of them. And if I may give my conjecture, this was the reason why our Lord tells His disciples, that it was expedient for Him to go away and to send the comforter or Paraclete,[92] who was not to come till Christ was departed. As much as to say, that they could not be complete Christians till they had a full and perfect faith in the messiah, which they could not have but by those evidences upon which such a faith was founded, and this could not be till all that was foretold of the messiah was accomplished, and that in particular which was the last act of His mission, the consummation of this great work, His pouring out His spirit upon them, who should work in their hearts a complete faith in Him, fully convincing the world of the truth of His mission, and rendering all those inexcusable who rejected it. The sending of the holy ghost therefore was as necessary to be believed as the coming of the messiah, as has been already shown from St. Paul's authority, and as appears from the very plan of the Christian religion. What was it that persuaded mankind to receive the doctrine of the messiah, but the great advantages they expected by it? Such as "the remission of sins," "the communion of saints," "the resurrection of the body," and "the life everlasting"? And what could engage them to obey as well as to believe, obedience being as requisite as faith? What but the belief that the son of man would come in the glory of the father, "to judge both the quick and the dead"; at whose coming all men shall rise again with their bodies, and shall give an account of their own works. And whoever believed these truths and hoped for these advantages, was required by the author of them to initiate himself into the Christian community, or the "holy catholic church."[93]

367. *Belief of the messiah put for the whole Christian faith as including it.* So that to sum up all in a word, whoever believed that

91. Astell cites from the Apostles' Creed in the Church of England, *Book of Common Prayer*, 44, 55.

92. Paraclete] "a title given to the holy spirit ... an advocate, intercessor; a helper or comforter" (*OED*).

93. Astell quotes from the Apostles' Creed in the Church of England, *Book of Common Prayer*, 44, 55.

"Jesus was the messiah," and professed themselves "subjects of the messiah's kingdom,"[94] did hereby engage to worship God after that manner which was enjoined by the messiah. Into whose religion they could not be "initiated" but by acknowledging father, son, and holy ghost, the object of the Christian worship, whose service they engaged in, and into whose "kingdom they entered themselves" by that solemn and divine rite.[95] And thus did "our savior make the one invisible true God," father, son, and holy ghost, "known to the world," and by this "clear revelation dispel the darkness" in which He "found the world."[96] Hence is this proposition, that "Jesus is the messiah," so often put for the whole of the Christian faith, and faith for the whole of the Christian duty. That faith is put for the whole of religion is plain from that text our author takes notice of, page 95,[97] that is, Romans 10:8–9, as well as from other passages of holy scripture: "though obeying the law of the messiah" our "king," be "no less required, than" our "believing that Jesus is the messiah."[98] And now I leave it to your Ladyship, and to all who will give themselves the trouble to read these papers, to determine upon a fair and unprejudiced examination, whether or not I have made good what I undertook to prove §360? Whether I have hit the meaning of the author of the *Reasonableness of Christianity*; or which of us "has mistaken the sense and tenor of the gospel"?[99]

368. *Why this author is here considered.* I do not accuse that author of any "tang of prepossession or fancy"; any "footsteps of pride or vanity; any touch of ostentation or ambition," "anything tending to his own by-interest, or that of a party"; as if these had "tempted" him "to mix any conceits" with the Christian religion, or to give any wrong turn to the faith of the gospel.[100] And I hope I have not treated him otherwise than becomes a Christian, whose charity is the substance of what good breeding is only the shadow and counterfeit. Whether he be the same person who writ *A Discourse concerning the Love of God*,

94. Astell's marginal note: Locke, *Reasonableness of Christianity*, 200 [111].

95. Astell's marginal note: Locke, *Reasonableness of Christianity*, 199 [111].

96. Astell's marginal note: Locke, *Reasonableness of Christianity*, 263 [145].

97. Locke, *Reasonableness of Christianity*, 95 [59–60].

98. Astell's marginal note: Locke, *Reasonableness of Christianity*, 93 [58].

99. Astell's marginal note: Locke, *Reasonableness of Christianity*, Preface [3].

100. Astell's marginal note: Locke, *Reasonableness of Christianity*, 284–85 [159].

or who is the author, it is not my business to enquire, since he has not thought fit to discover himself.[101] Nor am I about to "complain" or make reprisals, whatever occasion might be given by that *Discourse*. I found nothing in it to make me change my judgment about the point in question, as will appear presently. The argument I knew was in better hands than mine,[102] and I could not think it proper (after some people's fashion) to trouble the world with *Answers* and *Replies* filled with little but "personal reflections," such as show rather the slip of the manager than the weakness of the cause.[103] The justifying one's own opinions, merely as they are one's own, being a very poor employment, which I shall leave to them who like it.[104] But having now an opportunity to clear up some important truths, which is all I am concerned for, I thought it not amiss to bestow a few pages on this author,[105] and hope what has been said will not appear impertinent nor foreign to my subject. Especially since the *Lady's Religion* seems to be little else but an abstract of the *Reasonableness of Christianity*, with all those disadvantages that usually attend abridgments.

369. *What hypothesis best answers the cavils against Christ's divinity.* I will not "conjecture" what makes some people so warm against the hypothesis of "seeing all things in God," nor why after so much discourse about ideas, they are so hard to be reconciled to an ideal world.[106] But this I may say with due submission to better

101. Masham was in fact the author of the *Discourse*, not Locke.

102. Astell refers to John Norris and his argument concerning the moral implications of Nicolas Malebranche's occasionalism and his theory of vision in God in his "Discourse concerning the Measure of Divine Love," in his *Practical Discourses* (1693).

103. Astell obliquely refers to the Locke-Stillingfleet debate, including Locke's *Letter to the Bishop of Worcester* (1697), Edward Stillingfleet's *Answer to Mr. Locke's Letter* (1697), Locke's *Reply* (1697), Stillingfleet's *Answer to Mr. Locke's second letter* (1698), and Locke's *Second Reply* (1699). Locke begins his final response with an extended complaint about Stillingfleet's remarks on "personal matters." For details on this debate, see the "Historical-Intellectual Context" section of the introduction to the present volume.

104. In the first edition, this sentence has the qualification "being *in my mind* a very poor employment" (my italics).

105. Astell refers to Masham.

106. Astell alludes to Masham and Locke's support for the "new way of ideas" and their opposition to the theories of Nicolas Malebranche and John Norris concerning a world of ideas eternally existing in the mind of God.

judgments, that that hypothesis and what is built upon it, gives a better answer than any hypothesis I have met with, to the trifling and unreasonable objections, for so I will presume to call them, though they are the strongest that can be made by the greatest pretenders to reason, against the divinity of the son of God. Some have told us that "the chiefest good of man is the best design of God";[107] I cannot answer for the thoughts they seem to have of God and of themselves: but this I know, that they who are conversant in that hypothesis, have too awful a sense of the divine majesty to endure so presumptuous a supposition. They know that God is His own design and end, and that there is no other worthy of Him. For since there neither is nor can be, any comparison between the creator and His creatures, far be it from us to think so unworthily of God, and so arrogantly of ourselves, as to suppose that "His wisdom contrived all things for our use, or supports them for our satisfaction,"[108] who are "before Him as nothing," who "are counted to Him as less than nothing and vanity,"[109] who are not worthy of His notice but in and through His son our Lord, *by* whom, and *for* whom, "were all things created," and *by* whom "all things consist."[110] The relation we bear to the wisdom of the father, the son of His love, gives us indeed a dignity which otherwise we have no pretense to. It makes us *something*, something considerable even in God's eyes. And in this respect and upon this account, the creation and chiefest good of man is a design worthy of God, I know not how we shall be able to prove it so on any other.

370. *That God is the sole object of our love, a doctrine unreasonably opposed.* Having affirmed §122 that love to God is the natural effect of true faith, and if it is sincere, will certainly produce universal obedience, it may not be amiss to remove certain prejudices,[111] for Christians are not it seems agreed, wherein this love consists, nor what is the extent of it. I need not repeat to your Ladyship my thoughts in this matter; and shall leave it to your own judgment, and to every equitable person whether the affirming God to be the sole object of our love, as

107. Astell's marginal note: *Lady's Religion*, 5.

108. *Lady's Religion*, 56.

109. Astell's marginal note: Is 40:17.

110. Astell's marginal note: Col 1:16, and so on. [Astell also refers to Col 1:17.]

111. These opening remarks are not in the first edition.

love imports the motion, especially voluntary motion and tendency of the mind to its true good, be so "unserviceable" to religion,[112] such a "perplexing the duties of morality," and rendering them impractical, and in fine, so very dangerous as to shake and unsettle the grounds of true piety, as some would represent it.[113] All the proof they have hitherto brought to make good these heavy accusations, as far as I can see, amounting to no more, than that they mistake the matter and fight with their own shadows; or that it is not a generally received opinion; "and that every man's experience confutes this every day."[114] Which last I allow them, just so much and no more than they will allow me, that "the daily sense and experience of mankind" disproves what a great philosopher asserts when he tells us, that "flame" is not "hot and light," nor "snow white and cold," nor "manna white and sweet":[115] for the most of those with whom we discourse about the matter, will neither be convinced by his authority, nor which is more by his reasons, which they think they have sufficiently answered when they oppose to them what they call their sense and their experience.

371. *They who find fault with it do not establish a better.* This is not a place to take notice, how they who are so severe upon their neighbors for being wanting (even in private letters writ without a design of being published)[116] in that exactness of "expression" which ought to be found in "philosophical disquisitions,"[117] do not express their own notion of love so as to take in all that Christianity requires. For the love[118] of our enemies is by no means consistent with that

112. Astell's marginal note: Masham, *Discourse*, Preface.

113. Astell's marginal note: Also Masham, *Discourse*, 15, 77, 119, and so on.

114. Astell's marginal note: Masham, *Discourse*, 25, 92.

115. Astell's marginal note: See Locke, *Essay*, II.viii.[16–18]. [Astell refers to Locke's chapter "Simple Ideas" and his famous theory of secondary qualities, the view that our representative ideas of sensible objects bear no resemblance to the qualities inherent in those objects, even though the objects themselves have the power to produce those ideas in our minds.]

116. Astell refers to her 1693–94 correspondence with Norris, later published as *Letters Concerning the Love of God* (1695).

117. Astell's marginal note: Masham, *Discourse*, 27.

118. In the first edition, this part reads "do themselves confound the notion of love with the sentiment of pleasure, by making love to 'consist barely in the act of the mind toward that which pleases' [Masham, *Discourse*, 51]. I shall only observe, as more proper to my present

account of love that is given by our great men, nor even possible upon their principles. They tell us, that "love is nothing else but that disposition of mind we find in ourselves towards anything we are pleased with"; and that without this "principle of love to our neighbor, we can't discharge what we owe to him,"[119] and that "wishing well" is not love, "but a different act consequent to love."[120] Now if "we cannot love but what we are pleased with,"[121] and that it is certain, for reason, as well as "the experience of mankind,"[122] assures us, that we cannot be pleased with our enemies, consequently we cannot love them. "Love," according to our author, "naturally draws desire after it,"[123] and they who "say we ought not to be so pleased, deny that we ought to love. For we cannot love but what we are pleased with";[124] therefore, say I, if our author's account of love be right, we must either be pleased with our enemies, or we must not love them. And if it is not possible to be pleased with them, it is also impossible to love them.

372. *Their account of love inconsistent with love of enemies, particularly persecutors.* Suppose our enemy is a persecutor, and invades that "fundamental, sacred and unalterable law of self-preservation,"[125] as some call it, persecution is "no way desirable to us" according to their principles, and much less the persecutor; so that "it is manifestly impossible and contradictious that we should rejoice and take complaisance in him." Now if we "love our neighbor as ourselves, their being and well-being must necessarily be desirable to us."[126] But the being and much less the well-being of a persecutor can't be desirable. A persecutor who would deprive us of our dear and desirable estates, offices, and employments, our dearer lives perhaps (over which we

---

business, that the love," instead of "do not express their own notion of love so as to take in all that Christianity requires. For the love."

119. Astell's marginal note: Masham, *Discourse*, 18, 51, 89; 47, 48.

120. Astell's marginal note: Masham, *Discourse*, 25.

121. Astell's marginal note: Masham, *Discourse*, 24. See also 50.

122. Masham, *Discourse*, 92.

123. Astell's marginal note: Masham, *Discourse*, 16.

124. Astell's marginal note: Masham, *Discourse*, 24.

125. Astell's marginal note: Locke, *Two Treatises*, II.149.

126. Astell's marginal note: Masham, *Discourse*, 50.

ourselves "have no power,"[127] therefore how should he come by it, though we invested him with all the power we had, on condition he kept his compact?) and as we *say*, our dearest religion! It is therefore utterly impossible, if the former principles be true, and contrary to the nature of things, to love a persecutor. We may wish him so well indeed, as to deprive him of the power to persecute, we may tie his hands, or to make sure work, throw him out if we are able, in great kindness to him and in a little to ourselves without question! But none of this is love, for according to our author "wishing well" is not "loving," though it may follow from love. And besides it is not a little paradoxical, and a thought that none could have fallen into but those free thinkers who are got above the "alms basket,"[128] and the slavish principles of former Christians, to suppose we wish well to a man when we do him all the hurt we can! But to submit to and bear with a persecutor, "the common enemy and pest of mankind,"[129] much more to delight, to rejoice, and take complaisance in him, is contrary to all sense and reason, to "our just and natural rights,"[130] and can go down with none but "such servile flatterers," who would have all "men born to what their mean souls have fitted them, slavery"![131]

373. *But Christianity requires us to love our enemies and persecutors.* And yet for all this, so it happens, that Christ has commanded us to "love our enemies,"[132] even our persecutors, if our translation of the Bible is right;[133] and we know "God has laid no traps or snares to render us miserable, nor does He require impossible performances from us."[134] It follows then, that either the translators, out of slavish

127. Astell's marginal note: Locke, *Two Treatises*, II.23.

128. Astell alludes to Locke's "Epistle to the Reader" in his *Essay*: "Thus he who has raised himself above the alms-basket, and not content to live lazily on scraps of begged opinions, sets his own thoughts on work, to find and follow truth, will (whatever he lights on) not miss the hunter's satisfaction" (6).

129. Locke, *Two Treatises*, II.230.

130. Astell quotes from the preface to the *Two Treatises*, where Locke refers to "the people of England" and their "love of their just and natural rights" (137).

131. Astell's marginal note: Locke, *Two Treatises*, II.239.

132. Astell's marginal note: Mt 5:44.

133. "good" in first edition.

134. Astell's marginal note: Masham, *Discourse*, 57.

principles, and to curry favor with that arbitrary prince who employed them in that translation,[135] have corrupted the sacred text: or else that everything is not true which we find in the *Discourses* of our modern authors, who not only refine upon philosophy, by which they do service to the world; and upon politics, by which they mean to serve their party; but even upon Christianity itself, pretending to give us a more "reasonable" account of it, by which they mean somewhat more agreeable to their genius and conveniency; for their systems, so far as I can find, do no manner of "service to decaying piety, and mistaken and slandered Christianity."[136]

374. *Passive doctrines.* It must needs be a strange kind of love to enemies that is without any sort of desire or goodwill, since by their own confession, "so far as the object of our love admits of both,"[137] love is never without them. And according to their systems, the love of enemies, of persecutors at least, is not among "those admired and beneficial virtues that support and profit society."[138] Though according to others, the peace of the world is promoted by nothing so much as by the meek, forgiving, and if one dare say it, the "passive" doctrines which are in a most peculiar manner the doctrines of the gospel. But "certainly to persuade men that God requires what they find impossible to perform," or which is the same thing, to say, that what God has commanded is "opposite to their very constitution and being in this world, is to make religion," and, so far as we can, the author as well as "the teachers of it ridiculous,"[139] to render the divine law precarious, and to warp it upon all occasions to our own corrupt affections and pretended necessities.

375. *Absurdities.* Indeed if their account of love be right, it is ridiculous to give any precepts concerning it. For it is certain "we shall be pleased with that which pleases," whether or not it be commanded:

135. Astell refers with irony to James I, king of England (1566–1625), the monarch who authorized the English translation of the Bible that is now known as the King James Bible.

136. Locke, *Vindication*, 10 [13]. Here Astell also obliquely alludes to Locke's *Essay concerning Human Understanding* (his work of philosophy), his *Two Treatises* (his work of politics), and his *Reasonableness of Christianity* (his work on Christianity), respectively.

137. Astell's marginal note: Masham, *Discourse*, 51.

138. Astell's marginal note: Masham, *Discourse*, 123.

139. Astell's marginal note: Masham, *Discourse*, 119.

and though we are enjoined ever so often, "it is not possible to be pleased with that which does not please."[140] So that if by "disposition of mind towards that which pleases"[141] be meant the bare sentiment of pleasure, love in this sense is no more in our power than the motion of our pulse, and therefore can't be under command. But if by "act or disposition of mind" be meant the voluntary motion of the mind toward that which pleases, this is neither more nor less, than the particular determination of what others have called "the original bent and endeavor of the soul towards good in general";[142] only this last is the better expression because the clearer. For it is not to be supposed that the men of the former way intend to affirm, that the mind has any disposition to be pleased with evil, or at least with anything that appears so to it.

376. *Absurdities*. It is also to be observed, that whatever Moses and the Jews might understand by *love*, they could not take it in his sense who writ the *Discourse concerning the Love of God*. For when it was said by Moses, "thou shalt love thy neighbor," there could be no sense in what the Jews added, "and hate thine enemy," if delight and complaisance were meant by love.[143] For what occasion for an allowance to do that which must necessarily be done, or injunction not to do that which was impossible for them to do? For if "we necessarily love whatever is accompanied with pleasure";[144] we as necessarily hate whatever is accompanied with pain, or displeasure. So that it need not be said to any people, especially not to the Jews, you shall "hate thine enemy," for we "need little caution not to desire, or not" to be pleased with that "which is not desirable, or (which is here equivalent) not

140. Astell's marginal note: Masham, *Discourse*, 17, 90. [Astell targets Masham's remarks that "we need little caution not to desire what is not desirable, or ... not pleasing to us" (17) and that "we must not be pleased with anything but what pleases us" (90).]

141. Astell's marginal note: Masham, *Discourse*, 50.

142. Astell quotes John Norris's definition of love in his "Discourse Concerning the Measure of Divine Love," in the third volume of his *Practical Discourses Upon several Divine Subjects* (London: S. Manship, 1693). Love, he says, is a "motion of the soul" or "that original weight, bent, or endeavor whereby the soul of man stands inclined and is moved forwards to good in general or *happiness*" ("Discourse," 13).

143. Astell's marginal note: Mt 5:43.

144. Astell's marginal note: Masham, *Discourse*, 88.

pleasing to us."[145] All which considered, as I "imagine" (for one whose "reason is weak" and "imagination stronger"[146] must not pretend to *understand*) there is a manifest absurdity and contradiction somewhere, we are sure it is not in the precepts of the gospel, let those who are fallen into it get clear of it as they can. While I make no scruple to say, without fear of losing myself in a "pompous rhapsody,"[147] that the soul debases herself, when she sets her affections on anything but her creator. It being a very vulgar way of speech that a man debases himself, if being allowed to court the mistress he should make his addresses to the maid, even though she were his equal, much more if she were very much his inferior. And since the courtly prophet has said, that "all nations are as nothing before God, and they are counted to Him less than nothing and vanity,"[148] I am under no apprehension that by saying the same thing, or to the same purpose, I have "complimented God with the contempt of His works."[149]

377. *Our deplorable defection from genuine Christianity.* Some men indeed have writ of love, as if they knew nothing of it but what they learn from good eating and the like sensations. And for reasons to themselves best known, they write *Discourses* to persuade us, that we are under no necessity of taking our affections off the creature to place them solely on the creator.[150] Though the holy scripture requires us to "set our affections on things above not on things on the earth," and for this reason, because we "are dead and our life is hid with Christ in God."[151] Nor do I desire to stretch the love of God further than the true importance of this text. My ignorance in the sacred languages, besides

145. Astell's marginal note: Masham, *Discourse*, 17.

146. Astell's marginal note: Masham, *Discourse*, 120. [Astell wryly invokes Masham's remark that Norris's opinions seem to encourage an excess of devotion "especially amongst those whose imaginations are stronger than their reason" (Masham, *Discourse*, 120).]

147. Astell's marginal note: Masham, *Discourse*, 27.

148. Astell's marginal note: Is 40:17.

149. Astell's marginal note: Masham, *Discourse*, 27.

150. Astell possibly refers not only to Masham's *Discourse* but also to Daniel Whitby, *A Discourse of the Love of God. Showing, That it is well consistent with some Love or Desire of the Creature* (London: Awnsham and John Churchill, 1697), another response to the Astell-Norris *Letters*.

151. Astell's marginal note: Col 3:2–3.

all other disadvantages, makes me incapable of expounding scripture with the learned; but this is certain (or else we know nothing) that the practical Christianity of the apostles and the primitive Christians, was very different from what is practiced nowadays. For they gladly parted with "all for the gospel's sake," and "rejoiced" in nothing so much as "that they were counted worthy to suffer for the name of Christ," so little fond were they of the goods of this life, or even of life itself.[152] Whereas we dread nothing more, I need not say "than resisting unto blood," and "taking up our cross and following Christ,"[153] but, than running the least hazard, even in our estates, through a firm adherence to the precepts[154] of the gospel. And because we do not practice them, we take the boldness from hence to affirm, that they ought not to be practiced. The most beautiful and perfective doctrines of our most holy religion, being ridiculed and hooted out of the world by numbers and noise!

378. *How we ought to love God, and may love creatures.* But to pass on and draw a veil over our shame—suppose your Ladyship, or any other good Christian, is addicted to study, or if the expression be more acceptable to anybody, I will say *loves* study. And will also allow that you love it because it pleases. But why does it please? But because it enlarges and betters your mind, by putting you in possession of truth, which is your true good, that is indeed of God Himself who is "the truth and the life."[155] Your spirits fail and you grow faint, you eat and drink, or if they like it better, you *love* to eat and drink upon this occasion; and why so? Not for the mere pleasure of eating and drinking, this, I may say without a "rhapsody,"[156] were below a rational, much more a Christian mind. Though it is certain you feel pleasure in it, and you thank God for it, since by this easy sensible way, without engaging yourself in the troublesome examination of the state of your body and the suitableness of the nourishment, you eat and drink what will support it. But you do this only to keep your body in health that it may be able to serve your mind, that both may serve

152. Astell's marginal note: Phil 3:7–8; Acts 4:34, 5:41.

153. Astell's marginal note: Heb 12:4; Mt 16:24–25.

154. "truths" in first edition.

155. Jn 14:6.

156. Masham, *Discourse*, 27.

their redeemer, in which service all your happiness consists. And as great pains usually withdraw our attention from little ones, so do greater pleasures extinguish our sense of the lesser. Having therefore upon your mind that truly rational and sublime pleasure, of approving yourself to God and enjoying Him, you are not at leisure to attend the little poignancy[157] of meat and drink, though the health and soundness of your constitution makes these as relishing to you as to anybody. If meditation and a just disquisition of truth has carried you beyond the prejudices of sense, you are convinced that God is the true efficient cause of all our good, of all our pleasing sensations,[158] and that without any reflection on the purity of His nature. You look through the creature to the creator as the author of all your delight, and thus every morsel gives a double pleasure, considering the hand that feeds you, or to speak more correctly, the power of God giving you diverse modifications. And where is the hurt of all this, that our modern divines and philosophers should make such an outcry against it, as if the loving God in this manner were destructive of all religion, and even of morality, and would do all those strange things the learned are pleased to charge it with!

379. *Monasteries.* Among which, what they seem most afraid of, is dispeopling the world and driving folks into "monasteries,"[159] though I see none among us for them to run into were they ever so much inclined; but have heard it generally complained of by very good Protestants, that monasteries were abolished instead of being reformed:[160] and though none that I know of plead for monasteries, strictly so called, in England, or for anything else but a reasonable

157. poignancy] pungency.

158. Astell possibly alludes to Malebranchean occasionalism, the theory that God is the only true and proper cause of sensations in the mind.

159. Astell's marginal note: Masham, *Discourse*, 120. [Astell addresses Masham's criticisms of Norris and Malebranche, especially the claim that their philosophy "can end in nothing but monasteries, and hermitages; with all those sottish and wicked superstitions which have accompanied them wherever they have been in use" (Masham, *Discourse*, 120).]

160. Astell may have in mind Richard Allestree and Clement Barksdale. In his *Ladies' Calling*, Allestree writes: "As for the religious orders of virgins, in the present Roman Church, though some of those very great abuses have crept in; yet I think it were to be wished, that those who suppressed them in this nation, had confined themselves within the bounds of a reformation, by choosing rather to rectify and regulate, than abolish them" (157). Clement

provision for the education of one half of mankind, and for a safe retreat for so long and no longer than our circumstances make it requisite.[161] As is so plainly expressed in what has been said on this subject,[162] that none can mistake the meaning, without great disingenuity and an eager desire to cavil. But generous designs for the glory of God and the good of mankind, have been opposed in all ages (even by those who pretend to be the true patriots) by supposed and far-fetched dangers, and by misrepresentations to raise the mob and popular prejudices against them, since reason will not furnish out any objection.[163]

380. *Queen Anne.* But may we not hope from the magnificence of a truly glorious prince,[164] every year of whose reign may be reckoned, not by the addition of new extortions and oppressions to drain her subjects and enrich foreigners, but by an increase of new bounties and acts of goodness to her own people, as well as a generous exertion of her power to establish the tranquility of Europe; that since her subjects in general have had so liberal a portion of her royal beneficence, and the clergy more particularly,[165] an act that will embalm her majesty's name to future generations, and sound her praise louder

Barksdale cites Allestree's remark with approval in the postscript to his *Letter Touching a Colledge of Maids; or, A Virgin-Society* (London: n.p., 1675), A4r.

161. Astell pointedly refers to her proposal for an academy of higher learning for women, first put forward in her *Serious Proposal to the Ladies* of 1694. She describes her academy or "monastery" as "a retreat from the world" (Astell, *Proposal I*, 18). In the second *Proposal*, Astell emphasizes that "They must either be very ignorant or very malicious who pretend that we would imitate foreign monasteries ... our institution is more *academical* than *monastic*" (Astell, *Proposal II*, 232).

162. The first edition reads "in this business" instead of "on this subject."

163. In his 1752 biography of Astell, George Ballard reports that "a certain great lady" intended to fund Astell's female academy but was dissuaded by Gilbert Burnet, the bishop of Salisbury, who informed the lady that it "would look like preparing a way for popish orders" and that "it would be reputed a nunnery" (*Memoirs of Several Ladies*, 383). Burnet (1643–1715) was a Whig and a man of considerable power and influence in court circles. He may be the pretender to true patriotism that Astell has in mind here. For details on Burnet, see Martin Greig's biography in *ODNB*, s.v. "Burnet, Gilbert," http://www.oxforddnb.com/view/article/4061 (accessed November 8, 2012).

164. Queen Anne herself. In Astell's time, the term "prince" applied to female as well as male sovereigns.

165. Astell alludes to "Queen Anne's Bounty," a charity fund established in 1704 to supplement the income of poor members of the Anglican clergy.

than all the ravages and victories of usurping and ambitious men, nay even than her own glorious victories, truly glorious in that they do not dispossess a rightful owner, but secure his empire; "while the name of the wicked" who dispossess lawful sovereigns, who destroy God's heritage, and root up the order and government of His church, "shall rot":[166] may we not hope that she will not do less for her own sex than she has already done for the other; but that the next year of her majesty's annals will bear date, from her maternal and royal care of the most helpless and most neglected part of her subjects.[167] If she overlooks us we have no further prospect; for wherever other people may carry their views, we of the Church of England have no hope beyond our *present sovereign.*

381. *The only lawful restraint on the supreme magistrate.* I have neither forgot nor forsaken my subject by this seeming digression, for what but the love of God can justly restrain sovereign princes from being injurious, or excite them to be just and gracious to their people? They who think the awe of God's sovereignty but a poor restraint, and are therefore for subjecting His vicegerents to the coercion of their subjects,[168] against the laws of this nation as well as against the doctrine of the church, against scripture, and common sense, show too little regard to any religion, whatever they may talk about it, to be looked upon by any but a heedless mob as its defenders; and are *in truth,* what St. Paul and his fellow Christians were *falsely* accused of being, the "men that have turned the world upside down."[169]

382. *How the gospel provides for the quiet of the world.* From "whence come wars and fightings," brawlings as the margin reads,[170]

166. Prv 10:7.

167. The wording here recalls that of Astell's dedication to Anne (then Princess of Denmark) in the second *Proposal,* where she says, "I see no cause to fear that your Royal Highness will deny encouragement to that which has no other design than the bettering of the world, especially the most neglected part of it as to all real improvement, the ladies" (*Proposal II,* 117).

168. The first edition reads "subjecting them to the coercion of the people" instead of "subjecting His vicegerents to the coercion of their subjects."

169. Acts17:6.

170. Astell's marginal note: Jas 4:1. [Astell's translation of fightings as "brawlings" corresponds to the marginalia for James 4:1 in a 1696 version of the King James Bible, *The Holy Bible ... [with] Notes in the Margin*: "Or brawling."]

or in our modern expression "struggles for power," but from our "appetites,"[171] our eager desires after worldly things? And what remedy does the "gospel of peace" prescribe,[172] but that we should "use the world as not abusing it."[173] By which is meant, if we will allow the scripture to explain itself, the "using the world as though we used it not," being very indifferent, even "mortified," "dead" to it, "that the life of Jesus may be manifested in us."[174]

383. *What sort of love to the world our adversaries plead for.* But certainly the way of using the world mentioned in the 378th paragraph, is more like to restrain us from abusing it, than if we should say to ourselves, why may not we "satisfy" our "natural cravings" with the "good things of this world,"[175] which as we learn from the "common sense and experience of mankind," as well as from the *Discourses* of great men, "were given to be enjoyed"?[176] And what need of troubling ourselves with those "severe precepts" which none but "heads cast in metaphysical moulds" can understand, and such as have "privileges of nature" can practice;[177] which can't be talked of but by those whose "imaginations are stronger than their reason,"[178] who fly out in "an unintelligible" way of "pompous rhapsody" and "unpremeditated raptures," carrying "a show of some truth in the heart of the speaker which they have not strictly in themselves"?[179] Do not we "ask ourselves whether we are willing to part with any other good for God's sake"?[180] And do we not answer "we are willing"? But thanks be to

---

171. "pleasures" in first edition.

172. Eph 6:15; Rom 10:15.

173. Astell's marginal note: 1 Cor 7:31.

174. Astell's marginal note: Rom 8:13; Gal 6:14 and 5:24; Rom 6; Col 3:3.

175. Astell's marginal note: Masham, *Discourse*, 35.

176. Masham, *Discourse*, 92, 35.

177. Astell's marginal note: Masham, *Discourse*, 35. [Masham borrows the phrase "head cast in a *metaphysical mould*" from Norris himself; see John Norris, *Reflections upon the Conduct of Human Life: With Reference to the Study of Learning and Knowledge. In a Letter to the Excellent Lady, the Lady Masham* (1690), in Norris, *Philosophical and Theological Writings*, 3:41.]

178. Astell's marginal note: Masham, *Discourse*, 120.

179. Astell's marginal note: Masham, *Discourse*, 27.

180. Astell's marginal note: Masham, *Discourse*, 45.

providence and the "love of just and natural rights,"[181] the trying times of the gospel are past, we are delivered from that slavery, and as the world now goes, it is most for God's service that we keep what we have got, and add as much to it as we can. For this enables us to be patriots, to purchase heads and hands,[182] and to fight for religion upon occasion; and in the meanwhile to do abundance of good to mankind, by applying ourselves to *all* their inclinations whatever they be, that so we may bring them over to the righteous side! We know "we receive all our good from the hand of God,"[183] and this habitual knowledge is sufficient to secure our duty, while we freely entertain ourselves with the "present pleasure," so grateful to our senses, and which our Christian liberty allows us! We shall be wise enough to retreat in time, and to put a bridle on our desires when they grow inordinate. It may be difficult indeed for weak people to "proportion their desires to the worth of things,"[184] when the object has got possession of their hearts and strongly raised their passions, but we are too experienced and too well resolved to be thus overcome. Though we "act suitable to" our "nature and desire things that can be enjoyed," and thus go on in the "chase of pleasing ideas," yet we will not, no verily we will not be "led captive by them," but will keep them "under the government and direction of reason," which our indulged desires shall not at all impair![185]

384. *The consequences of it.* Were it not by such a process and way of arguing as this, there could not be so much sin and folly in the world as we must needs complain of. For the service of God is most reasonable in itself, and indeed most delightful to a rational nature. But we are not at leisure to hearken to reason, being taken up with pleasing sensations and the present pleasure whatever it be. All which is as good as acknowledged by our Discourser;[186] and I should be glad if he would condescend to show us a better way than was offered

181. Locke, *Two Treatises*, "The Preface," 137.

182. purchase heads and hands] obtain or acquire persons for our cause.

183. Masham, *Discourse*: "it is certain, that to believe … that we receive all our good from the hand of God; ought to be, and effectively is, the proper ground of our love of Him above all things" (26).

184. Astell's marginal note: Masham, *Discourse*, 53.

185. Astell's marginal note: Masham, *Discourse*, 53, 54.

186. Astell's marginal note: Masham, *Discourse*, 55 and so on, and 125.

above, whereby "the love of God and the interests of another life" may be "constantly our ruling and predominant passion."[187]

385. In the meantime, and to be as "intelligible" as I can, I desire only that our love to God may be compared with, and examined by that love which we have had to any of His creatures, upon whom we have sometimes set our hearts, or even the love we at present bear, to those whom we think we love with entire subordination to the love of God. For if we are more deeply and more lastingly affected with the gain or loss of a friend, or any temporal advantage or affliction whatever, than we are with our offenses against God, or the hopes of pardon; or with the loss, or the obtaining of His favor; I know not by what sort of reasoning we can conclude that we love Him above all things. There's a difficulty it is true, in setting our affections on things above and not on things on the earth, in being dead to sense and placing all our felicity in a spiritual and invisible object. But yet it may be done, and that without a "lively remorse" for pleasures that all of us reckon unallowable. What "turn" may be given to "the stream of some men's affections," or what "disgust" such a remorse may give them to "all sensible pleasures" I know not, they who have felt it are best able to account for it.[188] But this I can say, that consulting our own experience we shall find, that we never placed our hearts very much on any the most allowable object this world affords, but that in a little time it gave us sufficient reason as heartily to despise it. Whether from a remorse for our guilt in having loved *any* creature, or from a full demonstration of our folly in not "proportioning our desires to the worth of the thing";[189] I leave to our Discoursers to determine.

386. *Mr. Locke's supposition that it is possible for matter to think, considered.* As to matter's being capable of thought, a famous and ingenious author,[190] who does "neither say nor suppose, that all matter has naturally in it a faculty of thinking but the direct contrary";[191] does also say, that "it is possible, i.e., involves no contradiction, that God should if He pleases give to some parcels of matter a power

---

187. Astell's marginal note: Masham, *Discourse*, 55.

188. Astell's marginal note (first edition only): Masham, *Discourse*, 27.

189. Masham, *Discourse*, 52–53.

190. i.e., John Locke.

191. Astell's marginal note: Locke, *Third Letter*, 409.

of thinking."[192] And if so, then for ought we know, or can prove to the contrary, our minds may be nothing else but certain "parcels of matter" to which God has "given" this "power." I would not presume to charge this great writer, for whom I have a due esteem, with contradiction, he being such a master of thought and language; but if the "strength of my imagination" does not deceive me, there is something like it in some of his works. Though doubtless it will be thought the "weakness" of my "reason," and not want of consistency in him, that make me "imagine" it![193]

387. *What is impossible to any power whatever by Mr. L.'s principles.* This judicious writer in his excellent *Essay of Human Understanding* tells us, "that in some of our ideas there are certain relations, habitudes, and connections so visibly included in the nature of the ideas themselves, that we cannot conceive them separable from them, by *any power whatsoever.* Nor can we (as he goes on) conceive this connection to be *possibly* mutable, or to depend on any arbitrary power, which of choice made it thus, or *could* make it otherwise."[194] "Any power whatsoever," must as I "imagine," include the power of God, and therefore having so good an authority, we may "venture," in this case at least, to "limit the power of the omnipotent creator," and may say, He "cannot possibly do" that which "destroys" the "essence, or changes the essential properties of" things.[195] Or in the words of the *Essay*, "cannot separate that which is so included in the nature of an idea, that we can't conceive it separable": and by a parity of reason, can't add that which is so excluded from the nature of an idea, that we can't conceive the idea capable of that addition.

388. *His argument for matter's being capable of thought destroyed by his own principles.* Our author is pleased to instance in the idea of a "right-lined triangle, which necessarily carries with it an

192. Astell's marginal note: Locke, *Third Letter*, 430. [Locke's exact words are "it is possible, i.e. involves no contradiction, that God the omnipotent immaterial spirit should, if He pleases, give to some parcels of matter, disposed as He thinks fit, a power of thinking and moving" (Locke, *Third Letter*, 430).]

193. Astell borrows these disparaging comments from Masham, *Discourse*, 120.

194. Astell's marginal note: Locke, *Essay*, IV.iii.29. [The italics are Astell's.]

195. Astell's marginal note: Locke, *Third Letter*, 397.

equality of its angles to two right ones."[196] This property being necessary to it, as I humbly "imagine," because it is repugnant to the idea
of such a triangle, that its angles should be either greater or less. But
now should I with my "weak reason" and "strong imagination" affirm,
that "God may give to"[197] this triangle the property of including no
space, or of being equal to a square; nay, that He may "according to the
good pleasure of His omnipotency,"[198] give it a "speaking," a "walking,"
or "a dancing faculty";[199] and make it able to eat and drink; should I
tell our ingenious author, that to deny "God's power in this case, only
because he can't conceive the manner how," is "no less than an insolent
absurdity";[200] and a "limiting the power of the omnipotent creator."[201]
Should I "grant" that the faculty of speaking, or the property of being
equal to a square, "is not included in the essence of a triangle"; yet this
notwithstanding should stick to my "assertion," that "God if He pleases can superadd these excellencies," though I "have no more to say
to make it good," than that "whatever excellency, not contained in its
essence, be superadded to" a triangle, "it does not destroy the essence
of" a triangle "if it leaves it" a figure bounded by three right lines; for
"wherever that is there is the essence of" a triangle:[202] and that "if God
cannot join things together by connections inconceivable to us, we

196. Astell's marginal note: Locke, *Essay*, IV.iii.29.

197. Astell's marginal note: Locke, *Third Letter*, 397.

198. Astell's marginal note: Locke, *Third Letter*, 405.

199. Astell's marginal note: Locke, *Essay*, II.xxi.17. [Astell alludes to Locke's debunking of faculty psychology: "For if it be reasonable to suppose and talk of *faculties*, as distinct beings, that can act … it is fit that we should make a speaking *faculty*, and a walking *faculty*, and a dancing *faculty*" (*Essay*, II.xxi.17).]

200. Astell's marginal note: Locke, *Third Letter*, 402.

201. Astell's marginal note: Locke, *Third Letter*, 397 and 409.

202. Should … triangle] Astell adapts Locke's statements in *Third Letter*: "The idea of matter is an extended solid substance; wherever there is such a substance, there is matter; and the essence of matter, whatever other qualities not contained in that essence, it shall please God to superadd to it" (396–97) and "But if one ventures to go one step further and say, God may give to matter, thought, reason, and volition, as well as sense and spontaneous motion, there are men ready presently to limit the power of the omnipotent creator, and tell us, He cannot do it; because it destroys the essence, or 'changes the essential properties' of matter. To make good which assertion they have no more to say, but that thought and reason are not included in the essence of matter. I grant it; but whatever excellency, not contained in its essence, be

must deny even the consistency and being of matter itself."[203] Should I also add, that although the very ingenious Mr. L. in his *Essay* tells us, that connections visibly included in ideas, do not depend on any arbitrary power whatsoever, nor can be conceived separably by any power;[204] yet in his *Third Letter to the Bishop of Worcester*, he seems[205] of another mind, his reasonings there allowing us to conclude, that all the difficulties raised against a speaking or eating triangle, and one that is equal to a square, are "raised only from our ignorance or narrow conceptions," but "stand not at all in the way of the power of" God, "nor prove anything against his having actually endued some"[206] triangle with those properties ("though every" triangle *as a* triangle, "has them not")[207] "unless it can be proved that it contains a contradiction to suppose it."[208] Should I argue at this rate, would not that great master of good sense, despise such sort of discourses as the "rhapsodies" and "strong imaginations of" a silly woman? And the world it's like would not allow them to pass anywhere as the "philosophical disquisitions" of a free thinker, and a lover of truth, unless it pays a greater deference to names than things.[209] And yet I have all along used Mr. L.'s arguments, even his very words, only putting triangle in the place of matter.

389. *What is a contradiction according to Mr. L.* But let us see what it is that makes a *contradiction*, according to Mr. L's principles, that so by his excellent measures of reasoning we may determine, whether it be possible for omnipotency to make a triangle equal to a square, and that can eat and speak; since I should be as "glad" to dine and to discourse with a triangle, as Mr. L. would be to "get a demonstration of the soul's immateriality."[210] Mr. L. "thinks that we may

---

superadded to matter, it does not destroy the essence of matter, if it leaves it an extended solid substance; wherever that is, there is the essence of matter" (397–98).

203. Astell's marginal note: Locke, *Third Letter*, 405.

204. Astell's marginal note: Locke, *Essay*, IV.iii.29.

205. "is" in first edition.

206. Astell's marginal note: Locke, *Third Letter*, 405.

207. Astell's marginal note: Locke, *Third Letter*, 400.

208. Locke, *Third Letter*, 406.

209. Again, Astell uses the language of Masham, *Discourse*, 27, 120.

210. Astell's marginal note: Locke, *Third Letter*, 393.

say with due reverence," "that omnipotency can't make a substance to be solid and not solid at the same time";[211] which as I "imagine" is as much as to say, that *this* thing can't be *that*; or to be as plain as possible, that the idea I have of the table I write on representing it oblong, I can't perceive it to be round. That knowledge consists in the perception of the agreement or disagreement of ideas, is what Mr. L. affirms, and what none who think will deny.[212] So that a contradiction is a perception of such a disagreement between two propositions, that if the one be true the other must needs be false; and such an inconsistency between two ideas as that they cannot coexist. And though they may not be directly opposite as "solid and not solid," yet so far forth as they are different and distinct it is not possible that they should be the same, and to affirm that they are is a contradiction.

390. *Instance.* For instance, a sphere and a cube are not opposite, they are each of them figures, and solids; but being different and distinct, that piece of wax, which is now a cube, can't possibly in the same time be a sphere, any more than it can be "solid and not solid." And for the same reason, to say that a square is a triangle, or that an extended substance is a thinking substance, is as contradictory, as to say, that motion is rest, or that a "substance is solid and not solid at the same time."

391. *That it is impossible for matter to think, and a contradiction by his principles.* Mr. L. does not deny, that we have some knowledge of the "connection" or "repugnancy" that ideas have one with another, though "he thinks we know" this "but to a very small degree" with regard to bodies.[213] For indeed, unless we know the repugnancy of ideas, we could not know what a contradiction is. But yet as little as we know "as to incompatibility or repugnancy to co-existence" (your Ladyship I hope will pardon these hard words, which I only repeat from that polite and ingenious author) "we may know that any subject can have of

211. Astell's marginal note: Locke, *Third Letter*, 405.

212. See Locke, *Essay*, IV.ii.1–2.

213. Astell's marginal note: Locke, *Essay*, IV.iii.16. [Locke writes: "our knowledge concerning corporeal substances, will be very little advanced by any (hypotheses), till we are made to see what qualities and powers of bodies have a *necessary connection or repugnancy* one with another; which in the present state of philosophy, I think, we know but to a very small degree" (IV.iii.16).]

each sort of primary quality but one particular at once, e.g., each particular extension, figure, and so on, excludes all other of each kind." "It is impossible," says he, "that the very same particle of any body, should have two different figures and textures at the same time."[214] And therefore, unless he "proves" as well as "supposes it possible," that "though perception is not an essential property of matter,"[215] "yet some parcels of matter may be so ordered by omnipotence as to be endued with a faculty of thinking";[216] matter and thought being as incompatible as any two different figures and textures whatever; though it were too much for me to be "positive" on the force of my own "imagination," yet having so good authority as the *Essay of Human Understanding* on my side, I will presume to affirm, that it is impossible for "a solid substance to have qualities, perfections, and powers which have no natural or visible connection with solidity and extension";[217] and since there is no visible connection between matter and thought, it is "impossible for matter" or "any parcels of matter to think," at least for us to "suppose it contains a contradiction."[218] So that, in fine, I utterly despair of meeting with a triangle equal to a square, and that can eat and discourse; and I find it equally impossible for body to think. Thought and extension being as "incompatible" to the same substance, as the properties of a square and a triangle are at the same time.

392. *We judge of things not by the properties God may but by those He has given them.* Further, I know that a triangle is not a square, and that body is not mind, as "the child knows that the nurse that feeds it is neither the cat it plays with, nor the blackamoor[219] it is afraid of,"[220] and the child and I come by our knowledge after the same manner. But how is it that we distinguish one idea from another? Is it by the properties that God *may*, or by those he *has endued* it with? If by what God *may* do, then there's an end of knowledge, which consists in the perception of the agreement or disagreement of ideas. For upon

214. Astell's marginal note: Locke, *Essay*, [IV.iii.]15.

215. Astell's marginal note: Locke, *Third Letter*, 410.

216. Astell's marginal note: Locke, *Third Letter*, 416.

217. Astell's marginal note: Locke, *Third Letter*, 405.

218. Astell's marginal note: Locke, *Third Letter*, 406.

219. blackamoor] a black African or any dark-skinned person (*OED*).

220. Astell's marginal note: Locke, *Essay*, I.ii.25.

this supposition I have no way to distinguish one idea from another; and neither the child nor Mr. L. himself can say, whether omnipotency *may not* have endued the cat with the nurse's faculties. But if I am to distinguish ideas by their *essential properties*, then the not being able to discern these properties, and more especially my discerning a repugnancy between certain properties and certain ideas, is an unanswerable proof, that it is not possible for these ideas or the things they represent, to be endued with those properties. Unless God has been pleased to reveal that this is possible to His omnipotency; for if so, I must conclude that I only imagine and don't indeed perceive that repugnancy. And when Mr. L. or any other person can prove from divine revelation, that any parcels of matter do, or may think, I shall confess the "certainty" of the proposition, and be as fully persuaded of the truth of it, as if I were able to demonstrate it, till then they must excuse me from allowing it possible for body in general, or "for any parcels of" matter "to think."

393. *What Mr. Locke's arguments about matter amount to.* For I do not find that the arguments of the great Mr. L. who is best able to defend the cause, no not those he thought fit to use against so great and learned an adversary as the late Bishop Stillingfleet,[221] amount to any more than that God *can* do what we find He *has* done, that is, make another substance besides body, whose essential property, if not its very essence shall be thought, and can unite this thinking substance to body, which is what we call the union between soul and body. For if there is "nothing at all in" matter *as* matter "that thinks," then God's "bestowing on some parcels of" matter a power of thinking, is neither more nor less than the making an arbitrary union between body and something that is not body, whereby this *composite* has properties that matter as matter "is no way capable of."[222] So that it is not body that thinks, but the mind that is united to it, body being still as incapable of thought as ever it was.

221. Edward Stillingfleet, the bishop of Worcester and writer of theological works. On Stillingfleet, see Barry Till's biography in *ODNB*, s.v. "Stillingfleet, Edward," http://www. oxforddnb.com/view/article/26526 (accessed February 10, 2012).

222. Astell's marginal note: Locke, *Third Letter*, 408, 409.

394. *Some remarks on the Lady's Religion.* To add a few remarks on the *Lady's Religion*:[223] what the practice of the divine who wrote that letter was I know not, nor am I to judge of it, to his "own master he stands or falls";[224] but this I may say, that there are many divines who though they do all that in them lies to "defend the church by law established," are not for this reason at all less zealous in "promoting the common cause of serious piety," but rather the more so, the one being subservient to the other.[225] Whether or no he addicted himself to "superstitious appendages" and "by-interest" he best knows;[226] nor does any man serve the church by such ways, however he may serve himself. Our divine acquits the church of encouraging such practices, otherwise he could not continue what the title speaks him, "a divine of the Church of England." For a man of sincerity and candor must think as the French Prefacer does, that he could "not be silent on such an occasion without betraying his conscience."[227] To be sure he would not live in the church's bosom and secretly undermine her, for this is contrary to justice, ingenuity, and moral honesty, to say nothing of the simplicity and integrity of a Christian.

395. *What is said to be the design of that discourse.* His design, according to the French Prefacer, is to show, that the Christian religion ought to be accommodated to the meanest capacity, and in his own words, to "spare the needless trouble of reading abstruse and mysterious points of divinity."[228] I am so much of his mind, that should any learned divine tell me, "that it was generally believed of old that deity was made up of two coordinate powers," bringing Latin and Greek, nay, even Persian to prove it;[229] should he offer to inform me of the "original word" which we render "devils,"[230] and how great

223. The first edition reads, "And now give me leave, Madam, to add a few remarks on our divine's letter, and then I have done" instead of "To add a few remarks on the *Lady's Religion*."

224. Rom 14:4.

225. Astell's marginal note: *Lady's Religion*, 2.

226. *Lady's Religion*, 3.

227. *Lady's Religion*, "The Preface to the French Translation," A3v.

228. Astell's marginal note: *Lady's Religion*, 14.

229. Astell's marginal note: *Lady's Religion*, 60, 61.

230. Astell's marginal note: *Lady's Religion*, 64.

men have commented upon it: I would beg to be excused from enter-
ing into such "nice speculations," or "profound mysteries, which have
no direct tendency to improve my morals," and which therefore in
the opinion of the author of the *Lady's Religion*, might well be "passed
by."[231] For I only understand plain sense, being satisfied that this is
all that the gospel is designed to teach me; and that its sacred author
did not mean to trouble my head with curious criticisms and strained
interpretations.

396. *A passage in the French preface considered.* That Prefacer
also tells us, "that in the first ages of the church, bishops, true court
weathercocks, turned about with every little wind, to conform themselves to the pleasure of the prince."[232] To take no notice how well this
agrees with what he says a few pages after of rash and hasty judgment.
By the first ages of the church must be meant the first centuries. Now,
I confess I am but a very mean historian, and therefore possibly may
be mistaken, in supposing that the world was under heathen princes
until the reign of Constantine the Great, who flourished in the beginning of the third century. So that St. James and Simeon whom the
apostles made bishops of Jerusalem successively, together with those
other bishops ordained by them in all cities, of many of whom we
have honorable mention in the holy scripture, as St. Mark who was
bishop of Alexandria, Timothy of Ephesus, and after him Onesimus,
Titus of Crete, Silas of Corinth, Dionysius of Athens, Archippus of
Coloss, Epaphroditus of Philippi, Trophimus of Arles, Crescens of
Vienne, Aristobulus in Britain, Aristarchus, and after him Gaius of
Thessalonica, and Linus of Rome:[233] these holy men if the Prefacer
may be credited, conformed themselves to the pleasure of those heathen princes who held the empire at that time! Or else Nero and his
successors were Christians, and favorers of some little heresies, with

231. Astell's marginal note: *Lady's Religion*, 9.

232. *Lady's Religion*, "The Preface to the French Translation," A8r.

233. In their notes to appendix 3 in the Astell-Norris *Letters*, Taylor and New observe that
"Astell's source for her list of early Bishops up to 'the beginning of the Third Century' was
likely William Cave's *Apostolici, Or, the History, Lives, Acts, Death, and Martyrdom of Those
Who Were Contemporary with ... the Three First Ages of the Church* (1677)" (Astell and Norris, *Letters*, 258). It is also possible that Astell compiled the list herself, since (as she says) all
these early Christians are mentioned in the Bible.

which these "weathercock bishops" complied, either of which is a piece of criticism I must own I had not till now met with!

397. *Our divine's notion of faith.* I am also so dull, that as plain as our divine is, I can't apprehend what he means by faith, page 8. For if he understands no more by "faith in Christ" than our receiving the "Christian morals," and the "threats" and "promises" of the "gospel," in order to "practice," what becomes of the "narrations of" matters "of fact," which are part of the "Christian institution"?[234] And at that rate one might have faith in Christ without believing that there ever was such a person in the world, who was born of a virgin, lived an exemplary life, and died a bitter death for our redemption. But sure our divine could not mean to countenance so extravagant a proposition, nor will I suspect that he affects to be "dark" and "mysterious," because I won't suppose that he "has some indirect design in so doing."[235]

398. *Why controversies are become necessary.* It were to be wished that there were no controversies, "no writers and wranglers in religion, to fill it with niceties and dress it up with notions";[236] but that all of us, whether divines or others, "received the truth in the love thereof," "holding fast" the "form of sound words," set forth in holy writ, "in faith and love,"[237] "endeavoring to keep the unity of the spirit in the bond of peace."[238] But since the holy ghost has foretold, that "in the last days perilous times shall come,"[239] that "grievous wolves shall enter in among" Christians, "not sparing the flock"; and that even among the "elders of the church shall men arise, speaking perverse things to draw away disciples after them";[240] it is requisite for the governors of the church to "watch,"[241] "contending earnestly for the faith," "to convince and stop the mouths of the gainsayers."[242] Some

234. Astell's marginal note: *Lady's Religion*, 11.

235. Astell's marginal note: *Lady's Religion*, 10.

236. Astell's marginal note: Locke, *Reasonableness of Christianity*, 305 [169].

237. Astell's marginal note: 2 Tm 1:13.

238. Astell's marginal note: Eph 4:3.

239. Astell's marginal note: 2 Tm 3:1.

240. Astell's marginal note: Acts 20:29–30.

241. Astell's marginal note: 2 Tm 4:5.

242. Astell's marginal note: Jude 3. [Astell cites from Jude 1:3 and paraphrases Ti 1:9.]

controversies therefore are become necessary through the perverseness of "men of corrupt minds."[243]

399. *The object of divine worship controverted, though a matter of mere religion.* Our divine has not thought fit to let us know, what those "many books of controversial divinity" he has read treat of, so that for fear of falling under his censure of "rash judgment,"[244] I dare not guess at those "controversies" which he does not reckon to be matters of "mere religion."[245] But by the few controversies I have looked into, I find it has been disputed between us and the church of Rome, whether we should worship the consecrated elements in the Lord's supper? And whether we should pray to saints and angels? And by others, whether any but the great God ought to be worshipped? I know not how far our divine may have entered into these controversies, but certainly the "object" of divine worship is a matter of "mere religion"; and I think he ought to be so understood in his first instance of such matters, that is, "whether we should maintain in our hearts a high reverence and veneration for almighty God"?[246] It being very sure that God will not give His glory to another; and that no "divine person" whatever, though his "charity" and "heroic fortitude" be ever so great,[247] is to be worshipped, unless he be one of the three divine persons in the godhead. Whom the holy scripture expressly teaches us to adore, and also that God is jealous of His honor, and will not give it to another.[248]

400. *A supposition why our divine is so short.* It is like the reader[249] may think our divine might have given more instances of matters of "mere religion"; but it must be remembered, that he delights in being extremely concise, considering no doubt that he addresses to ladies, who are so taken up with those grand affairs and offices of life,

---

243. 1 Tm 6:5.

244. See *Lady's Religion*, "The Preface to the French Translation," A10r.

245. *Lady's Religion*, 21.

246. Astell's marginal note: *Lady's Religion*, 21.

247. Astell's marginal note: *Lady's Religion*, 36.

248. In the first edition, this sentence simply reads: "Whom the holy scripture expressly teaches us to adore with equal adoration."

249. "your Ladyship" in first edition.

dressing, visiting, and so on, together with the care of their "health"[250] and "beauty" the constant "works of their calling," that they have little time to "read" or "digest volumes," or to retire and converse with their own minds about matters of religion![251] Though with submission to better judgments, I will presume to say, that in a country where all are permitted to search after truth, there can hardly, if at all, be "orthodoxy of practice" without "orthodoxy of faith," these being the two constituent parts of the "one thing necessary."[252]

401. *Why this letter is so long.* That account of my religion which I have now given,[253] is not near so *short* as our divine's is, because in my poor opinion, he omitted many material and fundamental truths. "And as nobody can add to the fundamental articles of faith, nor make any other necessary but what God himself has made and declared to be so";[254] in like manner nobody can take from them. But though my religion is not so *short* as what he prescribes to the ladies, yet I hope it is "plain" and "practicable."[255] There are "no sublime notions or mysterious reasonings in it"; none "of the notions and language that the books and disputes of religion are filled with"; nor anything but "such plain propositions and short reasonings about things familiar" to our "minds," as need not "amaze" any "part of mankind,"[256] no not "the day laborers and tradesmen, the spinsters and dairy maids,"[257] who may very easily "comprehend" what a woman could write. A woman who has not the least reason to imagine that her understanding is any better than the rest of her sex's. All the difference, if there be any, arising only from her application, her disinterested, unprejudiced love to truth, and unwearied pursuit of it, notwithstanding all discouragements, which are in every woman's power as well as in hers. Nor did

---

250. Astell's marginal note: *Lady's Religion*, 29.

251. Astell's marginal note: *Lady's Religion*, 19, 20.

252. Astell's marginal note: *Lady's Religion*, 22.

253. The first edition reads "This account of my religion which I have given your Ladyship" instead of "That account of my religion which I have now given."

254. Astell's marginal note: Locke, *Reasonableness of Christianity*, 301 [168].

255. *Lady's Religion*, 9.

256. Astell's marginal note: Locke, *Reasonableness of Christianity*, 305, 306 [170].

257. Astell's marginal note: Locke, *Reasonableness of Christianity*, 282 [157].

she consult any[258] divine, or any other man, scarce any book except the Bible, on the subject of this letter, being willing to follow the thread of her own thoughts.

402. *The account here given of the gospel dispensation compared with that of an eminent and learned author.* Here I should have[259] ended, but that upon reading some *Sermons* (this Christmas, and while this sheet was in the press) *concerning the Divinity and Incarnation of our Blessed Savior,*[260] I could not be unconcerned when I found an account of the Christian dispensation so different from mine, given by so great an author, so deservedly celebrated for his good sense and just expression, the strength and clearness of his reasoning, and his natural and unaffected eloquence. I have endeavored "all along" (as he says he has done) to "take the express declarations, or at least the pregnant intimations of scripture for my ground and guide, in handling this argument,"[261] and I think those lively oracles allow me to say, that the design of the gospel, or of "the grace of God" offering "salvation to all men," and of Jesus Christ in giving "Himself for us," was "to redeem us from all iniquity,"[262] "from our vain conversation, received by tradition from our fathers";[263] "to be a light to the Gentiles, to open the blind eyes," or the dark and perverted understanding, as well as to "make straight the crooked" will,[264] and by this means to "purify to Himself a peculiar people zealous of good works";[265] in a word, to raise human nature to the utmost degree of perfection of which it is capable, to

---

258. The first edition reads "And I assure you, Madam, she consulted no" instead of "Nor did she consult any."

259. The first edition reads "And here your Ladyship's trouble had" instead of "Here I should have."

260. John Tillotson, *Sermons Concerning the Divinity and Incarnation of our Blessed Saviour,* 3rd ed. (London: Br. Aylmer and W. Rogers, 1702). Tillotson (1630–94) was archbishop of Canterbury and the much-respected author of numerous religious works. For further details, see Isabel Rivers's biography in the *ODNB,* s.v. "Tillotson, John," http://www.oxforddnb.com/view/article/27449 (accessed November 6, 2012).

261. Tillotson, *Sermons,* "Sermon 4: Concerning the Incarnation of Christ," 147, 114.

262. Astell's marginal note: Ti 2:11, and so on. [Astell also refers to Ti 2:14.]

263. Astell's marginal note: 1 Pt 1:18.

264. Astell's marginal note: Is 42:6–7 and 40:4.

265. Ti 2:14.

make us "perfect, as our heavenly father is perfect."[266] I likewise concluded from holy scripture, that the method God thought fit to take
to bring this to pass, was not by indulging or "complying" with us in
the "prejudices" we had fallen into through our adherence to sense,[267]
which had "alienated us from the life of God,"[268] and which was the
"main root and source" of the wickedness of mankind;[269] but by laying
the "axe unto the root of the tree," "by thoroughly purging His floor,"
and "burning up the chaff with unquenchable fire."[270] In short, by a full
and perfect reformation of the principles and manners of mankind, by
the spotless and exemplary life and death, and by the pure and most
exalted doctrine of His holy son, as has been shown (I think) in the
foregoing pages. Nor was I able to discern, either from scripture, or
from our natural notions of God, any reason why He was pleased to
condescend so far as to "send His" own eternal "son in the flesh," and
by making Him a sacrifice "for sin," to "condemn" and punish "sin in
the" human nature,[271] but only because "infinite wisdom" discerned
a "peculiar wisdom and fitness"[272] in this "method" above all others,
and saw not only a "great," but even the greatest "congruity and fitness
in the thing itself,"[273] so that upon the matter, it was absolutely the
best, and therefore the *only* way becoming the divine majesty. For, as
I humbly apprehend, there is not a greater "boldness and presumption" than in "affirming" that God does anything in vain,[274] or that He
would have been at the expense of so costly, so precious a sacrifice, if
the "business could have been done without it."[275]

403. But the great author just now mentioned, was it seems of
another mind, for he tells us, that "after all that has hitherto been said"

266. Astell's marginal note: Mt 5: *ult*. [*Ult*. is short for the Latin *ultimus*, meaning "last."
Astell paraphrases the last verse of Matthew (5:48).]

267. Tillotson, *Sermons*, 150.

268. Eph 4:18.

269. Tillotson, *Sermons*, 154.

270. Astell's marginal note: Mt 3:10, 12.

271. Astell's marginal note: Rom 8:3.

272. Tillotson, *Sermons*, 147.

273. Tillotson, *Sermons*, 170.

274. Tillotson, *Sermons*, 147.

275. Tillotson, *Sermons*, 146.

(by which I suppose is to be understood, either before the preaching of that sermon, or else in the foregoing sermons, in which he so clearly and fully, yet modestly proves the divinity of our Lord) "in answer to the objections against" God's way of saving mankind by Jesus Christ, "it may still seem very strange to a considering man, that God who could without all this circumstance and condescension, have done the business for which His son came into the world" should "make choice of this way."[276] *Strange*, not as this signifies admirable and wonderful, all God's works and ways, and this of man's redemption more especially, being strange in this sense, for God's "thoughts are not as our thoughts, nor *His* ways as *our* ways":[277] but *strange* as this imports odd, and not easy to be accounted for. And therefore this most learned and ingenious person, thinks it "necessary to give some account of this matter," "to enquire into the reasons of this dispensation, and to assign them particularly if" he "can."[278] And the only reason given by so masterly a hand, "upon a due consideration is,"[279] "God's gracious compliance with the weakness and common prejudices of mankind," "especially in the heathen world,"[280] by "accommodating the manner and circumstances of this dispensation to the most common and deeply radicated[281] prejudices of mankind concerning God and religion," that so He might "rectify more easily their wrong apprehensions by gratifying them in some measure."[282] And he tells us that "it would be great boldness and presumption to affirm, that God could not have brought about the salvation of men, by any other way, than by this very way in which He has done it."[283]

404. *Apology for dissenting, mischiefs of blind obedience.* I am by no means fond of dissenting from, much less of opposing the opinion of a man of so great and so established a character, who whether or no he be in the right, will certainly be said to be so by the most, who judge

276. Astell's marginal note: Tillotson, *Sermons*, 146.

277. Is 55:8.

278. Astell's marginal note: Tillotson, *Sermons*, 148.

279. Astell's marginal note: Tillotson, *Sermons*, 149.

280. Astell's marginal note: Tillotson, *Sermons*, 149, 150, 151.

281. radicated] established.

282. Astell's marginal note: Tillotson, *Sermons*, 150, 151.

283. Astell's marginal note: Tillotson, *Sermons*, 147.

by names and not by reason. Nor will it seem a little invidious for one of no consideration to differ from so eminent a person, much more for a woman to question, though ever so modestly, the authority of such a great man. And to me the greatest difficulty of all, is in starting any objection against an author when he has left the world, and therefore can't explain and answer for himself, which is a misfortune I am already fallen into (with relation to Mr. L.) by these papers being so long in the press.[284] But the cause of God and of religion will carry one through all difficulties, and answer all inconveniencies. And the mischiefs of a blind adherence to authority are so many and so great, and have occasioned such a swarm of Popish errors and superstitions, that none who are zealous for the Reformation, can reasonably be offended at anyone though ever so unnoted, who decently examines an opinion that comes recommended by ever so great a name. Indeed, the greater the name, the more dangerous the opinion if it is erroneous; for errors would do little or no hurt, if it were not for the veneration that is paid to the hand that recommends them. For my own part, I thank God, I am not considerable enough to countenance[285] an error, but I am much afraid of doing an injury to truth by appearing on her side; though all unprejudiced persons must needs allow, that a *proposition* is not the less true for being offered by a woman, or the more true for being delivered by the greatest man. And whether or not I am in the right, if I can but prevail with my fellow Christians, to receive no man's opinion on his bare word, nor to swallow his arguments without examining them, I shall do no little service to mankind. And if anyone will suppose that vanity was the motive to this undertaking, they may hurt themselves but not me by such a thought, so long as I know the contrary.

405. *Reasons for dissenting. First, for the honor of God and the Christian religion.* With all due respect therefore to the memory of that great man,[286] I must beg leave to adhere to my own account of the Christian dispensation in opposition to his, and that for the following reasons. First, because his account seems to me, not to make for the honor of God and of the Christian religion. A dispensation of

284. Locke died on October 28, 1704.
285. countenance] confirm.
286. John Tillotson.

which such great and glorious things are spoken by the sacred writers, the "method" and "circumstances" of which were prophesied of, very minutely, so long before, and which was ushered into the world with so great solemnity, not of worldly pomp and parade, which is most "accommodated" to the "common and deeply radicated prejudices of mankind,"[287] but with demonstration of the wisdom, the power and spirit of God. A "most perfect institution," not only "as to the main and substance of it," and as to its "being the law of nature revived and perfected";[288] but "most perfect" in all its "circumstances, method, and manner," for it is the "manifold wisdom of God, according to the eternal purpose which He purposed in Christ Jesus our Lord."[289] "Eternal purpose," and therefore, besides all other reasons, this "divine counsel and action" must be "taken from God Himself" alone, and can't be "assigned" to any creature, or the actions of any creature, much less to the "gross prejudices of men."[290] It is a question whether a wise man would contrive any great and momentous work after the model of vulgar prejudices: and I think it is out of question, that a "compliance" with people's "prejudices," is more like to continue than to cure them, at least it will not cure them effectually. For it is the blending truth and error, good and evil, that does the greatest mischief to mankind; because were error and evil separated from all manner of truth and good, their deformity would so much appear that they would find no followers. But we are told, that "the dispensation of God towards the Jewish nation, was full of condescension to their prejudices"; and that "the religion and laws which God gave them, were far from being the best and most perfect in themselves."[291] It is not to be denied, that absolutely considered, the Jewish religion was not the best, for it is not to be compared to the Christian: but then, upon the whole matter, it was most subservient to the grand design of the Almighty, even to the manifestation of His son, and His instituting a religion absolutely holy, just, and good. A religion suitable to the nature of God, who

---

287. Astell's marginal note: Tillotson, *Sermons*, 150.

288. Astell's marginal note: Tillotson, *Sermons*, 149.

289. Astell's marginal note: Eph 3:10[–11].

290. Astell's marginal note: Tillotson, *Sermons*, 147.

291. Astell's marginal note: Tillotson, *Sermons*, 148, 149.

"is a spirit," and "will be worshipped in spirit and truth"[292] under this dispensation, and not in ways "accommodated" to "the superstitions," the "prejudices," and "gross apprehensions of mankind."[293] And in this sense, that is with relation to what was to follow, even the Jewish religion was "perfect," as David tells us, and as might be made appear, but that it would carry us too far. Nor did God at all comply with the reigning prejudice of the Jews, when His son appeared in the world, whom they expected with all the grandeur and majesty of a great temporal prince. Let it also be considered, how precarious and of how little value to any considering person, that institution must needs be, which takes its rise from the "prejudices of mankind," their "gross and erroneous notions,"[294] and which can't otherwise be accounted for? How little it is for the reputation of the gospel mysteries, or the honor of their divine author, to have it said, that "since the world had such an admiration for mysteries"—"most of which were either very odd and fantastical, or very lewd and impure, or very inhumane and cruel, and every way unworthy of the deity,"—therefore they shall have a "mystery indeed, a mystery beyond all dispute, and beyond all comparison"![295] Suppose men had not been infected with these prejudices, then according to this account, there could have been no sufficient reason assigned for the gospel dispensation, no "answer" given to the "objections" made "against it," that could remove the wonder of "a considering man"?[296] Or suppose the reason assigned is found to be weak, and unworthy the divine majesty? We are told indeed, that we ought to be "satisfied with the wisdom and fitness of the way God has been pleased to pitch upon, whether the particular reasons appear to us or no."[297] But we are also told that there is no absolute necessity for "this very way, God could have done the business without it,"[298] to "affirm that *He* could not," is said to be "a great presumption and boldness";[299] and that the

292. Jn 4:23–24.

293. Tillotson, *Sermons*, 148, 150, 151.

294. Astell's marginal note: Tillotson, *Sermons*, 150. See also 151.

295. Astell's marginal note: Tillotson, *Sermons*, 153, 154.

296. Tillotson, *Sermons*, 146.

297. Astell's marginal note: Tillotson, *Sermons*, 147.

298. Astell's marginal note: Tillotson, *Sermons*, 146.

299. Tillotson, *Sermons*, 147.

"reverence due" to "mysteries and miracles in religion," is only "where they are certain and necessary in the nature and reason of the thing; but neither of them are easily to be admitted without necessity, and very good evidence."[300] The conclusions that follow from this account are harder than I care to make, and therefore without further remarks, I shall pass on to the second reason why I stick to my own, and can't submit to this great man's. And that is,

406. *Second, his supposition not agreeable to holy scripture.* Because his supposition[301] is not agreeable to the account that is given of the gospel dispensation in holy scripture. For in these sacred pages, we have a most august character of that great and glorious dispensation, which is said to be "the exceeding greatness of God's power," and "the exceeding riches of His grace," "wherein He has abounded towards us in all wisdom and prudence."[302] It is called the "wisdom of God," and "the power of God unto salvation";[303] indeed all the works and ways of God are made to center in it, "wherein are hid all the treasures of wisdom and knowledge."[304] And the preaching of the gospel is said to be the making "known the riches of the glory of the mystery," "which from the beginning of the world," "from ages and generations has been hid in God," and therefore did not, could not take its rise from "the prejudices of men" which are but of yesterday.[305] Christ is called "the lamb slain from the foundation of the world,"[306] nay, He is said to be "foreordained" even *before* its "foundation."[307] The "messiah," who being the eternal son of God was pleased to assume human nature, and by this means to become "a visible and sensible deity," and by making "expiation for the sins of men," and by suffering in their stead, to be their greatest "benefactor," and the "only mediator between God" and sinful "men," was promised to Adam immediately

---

300. Astell's marginal note: Tillotson, *Sermons*, 148.

301. "reason" in first edition.

302. Astell's marginal note: Eph 1:19, 2:7, 1:7–8.

303. Astell's marginal note: 1 Cor 2:7; Rom 1:16.

304. Astell's marginal note: Col 2:3.

305. Astell's marginal note: Eph 3:9; Col 1:26–27.

306. Astell's marginal note: Rv 13:8.

307. Astell's marginal note: 1 Pt 1:20.

after the fall;[308] and therefore, as I humbly apprehend, none of the "instances" given by our great and ingenious author, do in the least make it "appear," to anyone who reads and considers the holy scripture, that "God has complied" with the "prejudices" of men, "in the dispensation of the gospel," or that the "reasons" of it are at all derived from the "common notions of the heathen world."[309]

407. *Neither consistent with what he elsewhere says of expiation.* As concerning expiation, this great person himself allows, that "the notion of the expiation of sin," "by sacrifices, seems to have obtained very early in the world"—and "to have had its original from the first parents of mankind."[310] And which is yet more, in another sermon, he is pleased to assign "the method and dispensation which the wisdom of God pitched upon" for "the forgiveness" of sin, as the "reason" why God "seems either to have possessed mankind with this principle, or to have permitted them to be so persuaded, that sin was not to be expiated but by blood."[311] So that according to his own reasoning, this "notion concerning expiation" can't well be called a "prejudice"; much less can it be assigned as the reason why God "so far complied, as once for all to have a general atonement,"[312] unless we go in a circle, making this "method" of "a sacrifice" in the sinner's "stead," and this "notion and principle" that without shedding of blood there is no remission, reciprocally the reason for each other.

408. *Lastly, it is contrary to our natural notions of God.*[313] In the last place, that God should institute the Christian religion in "compliance" with the "gross apprehensions," and "prejudices of mankind,"[314] is not at all consistent with the natural notions we have of God. For that God does nothing in vain; and that He always does what is best, best in its kind though not always so in degree, I take to be as evident

308. Astell's marginal note: Gn 3:15.

309. Astell's marginal note: Tillotson, *Sermons*, 152, and so on.

310. Astell's marginal note: Tillotson, *Sermons*, 155, 156.

311. Astell's marginal note: Concerning the Sacrifice and Satisfaction of Christ. [Sermon 5 in Tillotson, *Sermons*, 205.]

312. Tillotson, *Sermons*, 156.

313. In the first edition, the order of sentences in this final paragraph is slightly different, but the sentiments are the same.

314. Tillotson, *Sermons*, 151.

truths as any axiom in the mathematics. God cannot act but for the wisest and best end, that is for His own glory, neither can He take the reason of any of His actions from without, much less, the reason of this glorious dispensation, which is the chief of the works of God, from so mean a cause, to say no worse, as the "weak, and gross, and wrong apprehensions of mankind."[315] Nor does this great man in reality, though he does in words, deny the *necessity* of the Christian dispensation, or that God "could not have brought about the salvation of men by any other way." For when we say that God cannot do a thing, we do not at all question almighty power, or "set" any sort of "limits to infinite wisdom";[316] we only question the fitness of the thing to be done, and mean no more than that such a thing is not suitable to the perfection of the divine nature. For to say that God cannot sin, that He can't deceive nor be deceived, is no limitation of His wisdom or power, because to be capable of those were an argument of imperfection. And to do what is less wise, or less just, or good, than something else that might be done in those circumstances, is not consistent with the nature of an all-perfect being, who because He is infinite in all perfection, always does what is best. So that if this great man, allows the "truth of" the mystery of our redemption, he must allow the "necessity" of it. Because if there was "a peculiar wisdom and fitness" in this method, as he allows, then this wisdom and fitness, and not a "compliance with the prejudices of men," determined God to act thus, and was the true reason why He could not, the perfection of His nature considered, act otherwise, or "do the business," that is, effect the salvation of mankind, any "other way."[317] And one can't in decency suppose, that a great and learned divine, who has offered so many good arguments against the Arians and Socinians in his sermons, can admit a doubt concerning the "divinity and incarnation of our blessed savior," and the great mystery of our redemption. Indeed he himself modestly calls his arguments "prejudices." Whereas were they only "prejudices," it would not make any man more in the right, he would only be rendered the more unhappy, by their being "invincible."

315. Astell's marginal note: Tillotson, *Sermons*, 151.

316. Astell's marginal note: Tillotson, *Sermons*, 146, 147.

317. Tillotson, *Sermons*, 147, 150, 146.

Index

This is the index from the 1717 second edition of Astell's *Christian Religion*. The numbers in this index refer to subsections (§§) and not page numbers. I have modernized the spelling and typography of the text, and made several changes to the arrangement of entries to bring them into alphabetical and numerical order. In accordance with modern style, I have separated out entries for the letters *i* and *j*, and *u* and *v*. In keeping with Astell's second edition, I have placed the index directly after the main text.

---

1. "affectations" in first edition.

2. In the first edition, this line is preceded by the entry "Lady, 1."

Paul, St., 1, 28, 56, 66, 73, 213, 321, 345, 346, 362
peace, 135, 213
peace-making, 101
penalty, 76
penetration, 265
people, 34, 142, 381
perception of God, 7
perfection, 7, 8, 10, 26, 77, 78, 159, 236, 237, 321; design of the gospel, 99, 334, 402; of human nature, 268; motive to it, 203; required, 94, 95; should thirst after it, 259; whence, 95, 159
persecution, 101, 102, 162, 210, 211
persecutor, 211, 372
perseverance, 226
person, 272, 273
Peter, St., 1, 28, 56; his fall, 165, 224
Pharisees, 38
Philip, 56
philosophy, 62, 66
Phineas, 189
physician, 1
pity, 254
plays, 260
pleasing men, 280
pleasure, 41, 79, 99, 106, 177, 245, 261, 282, 306, 308, 311; divine, 160, 161, 202, 254, 307; present, 90, 99, 149, 162, 203, 213, 250, 384; sensual, 101
plenty, 312

poetry, 260
poor, 111, 222, 316
popery, 28, 55
popish errors, 404
poverty, 162, 316
power, 7, 199, 318, 387
practical atheism, 133
practice, 19, 110, 252, 293
praise, 284, 300, 302, 321; of God, 277, *and so on*; of men, 277, *and so on*, 316
prayer, 130, 210, 292, 293
preach, 56
precepts, 189
prejudice, 4, 25, 250, 251, 253, 402, *and so on*
prerogative, 266
Presbyterians, 55
present, the, 90
presumption, 135, 165, 254, 324, 402
pretensions ridiculous, 141; to religion, 347
pride and its effects, 156, 179, 181, 203, 237, 250–53, 254, 258, 303; what, 140, *and so on*; what not so, 100, 108, 149
priestcraft, 92, 129, 356
primitive Christians, 377
principles, 37, 43, 192, 193, 251, 327
private, 172; duties, 292, 293
private interest, 331
privilege, 34, 234, 266
probation, 262, 306
professions, 193

Bibliography

Manuscripts

[Astell, Mary]. "A Collection of Poems humbly presented and Dedicated To the most Reverend Father in God William By Divine Providence Lord Archbishop of Canterbury and so on" (1689). Rawlinson Manuscripts. Rawl. MSS Poet. 154:50–97. Bodleian Library, Oxford.

Astell, Mary, and George Hickes. "The Controversy betwixt Dr. Hickes and Mrs. Mary Astell." In "The Genuine Remains of the late Pious and Learned George Hickes D. D. and Suffragen Bishop of Thetford," edited by Thomas Bedford. Papers of George Hickes, MS 3171. Lambeth Palace Library, London.

Ballard Collection. Bodleian Library, Oxford.

Printed Works

Acworth, Richard. *The Philosophy of John Norris of Bemerton (1657–1712)*. New York: Georg Olms Verlag, 1979.

[Allestree, Richard]. *The Causes of the Decay of Christian Piety*. In *The Works of the Learned and Pious Author of the Whole Duty of Man*. London: Roger Norton, 1704.

_____. *The Ladies Calling In Two Parts. By the Author of the Whole Duty of Man, &c. The Seventh Impression.* Oxford: at the Theater, 1700.

_____. *The Whole Duty of Man*. In *The Works of the Learned and Pious Author of the Whole Duty of Man*. London: Roger Norton, 1704.

Apetrei, Sarah. "'Call No Man Master Upon Earth': Mary Astell's Tory Feminism and an Unknown Correspondence." *Eighteenth-Century Studies* 41, no. 4 (2008): 507–23.

_____. *Women, Feminism, and Religion in Early Enlightenment England*. Cambridge: Cambridge University Press, 2010.

Arber, Edward. *The Term Catalogues, 1668–1709 A.D.; with a Number for Easter Term, 1711 A.D.* 3 vols. London: Professor Edward Arber, 1903–6.

Arnauld, Antoine, and Pierre Nicole. *Logic or the Art of Thinking.* Translated and edited by Jill Vance Buroker. Cambridge: Cambridge University Press, 1996.

Astell, Mary. *Bart'lemy Fair; or, An Enquiry after Wit; In which due Respect is had to a Letter Concerning Enthusiasm, To my LORD ***.* London: Richard Wilkin, 1709.

———. *The Christian Religion, As Professed by a Daughter Of The Church of England.* London: S.H. for R. Wilkin, 1705.

———. *The Christian Religion, As Professed by a Daughter of the Church of England.* 2nd ed. London: W.B. for R. Wilkin, at the King's-Head in St. Paul's-Church-Yard, 1717.

———. *The Christian Religion, as Professed by a Daughter of the Church of England. Containing Proper Directions for the due Behavior of Women in every Station of Life. With a few cursory Remarks on Archbishop Tillotson's Doctrine of the Satisfaction of Christ, &c. and on Mr. Locke's Reasonableness of Christianity. By the Author of the Proposal to the Ladies; and Reflections on Marriage, &c. The Third Edition.* London: W. Parker, at the King's-Head in St. Paul's Church-Yard, 1730.

———. *A Fair Way with the Dissenters.* In *Astell: Political Writings,* edited by Patricia Springborg. Cambridge: Cambridge University Press, 1996.

———. *A Fair Way with the Dissenters and their Patrons.* London: E. P. for Richard Wilkin, 1704.

———. *The First English Feminist: "Reflections Upon Marriage" and Other Writings by Mary Astell.* Edited by Bridget Hill. New York: St. Martin's Press, 1986.

———. *An Impartial Enquiry.* In *Astell: Political Writings,* edited by Patricia Springborg. Cambridge: Cambridge University Press, 1996.

———. *An Impartial Enquiry Into The Causes Of Rebellion and Civil War In This Kingdom.* London: E. P. for Richard Wilkin, 1704.

———. *Moderation truly Stated: Or, A Review of a Late Pamphlet, Entitled, Moderation a Vertue.* London: R. Wilkin, 1704.

_____. *Reflections upon Marriage*. In *Astell: Political Writings*, edited by Patricia Springborg. Cambridge: Cambridge University Press, 1996.

_____. *A Serious Proposal to the Ladies, For the Advancement of their True and Greatest Interest. By a Lover of her Sex*. London: R. Wilkin, 1694.

_____. *A Serious Proposal to the Ladies, Part II: Wherein a Method is Offered for the Improvement of their Minds*. London: Richard Wilkin, 1697.

_____. *A Serious Proposal to the Ladies, Parts I and II*. Edited by Patricia Springborg. Peterborough, ON: Broadview Press, 2002.

_____. *Some Reflections Upon Marriage, Occasioned by the Duke and Duchess of Mazarine's Case; which is also considered*. London: John Nutt, 1700.

[Astell, Mary], and John Norris. *Letters Concerning the Love of God, Between the Author of the Proposal to the Ladies and Mr. John Norris*. London: J. Norris for Samuel Manship and Richard Wilkin, 1695.

_____. *Letters Concerning the Love of God*. Edited by E. Derek Taylor and Melvyn New. Aldershot, UK: Ashgate, 2005.

Atterbury, Francis. *The Miscellaneous Works of Bishop Atterbury*. Edited by J. Nichols. 5 vols. London: J. Nichols, 1799.

Ballard, George. *Memoirs of Several Ladies of Great Britain (Who have been Celebrated for their Writings or Skill in the Learned Languages, Arts, and Sciences)*. Edited by Ruth Perry. Detroit, MI: Wayne State University Press, 1985.

Barksdale, Clement. *Letter Touching a Colledge of Maids; or, A Virgin-Society*. London: n.p., 1675.

Bibliotheca Selectissima; or, A Catalogue of Curious Books Contained in the Libraries of the Reverend Dr. Thomas Bayley late President of St. Mary Magdalen Coll. and the Reverend Dr. Henry Parkhurst, late Fellow of Corpus Christi Coll. in Oxford. London: n.p., 1706.

Birch, Thomas, ed. *Additions in the Second Edition of the Life of Archbishop Tillotson*. London: n.p., 1653?

Boyle, Deborah. "Mary Astell and Cartesian 'Scientia.'" In *The New Science and Women's Literary Discourse: Prefiguring Frankenstein*, edited by Judy Hayden, 99–112. New York: Palgrave Macmillan, 2011.

Boyle, Robert. *The Christian Virtuoso.* Vol. 8 of *The Works of Robert Boyle,* edited by Michael Hunter and Edward B. Davis. London: Pickering and Chatto, 2000.

_____. *The Christian Virtuoso: Showing, That by being Addicted to Experimental Philosophy, a Man is rather Assisted, than Indisposed, to be a Good Christian. The First Part.* London: Edw. Jones for John Taylor and John Wyat, 1690.

_____. *The Excellency of Theology.* Vol. 11 of *The Works of Robert Boyle,* edited by Michael Hunter and Edward B. Davis. London: Pickering and Chatto, 2000.

_____. *The Excellency of Theology, Compared with Natural Philosophy (as Both are Objects of Men's Study) Discoursed of In a Letter to a Friend.* London: T.N. for Henry Herringman, 1674.

Broad, Jacqueline. "Adversaries or Allies? Occasional Thoughts on the Masham-Astell Exchange." *Eighteenth-Century Thought* 1 (2003): 123–49.

_____. "Astell, Cartesian Ethics, and the Critique of Custom." In *Mary Astell: Reason, Gender, Faith,* edited by William Kolbrener and Michal Michelson, 165–80. Aldershot, UK: Ashgate, 2007.

_____. "Mary Astell (1666–1731)." *British Philosophers, 1500–1799,* edited by Philip B. Dematteis and Peter S. Fosl, 3–10. *Dictionary of Literary Biography* 252. Detroit, MI: Gale, 2002.

_____. "Mary Astell on Virtuous Friendship." *Parergon: Journal of the Australian and New Zealand Association for Medieval and Early Modern Studies* 26, no. 2 (2009): 65–86.

_____. *Women Philosophers of the Seventeenth Century.* Cambridge: Cambridge University Press, 2002.

Broad, Jacqueline, and Karen Green. *A History of Women's Political Thought in Europe, 1400–1700.* Cambridge: Cambridge University Press, 2009.

Brown, Michael. *A Political Biography of John Toland.* London: Pickering and Chatto, 2012.

Buickerood, James G. "What Is It with Damaris, Lady Masham? The Historiography of One Early Modern Woman Philosopher." *Locke Studies* 5 (2005): 179–214.

Christopherson, H. O. *A Bibliographical Introduction to the Study of John Locke*. New York: Burt Franklin, 1968.

Chudleigh, Mary. *The Poems and Prose of Mary, Lady Chudleigh*. Edited by Margaret J. M. Ezell. New York: Oxford University Press, 1993.

Church of England. *The Book of Common Prayer, and Administrations of the Sacraments and other Rites and Ceremonies of the Church according to the Use of the Church of England*. Oxford: Oxford University Press, [1952–70].

Clarke, Samuel. *A Demonstration of the Being and Attributes of God, and Other Writings*. Edited by Ezio Vailati. Cambridge Texts in the History of Philosophy. Cambridge: Cambridge University Press, 1998.

Connolly, S. J. "Hickman, Charles." *ODNB*, http://www.oxforddnb.com/view/article/13210 (accessed January 20, 2012).

Coventry, Ann. *The Right Honourable Ann Countess of Coventry's Meditations and Reflections, Moral and Divine*. London: B. Aylmer and W. Rogers, 1707.

Davenant, Charles. *Essays upon Peace at Home, and War Abroad. In Two Parts*. 2nd ed. London: James Knapton, 1704.

Descartes, René. *The Passions of the Soule In three Books. The first, Treating of the Passions in Generall, and occasionally of the whole nature of man. The second, Of the Number, and order of the Passions, and the explication of the six Primitive ones. The third, of Particular Passions. By R. des Cartes. And Translated out of French into English*. London: A.C., 1650.

———. *The Philosophical Writings of Descartes*. Translated by John Cottingham, Robert Stoothoff, and Dugald Murdoch. Vol. 1, *Passions of the Soul* and *Principles of Philosophy*. Cambridge: Cambridge University Press, 1985.

Edwards, John. *Some Thoughts Concerning the Several Causes and Occasions of Atheism, Especially in the Present Age. With some Brief Reflections on Socinianism: And on a Late Book, Entitled The Reasonableness of Christianity as delivered in the Scriptures*. Facsimile edition. New York: Garland, 1984.

Elisabeth, Princess of Bohemia, and René Descartes. *The Correspondence between Princess Elisabeth of Bohemia and René*

Descartes. Edited and translated by Lisa Shapiro. Other Voice in Early Modern Europe. Chicago: University of Chicago Press, 2007.

Ellenzweig, Sarah. "The Love of God and the Radical Enlightenment: Mary Astell's Brush with Spinoza." *Journal of the History of Ideas* 64, no. 3 (2003): 379–97.

Gailhard, John. *The Epistle and Preface to the Book against the Blasphemous Socinian Heresie Vindicated; And the Charge therein against Socinianism, made Good*. London: J. Hartley, 1698.

Goldie, Mark. "Mary Astell and John Locke." In *Mary Astell: Reason, Gender, Faith*, edited by William Kolbrener and Michal Michelson, 65–85. Aldershot, UK: Ashgate, 2007.

_____. "The Political Thought of the Anglican Revolution." In *The Revolutions of 1688: The Andrew Browning Lectures 1988*, edited by Robert Beddard, 102–36. Oxford: Clarendon Press, 1991.

Greig, Martin. "Burnet, Gilbert." *ODNB*. http://www.oxforddnb.com/view/article/4061 (accessed November 8, 2012).

Grew, Nehemiah. *Cosmologia Sacra; or, A Discourse of the Universe As it is the Creature and Kingdom of God*. London: W. Rogers, S. Smith, and B. Walford, 1701.

Handley, Stuart. "Stephens, William." *ODNB*. http://www.oxforddnb.com/view/article/26395 (accessed March 4, 2011).

Hickes, George. "The Postscript by the Translator. To Antiope." In François Fénelon, *Instructions for the Education of a Daughter, By the Author of Telemachus. To which is added A Small Tract of Instructions for the Conduct of Young Ladies of the Highest Rank. With Suitable Devotions Annexed. Done into English, and Revised by Dr. George Hickes*. London: Jonah Bowyer, 1707.

Hickman, Charles. *Fourteen Sermons Preached, at St James's Church in Westminster*. London: James Orme, 1700.

The Holy Bible, Containing the Old Testament and the New: Newly translated out of the Original Tongues and with the former Translations diligently Compared and Revised. By his Majesties Special Command. Here are added to the former Notes in the Margin. Edinburgh: Heirs and Successors of Andrew Anderson, 1696.

Howard, John. *Orthodoxy in Faith, and Uprightness in Life and Conversation*. London: Jonah Bowyer, 1713.

King, Peter. *The History of the Apostles Creed: With Critical Observations on its Several Articles.* 3rd ed. London: W. B. for Jonathan Robinson and John Wyat, 1711.

Kolbrener, William, and Michal Michelson, eds. *Mary Astell: Reason, Gender, Faith.* Aldershot, UK: Ashgate, 2007.

A Lady's Religion: In a Letter to the Honorable My Lady Howard. The Second Edition. To which is added, a Second Letter to the same Lady, concerning the Import of Fear in Religion. By a Divine of the Church of England. 2nd ed. London: A. and J. Churchill, 1704.

Lamprecht, Sterling P. "The Role of Descartes in Seventeenth-Century England." *Studies in the History of Ideas* 3 (1935): 181–240.

Locke, John. *An Essay Concerning Human Understanding.* Edited by Peter H. Nidditch. Clarendon Edition of the Works of John Locke. Oxford: Clarendon Press, 1975.

———. *Mr. Locke's Reply to the Right Reverend the Lord Bishop of Worcester's Answer to his Second Letter.* London: H.C. for A. and J. Churchill, and E. Castle, 1699.

———. *A Paraphrase and Notes on the Epistles of St Paul to the Galatians, 1 and 2 Corinthians, Romans, Ephesians.* Edited by Arthur W. Wainwright. 2 vols. Clarendon Edition of the Works of John Locke. Oxford: Clarendon Press, 1987.

———. *The Reasonableness of Christianity, As delivered in the Scriptures.* 2nd ed. London: Awnsham and John Churchill, 1696.

———. *The Reasonableness of Christianity as Delivered in the Scriptures.* Edited and introduced by John C. Higgins-Biddle. Clarendon Edition of the Works of John Locke. Oxford: Clarendon Press, 1999.

———. *Two Treatises of Government.* Edited by Peter Laslett. Cambridge Texts in the History of Political Thought. Cambridge: Cambridge University Press, 1988.

———. *A Vindication of the Reasonableness of Christianity, &c. From Mr Edwards's Reflections.* London: Awnsham and John Churchil, 1695.

———. *Vindications of the Reasonableness of Christianity.* Edited by Victor Nuovo. Clarendon Edition of the Works of John Locke. Oxford: Clarendon Press, 2012.

London Evening Post no. 553 (June 12–15, 1731).

MacDonald, Lynn, ed. *Women Theorists on Society and Politics.* Waterloo, ON: Wilfrid Laurier University Press, 1998.

MacKinnon, Flora Isabel. *The Philosophy of John Norris.* Philosophical Monographs series 1. Baltimore, MD: Psychological Review Publications, 1910.

Makin, Bathsua. *An Essay to Revive the Antient Education of Gentlewomen, In Religion, Manners, Arts & Tongues. With An Answer to the Objections against this Way of Education.* London: J.D., 1673.

Mander, W. J. *The Philosophy of John Norris.* Oxford: Oxford University Press, 2008.

[Masham, Damaris]. *Discourse concerning the Love of God.* London: Awnsham and John Churchil, 1696.

_____. *The Philosophical Works of Damaris, Lady Masham.* Introduced by James G. Buickerood. Bristol, UK: Thoemmes Continuum, 2004.

Maslen, Keith, and John Lancaster, eds. *The Bowyer Ledgers: The Printing Accounts of William Bowyer Father and Son. Reproduced on Microfiche. With a Checklist of Bowyer Printing 1699–1777, a Commentary, Indexes, and Appendices.* London: Bibliographical Society; New York: Bibliographical Society of America, 1991.

McGee, J. Sears, "Sanderson, Robert." *ODNB.* http://www.oxforddnb.com/view/article/24627 (accessed January 20, 2012).

Mendelson, Sara H. "Pakington [*née* Coventry], Dorothy." *ODNB.* http://www.oxforddnb.com/view/article/21142 (accessed January 16, 2012).

Milton, John. "Pierre Coste, John Locke, and the Third Earl of Shaftesbury." In *Studies on Locke: Sources, Contemporaries, and Legacy,* edited by Sarah Hutton and Paul Schuurman, 195–223. International Archives of the History of Ideas/Archives internationals d'histoire des idées 197. Dordrecht: Springer, 2008.

More, Henry. *An Account of Virtue: Or, Dr. Henry More's Abridgment of Morals, Put into English.* Translated by Edward Southwell. Bristol, UK: Thoemmes Press, 1997.

Myers, Joanne E. "Enthusiastic Improvement: Mary Astell and Damaris Masham on Sociability." *Hypatia: A Journal of Feminist Philosophy* 28 (forthcoming).

[Nelson, Robert]. *The Necessity of Church-Communion Vindicated, From the Scandalous Aspersions of a late Pamphlet, Entitled, the Principle of the Protestant Reformation explained.* London: A. and J. Churchil, 1705.

Norris, John. *An Essay Towards the Theory of the Ideal or Intelligible World. Being the Relative Part of it. Wherein the Intelligible World is considered with relation to Human Understanding. Whereof some Account is here attempted and proposed. Part II.* Vol. 7 of *Philosophical and Theological Writings*, edited and introduced by Richard Acworth. Bristol, UK: Thoemmes Press, 2001.

_____. *An Essay Towards the Theory of the Ideal or Intelligible World. Designed for Two Parts. The First considering it Absolutely in itself, and the Second in Relation to Human Understanding. Part I.* Vol. 6 of *Philosophical and Theological Writings*, edited and introduced by Richard Acworth. Bristol, UK: Thoemmes Press, 2001.

_____. *Practical Discourses upon Several Divine Subjects.* London: S. Manship, 1691.

_____. *Practical Discourses upon Several Divine Subjects.* London: S. Manship, 1693.

_____. *Reflections upon the Conduct of Human Life: With Reference to the Study of Learning and Knowledge. In a Letter to the Excellent Lady, the Lady Masham.* Vol. 3 of *Philosophical and Theological Writings*, edited and introduced by Richard Acworth. Bristol, UK: Thoemmes Press, 2001.

_____. *Theory and Regulation of Love. A Moral Essay.* Vol. 2 of *Philosophical and Theological Writings*, edited and introduced by Richard Acworth. Bristol, UK: Thoemmes Press, 2001.

O'Neill, Eileen. "Mary Astell on the Causation of Sensation." In *Mary Astell: Reason, Gender, Faith*, edited by William Kolbrener and Michal Michelson, 145–63. Aldershot, UK: Ashgate, 2007.

Oxford Dictionary of National Biography, online edition. Oxford: Oxford University Press, 2008. http://www.oxforddnb.com.

Oxford English Dictionary Online. Oxford: Oxford University Press, 2012. http://www.oed.com.

Pascal, Blaise. *Pensées.* Translated by W. F. Trotter. Online edition. Adelaide: University of Adelaide Library, 2012. http://ebooks.adelaide.edu.au/p/pascal/blaise/p27pe/index.html.

Perry, Ruth. *The Celebrated Mary Astell: An Early English Feminist.* Chicago, IL: University of Chicago Press, 1986.

Plutarch. *Moralia: Volume I.* Translated by Frank Cole Babbitt. Loeb Classical Library No. 197. Cambridge, MA: Harvard University Press, 1927.

The Principle of the Protestant Reformation Explained In A Letter of Resolution Concerning Church-Communion. London: n.p., 1704.

Reresby, Tamworth. *A Miscellany of Ingenious Thoughts and Reflections.* London: H. Meere, 1721.

Rivers, Isabel. "Tillotson, John." *ODNB.* http://www.oxforddnb.com/view/article/27449 (accessed November 6, 2012).

Sanderson, Robert. *XXXIV Sermons. Viz., XVI. Ad Aulam. IV. Clerum. VI. Magistratum. VIII. Populum. By the Right Reverend Father in God, Robert Sanderson, Late Lord Bishop of Lincoln.* 5th ed. London: A. Seil, 1671.

Smith, Florence M. *Mary Astell.* New York: Columbia University Press, 1916.

Smith, Hannah. "Mary Astell, *A Serious Proposal to the Ladies* (1694), and the Anglican Reformation of Manners in Late-Seventeenth-Century England." In *Mary Astell: Reason, Gender, Faith,* edited by William Kolbrener and Michal Michelson, 31–47. Aldershot, UK: Ashgate, 2007.

Smith, Hilda L., Mihoko Suzuki, and Susan Wiseman, eds. *Women's Political Writings, 1610–1725.* Vol. 4. London: Pickering and Chatto, 2007.

Sowaal, Alice. "Mary Astell's *Serious Proposal:* Mind, Method, and Custom." *Philosophy Compass* 2 (2007): 227–43.

Springborg, Patricia. "Astell, Masham, and Locke: Religion and Politics." In *Women Writers and the Early Modern British Political Tradition,* edited by Hilda L. Smith, 105–25. Cambridge: Cambridge University Press, 1998.

_____. *Mary Astell: Theorist of Freedom from Domination.* Cambridge: Cambridge University Press, 2005.

Spurr, John. "Allestree, Richard." *ODNB.* http://www.oxforddnb.com/view/article/395 (accessed February 28, 2011).

Squadrito, Kathleen M. "Mary Astell." In Vol. 3 of *A History of Women Philosophers*, edited by Mary Ellen Waithe, 87–99. Dordrecht: Kluwer Academic Publishers, 1991.

_____. "Mary Astell's Critique of Locke's View of Thinking Matter." *Journal of the History of Philosophy* 25 (1987): 433–39.

Steele, Richard. *The Lying Lover; or, The Ladies Friendship*. London: Bernard Lintott, 1704.

[Stephens, Edward]. *Necessary Correction for an Insolent Deist: In Answer to an Impious Pamphlet, the Principle of the Protestant Reformation Explained in a Letter of Resolution concerning Church Communion*. London?: n.p., 1705?

Stillingfleet, Edward. *A Discourse in Vindication of the Doctrine of the Trinity*. London: J. H. for Henry Mortlock, 1697.

Sutherland, Christine Mason. *The Eloquence of Mary Astell*. Calgary, AB: University of Calgary Press, 2005.

Taylor, E. Derek. "Mary Astell's Ironic Assault on John Locke's Theory of Matter." *Journal of the History of Ideas* 62, no. 3 (2001): 505–22.

_____. "Mary Astell's Work towards a New Edition of *A Serious Proposal to the Ladies, Part II*." *Studies in Bibliography* 57 (2005–6): 197–232.

Teague, Frances. *Bathsua Makin, Woman of Learning*. Lewisburg, PA: Bucknell University Press; London: Associated Presses, 1998.

_____. "Makin, Bathsua." *ODNB*. http://www.oxforddnb.com/view/article/17849 (accessed November 8, 2012).

Till, Barry. "Stillingfleet, Edward." *ODNB*. http://www.oxforddnb.com/view/article/26526 (accessed February 10, 2012).

Tillotson, John. *Sermons Concerning the Divinity and Incarnation of our Blessed Saviour*. 3rd ed. London: Br. Aylmer and W. Rogers, 1702.

[Toland, John]. *Christianity not Mysterious: Or, A Treatise Showing, That there is nothing in the Gospel Contrary to Reason, Nor Above it: And that no Christian Doctrine can be properly called a Mystery*. London: n.p., 1696.

_____. *John Toland's Christianity not Mysterious: Text, Associated Works, and Critical Essays*. Edited by Philip McGuinness, Alan Harrison, and Richard Kearney. Dublin: Lilliput Press, 1997.

Waterland, Daniel. *Advice to a Young Student. With a Method of Study for the Four First Years.* London: John Crownfield, 1730.

Whitby, Daniel. *A Discourse of the Love of God. Showing, That it is well consistent with some Love or Desire of the Creature.* London: Awnsham and John Churchill, 1697.

Wilson, Catherine. "Love of God and Love of Creatures: The Masham-Astell Debate." *History of Philosophy Quarterly* 21, no. 3 (2004): 281–98.

Yolton, Jean. "Authorship of *A Lady's Religion* (1697)." *Notes and Queries* 38, no. 2 (June 1991): 177.

Yolton, John. *Thinking Matter: Materialism in Eighteenth-Century Britain.* Minneapolis: University of Minnesota Press, 1983.